Alfred Dreyfus:

Man, Milieu, Mentality and *Midrash*

Norman Simms

Reference Library of Jewish Intellectual History

ALFRED DREYFUS:

MAN, MILIEU, MENTALITY AND *MIDRASH*

Norman SIMMS

Boston 2012

Library of Congress Cataloging-in-Publication Data:
A catalog record for this title is available from the Library of Congress.

ISBN 978-1-936235-39-1

Book design by Adell Medovoy

On the cover: Woodcut by Martha Simms based on Alfred Dreyfus' drawings in his prison *cahiers* from Devil's Island.

Published by Academic Studies Press in 2012
28 Montfern Avenue
Brighton, MA 02135, USA

press@academicstudiespress.com
www.academicstudiespress.com

Special thanks for their advice and support to

Ira Bing, Maru Bing, Athena Chambers, Phyllis Chesler Norbert Col, José Faur, Nancy Kobrin, Robert Liris and, as always and, especially, Martha Simms.

....les verres deformants qui interposent entre notre conscience et le monde extérnel...

...distorting mirrors stand between our consciousness and the external world...

—Octave Mirbeau[1]

Il y a plusieurs types juifs, mais malgré les croisements et les mélanges, on peut soutenir, contre Renan, que la pérennité de ces types est incontestable. Si, donc nous rectifions l'idée que philo et antisémites se font de la race juive, on peut dire que l'identité des origines, constitue déjà un lien entre les juifs.

There are many kinds of Jews, but despite all the crossings and mixtures, it is possible to argue, against Renan, that the perenity of these kinds is incontestable. If, then, we correct the idea that the philo- and anti-Semites make about the Jewish race, we can say that the identity of their origins constitutes already a connection between Jews.

—Bernard Lazare[2]

---

1 Cited by Pierre Michel and Jean-François Nivet, eds., *Octave Mirbeau, Combats esthétiques*, I, 1877-1892 (Paris: Séguier, 1990), Introduction: "Mirbeau Critique d'Art," 32.

2 Bernard Lazre, *Le nationaliosme juif.* Publications du "KadimaH" N°. 1 (Paris: Associations des Etudiants Israelites Russes, 1898), 2.

TABLE OF CONTENTS

Prologue

What you are about to read is the first of several new book-length studies of Alfred Dreyfus. This first in the series clears the ground of many assumptions, guesses set out as facts, and interesting ideas that have not been followed through to their logical conclusions. What are new are not so much facts as two new factors: to begin with, my concern is much less about the Dreyfus Affair than it is about the man's life and personality, along with that of his wife, Lucie, and of their closest relatives and friends. But my book is neither a biography of the Dreyfus family and its association with the Hadamards, Lucie's family, nor a social or intellectual history of the *fin de siècle* in France, the setting of the Affair. This is because of the second new factor, my concern with the intellectual, emotional and spiritual qualities of the man Alfred Dreyfus as evidenced in his writings—his letters to Lucie and hers to him, his several journals, and his prison workbooks composed on Devil's Island, approximately half of which have been saved from destruction. In other words, I am presenting a book about Dreyfus as a late nineteenth-century writer, a thinker, a scientist and a poet, a critic and a historian, and, not least, as a Jew.

The essential approach to Dreyfus's achievements I take is similar to the parameters established by Vincenso Calfa, the translator of Jules Michelet's *The Bible of Humanity*:

> The circumscribed frame of the narrative is broken.... history becomes a poem, and even when he keeps within the limits of pure narrative, his vivid imagination is not slackened. The images are so lively, the manner so rapid, the quick invention so happy and so wild that the objects appear to be born again with all their colors, motions, and forms, and pass before our eyes as a phantasmagoria of luminous pictures.[1]

1 Vincenso Calfa, "Life and Works of Michelet" in Jules Michelet. *The Bible of Humanity* (1864), trans. Vincenzo Calfa (New York: J.W. Bouton and London: B. Quarditch, 1877), xvii.

Though Calfa's remarks deal specifically with Michelet's style of writing, as much in his historical studies as in his more adventurous books on aspects of nature and people, there are at least two reasons why it is appropriate to cite them in regard to the life of Alfred Dreyfus. First, because Dreyfus describes what happened to him during the period from 1894 to 1906 as a phantasmagoria; and second, because Michelet is one of the writers he singles out as most influential to the nineteenth century and by implication to himself. In addition, when the love letters written by Lucie and Alfred to one another are carefully studied for the dynamics of their energy, intimacy and implied creation of a mystical relationship, and also when we examine closely the three-fold phenomena of his fifteen surviving *cahiers*—the essays and commentaries on a variety of historical, scientific, aesthetic and moral issues; the formulae and equations of mathematics and physics he works out; and the thousands of strange drawings that fill up scores of pages—there seems no better word to describe the results than phantasmagoria. Finally, his biography itself, with all of its starts and interruptions, its periods of seeming ordinariness, its outbreaks of nightmarish pain and humiliation, and its many disturbing blank spots, may also be appropriately designated by this same term.

In the second volume of this projected series, I will examine more closely the letters, journals and workbooks to see how they stabilize the now standard view of Alfred Dreyfus. Rather than being out of the picture as an individual of no particular intellectual merits and achievements, he will be shown to be a remarkable man who, under the extreme constraints of his imprisonment—exile, solitary confinement, and physical torture—prevented himself from going mad by discovering in his own mind a rational and critical consolidation of nineteenth-century philosophy and aesthetics. He was not an advanced author, but he was a deep thinker. He was also not a practicing Jew but he was a Jewish thinker. In other words, as his writings define him, instead of the rather middle-class conformist and technician most historians have assumed him to be, if they spent any time at all on his personality and feelings during the long ordeal he went through, close reading of his epistles and *cahiers* reveal an interesting man who was anything but ordinary.

In the third volume in this series, there will be a study of Alfred Dreyfus as a lover, a poet, a moral historian and a midrashist. All of these unexpected aspects of his personality will then be set in the context of his favourite European authors, not merely the figures of William Shakespeare and Michel de Montaigne, who historians have claimed were the sources of his thought, but the four writers he repeatedly cited and claimed as his key influences—Jules Michelet, Hippolyte Taine, Ernest Renan and Paul Bourget. Interestingly, Dreyfus hardly mentions any of the authors who emerged during the Affair to be his chief supporters, such as Emile Zola, Bernard Lévy and Marcel Proust. Moreover, thanks to his wife Lucie's influence and the circle of relations and friends on her side, the Hadamards, Alfred knew what was happening in the arts, music and literature, although his tastes were not for the *avant garde*, and his standards stemmed from the rabbinical culture of Alsace where his family had its roots. The mystery remains, however: why, given the great range of writing displayed in the prison *cahiers* and the meticulous record of his struggle for complete rehabilitation, does Alfred Dreyfus virtually fade from view after 1906, with only a few appearances in public until his death in 1935? From the time he was restored to his service in the Army and awarded the *Legion d'honneur*, we know more about his wife Lucie and their children Jeanne and Pierre than we do about Alfred. What can explain this? Was he a broken man, too exhausted by his ordeal, too depressed by his failures, to receive the full recognition he felt he deserved, and therefore unable or unwilling to speak in public, or to write to a public he could no longer trust?

Chapter One: Introduction

PART 1: DIFFRACTION OF LIGHT RAYS

L'Objet d'Histoire, objet mnésique, contient un amalgame de faits établis scientifiquement et de rumeurs fascinantes et non fondées. Ces attentes entre le vrai et le faux vont provoquer une mise en veille de la rationalité, voire une fascination trouble sur le réel qui tend à se dérober.

—Robert Liris[1]

We don't see as much of the world as we think we see . . . . We focus our attention on a few things that we want to see and the result of that is that we have to filter out things that we don't care about. And we sometimes also filter out things that we might care about. This is known as inattentional blindness.

—Daniel Simons[2]

A few words before I start. Actually, I have already started. You can see that by the various little citations preceding the beginning of my text. Although I will explain the whole method in due course, from chapter to chapter, if you need to be prepared to follow the argument, already the main themes should be evident. Things in this world and in the world of experience that Alfred Dreyfus, his wife, other members of his family, and his closest friends and associates underwent were not always as they seemed—or as they seem to us when we try

---

1 Robert Liris, "La Tour foudroyée: Image factuelle ou Object d'Histoire" *Mentalities/Mentalités* 25:1–2 (2011), "The historical object, the mnemonic object, consists of an amalgam of scientifically established facts and fascinating and unfounded rumors. The tensions between the true and the false set off a wake-up call from rationality, and that in itself stirs up a troubling fascination inside reality which then tends to scurry away in darkness."

2 Cited in an interview between Alok Juha and Daniel Simons, "Gorillas in our midst—but they're easily missed: A famous study has forced us to question how our brains see the world around us," published on the Perspectives page of *The New Zealand Herald* (4 August 2010), based on *The Invisible Gorilla and Other Ways Our Intuitions Deceive Us* by Daniel Simons and Christopher Chabris (New York: Crown Publishing Group/Random House, 1998).

to read the documents of the period.

There are many reasons for these discrepancies, which this book will address often indirectly rather than directly because I don't see how they can be addressed effectively in any other way. Part of the reason is that everyone in Western and Central Europe in the final years of the nineteenth century and the early decades of the twentieth was undergoing an epistemological change in the way they could feel, see, think about, imagine, and write about themselves and the world they lived in. Some of the changes were relatively minor and due to technological transformations—from telegraphy to railroads and steamboats, photography and urban architecture; some were more profound, more deeply embedded in the very affective and cognitive mechanisms of perception and articulation—from aesthetics to physics and psychology. Some were even more hidden in the shadows of history and the blinding brightness of new social relationships, changes a long time brewing and beginning to emerge to consciousness in a series of traumatic shocks in political events, wars, and personal crises.

The Dreyfus Affair was one of those occurrences that seem suddenly to bring to light what had been unnoticed and that called for ways of seeing, speaking, writing, and acting that would have been unthinkable and unimaginable before.

Things before Words

> *Utilize as best you can the transformations of the universe into a local section; use the process by which time is canned and called a newspaper. The world has become uglier since it began to look into a mirror every day; so let us settle for the mirror and do without an inspection of the original. It is uplifting to lose one's faith in a reality which looks the way it is described in a newspaper. He who sleeps away half a day has won half a life.*
>
> —Karl Kraus[3]

3 Karl Kraus, "In Praise of a Topsy-Turvy Life-Style" in *In These Great Times: A Karl Kraus Reader*, ed. Harry Zohn, trans. Joseph Fabry, Max Knighty, Karl F. Ross, and Harry Zohn (Chicago, IL: University of Chicago Press, 1984 [1976]), 37.

This section contains a rough summary of received opinions. After I set forth this narrative of events, I will put the words and the beliefs through a prism to see what patterns of light and darkness the rays break up into. Now we see through a glass or mirror only in enigmatic reasons and concepts; then we shall start to see more clearly the various midrashic faces or facets of the man, the milieu and the mentality.

The Dreyfus Affair, one of the shaping events of the modern age, occurred over a twelve-year period, from 1894 to 1906. This event began in France twenty years before the outbreak of World War I, but came to involve the rest of Europe and North America, with repercussions as far away as Australia and New Zealand. The affair that bears his name concerned a young artillery officer in the French Army named Alfred Dreyfus.

He was in his early thirties, comfortably married with two children, and at the beginning of a brilliant military career. Everything fell apart one morning, however, when Dreyfus was summoned to his office in the Intelligence Department and accused of offering to sell military secrets to the German embassy in Paris. With virtually no proof at all—and what little evidence was at first adduced and then used covertly at his court-martial a few months later proved to be either irrelevant, ambiguous, or forged—Dreyfus was found guilty of treason, stripped of his rank as a captain, and sent to perpetual incarceration in solitary confinement on Devil's Island, a former leper colony and an unpopulated outcrop of rock near the French colony of Cayenne or French Guiana on the northeastern coast of South America.

The morning he was arrested, it was as though he had been lifted up out of his normal life and suddenly found himself in a five-year-long nightmare, an absurd and grotesque dream—or a mad and fantastic silent film, of the type which was just beginning to be made at exactly the same time by men like Georges Méliès. In other words, a theatre of grotesque illusions, a horror movie, a nightmare.

But this event was no simple *phantasmagoria*. It was all very real, all too real. Alfred Dreyfus had been set up, framed, and scapegoated because he was a Jew. Although he was a dashing young officer who rode his horse every morning before going to the office at military headquarters, although he was a comfortably middle-class husband married to a rich and educated wife, although he seemed to be a normal Frenchman of the late nineteenth century, to the anti-Semites in France he was an ugly stage Jew with a hooked nose and disgusting habits, and he was caricatured almost daily in the press and on posters as a dangerous non-Aryan monster[4] who could never fit in and who threatened Christian France. He was hated by screaming mobs in the streets, who called out, "Down with the traitor! Death to Dreyfus! Death to the Jews!"[5]

At first, only his wife, immediate family, and a few close friends believed that there had been a miscarriage of justice, a mistake, an error in the procedures of the court-martial. Most people in France, including most French Jews, simply accepted the verdict of the military tribunal. But Edouard Drumont and the anti-Semitic press and a political opposition made up of an unholy alliance of Boulangists or disgruntled monarchists, angry Jesuits and fearful Catholic priests, and all sorts of jingoistic patriots began to whip up strong feelings both in the streets and in the chambers of the French parliament.

From 1894 through 1897, not many people inside or outside the Jewish community of France seemed to care—except Alfred's wife, Lucie, and older brother, Mathieu Dreyfus, and their extended families, along with just one or two other allies. Again, as is now widely known, this early inner circle of Dreyfusards pledged their time, their fortunes, and their lives to the cause of proving Alfred Dreyfus innocent and bringing him back from Devil's Island for a revision of the verdict against him. Most of the Jewish community in France, it seems, did not believe, or did not want to believe, that he was innocent, because to do so would question their loyalty to the French Republic. Many feared, as too often happens even today, that taking a public stand would draw too much attention to themselves as Jews. A few probably also considered themselves more French than Jewish or not even really Jewish at all, and to protect their own status and to prove in public their separation from the organized synagogues and rabbinical institutions, they even spoke out as anti-Dreyfusards. Some of them perhaps honestly believed that whether he was innocent or not, the best course for France was to accept the verdict of the military courts

4 Although this Germanic terminology was not used often in France, the label Semite was applied regularly to Jews, and the Semite is always implicitly contrasted to the Aryan or whatever is currently fashionable for the nationalist racial ideal. Gobineau was not cited often in the last decades of the nineteenth century.

5 Romain Rolland: "Just look at your old Dreyfus affair. You shouted loud enough: 'Death! Blood! Slaughter!' . . . Oh! you Gascons! Spittle and ink! But how many drops of blood?'" (*Jean Christophe*, vol. III, 228).

and to respect the opinions of the men in government.

Yet gradually, through the second half of the 1890s, the truth began to emerge—that there was a strong possibility that Dreyfus had been framed by a small clique of envious officers, that the real spy and traitor was a rather unsavoury character of Hungarian descent named Charles Marie Ferdinand Walsin Esterhazy, that the officers in the French high command were lying and forging documents to protect one another, and that this corruption went right up into the offices of cabinet ministers and even, it seemed, to the president of the republic. So by 1898, a great wave of reaction had began to form, calling for, on the one hand, a revision of Dreyfus's verdict from the court-martial and, on the other, for a radical change in government and a separation of church and state in France.

Despite the emergence of a new class or category of people, the intellectuals, who spoke out for Dreyfus and signed their names to petitions,[6] the military, the government, and the clergy tried to bluff it out, using all the means at their disposal—not only newspapers and books but new media as well, such as motion pictures, illustrated postcards, wax museums, vaudeville shows, and street parades. Matters reached a head, however, when the most popular and important novelist of the day, Emile Zola, published a scathing attack on the whole of the establishment. In a full-page open letter in the press, Zola's *J'Accuse* (*I Accuse*) forced the issue into the public arena. In the following days, weeks, and months, a new kind of group came into being—the intellectuals. Students and professors, doctors and lawyers, and writers and artists signed petitions almost every day in the newspapers, calling for a revision of the original verdict.

But while there were also mobs screaming in the streets for the death of the traitor Dreyfus, the Jew, and all the Jews, there also seemed to be professional men and women, cultural leaders, and university-trained people, also intellectuals, arguing that the honour of the army must precede that of an individual, that the ideals of France were worth more

---

6 Romain Rolland: "There were famous men among them men who had been wrenched away from their stylistic labors and plunged into public meetings by the Dreyfus affair . . . . There was now a mob of writing men all engrossed in politics, and claiming to control the affairs of the State. On the slightest excuse they would form societies, issue manifestoes, save the Capitol. After the intellectuals of the advance guard came the intellectuals of the rear: they were very much of a muchness. Each of the two parties regarded the other as intellectual and themselves as intelligent" (*Jean Christophe*, vol. III, 179).

than simple justice, and that if Dreyfus were found innocent, then the whole of the military leadership and most of the government would have to resign—something untenable.

Several other related trials took place in the 1890s, all part of the Dreyfus Affair—that of Emil Zola, the novelist who had spoken out so bravely; of Colonel Georges Picquart, the military officer whose investigations had confirmed Dreyfus's innocence; and of the infamous Esterhazy, the real culprit, all against the Dreyfusards—until a second court-martial for Dreyfus took place. Each trial resulted in victory not for the Dreyfusards but for the anti-Dreyfusards. Even Colonel Henry's suicide[7] raised more sympathy for the case against Dreyfus, rather than undercutting it.

In 1898, in the provincial city of Rennes, for a second time, to the dismay of the intellectuals and of liberal, progressive men and women around the world, Alfred Dreyfus was found guilty again—but this time, adding insult to injury, with what was called extenuating circumstances. Picquart was found guilty in his trial, and Esterhazy was declared innocent in his. As for Alfred, twice condemned by military tribunals, even after the civilian court of appeals had found the evidence insufficient to accept the original verdict and thus set the stage for the second Rennes trial, the offer of a pardon was too good to be turned down on principle: his family and friends were convinced that his health and sanity could not be risked again. How could they allow him to be sent back to Devil's Island for another day, let alone another five or ten years? Thankfully, there was by then a new, more liberal government in Paris embarrassed by the whole affair, and so a few days later, Dreyfus was indeed pardoned. Yet the struggle for his exoneration carried on for several more years until 1906, and eventually he was brought back into the army, promoted, and given the *Legion d'honneur*. Yet none of those responsible for the crimes of perjury, deception, and worse were

7 A documentary film by Jean Cherasse made in 1975, *Dreyfus: L'Intolerable vérité* (rereleased in 2006 for the centenary of Alfred Dreyfus's rehabilitation on DVD by Janus Diffusion and available at http://www.horsfilm.com), alludes to questions raised about the veracity of this culprit's death as self-inflicted, not least because the colonel's corpse was never subjected to a postmortem examination. Like the accidental death of Emile Zola by asphyxiation due to a malfunctioning gas heater in his home or the failure of police to apprehend the would-be assassin of Dreyfus's lawyer during the Rennes trial, this is one of the still-unsolved mysteries associated with the affair. (On the theory that Zola was murdered by an anti-Dreyfusard workman, see Frederick Brown, *Zola: A Life* [New York: Farrar, Straus and Giroux, 1996]).

brought to account, except for a few who committed suicide.

In hindsight, we can see that justice was not done, peace was not restored, and the truth was not fully known or given its proper due. The great paradox of the affair, then and now, is that while Dreyfus and the Dreyfusards wrestled with the monsters in their nightmare as though the enigma of his persecution still lay in an unresolved distortion of justice—the judicial error and the mystery of why the powers-that-be still suspected him of treason—the anti-Dreyfusards and the old Dreyfusards who grew weary of his whining and moaning did know the truth: it was because Alfred belonged to the Jews—that unassimilable, annoying, untrustworthy other.

The Narrative of the Case

> *This is not a book. A book, even a bad book, is a serious affair. A phrase that might be excellent in the fourth chapter would be all wrong in the second, and it's not everybody who knows the trick.*
>
> —Paul Gauguin[8]

One definition of a myth is "what everyone says." The ancient Greeks and Romans did not use this term because what we see as *mythos* in the sense of lies or false stories or fantastic explanations for things they could not otherwise understand, they called histories, in other words what everybody says and consequently believes. They are not books or formal, rational arguments, *logoi*. The argument I am making here is only a *book* in a superficial sense: it is a way of playing with the words of the narrative everyone says they know and believe. I am not trying to say it is false, but that this so-called history of Alfred Dreyfus and the affair that bears his name is not "the truth, the whole truth, and nothing but the truth." Much if not most of what is found in history books is true today. However, not all the truth appears in them, and there are some untruths mixed up in the official narrative. Most of all, what is left out in Dreyfus's history is Alfred Dreyfus himself, the man, as well as

8 Paul Gauguin, *The Intimate Journals* (London, Boston, Sydney, and Henley: KPI/Pacific Basin Books, 1985 [1983]; orig. trans. 1923; orig. French 1903), 1. Then a few pages later, he adds, "Besides, even if he has no serious readers, the author of a book must be serious" (4).

his wife Lucie, and how they formed a new milieu in writing for themselves, and how this milieu, as we shall see, is a midrashic one. To begin with, as I have already begun to do, my words and processes will seem to come less out of Jewish techniques of reading and more out of the shifts in optics and aesthetics occurring in the nineteenth century. The other thing left out is more than just that Dreyfus was a *Jew*, but that he was *Jewish*. Though he thought of himself as an assimilated Frenchman and tried to dismiss the anti-Semites howling out on the streets as irrelevant fools, he thought and felt like a Jew, guided more and more by his wife Lucie in her letters. Whatever he may have believed about himself, the Jew-haters saw him as Jewish and thus absolutely unassimilable. They read the clues in his actions and words, and so we have to take their interpretations seriously because their bigotry and ignorance was in response to qualities in his personality, his milieu, and his mentality, which was different, alien, special. Drumont and his colleagues were wrong about Dreyfus being a spy, part of a conspiracy by the enemies of France, and a figure of evil, but they were right about him being Jewish. In due course, my book will address the questions about what it meant to be Jewish in France at the end of the nineteenth century and what traditional resources of rabbinical knowledge and analysis Alfred could have drawn on, even if he did not know he was doing so.

As I said above, one of the shaping events of the modern age occurred over a twelve-year period, from 1894 to 1906. To know what a "shaping event" is, we need to pass the received opinions (which the midrashic rabbis called *pshat*) through a number of epistemological and aesthetic filters, that is, to diffract the light rays—to break them up through a moral filter, so as to reveal what has not been noticed before, or what could not even be seen because of the shadows out there in archival reality and inside the mind of the participants in these events. This momentous set of events did indeed begin in France twenty years before the outbreak of World War I, and come to involve the rest of Europe and North America, and even Australia and New Zealand. The life of a promising young artillery officer and family man began to fall apart upon the accusation that he had offered to sell military secrets to the German embassy in Paris. As everyone now knows or thinks they know, despite the extraordinarily weak and falsified case against him, Dreyfus was found guilty of treason and punished: stripped of his rank as a captain and sent to perpetual incarceration in solitary confinement on Devil's Island. His arrest seemed to remove Dreyfus from his normal life and into a world of insanity, reminiscent of the worlds men like Georges Méliès were just beginning to create in cinema with the new instruments in the world's techological toolbox. Dreyfus did not know about these technological advances in optics, but he sensed in his deepest soul that something had changed and that he could no longer trust his own perceptions or his mind to make sense of what he was experiencing.

But although Dreyfus himself later used the word *phantasmagoria* to describe the experience, it did not fit that definition in truth. It is clear that he was set up, framed, and scapegoated because, despite his profession, despite his behavior, and despite his lack of religious conviction, to France's anti-Semites he remained a Jew, wearing an ugly mask with the features anti-Semites throughout recent history have given to members of his class.

The absurdity of all this resonates close to home now for us. In late October 2011, another Jew, also a Frenchman, a soldier, and an innocent young man, was released from five years of imprisonment, five years of torture and solitary confinement, five years kept out of the sunshine, with no contact with the outside world. When he was released, he looked emaciated, weak, confused, hardly able to stand erect, fumbling in his speech. In many ways this young Israeli, Gilad Shalit, is like Alfred Dreyfus. There are, of course, many important differences, but a central similarity is the fact that Gilad, like Alfred, was transported from normal life to a nightmare existence. The differences mainly serve to remind us about what was unique in Dreyfus's case—that the young Israeli was not left alone by his nation and that his plight did not split the intellectuals from the ordinary citizens of France. The modern instance also alerts us to the fact that for a Jew, while certain specific circumstances shift and reconfigure themselves through the books of history, there is also something unique in the experience of hatred in the world, as though that world of prejudice and cruelty could at least temporarily override rationality and justice.

How so?

Because the military tribunal, made up of respected French military officers, produced a unanimous verdict, it was at first difficult to persuade any members of society at all that it had been in error. As Eli Wiesel, one of the leading moralists and witnesses to the Holocaust in our times, points out often, anti-Semitism is a form of moral, that is, pyschological, contagion that goes from cell to cell, person to person, and nation to nation, and no cynical or hard-headed economic or materialistic explanations can explain what it is or why it happens.

In 1898, when the second court martial was at last held, Alfred Dreyfus was shockingly found guilty again, with "extenuating circumstances." The main extenuating circumstance, as his supporters could clearly see, was that Dreyfus was innocent. It was a joke, a shock, an abuse of logic, a perversion of justice.

These flagrant distortions of the truth could not be accepted, and yet they were and by many, for they were believed to belong to a higher truth, that of reasons of state, the honour of the Army, the glory of France, and the integrity of the Church, The culture shock, the abuse of reason, flabberghasts us only in retrospect, although many Dreyfusards, like Emile Gallé the *art nouveau* glass-maker, believed the world was coming to an end.

Words before Things

> *Someone must have been telling lies about Joseph K., for without having done anything wrong he was arrested one fine morning.*
>
> —Franz Kafka, *The Trial*[9]

Hundreds, if not thousands, of books concerning the Dreyfus Affair already exist—many of them quite thorough and up-to-date. Such books deal with history, sociology, law, politics, aesthetics, and morality. In what is an example of a collective scale of "inattentional blindness,"[10] these academic historians, their publishers, editors, reviewers, and general readers tend not to see what is most significant about the affair. This would include not only what the mobs in the streets of the big cities and towns of France during the late 1890s considered central, and the popular anti-Semitic press screamed day after day in their headlines and editorials—the fact that Dreyfus was a Jew and the treason he was as-

9 Franz Kafka, *The Trial*, definitive edition, with an epilogue by Max Brod, trans. Willa and Edwin Muir (London: Secker and Warburg, 1950); *Der Prozess* (Berlin: Verlag die Schmiede, 1925), 7.

10 This is a term coined by Daniel Simons and Christopher Chabris in the late 1990s after a series of experiments in which a gorilla passed unseen through a room of students concentrating on tasks that they thought was the point of the experiment; to be discussed later in this book.

sumed to have committed was part of an age-old rabbinical conspiracy, and also that Alfred Dreyfus and his family, as well as the family of his wife, Lucie, were wrenched out of their normal lives and forced by circumstances to reinvent themselves. This process that was only partly typical of how other educated, middle-class, assimilated Jewish families in Western Europe had to conduct themselves in public and at home—and in their own most private, intimate moments. Exactly what was the normal life of Captain and Madame Dreyfus before his arrest? How Jewish were they? How aware and concerned were they about the matters Alfred chose to write about in his prison notebooks of 1898, such as contemporary psychology, aesthetic theory, historiography, imperial and colonial developments, and political economy, for instance? Have they and we missed the gorilla standing in the middle of the scene?

The Dreyfus Affair as a political phenomenon, to be sure, grew out of attitudes and opinions that were already in the process of changing by the final decade of the nineteenth century—and these attitudes and opinions had been part of people's minds and were ordinary everyday ways of seeing the world[11] and were reflected as well in the more refined perceptions and feelings of the arts, the sciences, and the philosophies of the period. The affair also did concern the issues that the Dreyfusards believed were under threat—liberty, equality, and fraternity, along with justice and secularism and scientific reason. On the other hand, did it not also deal with the issues the anti-Dreyfusards believed in—the traditional values of rural France, the dignity of the army as the backbone of the nation, the spiritual power of the Catholic Church and its institutions, the threats made by modernity, not least the industrial revolution, the transformation of the economy from agriculture to urban productivity, and the breakdown of the family and the community? It would be egregious to dismiss all the opponents of Dreyfus as ignorant, fanatical lunatics, just as it would be to idealize the Dreyfusards all as sincere, intellectual, and tolerant citizens. There were fools and cynics on both sides.

One phrase in the lectures of Jakob Burckhardt clears the air by blow-

---

11 Here is what John Rewald says in an analogous situation: "Thus the new phase in the history of art inaugurated by the impressionist exhibition of 1874 was not a sudden outbreak of iconoclastic tendencies; it was the culmination of a slow and consistent evolution" ("Introduction," *The History of Impressionism*, 4th rev. ed. [New York: The Museum of Modern Art/Boston: New York Graphic Society, 1980 (1973), orig. 1946], 8).

ing away the smoke and the mists of illusion that fill the places where the Dreyfus Affair is still discussed. The nineteenth-century Swiss historian says, almost in passing, that after 1870, the French, even France itself, became afraid of its own shadow.[12] The shadow represents the illusions and impressions that hovered over the realities of life itself so that this is a way of saying that France became fearful of itself. The nature of the fear was the terror of modernity, and behind it still further is the anxiety of the *fin de siècle*. Was the image of Alfred Dreyfus the scapegoat for the shadow of France? Was the Dreyfus Affair a phantasmagoria displayed when the magic lantern of his story—his arrest, his condemnation, his exile, his long years on Devil's Island, his return for a revision of his trial, and the defeats again and again of his fight for honour—was projected on those smoky clouds in the darkness of the 1890s? Can we say that the whole experience of his ordeal was not so much a tragedy by Racine or Corneille or even his beloved Shakespeare, nor even a philosophical novel or allegorical tale of rationality and justice versus obscurantism and demagoguery, but more like the bizarre and grotesque films of Georges Méliès, a pioneering French cinematographer who portrayed fantastic journeys to the moon, visions of men whose heads explode, and choreographed pictures of dancing musical notes played by half-clad young women? These shadowy mechanized pictures are always in motion, shadows scattering and colliding into one another like atoms, creating the impression of a reality undermined by its power of fantasy.

This book will try to engage with many of these changes in the social and intellectual milieu in the processes of transformation of those mentalities that constitute the national consciousness and its imagination, as they push and pull, influence, and reshape each other. This book demonstrates that *midrash* is at once an analytical tool we can use to discuss the Dreyfus Affair and the people involved in it, as well as an epistemological stratagem used by Jews, consciously or not, to survive in a non-Jewish and often anti-Jewish world. It will consequently also be a book about the isolated life imposed on Dreyfus by the military and prison authorities or rather projected on to him by all of French society, while he bravely tried to maintain his inner dignity and sanity, and how, through his love for his wife, Lucie, and her active efforts on his behalf,

12 Burkhardt, Jacob, *Force and Freedom: Reflections on History*, ed. James Hastings Nichols (Boston, MA: Beacon Press, 1964 [Pantheon Books, 1943]).

he generated a whole new moral dimension of reality for the both of them.[13] Their mutual efforts form part of the midrashic transformation of their milieu, through acts of *tikkun ha'olam* and *tikkun ha'nefesh*, the repair or correction of the world and of their souls.

Man: *L'Humanité*

> *By extension, the term "children" can designate something born of the mind, like opinions (GP, I:7, p. 32). The "children" who will bear the brunt of God's wrath are now identified with a facet of Jacob's personality. Jacob's thought processes and intellectual maturity will be frustrated to some extent by the natural progression of history as represented by the four kingdoms.*
>
> —James Arthur Diamond[14]

Although this book is neither a history nor a biography, it is about Alfred Dreyfus the man[15]—the military officer, the husband, the father, the son, the man of his time, and the Jew—and so it is an anthropology in the old sense of a study of man as a moral being, a *mensch*. Instead of bearing the sexist burden of terms like *macho* and *patriarchal*, this sense of *mankind* stands proudly in the domain of humanity and humanism. The analysis here follows the kind shown by Diamond in his analysis of the interpretative techniques and strategies used by Maimonides in his monumental *Guide of the Perplexed*. These methods of analysis and midrashing are also central to my own way of understanding the Dreyfus Affair and the way in which I read the statements and actions that constitute it. For instance, right here, I am modelling my argument on

---

13 Unlike the Proust family, in which Jeanne née Weil seems not to have practiced the Judaism of her family and ensured that her sons, Marcel and Robert, were brought up with knowledge of Catholicism, the families of Alfred and particularly Lucie were still observant, at least to the point of being married by a rabbi, celebrating the main Jewish holidays of the year, and teaching their children the basic forms of worship. Cf. Evelyne Bloch-Dono, *Madame Proust* (Paris: Grasset, 2004), 15.

14 James Arthur Diamond, *Maimonides and the Hermeneutic of Concealment: Deciphering Scripture and Midrash in* The Guide of the Perplexed (Albany, NY: SUNY Press, 2002), 128. In Diamond's statement, *GP* stands for *The Guide of the Perplexed*.

15 A year before this book appeared, some booksellers were already advertising it online, and I found one of them had included it in their "masculine" titles, which I came to discover meant it had something to do with gay men's lifestyles.

what the Rambam (that is, Maimonides) does with the figure of the *sulam* (ladder) and *semel* (statue), both spelled the same in Hebrew as *SML*.

> This type of wordplay seems to be best suited for plumbing the depths of cryptic visual objects that are encoded with secrets or matters pertaining to *ma'asseh ber'eshit* [the narrative of the creation recounted in the opening chapters of Genesis] and *merkavah* [the elaborate apocalyptic image of the chariot of God described in Ezekiel].[16]

In fact, in order to plumb the depths of the Dreyfus Affair, it becomes necessary to treat words and phrases, as well as imagery and rhetorical tropes, in ways quite dissimilar to those usually used by social scientists and deconstructionists. Gradually, through our midrashic reading of the relevant documents, it will be possible to see how Alfred Dreyfus worked within the paradigm of *melitza*, rabbinical rhetoric and poetics, what José Faur calls "horizontal dialectics."[17]

So, in one sense, I will be using a lot of old words, or familiar words in their older senses. However, I will be going out of my way to avoid contemporary usages, jargons, and neologisms because their inaccuracy is part of what I see as a disastrous loss of historical sensibility and knowledge, a shameful lack of sensitivity in thinking and feeling, and a terrible loss of great areas of what used to be common human experiences, the very places in the life of the man—and of the mankind, humanity, *humanité*—Dreyfus cared about and suffered for. For instance, when he writes about morals, he means not simply sexual habits and attitudes, but instead, as it used to mean, a concept that includes psychology, public ethics, and private self-control and integrity. Morals are thus closely related to the anthropology first mentioned, part of the experience of and the value in *humanité*. It is these now virtually unfamiliar and disparaged concepts from which arises another old word, *honour*, with the dignity, integrity, sense of loyalty, duty, and pride that it embodies.

I also try to avoid the incomplete passive structures of sentences. This way of forming syntax removes active, responsible human agents from the world and replaces them with allegorical personifications of abstract

16 Diamond, *Maimionides and the Hermeneutics of Concealment*, 87.

17 Faur, *The Horizontal Society*, section IV, introductory remarks.

and linguistic constructs. Thus, instead of arguments and struggles between individuals and groups representing living interests, even when much of what is at stake is unconscious or poorly misunderstood, the universe is conceived by this postmodernist discourse as merely paradigm shifting and "societal" powers wrestling with one another in an endless and quite meaningless tussle. Again, the consequence of such malformations creates something beyond the awkwardness, weakness, or infelicity of style that would occur if it were merely an occasional lapse; as a persistent and pervasive feature of the current scholarly language, it marks out huge areas of what Alfred Dreyfus saw to be *l'inanité, la déraison humaine, cette légende imbécile, une pretendue bonne foi . . .*[18]

Milieu: The Ambient World

> *On n'a peut-être pas assez remarqué que, bien avant 1914 et alors qu'elle n'avait aucun sens de la gravité de l'heure, la société française ne connaissait plus l'ironie.*
>
> —Julien Benda[19]

The study will have at its centre less the *Affair Dreyfus* than *l'homme Dreyfus*, the man Alfred Dreyfus—one who is not only elusive but also often effectively absent from many accounts, which at best take him as a symbol or a cipher, whereas he was instead a person of flesh and blood, a man of intellect and emotions, a son, a father, a brother, and a husband, and he was a part of a family, a community, a nation: a secular Jew and a patriotic Frenchman, a soldier, an engineer, an intellectual, and a man of his period. Indeed, Dreyfus was very much a man with a history and a place.

Ironic? The newspapers, even those somewhat inclined at first to hesitate at proclaiming his guilt, called him "the zinc man" in the press, and even after he returned home from Devil's Island for the revision of his trial, alluding to what they thought was his lack of feeling, his fail-

18 These phrases are taken almost at random from the pages of Dreyfus's *carnets* of 1899–1907, volumes which are to be discussed at greater length further into this book.

19 Julien Benda, *Belphegor: Essai sur l'esthétique de la présente société française*, 2eme éd. (Paris: Emile-Paul Frères, 1924), 130–131. "Perhaps it hadn't been noticed enough but well before 1914 and because it had no sense at all of the seriousness of the times, French society no longer recognized irony."

ure to display the passions of a true-born Frenchman, they blamed him for not breaking through the icy hatred of his accusers and judges. For those who didn't know him, Dreyfus was aloof, taciturn, and stiff in a military way. But even for those in his family and the allies who began to study his case, Dreyfus was not a warm, emotionally expressive man. He was a friend to few, and yet, as we will come to see him, extrapolating from his own writings during his imprisonment back to the more carefree days of his early marriage, a man with wide tastes in books and art.

During the affair and especially afterwards, to be sure, Alfred Dreyfus changed—how could he not? His circle of acquaintances grew, his view of the world matured, and his inner world went through a transformation. But these changes were not known to most people outside his family, even as it expanded to include those who had rallied to his cause and those whose children married his own. What he exposed to the outside world was unspeakable: for amongst these Dreyfusards were many former supporters who, following his acceptance of the pardon, could see no reason to remain loyal to a man who seemed to betray *their* cause. Their goals were ideological and political in ways that did not fit with a military man, a believer in moral values, and a Jew. These socialists, anarchists, and progressives saw in Dreyfus's personal campaign for total rehabilitation something better kept private because otherwise it would just prove annoying, if not downright dangerous to their new cause in government.

Though often categorized as a loner, a solitary, unsocial being, Dreyfus was very much a social being—son, brother, husband, father—and his solitary self was a protective screen, while his unsociableness was an illusion, a mask of a person isolated within himself almost to the point of autism which he was forced to wear by circumstances, by the pressure of the press, and by the trick of the anti-Semites. Like the man in Méliès's film whose head grows larger and larger until it at last explodes, Dreyfus's autistic image is an illusion, and he was seen, because he was expected to be seen, wearing this and related masks.

While he balked at accepting the pardon offered in 1899 following the second condemnation at Rennes, he did in the end accept it, to the chagrin of those supporters who wanted him to remain the victim and the martyr, to wear the mask of the drama they wished to keep producing to their own political ends, while he took the role offered on the understanding that, no matter how it was hidden from the spectators, he would keep up the fight for his dignity and his good name.

These changing masks and the changeable qualities they projected and hid together constitute his milieu or the matrix in which he lived—and may be termed, in the sense in which Dreyfus came to use the term in regard to his life, *artistic*. To outsiders, Dreyfus, the zinc marionette, whether they actually knew him in person or not, was a symbol and a cipher, and it is important to analyse those roles carefully. The symbol was a sign of issues in politics and philosophy that were swirling around society in the long aftermath of the disastrous Franco-Prussian War of 1870 and the lead-up to the Great War of 1914–1918, *la der des der.*[20] The was being a less clear and more dreamlike indicator of the anxieties and other stresses that haunted the *fin du siècle*, that first period between wars, what Léon Daudet called *l'entre-deux-guerres*.[21] This was not a one-man show at all, although sometimes it seemed like a no-man show—the affair without Dreyfus—but a complex interactive performance wherein multiple mentalities, with their fluid imaginations and shifting, dynamic ideologies played off against one another.

Mentalités

> *The Dreyfus Affair left him [Daniel Halévy] very much changed, subject to spells of amnesia and melancholia.*
>
> —Mina Curtiss[22]

But this book is perhaps more interested in two other things, although it does not leave aside completely the question of milieu. Like Daniel Halévy, many, if not most, Frenchmen and women were morally ill, mentally disturbed by the affair, although as we have said—and will explain in due course—they projected their disease onto one man on a faraway Devil's Island. One of the matters we push to the fore of the milieu is the mentality, or rather mentalities, which made the Dreyfus Af-

---

20 The War to End All Wars, *la dernière des dernières*; cf. Robert Liris, *L'Ordinaire de Vichy. 1940–1942* (Bellerive sur Allier: Privately Published, 2010), 67.

21 Léon Daudet, *L'entre-deux-guerres: souvenirs* (Paris: Nouvelle Librairie Nationale, 1915). This confused and degenerated generation between 1870 and 1914 is not to be confused with the interwar period from 1919 to 1939.

22 Daniel Halévy, *My Friend Degas*, trans. and ed. Mina Curtiss (Middletown, CT: Wesley University Press, 1964) n. 7, 33; original edition of Halévy's memoir entitled *Degas parle* (Paris: La Palestine, 1960).

fair possible. The affair was more than an isolated instance of a "judicial error" or a localized grievance lodged by his family and friends. It was something that gave historical shape and substance to an era—the people, the events, and the ideas current during a given period of historical and existential time—and was an organizing concept in an ideology, sometimes virtually a vivid narrative in the sense of a myth, and thus a suite of intertwining affective and cognitive tensions that wound over more than a dozen years from 1894 to 1906, playing itself out through that kind of intelligence we have called elsewhere mentalities. In other words, they may be envisioned as subatomic particles constituted of energy, mass, and antimatter described metaphorically as the spoken and the unspeakable, the seen and the unseeable, the conceivable and the inconceivable, the imagined and the unimaginable, and the experienced and the unconscious.

The expression "intelligence" is to be taken in a dynamic sense, as it was used by one of Dreyfus's favourite authors, Hippolyte Taine. In *On Intelligence*, Taine defines the seen, the conceivable and the imagined as "a true hallucination"; in other words, what the mind comes to know it has to reconstruct from the confused sensations of experience and the stock of memory sensations it brings up at such a point of sensory arousal. Yet this mental image or hallucination is unseeable, inconceivable and unimaginable outside the mind—as are the more fantastic hallucinations created by the mind, unless somehow they are confirmed by other persons and tested against external objects and forces. Unlike Plato, who would consequently banish poets from his ideal City because they compounded the hallucinatory effect of unreliable imitations of vague impressions of ideas, or Kant, who could find no reliable means of confirming the unreliability of sensory experience, Taine offers an Enlightenment solution, at least a practical working proposition through scientific and rational training of the mind. Dreyfus, who had had unquestioned faith in the methods of science and technology, comes to doubt the reality of what is happening to him, and seeks, partly through acts of the imagination, partly through love-driven dialectical conversations with his wife Lucie, and partly through an intellectual ordering of his mind, including, as we shall show in a further study, the reiteration of variations on particular doodles or row on row of drawings that are related but never the same, to maintain his sanity, his emotions, and his sense of faith in Truth and Justice. Intelligence combines for Dreyfus, as it does for Taine, both poetry and science, creative thought and rational proofs.

Thus, it is not so much the world of feelings and ideas (a *world picture* or *Weltanchauung*) as it is the realm where feelings and ideas come in and out of existence and awareness. This is the mentality in which the affair can only be spoken about, thought about, and imagined precisely in relation to textual gaps and silences, historical surrogates, and mistakes, in philosophical fringes and thus heard, read, and perceived between the lines, as well as in denials and misunderstandings. But how does one write about such things?

Midrash

> *I staggered through a world whose signs remained as inscrutable to me as Etruscan script. Unlike the tourist, for whom such things may be a piquant form of alienation, I was dependent on this world full of riddles.*
>
> —Jean Améry [23]

> *From Dreyfus's point of view the world had turned upside down, and it proved too much for him to endure. He went temporarily mad, screaming his innocence and banging his head against the walls of his cell until it was bloody.*
>
> —Michael Kurland[24]

What does it mean to be in a wonderland of riddles and nightmares, where nothing seems to make sense at all and where interpretations are violent and bloody? Is this *midrash* or *mishmash* or *mishigas*?[25] Here

---

23 Jean Amery, *At the Mind's Limits: Contemplations by a Survivor on Auschwitz and Its Realities*, trans. Sidney Rosenfeld and Stella P. Rosenfeld (Bloomington and Indianapolis, IN: Indiana University Press, 1980; 1977), 47.

24 Michael Kurland, "An Account of the Ordeal of Alfred Dreyfus," *Knol* (13 September 2008), 10 online at http://knol.google.com/k/michael-kurland/dreyfu[alfred/1m3ftpwcv6va/3.

25 In contemporary usage, *midrash* has almost come to replace *aggadah* as the term for a rabbinical story or riddle or poem that helps to explicate a sacred passage, indicate how a law may be applied, or demonstrate the process of analysis needed to engage with a revealed message. It is also usual to define *aggadah* in relation to *halachah*, the legal explication or application itself, in the sense that whatever is not *halachah* is *aggadah* and vice versa. This kind of ambiguous and relatively open-ended definition, however, does not help us move to the term *midrash* outside the strict historical boundaries of rabbinical discourse nor promote understanding of the term *midrashing*,

where the sense is deeply implicated in specific historical examples of rabbinical exegeses, I am concerned mostly with how the term *midrash* developed. Scholars have noted evidence of the *midrash* being understood as both the thing produced and the techniques of analysis, interpretation, and application found already in Hebrew scriptures, as well as in legal and homiletic books outside the strictly authorized documents of the Oral Torah. Hence, it can be extrapolated without too much effort to be a verb—*to midrash, to be midrashed*, that is—a process of acting in the world both psychologically and politically.

Though related to the classical Greek and Roman and Christian legal discourses of allegory, parable, metaphor, metonymy, and so forth—the figures of thought and speech that constitute the colours of rhetoric—the *midrash* is more dynamic, fluid, witty, ingenious, and radical. Alphabetic letters (their shapes, their sizes, and their actual placements on the page), lexical units or words (sounded, seen, and organized in relation to one another), syntax and grammar (logically, historically, and wittily conceived), and allusiveness (near and far-fetched, adjusted and re-created) are in a *midrash* fissured, scattered, reassembled, but also turned upside down, inside out, and backwards, so that the meaning is as much a hallucination as the reality is a counterhallucination.

The *midrash*, turned from noun (a historical and specifically rabbinical mode of exegesis or discourse, a genre) to a verb (a transformation of the world and of the self's place in it), in regard to the Dreyfus Affair and to Alfred Dreyfus the man or the mensch, is a way of using a very

---

a verb to indicate how the mentality of rabbinical exegesis in this poetic, speculative, and creative sense can be seen in social and individual actions. Another drawback in the use of the aggadah-halachah pairing can be shown to be historical and culture-specific. As David Shasha puts it, introducing Leon Wieseltier's review of Rabbi Adin Steinsaltz's now completed translation into modern Hebrew of the Talmud, "There is no evidence in the Ashkenazi tradition between Halakha and Aggada because both of them serve to express the Divine truth in a literal way." He then adds, by way of contrast—and he is again exaggerating for the sake of a polemical argument, or at least one hopes he is—"In the Maimonidean tradition—rejected by the Ashkenazim—Halakha is binding after the ruling of the Sage or rabbinical court while Aggada is a more open-ended creative process." From my perspective, this kind of mutually exclusive thinking may perhaps be temporarily true in regard to certain hard-line conservative elements in the Orthodox branch of Ashkenazi Judaism but does not square with the more inclusive and longer historical perspective. Even Shasha himself also often complains that contemporary Sephardim, especially the subcategory of Arabic-speaking Syrian Jews to which he belongs, have allowed themselves to give away their own ancient traditions centered on Maimonides and other wise men. David Shasha, "SHU Classic Article Revisited: Leon Wieseltier on the Steinsaltz Talmud" (1989) available through davidsha@googlegroups.com (11 November 2010). A *mishmash* is a mixed-up thing, a *balagan*, as they say in Hebrew, and a *mishigas* is a crazy thing.

Jewish word for a very Jewish experience and a common type of modern Jew, and because of that, this book takes very seriously the role that anti-Semitism played in causing, giving shape and substance to, and providing the continuing influence for the affair, for *midrash* is not only a historical phenomenon, an ancient rabbinical artefact, a way of interpreting scripture and shaping the law; it may be the term we have come to use for an insidious, counterintuitive, uncreating way of imagining Jews living in and experiencing the non-Jewish or anti-Jewish world of the late nineteenth century in France and elsewhere in Europe.

Since so much scholarship on the Dreyfus Affair tends to denominate the *Jewish background*, placing it in the margins of history and conceptual thought, treating it as a nasty and annoying background noise to the reality of the events and the personages that constitute the events and ideas they want to deal with,[26] this book will have to dwell on the anti-Semitism.[27] We have to ask more than *who* were its proponents or *why* they believed that Jews had invaded France and were ruining its traditional values and institutions, but also *how* these false perceptions were generated and maintained for generation after generation, and *what* were the epistemological and aesthetic consequences of these distortions. Such recurrent anti-Jewish prejudices can be used to explain partly why justice was traduced in the affair, in trial after trial, for there were many; why documents were forged; why witnesses perjured themselves; why otherwise normal and orderly people rioted in the streets; and why old friends and relations—artists and intellectuals both—split apart over the affair, but they won't explain why these distorted and insane ideas took hold and seemed convincing and rational.

How were the Dreyfusards and the anti-Dreyfusards convinced by the same apparent evidence either to act or not to act—almost everyone had a point of view, but not everyone wrote letters to the paper, signed petitions, joined a league, contributed money, or marched in the boulevards—and how did they attempt to persuade others that Jews were or were not an alien presence to be removed by all necessary means from the heart of the nation? Indeed, what was the heart and what was the nation? And did all that hullabaloo mean that the two sides in the great

26 How much of this "wanting" can be measured will be discussed later in this book, where we deal with the limitations of the current critical imagination.

27 Including a cloying and equally distorting philo-Judaism to be found in many booklets, pamphlets, and letters of the period.

conflict between the Dreyfusards and the anti-Dreyfusards divided along a pattern of Jews and their allies on one side against Judeophobes and their ignorant dupes on the other, good guys against bad guys, and progressive intellectuals against reactionary fools? This book looks at a much more dynamic and unstable field of activity wherein the people and the issues become more complicated and confused. Part of my argument will be, as another of Dreyfus's favourite authors, Gabriel Tarde, put it, that each party imitated the other so that their intelligences and mentalities were entangled by an interpsychic experience. This book will therefore also attempt to show that the best way to understand this kind of complexity is that of the *midrash*.

Midrash, as we shall show at greater length later in the course of this book, developed in the period when the books of scripture were being redacted and rewritten for inclusion in the formally collected national archives or library, the *morasha*. The ancient collections of oral traditions, written documents, and commentaries were put together in the sense of proclaiming them as sources of the law, historical justifications and authorizations of the applied interpretations of such law, and ancillary discussions and exemplifications of these practical readings.

In a sense, then, the very constitutive attribution of national status and legal acceptance by the representatives of the community made the formulation of scripture a political event: the formation of nationality at the moment of the giving and the reception of the law at Sinai and its acclamation by the people assembled, and then later, with the destruction of the temple and the permission to set up a constitutional assembly, as it were, with the eventual formulation of a *nation in exile*. This conceptual development precedes the institutionalization of a canon in the years following the destruction of the Jewish political state, the loss of the temple in Jerusalem as a site of cultic practice, and the pillaging and burning of the *morasha* itself as a depository and clearinghouse of authoritatively copied documents. *Midrash*, as the process of formulation, constitutes these very stages in production: (a) transcription and collection of traditional oral and written materials of national-historical importance regarding the functioning of the kingdom and the temple, including supplemental traditions needed to understand, interpret, and formulate additional texts; (b) direction for constant redaction, annotation, and correction or adjustment of texts put together to ensure coherence, consistency, and correctness of texts presented for discussion and debate by various scholarly, judicial, political, and spiritual groups; (c) the recording of such dialogues and debates, decisions made, and questions left unanswered.[28]

In another sense, the *midrash* represents the collections of rabbinical texts produced and promulgated subsequent to the loss of the political-juridical state, the priestly temple, and the national archives. The midrashic process is therefore separated from the dynamic production of primary documents, now assumed to be in another category of authority, as a canon takes shape, a process that comes to its conclusion when the Masoretic schools establish the final forms of the Tanakh. Further enhancements, internal questionings, and discussions of meaning and application constitute a body of work deemed in a state of orality—that is, open to continuous development. In particular, amongst all these rabbinical writings, *midrash* is identified with only one generic type. It is partly designated by what it is not: *midrash* per se is not Mishnah, Gemarah, Talmud, and so forth, even though in these kinds of debates, poetic enhancements, or philosophical speculations, midrashic exercises may be found. The word *midrash* designates both particular procedures of exegetical discussion and narrative or lyrical development and the corpus of such works produced under rabbinical authority and practice.

In this book, as in others I have written,[29] *midrash* is used in the sense of a process of thought, of imagination, and of action in the real world. In other words, (a) it is a way of thinking about religious and secular texts; social, political, and psychological ideas; scientific or art-conceptual problems; and other intellectual matters; (b) a creative mode of re-visioning the world of existential experience and speculative evaluation of nature and history; and (c) a set of practical and ironic strategies for acting as an individual or group in a society or civilization that is no longer aware of or in agreement with Jewish legal or moral values, historical traditions, and social relationships.

---

28 One might add that on the one hand, the law is, in José Faur's term, "the hyperspace where God's revelation unfolds" and Heinrich Heine's *aperçu* that the Torah is the "portable homeland of the Jews." Putting these together, we can see how Alfred Dreyfus in the thousands of pages of letters, journal entries, and workbook folios created a unique Promised Land of Truth and Justice for himself and Lucie over the long years of the affair from 1894 to 1906.

29 See the bibliography at the end for a list of relevant titles.

PART 2: THE DREYFUS TEXTS

For him [Paul Bourget] . . . the Will is . . . a state of final consciousness which results from the co-ordination, more or less complex, of a group of conscious, subconscious or unconscious states, which in combination translate themselves by an action or an inhibition; a state of consciousness which causes nothing; which establishes a situation, but does not constitute it.

—Anatole France[30]

Le rôle du commentaire n'est pas d'expliciter un texte, mais de le construire. Le rapport du commentaire avec le texte n'est alors évidemment pas celui d'une déduction.

—Marc-Alain Ouaknin[31]

Alfred Dreyfus has left us three categories of document for analysis: letters, journals, and workbooks. Lucie Dreyfus has also left us many letters, some of which were not edited and published until very recently, and some of them form themselves into suites of what can be called a virtual journal; her writings also require careful analysis. Above all, the relationship between these various letters, journals, workbooks, and other writings has to be seen in itself as a mode of composition, one not always intended or recognized by the writer and his or her immediate audience.

While many of the thousands of books written about the affair barely touch on the man at the centre of the controversy, the best way to get in touch with who he was and what he became during the long ordeal he underwent lies in a close reading of the documents produced during his imprisonment and, to a lesser extent, in the years following. Alfred Dreyfus was not a man of letters and certainly not a literary figure, whether as a writer of essays or fiction or as a critic and commentator; by profession he was a captain of artillery. Yet as the written evidence

---

30 Anatole France, "Science and Morals" (an essay on Paul Bourget's *La disciple), Of Life and Letters*, third series, trans. Bernard Miall (London: John Lane, The Bodley Head Ltd., 1924), 72.

31 "The role of the commentary is not to explain a text but to construct it. The relationship of the commentary with a text, then, is evidently not that of a deduction." Marc-Alain Ouaknin, *Lire aux éclats: éloge de la caresse*, 3eme ed. (Paris: Quai Voltaire, 1992), x.

discloses—sometimes quite surprisingly, given all that has been said about him for more than a hundred years—he was well-read; studied literary, historical, and moral (in the older sense that combines our modern notion of private ethical concerns and psychology) books; and had quite definite opinions about these texts. He often expressed the view, too, that art and history were primary sources of knowledge and moral guidance, at the same time as he valued science, technology, and mathematics.

There is a further surprise in what he read and how he responded to the authors he studied, and that is that although he does not seem to be interested in the novels, poets, dramatists, and essayists of the *fin de siècle*, he was aware of up-to-date critical and psychological issues and arguments. His knowledge of the fine arts—painting, sculpture, music, dance, and so on—seems virtually nonexistent, and yet he declares himself a lover of aesthetics and the artistic temperament. Even more than that, considering how in this book we stress the centrality of Judaism and anti-Semitism in the events and the conceptualization of the affair, he virtually never speaks of himself as a Jew, directly or indirectly, and seems not to recognize that the charges against him and the opposition to his figurative role in the Europe-wide debates stemmed from the rise in anti-Semitism as a pseudoscience, a political ideology, and social exclusionary principle, and yet examining the various documents he wrote and occasionally edited—except, of course, those he removed from the public record and thus kept from publication—through a midrashic lens, we can discern patterns of thought, points of historical convergence and allusive lines of "magnetic" influence that do indeed mark him out as a Jew and establish his role in what was still mythically conceivable: the affair as an all-Jewish phenomenon. More scientifically, the explanatory figure has to do with light rays passing through prismatic lenses, each ray being diffracted through the other and thus exposing the constituent bands of light, not only those usually visible as in Newton's model of colours, but the normally unseen range, from the ultraviolet and infrared at each end of the prism to the energetic powers of x-rays, the discovery of which fascinated Dreyfus.

First of all, he wrote a large number of letters to family and friends, the bulk of which is correspondence to his wife, Lucie, from the time of his arrest in 1894 right through until his release on a pardon in 1898. Those from Lucie have only recently been edited and made public in an accessible form. Thus, we have to see the epistolary exchange as precisely that, a process of double creation and mutual support through love and loyalty. Yet, without detracting from their intrinsic value as domestic, intimate, highly personal expressions of feeling between a wife and her husband, the letters, set against any number of more "normal" affectionate relationships in historical or fictional circumstances, take on a very distinct characteristic. In part, they have to be registered and filtered through the critical gaze of historical research, following the various editorial schemes through which they have been collected, selected, and annotated as suites of communication.

Thus, to begin with, these letters should be read in two forms: one, in their original form, with all their rough edges and incompleteness, as they have more recently been published; or two, in the context of various selected editions, with and without the comments of Dreyfus himself or different external hands, some of them participants in the affair, and some more modern editors. However, whether read as an epistolary sequence along a trajectory of narrative development, albeit with many gaps and repetitions occasioned by frustration and the desire to rearticulate key words and concepts by either or both of the writers, or as a series of discrete, separate, and occasional moments of experience, the letters cannot be fully appreciated outside of a larger context, a consideration, that is, of how they swerve away from traditional love letters, prison writings, and diaries or journals of despair and/or defiance.

From almost the very first letters sent before Alfred was shipped to Devil's Island, the letters of the man and his wife have a different tone, content, and function than what would have been expected from them—or anyone under similar conditions. As we shall see later in this book, these conditions include an awareness of constant surveillance and censorship, a need for each of the pair to withhold vital aspects of their own situation and understanding—or lack of understanding—of what was going on. There is a felt need to assume, presume, or intuit circumstances and attitudes in the other's situation so as to shape the words of one's own epistle and thus to affirm, confirm and induce necessary responses, and then, not least or last, to attain to a sensitivity perhaps as unconscious/conscious of deeper Jewish values, aspirations, and traditional modes of entering into *zman cherusenu*, the time of our remembrance. This last matter of time and memory will be shown to be analogous to aesthetic and psychological strategies undertaken by Marcel Proust in his *A la recherche du temps perdu*.

Even more, the reading of the letters between Alfred and Lucie has to be undertaken within a frame of reference that understands the epistles as only part of their textual relationship. In a general sort of way, scholars have been aware of this, in the sense that they know that Alfred did more than write letters to Lucie: he kept a journal of his acts, thoughts, and feelings while he was separated from his wife and as he prepared to rehabilitate his name and the honour of his family after his return to France and the disaster of the second court-martial in Rennes, and Alfred also undertook some of the editorial work of preparing those letters and journals for publication—that is, he helped to select letters, write explanatory and polemical introductions, and provide annotations. Only recently have historians and editors sought to see that the *cahiers* (workbooks) and *carnets* (journals) do more than amplify or supplement the letters. These notebooks and workbooks contain in themselves a variety of forms of expression, some of them verbal texts, some nonverbal mathematical equations and chemical formulae, and some of them drawings of a number of kinds from geometrical shapes, to iterative doodles and playful design-making.

The second category of documentation may be found in the journals (*carnets*) kept by Dreyfus during and after his imprisonment on Devil's Island. These also have been edited and annotated by the author himself, members of his family, and later scholarly commentators. Most of this material has either disappeared altogether, is hinted at in reports made by various prison and government officials charged with monitoring Dreyfus's activities while in exile,[32] or is contained in fragments and as trial sketches in the *cahiers*, in the same way as there may be found a few sentences or outlines of letters to be written to Lucie, other family members, or political officials in Paris.

The third kind of evidence is found in the extant *cahiers* or workbooks brought back from his years in exile in the French penal colony in Cayenne, South America. Most were either lost or destroyed by Dreyfus himself and have only recently been made available in a selected, part-

32 Faur: "Jews were the first (and only) people going into *Galut* ('Exile') that introduced a new doctrine in international law and diplomacy: a nation is not extinguished by the fiat of sword and banishment. A vanquished nation, ejected from its territory could preserve its political identity as long as it administers its internal affairs according to its *own legal and political institutions*" (*The Horizontal Society*, Section II, 21).

facsimile and part-transcribed format. These fifteen surviving manuscript texts are the most interesting now because they are the last to be made public in an accessible form. Unfortunately, the latest editors, while transcribing the verbal texts and numerical exercises, do not reproduce all the pages filled with Dreyfus's doodles—either in the opening section devoted to photo-reproduction of the original documents or the transcribed and printed version of the workbooks. The editors do indicate where the drawings are placed in relation to the essays and mathematical ciphers, and so we can imagine to a greater degree than ever the total impression the books have as physical objects and artefacts of Dreyfus's last two years on Devil's Island.

Allowing for these gaps in our knowledge, it is now possible to attempt a new reading of the whole body of evidence in its various forms and to show it to be, not so much a *Gesamtkunstwerk*, a collective and synthetic work of art, even if it's more like a *satura* or confused hodgepodge than an aesthetically conceived or logically organized whole, as what Dreyfus hints at and once actually designates *une fantasmagorie*, a phantasmagoria. It can also be approached as a kind of social dance of reason, a *mazurka* of mentalities.

Reading, Analysis, and Interpretation

> *En effet dans les premières Tables il est dit:* Zakhor ét yom hachabbat; *dans les Secondes,* Zakhor *est remplacé par* Chamor *"garde" au lieu de "souviens-toi!"*
>
> —Marc-Alain Ouaknin[33]

While the early historians of religion in the nineteenth century were busy discovering that Hebrews had once been like their surrounding neighbours in regard to archaic rituals of bloody sacrifice, temple prostitution, and other forms of ceremonial violence, they tended to do so, if they were Christians, out of a duty to exalt the religion of Jesus and depict the early Church as justly leaving the Jews either behind in the cellars of history, or in the shadows of modernity, where they could only

33 "In effect, in the first Tables [of the Law] it is said *Zakhor ét yom hachabbat* [Remember the Day of the Sabbath]; in the second, *Zakhor* is replaced by *Chamor* 'guard' in place of 'thou shalt remember!'": Ouaknin, *Lire aux éclats*, 100.

survive by becoming less and less Jewish in their minds, hearts, and souls. And if they were Jews, as indeed many were when the century came to a close, they sought to prove that Judaism had now cleansed itself of all such ancient detritus and could stand tall as a purified, moral system, ready to support the modern world and share in its progress.

Yet at the same time, outside of the arena of these new anthropological and sociological arguments, in the real world of modern life, Jews in the Western nations, such as France, Germany, and even Italy were doing what their ancestors had always done: engaging with the ideas and the institutions of the peoples they lived amongst in such a way as to keep developing their Jewish beliefs and practices and carefully accepting and modifying "the knowledge of the nations"—and nowhere more clearly than amongst those assimilated and more or less occulted or veiled Jews whose achievements in the arts, literature, theatre, and music, as well as in the sciences and technologies of psychology, architecture, medicine, mathematics, physics, astronomy, and mechanics, enhanced the entire spectrum of twentieth-century culture and society. This means that the studies of Israel Bédarride, Franz Cumont, Theodor Reinach, Marie Joseph Lagrange, Ernest Renan, and a host of others could at best be seen as opening the eyes of modern men and women—ordinary middle-class educated folk, as well as those with more literary or aesthetic sensibilities—to the way in which there was a continuum of relations and developments from the archaic Semitic civilizations of the Near and Middle East through the great prophetic and mystical reforms in proximity of time and space to the classical cultures of ancient Greece and Rome, the constant refinements and variations in late antiquity, the Middle Ages, and the Renaissance and into the Enlightenment and the Romantic periods.

Simultaneously, however, and usually completely outside the scholarly intentions or conception of the writers themselves, these same tomes by Jewish and non-Jewish authors provided grist for the mill of the new forms of anti-Semitism, which seized open the paradigms of evolution and the struggle for existence to build up myths of exclusive and progressive nationalism, racial classifications of humanity, and notions of moral degeneration, the dangers of biological impurities in language and ideas, and the pernicious operation of unseen organisms and organizations.

The dialectical tensions between these two ways of seeing the history of Judaism form, to a large degree, the matrix in which the Dreyfus Affair came into being and then played itself out. Nevertheless, insofar as a Jewish perspective may be found through which to view the major players, events, and ideas of this set of phenomena—this kaleidoscope of ideas, this phantasmagoria of illusions, and this swirling mazurka of social relationships—we have to explain what a *midrash* is and how it functions. And to do that, it is needful to set out a scheme of Jewish cultural development somewhat different from the Christian patterns of spiritual triumphalism or condescending tolerance normally applied.[34]

Judaism was constituted out of archaic rituals and ancient beliefs by refocusing all its efforts on the law and its interpretation, which meant on the study and analysis of texts. While the word became central to the exercise and practice of the new constitution for the nation of Israel, the primary text, received in the revelation of Sinai by Moses our teacher and handed on to the elders, sages, and rabbis of the great tradition, was not to be taken as a fixed, immutable thing, an idol, for not only were there two *luchot ha-brit*, two tables of the law, but two versions of the tables, one inscribed by the hand of God and then broken by Moses in his righteous indignation against the idolatrous worship of the golden calf and one written as he took dictation from the voice of God. The fragments and the dust of the broken tables were collected and stored in the moveable Ark of the Covenant and then in the Holy of Holies of the two temples in Jerusalem.

Simultaneous with the donation of the stone tablets on which the primary words of Torah were written, there was another ongoing oral revelation of the Torah, that which continues in all discussions, debates, and public readings of the law. Combining the written Torah with the oral Torah creates the Talmud, and there were two versions developed, one for the land of Israel called *Yerushalmi*, the Talmud of Jerusalem, and one for the Diaspora or Exile, called *Bavli*, the Talmud of Babylonia. All of these texts form into a multilayered, intertextual machine for thinking—a complex lens to see through, a mechanism for generating ideas and mental images, and a continuously flowing river of interpretation through conversation, debate, and questioning.

---

34 Faur: "In my view, given that we are all endowed with the image of God within, it would be sacrilegious to presume that anyone has the right to impose his sense of sacrality on anyone else. God alone, who sees into the hearts of men, can know who is righteous (see 1Sam 16:7, cf. MT *Teshuba* 3:2)," *The Horizontal Society*, Section II, 25.

Several important clues as to how texts are created, transmitted, discussed, and reproduced in Jewish tradition need to be teased out from this overly condensed scheme. Texts are, to begin with, actual physical objects, generated in specific historical times and places, and then, though they are reproduced, the secondary—*mishnaic*, *deuteronomic*[35]—objects do not totally replace the originals, for the originals, even if broken, annihilated, or hidden, remain intact in memory, a memory that includes the original time and place but includes them in such a way that they continue to draw into themselves, through reading and interpretation, those who hear, see, and understand these texts, meaning that the original time-place textuality is always expanding from its moment and space of creation. By continuous doubling, something quite distinct from the platonic horror of mimetic diminution occurs, for whereas Socrates, through his textualizing student Plato, fears that writing as an art(ifice) fixes the original dynamic idea of reality into a flat, virtually dead copy, withdrawn from its original social signification, destroying the mind's ability to encompass and transcend the mere moment of transcription, the rabbis and their predecessors experience and envision textualization as a creative and consequently divine action, with those primary energies and meanings flowing outwards and expanding to embrace ever more time and space, the moments and places embodied, and the individuals who participate in the explosive act.

Reading, study, argument, and application therefore form an ongoing dialectical process, moving forward towards as yet unachieved instants in history and backwards to the first and continuing explosion of creative energies. Variations and variations within variations spill forth, generating ever-renewing and transforming contexts for all that had preceded them, so that there can be no fixed eternal interpretation—that would be idolatrous and soul destroying. It is not, however, that every meaning is equivalent to all others, but that even small or erroneous interpretations are part of a cumulative, self-correcting whole, determined not by a secret and single truth hidden in the mystery of

35 Each term contains a sense of repetition, doubleness, duplication, reiteration, supplementariness, complementariness, and implemental repetition. Like the term *twin* in English, which can mean at once to have two versions of the same person or thing or one person or thing divided into two or a situation where the object or being is more than the sum of its part, that is, a wholly new kind of phenomenon distinct from whatever it was that doubled itself or split into two units, so too the learning that is *mishna-ed* is made into *shnay*, two, and the law (*nomos*) repeated by *deuteromonizing*, repeated and learned and readjusted to changed circumstances.

the created beginning but freely expanded and guided by its dynamism and dialectical connections to the existing traditions of logic, loyalty, and love.

A Mutual Admiration Society[36]

> *Every two or three weeks the jailer had brought me a letter from some of my family. It was previously submitted to the Commission and most roughly handled, as was too evident by the number of ERASURES in the blackest ink which appeared throughout. One day, however, instead of merely striking out a few passages, they drew the black line over the entire letter, with the exception of the words, "My DEAREST SILVIO," at the beginning, and the parting salutation at the close, "ALL UNITE IN KINDEST LOVE TO YOU."*
>
> —Silvio Pellico[37]

What Lucie and Alfred write to each other over the nearly five years of the captain's imprisonment and while he resided in at least three separate jails is, from a cold, almost cynical perspective, not much; their letters are repetitive, full of clichés, and superficial. However, what they say is not of great importance; there are elsewhere in the nineteenth century and earlier great and passionate love letters, soul-searching epistles from men in prison or exile, and well-crafted expressions of all kinds. What is significant in the letters lies in a number of factors emerging into focus only after repeated readings and intense scrutiny. One of these factors is how gradually and almost unconsciously each of the correspondents picks up clues from the other and repeats or anticipates the other's words, phrases and sentiments, reinforcing their mutual commitment to the main themes that underlie their relationship. A second factor is how, again gradually and without deliberate planning, they each come to realize the conditions under which the epistolary exchange has to be carried out—the censorious interference by various

36 The title of a 1956 song made by popular by Teresa Brewer, with words and music by Matt Dubey and Harold Karr.

37 Silvio Pellico, *My Ten Years' Imprisonment* (1833), trans. Thomas Roscoe (London: Cassell & Co., 1886) Chapter XXXII, 40. This was a book that the guards on Devil's Island were afraid Dreyfus would read.

prison and governmental officials; the delays in passing letters on so that there are gaps, clusters, and out-of-sequence arrivals; and the different degrees of epistemological repression and confusion between husband and wife, the one trying to hide the specifics of his discomfort and despair, the other forced to avoid revealing information forbidden by order of the men in charge of passing on the letters, since that would end the permission to write altogether and perhaps cause greater punishments, and also attempting to conceal as much as possible her own private anxieties and anguish.

One result of these factors is that time is annihilated since there is no real narrative of change or development to be recounted, other than expressions of pain caused by the seemingly hopeless and endless ordeal or remarks on how their two children, Pierre and Jeanne, are growing up, reacting to their own changed and confusing conditions. Similarly, though in a somewhat different sense of literalness and existential understanding, space is conflated and transformed for the pair of separated spouses. They each confess to feeling what the other does and consequently offer to inhabit a new imaginary realm of experience created by the words they exchange in letters, with these written words being transformed into sounds of imagined speech, and these imaginary conversations being contextualized by more tactile fantasies of being together again in a mixture of memories and anticipated restoration of normality, the words on the pages, the handwriting of the other seen and felt—until the censors realize this and try to stop the process of transformation by having the actual letters recopied before passing them on—and then in dreams of embraces and unification of their persons.

It is possible to see some of these transformations if we compare the words inscribed by one and then the other writer to a fictional conversation between two lovers in Ludovic Halévy's short romantic novel *L'Abbé Constantine*, published more than a decade before Lucie and Alfred began writing to one another.[38] In this fictional account set in 1881, a young Canadian woman, Mrs. Susie Scott, comes to France with her sister, Miss Bettina Percival, both having inherited an enormous amount of wealth from their father. At first, when they arrive in Paris, the older married sister and her younger single sister quickly

38 Ludovic Halévy, *The Abbé Constantin* (English translation 1882), no translator given.

become the talk and the toast of the town, thanks to their good looks, exotic oddity as free and vivacious American women, and the lure of their great fortunes. The younger sister, especially, attracts suitors of all sorts, mostly men with titles but little money, seeking to gain both a trophy wife and her untold millions of francs. But when the sisters decide to move to the country and buy up a series of farms, houses, and tenants once constituting a whole aristocratic estate, they also meet the old parish curate and his godson, Jean Reynaud, a young artillery officer of relatively humble origin.

Both sisters, seeking to ingratiate themselves with the *abbé*, show themselves to be generous, genial, and eager to fit into the community. The young *Canadienne*, Bettina, finds herself emotionally drawn to the handsome officer, finding him a welcome relief from the pretentious, snobbish, and gold-digging dandies of Paris and the various princes and lords who tried to win her hand and purse. In the climactic scene before the romantic ending to the novel, the lovers find themselves in an awkward, untoward impasse: the rich young woman fears that the man she loves will be too embarrassed to risk marrying her because it would humiliate him to be thought an adventurer just after her money, and she is also sure that he would be unwilling to enter the world of high society, in which he would have to play roles totally unsuited to his character. Jean, on his part, wishing to remain loyal to his military career, is afraid that the woman he loves would not want or should not live the life of an army wife, having to exist not only on his modest income but in a relatively unstable way, travelling from one posting to another, often to isolated and insalubrious parts of France or elsewhere in the world. While each is sure of his or her own love for the other, they cannot be sure of the other's commitment—nor whether it would be fair to force the other to give up their friends, ambitions, and cultural pleasures.

Only with the aid of the *curé* is the moral impasse broken. By the parish priest's gentle prodding, each one confesses to loving the other, and then, remarkably, gives the reasons for not wishing to harm the other's way of life. It is in this conversation, hardly realistic in its tones or execution, that the young woman states her willingness to enter into the humble conditions of an artillery officer's wife, her desire to support him in all his endeavours, and lack of any regrets for the gay lights of Paris and the artificialities of the high life. As she feels there can be an accommodation as well to her personal fortune insofar as she and he can live comfortably enough, perform together acts of Christian charity, and bring up any children without the snobbish artificialities they both dislike, a marriage is quickly agreed to and then occurs.

What is striking is how closely the words, phrases, and postures of these fictional lovers in Halevy's novel are echoed in the letters written by Lucie and Alfred Dreyfus. This remarkable similarity highlights the very different contexts and functions of the words themselves. For instance, the following lines from the novel describing Jean Reynaud's feelings before going away on military manoeuvres foreshadow words Dreyfus and his wife used:

> Jean is no longer tranquil; Jean is no longer happy. He sees approach with impatience, and at the same time with terror, the moment of his departure. With impatience—for he suffers an absolute martyrdom, he longs to escape from it; with terror—for to pass twenty days without seeing her, without speaking to her, without her in a word—what will become of him? Her! It is Bettina: he adores her![39]

Even more surprising are the words spoken by Bettina during the scene in which the priest guides the lovers towards an understanding and commitment to one another.

> "Jean, I know what you are, I know to what I should bind myself in marrying you, and I should be for you not only the loving and tender woman, but the courageous and constant wife. I know your entire life; your godfather [the Abbé Constantin] has related it to me. I know why you became a soldier; I know what duties, what sacrifices, the future may demand from you. Jean, do not suppose that I shall turn you from any of these sacrifices. If I could be disappointed with you for anything, it would be, perhaps, for this thought—oh, you must have had it—! That I should wish you free, and quite my own, that I should ask you to abandon your career. Never! Never!

39 Halévy, *The Abbé Constantin*, Ch. VIII, "Another Martyr to Millions," 59.

Understand well, I shall never ask such a thing of you."[40]

A short while after, Bettina makes another statement, one resonant with echoes from the book of Ruth, where the young Moabite new widow, returning with her mother-in-law, declares her commitment to be from then on a good and faithful Jewish daughter-in-law,[41] thus providing an indication of the allusive power inherent in Lucie Dreyfus's oath of loyalty to her husband:

> "When I can follow you, I will follow you; wherever you are will I be [and do] my duty, wherever you are will be my happiness. And if the day comes when you cannot take me, the day when you just go alone, well! Jean, on that day, I promise you to be brave, and not take your courage from you."[42]

It is uncanny how prescient these speeches are, although Halévy could have no inkling of what would happen to Alfred Dreyfus and his wife, nor what kind of letters they would write. The prescience extends to the language of military loyalty as a code for marital love and duty, as well as to the general pattern of development of the events Alfred and Lucie would be tested through.

Refuge in the *Cauchemar*

> *Alfred Dreyfus was very affected by the affair but he avoided showing his feelings. He was criticized for his attitude but it was a pure product of his generation. He was secular, rationalist and when he became the victim of injustice he thought that the truth would impose itself naturally.*
>
> —Pascal Ory[43]

---

40 Halévy, *The Abbé Constantin*, Ch. IX, "The Reward of Tender Courage," 83.

41 Ruth becomes the ancestor of King David and thus of the messianic line in ancient Israel. Her conversion has no other ritual than her promise to Naomi.

42 Halévy, *The Abbé Constantin*, Ch. IX, "The Reward of Tender Courage," 83.

43 Pascal Ory, in an interview with Shiri Sitbon, "Historian: 'French Jewry was Falsely Accused of Abandoning Dreyfus," online at http://ej[ress.org/printversion.aspx?idd=10064 (updated 4 August 2006) (read 19 May 2009).

One of the most frustrating aspects of reading Alfred Dreyfus's journals and *carnets* is the lengths to which he seems to go to avoid having to recognize that when all other hostilities against him are taken into consideration, the commonest feature—and the common denominator between his manifest enemies and many of his non-Jewish supporters—is anti-Semitism. Whether it is in his allowing to pass by without any notice the comment by Georges Clemenceau that Dreyfus is—like all other Semites, of which he is so typical—a bothersome annoyance, or his own annoyance at a police officer who comes to warn him of a suspected plot by a band of rabid Jew-haters to kidnap him on the street and probably spirit him away to be murdered, it is only by going to the modern footnotes appended to the edition of his *carnets* that we discover who these dangerous criminals are, as Dreyfus merely calls them nationalists.

Whereas in the letters to Lucie, as we have seen, the constant threat of censorship and thus the need to maintain a vigilance against any hint at their Jewishness[44] may justify the absence of any but the most subtle and covert hints of their religion and culture, the journals and the *carnets* emerge from a different set of circumstances altogether, and the strong sense of denial has to be found elsewhere than in what Pascal Ory calls "a pure product of his generation." Even in the prison notebooks, to be examined later in this book, the reasons for a similar silence and invisibility in regard to Dreyfus's religious heritage and spiritual or ethical concerns cannot be brushed aside as a consequence of his and his age's "secularism" or his own philosophical positivism, scientific rationalism, and indifference to Judaism. Without midrashing the texts we have, any interpretations would seem forced and against the grain.

Fourteen Prison *Cahiers*

> *Mirabeau always carried around within him the pains of his past; he had the glory but never the esteem and confidence [that should have gone with it] However, in the midst of all the disorder [of the late eighteenth century], Mirabeau*

44 It was not that everyone did not know that Lucie and Alfred were Jews, but that both of them attempted, as much as possible, to keep from calling attention to that fact, as any reference to holidays, customs, ritual objects, or Hebrew or Yiddish words would have been leaped on as evidence of a secret code and a plot for escape.

> *worked hard and educated himself; the three years that he spent in the dungeon of Vincennes were fertile years of study and meditation. It was at Vincennes that he wrote the famous Letters to Sophie, a kind of journal of his heart and intelligence, with a profundity, penetration and marvellous passion. When the Revolution began, Mirabeau was ready; his previous studies would serve [him in good stead], but it was not only as a great orator that this was revealed; it was as a statesman, endowed with a rare gift, as much for great things as for great words.*
>
> —Alfred Dreyfus, *Cahier* 14, Folio 4

In the last of the fourteen extant notebooks written while he was on Devil's Island, which is dated from 11 to 29 April, 1899, shortly before he finally returned to France to have his long-awaited second court-martial in Rennes, Dreyfus writes one of his many little essays on the leaders of the French Revolution, drawing from his favourite historians, such as Michelet and Thiers. In this brief meditation on Gabriel de Mirabeau (1749–1791), Dreyfus spends a full paragraph discussing his transformation into a great revolutionary orator, giving credit for this rise in character and rhetorical skills to the three years he spent in prison in the town of Vincennes, a period which he spent in intense study and meditation. Although Dreyfus does not detail what books and authors the Comte de Mirabeau focused on during those three years, what is implied mostly is that, like this famous historical figure who recreated himself as a revolutionary hero through his own efforts, Dreyfus was preparing for his own future by an analogous regimen of reading and meditation.

When we read this fourteenth *cahier* and the thirteen that precede it, we become aware of Dreyfus's rather complex regimen of self-education, as well as a sustained exercise in maintaining his sanity and emotional stability. He imagines himself to be not only in a kind of intellectual conversation with himself, on the one hand, but in a conversation with all the writers and books he was commenting on his notebooks on the other. His intellectual conversation with himself was in preparation for that hoped-for eventual return to France and normality, at which time he would have to speak and write on behalf of the principles for which he was being unjustly punished, although at this point he was not aware of the deep impact his case was making on the educated classes in the metropolis. The conversation with the other writers, as we shall make more clear as we proceed in our discussion, not only kept him in touch with and more worthy of being so involved with thinkers who provided the matrix of French civilization, but also allowed him to engage in a form of secularised adaptation of rabbinical discourse. This second aspect of his notebooks—with their puzzling mixture of brief commentaries, complex mathematical and scientific annotations and exercises, and strangely mesmerizing and ever-varying proliferation of drawings—is what we are calling by the neologism of *midrashing*—that is, turning the Talmudic Hebrew word *midrash* into a verb, to *midrash.*

Before the notebooks from the final year of his imprisonment on Devil's Island became available, it was thought that Dreyfus was a man of rather narrow learning, his mind formed by the military school he attended to make him an officer in the engineering corps. Scholars have presumed, because of his taciturn behaviour in court at his two trials, that he was not a cultured man able to express—or perhaps even to have—very deep thoughts or to engage with the wide range of ideas in literature, philosophy, and the arts flourishing at the end of the nineteenth century. But these *cahiers* from the years 1898 and 1899 put paid to such notions, as they reveal a Dreyfus far more sensitive, critical, and learned that previously envisaged.

In these surviving notebooks—those from the previous three or four years of his imprisonment were destroyed by Dreyfus himself—we see discussions of not only a very long list of Latin and Greek authors from the classical period and a range of French poets, dramatists, essayists, and novelists from the seventeenth, eighteenth, and nineteenth centuries, but also representative thinkers from elsewhere in Europe, references to painters, musicians and sculptors, and, of course, historians, political theorists, and psychologists. I say "of course" because this latter list underlies the ideas and opinions expressed in Dreyfus's subsequent journals, which were composed as part of the campaign to clear his name after the pardon granted at Rennes and, though these individuals are not mentioned by name, they are clearly alluded to, indirectly and directly.[45]

Although Dreyfus was a well-educated man with wide interests, there

45 See Appendix A for an index of names and authors written about or mentioned in the *cahiers*.

were limits to these interests and to his own scholarly skills. The prison workbooks, as we have noted several times, were prepared under trying circumstances and serve several functions other than those of intellectual note-taking or literary and philosophical musing on ideas important to their author. In my attempt to translate what the fifteen remaining notebooks contain, it quickly became clear that Dreyfus would lose track of his train of argument, repeat himself, seem to stutter, and return at long intervals to the same book, author, or idea to try to correct his understanding. In other words, just as it would be wrong to measure the value of these jottings in terms of any subsequent career in scholarship or creative literature—there is no such career in Dreyfus's life aside from his polemical and apologetic letters and journals meant to further his cause after the pardon and in a generally *ad hoc* manner—it would also be wrong to dismiss them as of merely passing interest and as a witness to his suffering in the tropical hell of Devil's Island. These books are of the essence in coming to an understanding of the man.

These *cahiers* seem at first glance to contain a miscellaneous series of reading notes and short commentaries on the various books he has been perusing while confined to his cell and with no one to converse with. However, as we shall see, we have to do more than enumerate, classify, and evaluate these authors and the ideas they generate in Dreyfus's mind as evidenced by his explicit comments. Putting aside short, incomplete fragments of trial letters to his wife, Lucie, and outlines of appeals to the commandant of the prison he is incarcerated in or to ministers back in Paris, for the most part Dreyfus writes about ideas, history, and scientific or aesthetic principles. Yet from time to time something else emerges which is of far greater significance for our understanding of the man and his place in the affair.

Occasionally, when he criticises one of the authors, he reveals an attitude quite distinct from that usually attributed to him, such as in his suggestion that the artistic personality and the work of art should be more than just factored into the history of eras and nations but taken as central matters. It also happens that he starts to discuss one particular author or book and then seems to slide inadvertently to another, and thus establishes new ideas, new contexts, and new perspectives, perspectives that moreover spring from memories of childhood, deeply personal tastes in the arts, and unexpected attitudes towards people, places, and historical events.

In his recently-published *Prison Notebooks* for 1898, Alfred Dreyfus obsessively writes his response to Ernst Renan's comment that in the future, literary history will effectively replace direct reading of great works of literature. Dreyfus finds himself forced to disagree with the renowned historian and critic, stating that direct reading—that is, direct contact and engagement with the masterworks of world literature—offers a profound access to the themes and experiences of human genius. Several important ideas emerge as we see Dreyfus, in his fifth year of imprisonment, exile, humiliation, and torture grappling with this seemingly abstract and purely intellectual problem. First, in coming back again and again, never really getting beyond the few points noted here, Dreyfus indicates how significant the idea is for him, representing not so much a problem in literary history or critical theory as a point around which his own shocking confrontation with history keeps running against a major impasse. Second, in finding himself forced to disagree with one of the truly pivotal figures of critical thinking in nineteenth-century France, Dreyfus indicates, probably without being fully aware of the implications of the blockage, that conventional middle-class thinking, as taught in schools and institutionalized elsewhere in the national consciousness, does not answer to his own transformed circumstances and thus serves as a sign, at least by hindsight to readers like ourselves, that there has been an existential shift in the paradigms of knowledge and imagination. Third, insofar as Dreyfus, normally a man of science and technology, a military practitioner in engineering and mathematics, now reads and rereads literature, literary history, philosophy, and the philosophy of history, he attempts to put himself on the side of creative, speculative, and aesthetic thinking.

Above all, what he comes back to again and again, in many forms, are the key themes of justice and truth, in Hebrew *Daat v'Emet*. Rather than appealing to the fundamental principles of the French Revolution and the republic (i.e., *Liberté, Egalité et Fraternité*), Alfred Dreyfus returns to these two key words, concepts, and values.[46] From time to time, he does speak of liberty, believes in the equality of peoples, and seeks to promote the notions of mutuality, charity, and tolerance. However, his

---

46 At this point, in a personal communication, Norbert Col wrote: "Most challenging this. Maurras would have agreed. His late disciple, Pierre Boutang, has a few fascinating remarks about this side in Maurras, and precisely related them to the Hebrew *seddaqah*," that is, to acts of charity and loving-kindness.

whole value system, insofar as we can piece it together from his writings, does not lean towards modern liberal principles as they have come to be understood in terms of socialism and anarchism, the conceptually leftist movements in his own time, which for the most part backed up his or rather his family and friends' efforts to have him released from imprisonment, his verdict revised and reversed, and his status in the army and his honour in the public eye restored.

On the one hand, perhaps most ironically, his own moral ideals were more akin to those of the intellectual anti-Dreyfusards, the traditionalists who believed in the importance of the state, the church, and the army, and who also favoured rule by intellectual and moral elites but not, of course, those who were bigoted, superstitious, and irrational. On the other hand, most surprisingly, his strong conviction in the power and rightness of justice and truth place him within the conceptual world of rabbinical or Talmudic Judaism, surprisingly because this source of values is the one he seems most determined not to speak about explicitly. In Judaism, these two great principles of the law are called *Daat* and *Emet*, and they resonate through liturgy, legal discussions and mystical speculations. In my close readings of the Dreyfus letters and *cahiers*, I hope to show that they are deeply and implicitly embedded in those documents as well.

Equations, Formulae, and Kabbalastic Signs

> *Il y aurait une très curieuse étude à faire sur le fantastique, sur l'*irréel *que dégage ce prodigieux ensemble de lignes, de formes et de couleurs, si magnifiquement réel, si mathématiquement coordonnés. Le fantastique n'est qu'une question de géométrie; voila ce qu'il faudrait prouver et ce que l'Exposition démontre.*
>
> —Octave Mirbeau[47]

Although Octave Mirbeau—novelist, art critic, and Dreyfusard[48]—was

47 "There is a very interesting study to be done on the fantastic, on the unreal which may be drawn out of the prodigious assembly of lines, forms and colors, utterly magnificent and mathematically coordinated. The fantastic is only a question of geometry; and there it is, that which ought to be proved, and that which the Exposition demonstrates." Octave Mirbeau, 372.

48 According to Norbert Col (in personal communications during December 2010), in France,

writing about the Universal Exhibition of 1889, which he saw very much as a "tumult of joy" or what we have called elsewhere generically a "Festival of Laughter," he can also be describing—and his modern editors see him very much as an accurate prophet of what is coming in the next few decades—the phantasmagoria of Alfred Dreyfus's prison notebooks. These fourteen *cahiers*, with their mixture—including pages of alternating sequences and overlapping presentations—of numerical equations and formulae, kabbalistic or arabesque doodles, and brief essays and commentaries on literature, historiography, philosophy, aesthetics, and science, are a new form of *fantasia*, a coordination of mathematics, technology, art, and morality. But although Mirbeau mockingly assesses the role of the exposition, with its wonders of modern technology and architecture, such as the Eiffel Tower and its surging crowds of drinking, eating, laughing, and babbling people, he takes no account of the real transformations occurring in the imagination and the subversive role played in such changes by the gradual leaking into the current of French history of Jewish ideas, attitudes, aspirations, anxieties, and ways of perceiving and evaluating reality.

Along with many of his compatriots on either side of the divide that yawns open so conspicuously during the Dreyfus Affair, Mirbeau is an anti-Semite. Not that he is a raging fanatic like Drumont, Maurras, or the crowds out on the streets in a riot of mockery and hatred, but he, like Degas and other intellectuals—even amongst those who temporarily and for politically strategic reasons joined the Dreyfusard cause—finds the Jews an annoying people. In fact, after Dreyfus's return to France, the second trial at Rennes, and the granting of a pardon, when his firm supporter Georges Clemenceau was approached to continue to help the captain gain full rehabilitation of his name, rank, and salary, he dismissed this annoying Jew, sick and tired of his whining and complaints.

Jews? An Annoying People!

> *Nouveau refus. Lebon m'explique, en termes plus embarrassés, qu'il lit toute la correspondance de D., mais qu'il n'est pas*

arguments still rage about whether or not Mirbeau was really an anti-Semite throughout his career or only in his early years, and whether or not the author came into his own during the time of the affair or not. Pierre Michel and Samuel Lair, young specialists, are now disputing these matters. I will leave the issue to resolve itself for a few years before venturing to give my opinion.

> *le seul à lire, qu'elle est soumise au ministère de la Guerre dont il se défi, où l'on bavarde, qu'elle est lue ensuite par le personnel pénitentiaire de la Guyane, dont il se défie encore plus, que, par conséquent, ma lettre risquerait d'être connue, et que, cela pourrait être pour moi,* Sémite, une cause d'ennuis.
>
> —Alfred Dreyfus[49]

This is one of the very few instances when Alfred Dreyfus or anyone calling him- or herself a supporter mentions the fact that the captain was a Jew and that much of the opposition, if not the vast majority of opposition, derived from anti-Semitic hatred. Here, capturing in the rhythms of his own syntax the pattern of deceit and duplicity ranged against him, Dreyfus writes how he was treated in André Lebon's ministerial office in 1899, soon after his pardon, when he had gathered enough strength of mind and will to begin the campaign for a more complete vindication of his innocence. Dreyfus wants to have all his letters, books, and papers from Devil's Island returned to him. "Another refusal," he starts off. "Lebon explained to me in embarrassing terms that he had read all of D.'s correspondence, and that he was not the only one to read it, that it was sent to the Minister of War who rubbished it, since it was blithering nonsense, and that it was also read by the officials of the Guiana Penal Colony who also rejected it, and consequently my letter risked being known and that would be, for me, a Semite, an annoying thing."

It is important here to watch the way Lebon dismisses Dreyfus's appeal to have his documents returned to him. Although many of the letters had already been published as part of the build-up to his second trial in Rennes and in order to garner support from a wider public based on his personal sufferings on Devil's Island for five years, as far as the government was concerned—from the Ministry in Paris to the colonial officials in Guiana—it was all blather and nonsense, *bavarde*. Then, continuing the condescending tone and the condescension due to a mere Jew, Lebon warns Dreyfus to watch out because all his efforts will just be *ennuis*, vexatious, bothersome, annoying to him and to the government, to the army, to France—to real and true Frenchmen.

49 Alfred Dreyfus, *Carnets (1899–1907)*, ed. Philippe Oriol (Paris: Calmann-Lévy. 1998), 56.

When the aged Senator Auguste Scheurer-Kestner, a convinced Dreyfusard, appealed to Lebon, he replied "that he would not be cast in the role of a jailer, which disgusts him," and yet, since "if you who are not a Semite" (*vous qui n'etes pas sémite*), insist, then he will pass the request on, but . . . and he goes on speaking of how tedious, annoying and vexatious the whole affair is.[50] In his report on what transpired in this encounter with the minister, the ancient and respected politician goes on citing this conversation with the Minister of Colonies:

> *"Je l'ai dû: ah! Mon métier me dégoût!" Puis, pour soulager sa conscience, il me dit qu'il ne croît pas à l'innocence de D. Qu'il a lu toutes ses letters et qu'elles ne l'ont pas ému, que c'est toujours la même chose, et dans les mêmes termes! "Et que voulez-vous donc que cela soit?"*[51]
>
> "I was forced to do that: ah! My profession disgusts me!" Then, to assuage his conscience, he told me that he did not believe in D's innocence. That he had read all his letters and that he was not moved by them, that it was always the same thing and in the same terms! "And what do you want me to do about that?"

Nothing about Dreyfus rouses Lebon's sympathies, and look what an annoying situation he has been put in by this troublemaker of a Yid. Reading the letters between Lucie and Alfred, which we will analyze at length to show how truly moving they are and how important they are for understanding the character of the man wrongly accused of treason, the mean-spirited little *apparatchik* cannot see anything in them but boring repetitions of puerile complaints. However, in correspondence with Joseph Reinach, Scheurer-Kestner shows a different way a non-Jew could respond to the same evidence. When the aged senator was told about the long period Dreyfus was kept in irons, he exclaimed, "*C'est hideux! Je suis étonné . . .*"[52] That was the way a mensch should react to the torture inflicted upon a loyal French officer. That was the way an en-

---

50 Dreyfus, *Carnets*, 57.

51 Dreyfus, *Carnets*, 58.

52 "That's hideous! I am astonished . . ." Dreyfus, *Carnets*, 305, n. 122.

lightened Frenchman of the late nineteenth and early twentieth century responded to the Dreyfus case. But what about those others, like Lebon?

Jews are, if you go by the comments of the government and judicial officials Dreyfus appealed to after his pardon, often explicitly called an annoying people. How so? The Semite asks too many questions. He doesn't accept words on the mere authority of the speaker but wants reasons. He is never satisfied. He should go home, be quiet, stay with his wife and children, and be satisfied with what he has. But this Semite and his brother keep badgering us. The Jew is therefore a troublemaker. He demands truth and justice. He is not like us; he is not part of the team which pulls together to protect the institution and each of us. Semites, the people in power complain, do not take words at face value. Words escape them in the sense that common associations, tonalities, and historical resonance are different to different kinds of people. It is not the words themselves but the social dynamic, the historical matrix, and the epistemological technologies that shape the flow of communication, the impasses, and the static that replaces understanding. The Dreyfus Affair occurred along the long and jagged fault line between these different modalities of thought, feeling, and experience.

Which Words Escape Them?

> *The reason why we need to remember the Dreyfus Affair now is that we failed to remember it the first time. We, the citizens of the world, did not pay attention to what was happening to the Jews in Nazi Germany because we were convinced that nothing so atrocious could really happen in the modern world. Our faith in the press and our ability to communicate almost instantaneously across vast distances led us to imagine that no large-scale injustice could go undetected for so long.*
>
> —Siouchо[53]

For Jews, assimilated and practicing their ancestral customs, words are phenomena quite different from what they are for their Christian com-

53 Sioucho, "'I'm not a Man: I'm a Cause'—The Story of Alfred Dreyfus in *J'Accuse*" (1 July 2001) *Epinions.com* (18 November 2010).

patriots in France and the rest of Western Europe. For the Jew, words are objects in which meanings are stored, but the meanings are active processes, particles of energy emanating from revealed truth and yet now confused by diverse interests and emotional states of being. The words are processes of meaning-creation, which have historical trajectories as well as unclear and confused explosions of irrational fear and desire, cries of pain and anxiety, soothing noises, and temporizing arguments. Words therefore cannot be totally detached from the occasions in which they are used or from the people and the institutions that use or abuse them; they are fragments of rhetorical discourse and shards of explanations that have shattered in the course of time. More urgently, words are sounds and appearances, open to etymological connotations and semantic slides and able to be fractured and reassembled by paronomasia and letter manipulation and other witty, ironic, and cynical inversions and reconfigurations.

Truth: *Emet*

> *The notion that the goal of Talmud is truth is un-Talmudic in spirit. It promises a finality, a definitiveness, a certainty, that the Talmud mocks on every page . . . . The objective of Talmud is not truth but thought.*
>
> —Leon Wieseltier

Like a refrain, in his appeals for a revision of the second court-martial at Rennes and those of his supporters for the first revision of the original military tribunal, the two words that appear throughout are *truth* and *justice*. But what does a Jew mean by the truth? In one sense, the truth is what is real and verifiable, what is not a lie or a distortion of what really happened. In another sense, it is what is in accord with the principles of the law and the patterns of history, putting aside as accidents and contingencies that which belongs only to the moment. Yet it is neither an absolute idea upon which all else is measured as real or valid nor an unreal manifestation of wish projected by the rich and powerful into the matrix of changeable, unsteady, and immeasurable events and experiences. Truth is certainly an ideal of just and compassionate probability in a world in which human reason cannot reach perfection.

Truth by itself, however, is not a statement or a fact settled once and for all or available *ab initio* and eternally revealed to those who know where and how to look for it. Rather, and this is the essence of a traditional Jewish approach, it is something dynamic and always renewing itself. For this reason, as Leon Wieseltier points out, the Talmud does not teach the truth but how to think, and, through thinking, to create the truth appropriate for this time and this place, which is not the same as for all times and all places. Yet that does not make a Jewish version of *emet* something relative or arbitrary—there are rules of logic, processes of argumentation, and a rhetoric of discourse with which to wrestle with the angel.

Even further, as will be opened up gradually like the facets of a precious stone, emitting its flashes of light in all directions, rabbinical *melitza*, or horizontal dialectics is, in Faur's words,

> a humanistic eloquence which springs from the Hebrew doctrine that every human being is created in God's image . . . . The essential *meliṣa* is a dialectic in which neither side must necessarily be wrong; or conversely that both sides may be indeed uttering "the words of the Living God.[54]

Justice: *Daat*

What does the Jew mean by *justice*?[55] He or she says it is an ideal of the law and of law but then doesn't treat it as an absolute abstraction, a general idea, a distant goal of perfection, but as an eternal idea to be realized in practice without being perfect for all times and places but for specific occasions and persons. In one construction of the term, justice is what is right and fair, what is commensurate and balances out differ-

54 Faur. *The Horizontal Society*, Section IV, Introductory Remarks.

55 If we were to ask, on the other hand, what was the official line on "justice" during most of the affair, we could do worse than turn to one of Anatole France's so-called profitable tales, that of "Crainquebille," wherein a magistrate explains his meaning of the word: "Justice is the sanction of established injustice. Was justice ever seen to oppose conquerors and usurpers? When an unlawful power arises, justice has only to recognize it and it becomes lawful. Form is everything" (in *Crainquebille Putois, Riquet and other Profitable Tales*, trans. Winifred Stephens [London: John Lane/The Bodley head, 1916, 1905], 29). A few lines later, the parody of the Dreyfus Affair is even more pungent: "Such would have doubtless been the words of President Bourriche, for he has a judicial mind and he knows what a magistrate owes to society. With order and regularity, he defends social principles. Justice is social. Only wrong-headed persons would make justice out to be human and reasonable" (30).

ent desires and objections, what is measured, and so what can be made most fitting to maintain peace and harmony between individuals and groups. In another construction, justice is what is lawful when the law confronts complicated and confused circumstances, different versions of reality, and thus adjusts itself for the moment to what is most beneficial for all in their various conditions. Still more, *justice* is the term used for decisions reached thoughtfully, deliberately, after dispassionate consideration, when most irrelevant interests have been put aside, but when the consequences of the decision are also thought through so as to avoid undue pain or suffering to parties not directly involved and without leading to even more disturbing disruptions to the good running of families and communities. Thus, although it would be cynical to define justice as merely the application of the wishes of the most powerful over those who have less influence or wealth, it also cannot be tipped totally on the side of mercy or compassion, although the judgement should avoid undue harshness and not over-reward persons or groups who are merely technically in the right.

Thus, both the concepts and processes of *emet* and *daat* are at once the matrix in which thought operates, the process of rational argumentation and analysis, and the rhetorical construct or figure of thought in which the interpretation and the application are for the time being realized. In brief, like the Talmud in its widest acceptance as Torah—from a specific word or passage in a text to an argument rehearsed in a witty and mutually respectful manner regarding the performance of wise and saintly deeds—it is a lens through which to see, a kaleidoscope to keep adjusting to the swirls of history and social revolution, and a moral mazurka, a dance of reason. Or to cite Franz Liszt in his remarks on Friedrich Chopin, following George Sand,[56] again one of those citations we

---

56 Taken from George Sand's *Lucrezia Floriani*. According to James Huneker's *Chopin: The Man and his Music*, Mr. A. B. Walkley, the English dramatic critic, after declaring that he would rather have lived during the Balzac epoch in Paris, continues in this entertaining vein:

> And then one might have had a chance of seeing George Sand in the thick of her amours. For my part I would certainly rather have met her than Pontius Pilate . . . . But, to my mind, the most fascinating chapter in this part of her history is the Chopin chapter, covering the next decade, or, roughly speaking, the 'forties'. She has revealed something of this time—naturally from her own point of view—in "Lucrezia Floriana" (1847). For it is, of course, one of the most notorious characteristics of George Sand that she invariably turned her loves into "copy." The mixture of passion and printer's

make only to keep adjusting the lens and focusing in a different way on the subject of our choice:

> His [Chopin's, but here read the Jew's] imagination [in the sense of a creative, midrashic process of thought] so filled with exquisite beauty [i.e., the beauty of the Law, in all its rational splendor and mystical power], seemed as it were holding a monologue [make that now a dialogue or a conversation or even an argument] with God himself; and when upon the radiant prism, in the contemplation of which he forgot everything else [instead of this mystical loss of self and rationality, read here: in which the Jews remember deeply, creatively and wittily], the phantasmagoria of the world [the great contraption that spews forth the claptrap of anti-Semitism and foolish ideas] cast even its disturbing shadow he [like Alfred Dreyfus confronted with the machinations of arrogance and racial hatred] was deeply pained, as if in the midst of a classical concert a shrieking old woman, in shrill and broken tones, should blend her vulgar musical motive with the divine thoughts of the great masters.[57]

Peace: *Shalom, Tikkun*

These concepts, as we have been showing, come close to, sometimes overlaps with, but are never exactly the same as, their Christian or secular, enlightened brethren. *Peace*, familiar in the greeting, and *farewell* (*shalom aleichem*), "Peace be unto you!" does not mean primarily a state

---

> ink in this lady's composition is surely one of the most curious blends ever offered to the palate of the epicure.

57 Liszt, *The Life of Chopin*, 208–209. The original French is somewhat different and therefore deserves its own midrashic interpretation: "*Il semblait noyer son imagination si exquise et, si belle dans un monologue avec Dieu même, et si parfois, sur le prisme radiaux où il s'oubliait, quelque incident faisait passer la petite lanterne magique du monde, il sentait un affreux malaise, comme si, au milieu d'un concert sublime, une vielle criarde venait mêler ses sons aigus et un motif musical vulgaire aux pensées divines des grands maîtres*" (chapter VII). It is not just the substitution of a magic lantern for the phantasmagoria, but the sublime rather than the classical concert the old woman interrupts with her shrieking. Broadhouse's translation draws out the implications of the figurative language we have interpreted in a new context and given a new Jewish accentuation.

of nonviolence and harmony with others, including states as well as individuals, but a harmonious, just, and equitable relationship, free of threats and constraints, drawing on the same root *sh-l-m* שלם that applies to paying a bill or a fair wage—to balance out a situation of temporary inequality, disequilibrium, or debt.

The opposite of war is justice, and justice is achieved when order is restored. This restoration, repair, and correction of an incongruity is called *tikkun*, deriving from the kabbalistic myth of the contraction of *time* and *space* (*tsimtsum*), the breaking of primary vessels of creative force, and their scattering like sparks; *tikkun* which consists of gathering up the hidden sparks, putting them back into an orderly flow of creativity, and reconciling the seemingly hostile and violent relationship between the infinite and the finite, brings about the conditions of *shalom*.

PART 3: THE MYTH OF THE UNTHINKABLE AND THE IMPOSSIBLE

> *They are the quintessence of what I detest most, people like her and her father. They are the incarnation of the modern world, in which there is nothing more despicable than these cosmopolitan adventurers, who play the grand seigneur with the millions filibustered in some stroke or other on the Bourse.*
>
> —Paul Bourget, *Cosmopolis*[58]

What happened to Alfred Dreyfus from the moment he was told of his arrest was impossible to believe, something unthinkable, and, as we can see in his reactions over the first few days when he raged in his cell,

58 Paul Bourget, *Cosmopolis* (1892), no trans. (Doylestown, PA: Wildside Press, 2010), 24. The speaker here is the Marquis Claude-François de Montfanon, a notorious aristocratic bigot, and he is speaking of Baron Justus Hafner and his daughter, "a young girl of almost sublime beauty . . . Her profile, of an Oriental purity . . . so much on the order of the Jewish type that it left scarcely a doubt as to the Hebrew origin of the creature . . ." (20–21). As Norbert Col remarked on reading this book in manuscript, Bourget, like others, from Walter Scott in *Ivanhoe*—but even before him in Shakespeare's *Merchant of Venice* with Shylock's daughter Jessica—temper their presentation of grotesque Jewish men with a titillating fascination for young Jewish girls. By the way, Col also points out that although he was an anti-Dreyfusard, Bourget was not a rabid bigot but came down on the side of the army because he could not believe French officers would deliberately lie or manipulate evidence. Unlike others, he did not equate Dreyfus's Jewishness with prima facie evidence of his treason. This matter is further discussed in relation to the essay on Bourget in the *cahiers*.

threw himself against the walls, and cried out in inarticulate despair, it was unspeakable. Such traumatic occasions are thankfully rare in life, even more so when they occur to a group of people, a whole community, or a nation. Gradually, as the news of what happened to Captain Dreyfus spread from his family through the Jewish community to the whole of France and then the rest of Europe and other parts of the so-called modern world, the trauma became general. It was moreover an increasing, cumulative trauma, only beginning with the shock of the arrest of a quiet, middle-class, assimilated Jew in Paris at the end of the nineteenth century and became more unbearable and unbelievable at each new turning point: his condemnation at the first court-martial, his degradation in public, his exile to Devil's Island, his solitary confinement and shackling to a bed, and his second condemnation at Rennes—and these are only the most salient events.

What began as a personal or family tragedy, seemingly based on a judicial error, soon re-formed into a national and international scandal as more and more evidence began to emerge of a conspiracy amongst Dreyfus's fellow officers and some members of the government until it reached into the highest echelons of the army and the leading members of the National Assembly and strained the loyalty and faith of the whole population in the ideals of the republic, in the integrity of the state, the church, and, yes, of the truth.

What does it feel like when the impossible happens, when the unspeakable has to be spoken, when the unimaginable is put into pictures, and when the inconceivable fits into the normative paradigms of thought and of rationality itself? Some of us have had such experiences, perhaps even more than once in our lives. Take the fall of the Berlin Wall and the rapid collapse of the Soviet Empire. I was teaching on an exchange agreement at the University of Ottawa at the time. There was to be a conference of various leaders from the countries of the Warsaw Pact in a building around the corner from the university, so I made sure to take a detour to pass by, coming and going, each day. I could not keep my eyes off the flags, all of them with the old hammer and sickle emblem either cut away or sewn over. It was unbelievable. My whole life, I had grown up on the paradigm of the Cold War, and whether one felt sympathy or not for the ideals of Communism, no one of my generation or that of my parents could have escaped the power of the conflict and the influence of the Iron Curtain that cut across Europe and the world.

I would come into the classroom trembling at what was happening a few hundred metres away, as the Warsaw Pact states disentangled themselves from the Soviet bloc and prepared to reenter history and European life. But the students, mostly young, middle-class Canadian kids from Ontario and Quebec—the University of Ottawa was a bilingual institution and still had structural memories of its recent transformation from a Catholic to a provincial college—seemed quite uninterested. These comfortable, smug young people, for all their supposed intelligence and imagination, could not see the big deal. They sniggered at my remarks about how these were days that were transforming the world, how we viewed history, what politics and economics could mean from now on, and where the truth of the past nearly ninety years would be found. It was therefore impossible for me to explain to them how deeply the ideas of the division between East and West had gone into every part of my consciousness and even, I am sure, unconsciousness; and how, although people had speculated on the eventual demise of what Ronald Reagan termed "the Evil Empire" and had spoken about possible scenarios over the next hundred years, basically most of the men and women I knew could not really believe that such an eventuality would happen in our lifetimes, if ever.

Or take another example, what happened on 11 September 2001. This was far more traumatic than the assassination of John F. Kennedy or the accidental death of Princess Di, events to which others have compared it, in the sense that for many people such dates are marked by everyone comparing where they were and what they were doing when they heard the news. The so-called 9/11 phenomenon digs deeper into the consciousness and the unconsciousness because it transformed—as some news broadcasters were able to say within hours of the terrorist attacks in New York City, Washington DC, and a lonely field in Pennsylvania—the way many of us think and feel about reality. If it didn't transform the thoughts and emotional reality of our lives, because those changes occur over a longer period of time, it was the moment that exposed the processes of change and made it impossible to use the previous discourses of rationality in history, politics, or aesthetics. I say this even though with each passing year—and I merely have to point to young students in my classes since then to demonstrate this—the trauma has been papered over by those who wish to deny that anything really world-changing happened, or who cannot live with the trauma and have already repressed it so deeply that they are angry and offended if you merely suggest it to them.

In a sense, what the several terrorist attacks revealed on that memorable day was what one could have—perhaps should have—made articulate a few months earlier in the ironically entitled 2001 "Anti-Racism" UN Conference held in Durban, South Africa. This festival of racial hatred, and especially vicious slandering of Israel and the United States by a wide range of nongovernmental organizations and national representatives to the United Nations, manifested the same declaration of war against what is known as the Judeo-Christian value system of the Western World, was a celebration of superstition, demagoguery, and envy—and led directly to the hijacked airliners that flew into the World Trade Center and the Pentagon and might have targeted the White House itself. It revealed the new distortion of all the language of human rights, democracy, and racial harmony that was responsible for the subsequent terrorist attacks in London, Madrid, Bali, and Mumbai. The bizarre alliance of Islamacist fanaticism, Marxist ideology separated from its old class analysis of dialectical materialism, anti-globalism, and other politically correct ideologies, all wrapped up in a Palestinian scarf, makes a nonsense of the traditional language and activities of liberalism in the West. It is now impossible to talk sensibly using any of the words and concepts that used to be filled with and resonate morality and responsibility.

I learned of the 9/11 attacks in the middle of the night, since I live in New Zealand, and realized that my wife was somewhere in the air en route to New York City, and so I had first to overcome a personal panic. I spent most of the night using the telephone and internet trying to locate members of my family and transmit messages from persons who, though near each other geographically, were cut off from news about each other's whereabouts and conditions. By the next morning, when I had to go to the university to teach, I was exhausted but somehow buoyed up by the adrenalin of panic.

There were two reactions that met me when I drove in that next morning. On the one hand, there was the deaf silence of most of my colleagues and students, who neither knew nor cared what had happened, and who treated the event when they bothered to find out about it—most never read newspapers, listened to the news on radio or television, or used the internet as a source of current events—as unimportant. Not one ventured to ask how my family in New York City was, where my wife was, or what I was feeling at the moment, although I was clearly shaken and upset. On the other hand, the politically aware minority, to a man, all expressed anti-American sentiments, smiled, and congratulated one another on the fact that "the big bully got a bloody nose" and "now they know how it feels." No sympathy for three thousand murder victims. No understanding of how deeply the event had shaken Americans' long-lasting confidence in the safety of their nation from foreign attack or invasion—that not since the war of 1812 had the Continental United States been hit by such an attack. Not even a recognition that that confidence has been built up since the late 1980s, with the sense that the Cold War was over and the world was safe from any major conflicts again.

But more than these political or military actions that shattered the myth of Fortress America, there was the other, deeper trauma of a total destabilization of our concept of reality. This might be a variation on Huntington's "Clash of Civilizations" or some notion of "the end of history." It was a trauma that meant that the Enlightenment was over and that the whole history of rationality, science, and secularism was teetering of collapse.

I do not mean to say, however, that the shocks experienced at the Fall of the Soviet Union or the terrorist attacks of 9/11 could be considered the most shattering experiences of the late twentieth and early twenty-first centuries and thus equivalent to that most enormous of all traumas, the Holocaust or Shoah. No more could, at least for a Jew, the episodes surrounding the Dreyfus Affair and then soon after the Mendel Beylis case in Czarist Russia be so considered. For many, to be sure, the outbreak of World War I was in itself the opening up of a deep abyss between the relative security and comfort of the nineteenth century and the seemingly endless violence of the twentieth. What we are talking about here are moments in existential history when individuals and groups of smaller or larger size pass through a liminal event that at once seems to bring to an end not so much the institutions and paradigms of one form of noetic universe or *Weltanschauung* as the realization that those organized and collective paradigms of knowledge can no longer be trusted; in fact, at such a moment, the vast inner dimensions of what had hitherto been unquestioned, usually unexpressed dimensions of truth and reality come to the surface and reveal themselves to be inconsistent, incoherent, and riddled with contradictions.

At the same time, as this experience of shock and disappointment begins to play itself across the consciousness of a community, a nation, or even a whole civilization, there is another realization crystallizing into awareness and seeking to take charge of how knowledge is generated, taught, preserved, and transformed into art and philosophy—the realization that already for a long time, perhaps even a generation or more, other paradigms have been created, new ways of seeing and feeling have been articulated, in both popular and elite cultures, and seemingly radical and rash modes of social relationship have started to stabilize themselves into patterns of normality and hence of acceptability. Yet since generations overlap, as Proust shows throughout *À la recherche du temps perdu*, individual and collective memories crisscross over each other, different memories inform various individuals and groups in asymmetrical ways, and denial and misprision often dominate over acceptance and clarity of perception.

For the narrator, Marcel, in Proust's *A la recherche de temps perdu*, the moments of realization burst forth unexpectedly and change the way in which he sees others, himself, and the world in which he lives, so that he can feel himself alive in many times and places at once, sometimes riding in a horse and carriage, sometimes driving in an automobile, encountering an aeroplane for the first time, walking through Paris during an aerial bombardment, sending messages with a servant, using a telegraph, writing a note for the pneumatic post, or using the telephone. Not that the accumulation of technological advances by itself can account for the transformation in the imagination and rationality of an age, but that such inventions are markers of more dynamic shifts occurring in the minds, the memories, the milieu, and the mentalities of the society.

Scattering Sparks of Memory

> *The artist expresses specifically what all our dreams tend to express in more fragmentary form, through symbolism rather than words. This symbolism is both highly personal and, at a deeper level, universal . . . This unconscious realm is the meeting place of aesthetics and psychological or biological inquiry, and symbolism is its means of delineation.*
>
> —Milton L. Miller[59]

59 Milton L. Miller, *Nostalgia: A Psychoanalytic Study of Marcel Proust* (Boston, MA: Houghton Mifflin

It is clear, of course, that Dreyfus was no artist and his tendencies were always towards the more scientific, positivistic philosophies of the late nineteenth century. Nevertheless, when the prisoner on Devil's Island comments on the authors he approves of, he does so with provisos, objections, and modifications, most of them expressing a recognition of the importance of the aesthetic perspective and the artist's role in society and history. Moreover, as should become more and more evident in this book, when we examine the full range of his thoughts in his various letters, notebooks, and journals, Dreyfus does not fully adhere to his own stated principles. This is not only because he knows that whatever he writes, even in personal, intimate letters to his wife, there is a manifest censorship by prison and other officials going on, making any allusion to radical ideas—and this could be as much a statement of antigovernment opinions as a hint at Jewish adherence to the Law of Moses as a guide to moral and ethical views, let alone to suspect anarchist tendencies in the aesthetic manifestos of the period—dangerous, at least in the sense of interfering with his search for a revision of his case in the military courts and in the parliamentary process but also because he is himself fearful of letting uncontrolled and uncontrollable thoughts and feelings emerge, and thus sliding into the despair and madness his situation could all too easily create.

Whereas Proust seems to have found both consolation and transformative power in his literary art, thus avoiding the threats of physical and psychological annihilation he so dreaded, Dreyfus struggled to make rational sense of what had happened to him and to maintain a sanity that would protect his wife and children along with his own honour. He knew that any concession to the savage rage and melancholia deep within himself—in what Jewish mystical tradition would call the *sitra achra*, the demonic other side—could be taken as a mark of guilt and stigmatize his family and himself with all the calumnies published in the anti-Semitic press.

Although I will consequently seem to wind the life experiences of Marcel Proust around those of Alfred Dreyfus, along with their families and circle of friends and acquaintances, it is not my intention to suggest that these men and their accomplishments are to be considered inter-

---

and Cambridge, MA: The Riverside Press, 1956), 258.

changeable—or that in any way they had more than the most tangential relationship with one another. At best, Proust was aware of Dreyfus's plight, sympathized with the cause of his revision, and helped collect signatures on a petition for the revision of the first court-martial's decision. Rather, I want to show—and in a very special way, the way of *midrash* which will be explained over the whole course of this book, occasionally in a theoretical discussion but more usually through application and demonstration—that both Proust's literary achievement and Dreyfus's ordeal are part of the way in which the impossible came to be possible. Once we know through our own experiences that the impossible can happen—because it has happened again and again, as suggested in my thumbnail sketches of how I came to understand the traumatic and shocking nature of liminal events, such as the Fall of the Berlin Wall or the breaking out of the War on Terror in the place where the Cold War had been—then we can try to unpack the levels of textuality and follow the threads of memory in the *midrash* of Alfred Dreyfus's life and the specific ordeal of his case.

An Age of Boredom and Anxiety

> *These two peoples, always in presence of each other, and living within the same walls, still had almost nothing in common . . . . They were two peoples that did not even understand each other, not having—so to speak—common ideas. . . . They reproached each other with injustice: each was just according to his own principles, and unjust according to the principles and beliefs of the other . . . . And yet there was something which formed a tie between these two peoples.*
>
> —Fustel de Coulanges[60]

Many writers say or at least imply that the last decades of the nineteenth century and the first thirteen years of the new century were marked by a great boredom and melancholy amongst the bourgeoisie, with the so-called Gay Nineties or Age of Salons and Banquets a misreading of the

60 Numa Denis Fustel de Coulanges, *The Ancient City: A Study on the Religion, Laws, and Institutions of Greece and Rome* (1864), trans. Willard Small (Garden City, NY: Doubleday Anchor Books, 1956; orig. trans. 1873), 296–297.

period. It would seem by such an assertion that, out of nowhere, at least in France, the Dreyfus Affair appeared, and suddenly in 1894 one people became divided, the Dreyfusards versus the anti-Dreyfusards. And then just as suddenly in 1906 all went silent again, the lights dimmed, and France drifted along as if in a dream until the Great War shattered everything once and for all. But this is, of course, a specious assertion. Even if we discount the suddenness of the affair or the shattering quality it had on French society, the fin de siècle was not all a *Belle Epoque*, a time when Paris, France, Europe, or the world deluded itself into thinking these were the best of times, that all was well, and that as many new inventions and discoveries as one could ever think of had been invented and discovered. Such a statement or vision or wish is untenable.

Any authors who speak like that seem to treat the society of the late nineteenth century as one in which life was staid, repressed, and smug, something like the Vienna of Stefan Zweig's lengthy autobiographical essay. However, judging by the innovations in the arts and sciences, the advances in technology and popular entertainment, and the radical twists and turns in literature, this was anything but a prim Victorian period. The question nevertheless remains: why in the midst of so much change and confusion, innovation, and struggle to assert traditional or mythical values and institutions, did so many people feel themselves to be men and women without qualities, individuals lost in the power of crowds and mobs, adults trapped in the memories of an abused childhood?

Stefan Zweig wrote a thesis entitled "Die Philosophie des Hippolyte Taine," pointing out in this way the direction in which we need to track down some of the paths through which mentalities travelled in the lives and events we are talking about in this book. Although thinkers like Hippolyte Taine and Ernest Renan have faded from the centres of attention of those who write about the Dreyfus Affair, they form part of the constellation of writers who created the matrix of ideas in which the mentalities and the imaginations that made the clash of personalities, institutions, and paradigms possible, and whose explosion and disintegration are the playing field where the affair was fought out. It is in the work of the forgotten writers, and often in the neglected books and essays of the authors we still care about, that the games and battles were contested—not in the works that are important to us, who come after the paradigms have shifted.

The Phantasmagoria

Le premier devoir de l'homme sincère est de ne pas influer sur ses propres opinions, de laisser la réalité se refléter en lui comme en la chambre noire de photographe, et d'assister en spectateur aux batailles intérieures que se livrent les idées au fond de sa conscience.

—Ernest Renan[61]

Lorsque seul, dans le silence, demi-couche dans un fauteuil, je me laisse aller à la rêverie, et que, par l'effacement des sensations ordinaires, la fantasmagorie interne devient intense, si le sommeil approche, mes images précises finissent par provoquer des hallucinations véritables.

—Hippolyte Taine[62]

During the months that followed our interviews and in which the book took shape, not only did I live completely involved in Proust, thanks to the voice I had been listening to, but I also saw and heard him in a way that at times was almost hallucinatory. Not once did I doubt that this was the real Proust.

—Georges Belmont[63]

---

61 Ernest Renan, "Examen de conscience philosophique" (September 1888) in *Souvenirs d'enfance et de jeunesse*, ed. Laudice Retat (Paris: GF Flammarion, 1973), 283. "The first duty of an honest man is not to be influenced by his own opinions, but to let reality be reflected in him as in a photographer's darkroom, and to observe passively and objectively the interior battles of ideas rising from the bottom of his consciousness" (my translation).

62 Hippolyte Taine, *De l'Intelligence*, volume 2 (Paris: Hachette, 1870); facsimile édition Lexington, KY: Biblibazaar, 2010), 35. "Alone and in silence, half-asleep in an easy chair, I let myself float into reverie and when, by the fading away of all normal sensations, the internal phantasmagoria becomes intense, if sleep approaches, my precise images end up by provoking veritable hallucinations" (my translation).

63 Georges Belmont, "Introduction" to Céleste Albaret, *Monsieur Proust*, trans. Barbara Bray (New York, NY: New York Review Books, 2003), xvi-xvii. Belmont recorded the interview with Alberet, who had been Proust's servant and confidant for seventeen years. She had an uncanny memory for details and tones of voice in the conversations she had with the great writer. Although she lacked a formal education, Albaret was extremely intelligent and intuitive and she could hold her own in discussions of Proust's book with the author and his artistic friends. Belmont's comment sets the stage for a double way of reading the character and the writings of Alfred Dreyfus undertaken in this book: first, close attention to specific details, an attempt to grasp the nuances of his style and tone, and a contextualizing of his emotional and intellectual documents within the creative and scientific writers of his time, and second, a midrashic enhancement of the text by various rabbinical techniques of exegesis explained over the course of this book.

There are two broad and distinct ways to look at truth, reality, memory, and history. In one, it is possible to imagine our minds as photographic lenses through which the facts of the outside world pass with minimal distortions and then register objectively on the screen or chemical plate of our minds as memory—things that can be recalled and discussed as accurate and truthful records of the past, our own and those of people; ideas; and institutions outside of us. The other way, more creative, poetic, and subjective, is to recognize that our experience of the world is always in flux, subject to transformations, distorted by conscious and unconscious pressures, our own and those of society around us, already limited and censored by language, culture, and political ideologies (including religion and aesthetic theories)—and to take this second vision as not always having a negative effect that at best leads to scepticism and at worst to cynicism and hedonistic behaviour, but also sometimes leads to something positive, that allows for artistic re-creation, scientific innovation, philosophical refinement, and other innovative and critical acts and dreams.[64]

The assumption usually is that even in dreamlike states, whether in hypnotic trances or private reverie, such as Taine imagines for himself, the images created are hallucinatory distortions of reality, anything, that is, but accurate and detailed depictions of reality so that while speculative interpretations of the natural world and human history are based on such false memories, they have at best a heuristic or aesthetic value and at worst a dangerous, insane influence on our lives. However, certainly by the 1890s, following the radical shifts in perception brought about by the impressionist painters and initiated by the advanced psychologism of Tarde, Bergson, and Freud, it was possible to conceive of an approach to memory, history, and poetry that avoided the incongruities and mutual exclusiveness of these two earlier perspectives, either truth or distortion, reality or madness, objectivity or interference.

Even Marcel Proust, who in *A la recherche du temps perdu* seems to dismiss the new cinematography as another form of photography, was

---

64 This is not the kind of argument that can be refuted as Dr. Johnson thought he did with Bishop Berkley by kicking a stone to prove that the outside world did exist; this kind of practical cynicism appears in ancient satires too where, for instance, Plato's thesis of the ideal of love is undercut by a husband and wife team of *kyniks* writhing in ecstasy on the floor in front of his students. Logic needs to be met by logic, as facts by facts.

merely a passive recorder of facts and so a distorter of the dynamic fluidity of lived experience, and yet this rejection of the technology of motion pictures misses the points where cinema can enhance, advance, and interpret finely the insights of his own concepts of time, reality, memory, and art. Proust took a negative stand against photography, which he identified with a positivist realism; he saw photographs as banal and bourgeois. But Méliès the magician promoted a more dynamic, playful sense with his moving pictures. They are illusions to be sure, but they take artificial reproduction of reality to a higher, more artistic reality. Two things happened when Daguerre found a way to fix fleeting images on metal plates to make what we call photographs. First, artists and philosophers realized that the pictures produced were different from artistic paintings or drawings, insofar as they could not reproduce nuances of colour or texture and did not distinguish between the significant and the insignificant elements in an image or the reality it supposedly reproduced, and yet they revealed details and aspects of the scene or object that had not been noticed before. Therefore, second, the camera could be more than just an aid to the artist in recalling persons, places or things for him or her to later reproduce as an aesthetic object: it could itself be a way of manipulating the memory of the reality experienced, revealing what had not been noticed, exploring the subtleties and interstices between shadows and light or colours—indeed, the shadows were themselves aspects of light and colour. For all his opposition, Proust actually worked in a cinematic way in both his narrative structures and in his exploration of the nuances of character and social reactions. Dreyfus was fascinated by the technology of photography and also of x-rays, and saw in the optical mechanics of transferring fleeting and seemingly confusing light and shades to fixed pictures a way of coming to terms with the phantasmagoria of his plight and the enigma of his arrest and guilty verdict.

Despite these theoretical speculations and the advances in everything from cosmology and psychiatric medicine to quantum physics and hypnotic techniques,[65] today most historians still approach the Dreyfus Affair through a lens of mid-nineteenth-century positivism,

65 This was precisely the period when spectacular advances were published in Einstein's essays on relativity, and related topics or Henri Bergson and Sigmund Freud were making their advances in two kinds of depth psychology.

taking the words, images, and events of the period as transparent, accurate, and true, and the result is that like those thinkers who were against Dreyfus and who we now know were deluded, hysterical, and delirious, they are still mistaking the ideological misperceptions of the popular press as reality.[66]

What I have found through a close reading of the recently published notebooks that Dreyfus kept during the years he was imprisoned on Devil's Island is that he was himself wrestling with the received ideas—because for all his faith in the republican values of reason, justice, and freedom, his existential reality could not sustain the consequences of that faith. He was reading a wide range of books, commenting on them critically, and posing new questions. To be sure, this initial reading of his notebooks cannot mark Dreyfus as a major innovative thinker of the period; he was, it seems, uninterested in many of those we today see as the avant-garde painters, musicians, novelists, and philosophers of the late nineteenth century, and he often expressed distaste for the aesthetic theories or political ideologies he was aware of. Nevertheless, he did not accept what he was reading—he made objections, he provided additional details to create new contexts, and he suggested other ideas and processes to apply. In a certain way, he played out the roles of the underground man, the man without qualities, the Kafkaesque victim of bureaucracy gone mad, the *artist manqué* . . .

Meditated on more soberly, however, Dreyfus was none of these—neither autistic nor artistic—and yet, as we shall argue throughout this book, he found himself both cast out of normality and cast into the role of anti-hero in a national theatre of the absurd, an externalized phantasmagorie.[67]

---

66 Which is not to call these historians of the last twenty-five years anti-Semitic or belonging to the various political ideologies that in the later phases of the affair, after supporting Dreyfus for their own strategic purposes, turned against him, but to say that the inability or refusal to interpret documents and actions in a more dynamic way, recognizing all the techniques in psychoanalysis or in Leo Strauss's modes of deciphering messages written during persecution, yields variants on the old canards about Dreyfus's character being dull and conventional or about the tediousness of his letters to Lucie. Worse are those who still write hundreds and thousands of pages about the juridical procedures and the political implications of the struggle for Alfred Dreyfus's rehabilitation and lament the "fact" that there is little or nothing to say about his personality.

67 Romain Rolland speaking of Russian revolutionaries but giving a sense of the matrix in which the affair was fought out in France: "It is not treachery so much as versatility, and it is thoroughly disinterested. There are so many men of action to whom action is a theater into which they bring their talents as comedians, quite honestly prepared at any moment to change their part!" (*Jean Christophe*, vol. III, 181).

My Book Is a *Midrash*

> Midrash, *as "witty" poetry, possesses malleability not available with doctrinaire teachings in the realm of Jewish law* (halakhah). *For this reason it is a suitable candidate for the kind of liberal and ambiguous usage Maimonides employs in the labyrinthine undertaking that constitutes the* Guide of the Perplexed.
>
> —James Arthur Diamond[68]

The way in which I *midrash* this study of Dreyfus is in truth four different ways, some overlapping, some alternating, some conflated, and some hinted at. While it is evident from previous discussions of what a traditional Jewish *midrash* was and how it works as a generic, epistemological tool, my own performance in this book about Alfred Dreyfus and the Dreyfus Affair is more restricted and is also modified to meet with the particular circumstances prevalent at the historical period of the captain's and the French nation's ordeal, as well as with the nature of the crises through which we went in the first decade of the twenty-first century, a hundred years later.

These midrashing techniques will be applied to the following kinds of texts: (a) books, letters, journals, memoirs, and essays by Alfred Dreyfus, other members of his family, and close associates or participants in the affair; (b) documents referred to, hinted at, or implicit in the writings of Alfred Dreyfus and Marcel Proust and other authors and artists who took aspects of the affair as major or minor subjects of their work; (c) historians, reporters, and analysts of the affair, especially those within the first ten to twenty years of its occurring—that is, from about 1894 to 1924; and (d) books, articles, essays, and other works by and about the anti-Semitists involved in or inspired by the affair.

First, the texts of written documents and the articulated memories of events are described in and of themselves. The exercise involves a series of close, etymological and cultural studies of the words, references, allusions, and echoes in the texts written by Dreyfus and his supporters. Words and phrases have to be seen not only in the specific contexts

---

68 Diamond, *Maimonides and the Hermeneutics of Concealment*, 3.

of their normal usage by these writers and their contemporaries, but also in wider and deeper contexts, so that implications and significance can be ascertained. They also have to be measured in their literal and figurative senses, perceived in patterns—what words they are normally associated with, and what words they stand related to as antonyms and variants in regard to tone, nuance, and hint. Thus, what may seem like casual, passing, or insignificant words and phrases can be charged with an electrical or magnetic energy that reconfigures the texts we are studying and hence the dramatization, memorial quality, and probative value of the man, the milieu, and the mentality of Alfred Dreyfus.

Next the study approaches the relationship of text to countertext (where there are two or more competing versions of the same supposed reality or subjective experiences), text to antitext (where the validation of one text does more than undermine the truth content in full or in part of its competitors but designates a different sort of reality that excludes the reality of the others by sheer rhetorical force, political censorship, or some deeper epistemological technique), or text and nontext (where the power of one textual experience invalidates, undermines, and consumes to the point of obliterating the memory, traces, and conceptual space of the others). Juxtapositions of these kinds of textual networks are made using the range of documents and authors mentioned by and commented upon by Dreyfus and his supporters. At first sight, many of these juxtapositions seem outrageous and far-fetched, but as we explore their analogies, often by intricate and witty discussions, aspects of the meanings not fully appreciated or even missed out upon completely should begin to surface and register in light of the larger picture emerging in this book. It is in this way that this book forces the reader to examine from new angles, new filters, and new measuring devices the matrix of the man and the affair.

Third, rather than setting two or more texts next to one another in order to see what is precipitated, crystallized, or destroyed by the epistemological phenomenon, we attempt a series of new contextualizations of passages and events from the books and authors mentioned by Dreyfus and his supporters. Much like the juxtapositions, the relocation brings new angles of appreciation and unexpected perspectives into focus, even creating paradigms of connectivity, analogy, and contrast that illuminate the pictures and arguments in the text. Normal, commonsense, and traditional readings, analyses, and interpretations are thus challenged by the new angles of vision, the new connectivities established, and the annihilation of previously assumed relationships and historical signs.

Most radical and shocking of all will be the fourth midrashic mode, which is a series of rhetorical conversations that undermine the apparent conventional integrity of the texts, especially the discourses of scholarship—history, psychology, and philosophy—in order to develop new perspectives. These dialogues may at times seem irrelevant, trivial, or transgressive. Although they are indeed made_up, they provide a number of tools to shatter entrenched truisms and unquestioned assumptions about Dreyfus and the affair. Their value is therefore less in their literal development inside this book than in their probing, discombobulating, and destabilizing faculties. They invite the historian and literary critic to participate in the formation of a more powerful conversation about the topics at the heart of this book.

A further word is also needed on what we mean by hints, oblique allusions, echoes, and similar techniques of *inadequation.* Alfred and Lucie Dreyfus, for instance, knew that when they wrote to each other, whatever they put into words in their letters would be subject to censorship, but they only learned through harsh experience what the consequences of mistakes, casual or unconscious, would be, and hence needed to work out—without direct communication and certainly without having previously agreed upon codes, signals, and experience—various ways of reassuring one another, of their complete love, loyalty, and trust in one another. While their correspondence was not perfect and was often fraught with frustrations, in the long run, over the five years in which they sent epistles to one another, they reproduced, totally without forethought or formal recognition, methods of writing that were firmly rooted in Jewish experience, particularly amongst those men and women caught up in contraptions such as the Inquisition. It is unlikely that either would have read books, such as Maimonides's *Guide of the Perplexed,* in which much of this tradition was discussed and analysed, although Maimonides too composed his book using these techniques to exemplify exactly what this mode of hiding knowledge and teaching students would entail.

My argument, tentative as it must perforce be, is that Marcel Proust became aware of this way of writing through his family background—the conversations he had and overheard with his mother, his grandfather, and their Jewish friends—and the books he read as he moved from preparatory short stories towards his major novel; and if Proust could absorb and modulate these techniques in the same period as the Dreyfus Affair was unfolding, so too could the Dreyfuses have become aware of them, albeit through less systematic means—partly from Lucie's parents and relatives, who were more attached to Jewish traditions than her husband's family and friends, and partly from hints he had picked up but not needed to think about before the shock of his arrest and the nightmare of his imprisonment.

This knowledge and skill in Dreyfus cannot be traced to specific moments or texts in his experience, however, and we are left with only two modes of proof: one is in the fact of what he did write in concord with Lucie—in other words, the proof is in the pudding; and the other is in the similarities between what this couple did in their letters and what the husband wrote alone in his notebooks, workbooks, and journals, and what Maimonides recommended and hundreds of Marrano, Crypto-Jewish, and Sephardic individuals and families did over the course of more than four hundred years when they had to keep their true identities a secret from church spies, inquisitorial officials, and suspicious relatives, friends, and neighbours. That these techniques were more or less suspected, if not always exposed and confirmed, can be seen in the responses of non-Jewish commentators, not least of whom were the prison guards and administrators who observed Dreyfus in captivity, searched his writings for criminal ideas, and reported regularly to their political masters in Paris.

I thus justify my own way of writing this book on the grounds that it is only by such imitation that the reader can properly grasp the phenomena we are studying and, even more, that it is only through this shattering of literary and scholarly conventions that the truth of Dreyfus's experience and the meaning of the affair can be understood, and thus, justice in a Jewish sense served.

In each of these four midrashings, but especially the second and third modalities, I will put into play the words, images, themes, and conceptions of anti-Semitism. Although usually dismissed as delusionary ravings or deliberate distortions of historical reality, such discourses and imaginations nevertheless are valuable both as markers of the hateful currents of the times, at times only partly audible or visible to the main players in the Dreyfus Affair, and as tracings of variant ways of thinking and feelings, as well as of seeing and articulating the existential truths of private and collective experiences—fears, anxieties, hopes, aspirations, desires, and so on. We show in this book that not all opponents of Dreyfus were raving maniacs or fanatics; many were intellectuals, and indeed some were themselves Jewish, or at least claimed Jewish relatives in their close family histories, formed part of the educated, professional elite, and were sometimes recognized leaders in the arts, sciences, and political movements of their time, and in most other ways of speaking, writing, and picturing the world were quite sane, perceptive, and sensitive. The manifestation of Judeophobia—something that also could be measured at various degrees of intensity at various stages of their lives or in different social or political venues—does, therefore, form part of the complex existential reality of the period.

Chapter Two: Bodies of Evidence

PART 1: AN ORCHESTRATED LITANY OF LIES[1]

> *A crowd scarcely distinguishes between the subjective and the objective. It accepts as real the images evoked in the mind, though they most often have only a very distant relation with the observed fact.*
>
> —Gustave Le Bon[2]

The whole Dreyfus Affair can, from one perspective, be seen as a long debate about the nature of evidence and thus about real and false documents, shredded papers glued together, and forgeries, interfered-with letters, secret and nonexistent pieces of paper, handwriting experts, and discrediting of testimony—about what does and what does not constitute the truth, the whole truth and nothing but the truth. From another perspective, sometimes that of hindsight and sometimes that of denial and wilful self-blindness and -deafness, it is about anti-Semitism, about the way the prosecutors in the drawn-out controversy do all they can to prove Dreyfus the Jew guilty because Jews must by virtue of their being Jews be traitors and liars. Most of the Dreyfusards do all they can to avoid dealing with this issue of anti-Semitism and to claim instead that the affair is about truth and justice, about the honour of individuals and

---

1 Justice Peter Mahon, *Royal Commission of Inquiry into the Erebus Disaster* (27 April 1981), examining the cover-ups used to protect Air New Zealand from full responsibility for the crash of a chartered tourist flight over Antarctica. As in the Dreyfus Affair, the arrogance of power came fully into play in a conspiracy of silence, duplicity, and pressure from both the New Zealand government and its national airlines. Amidst the claims and counterclaims, there were denials, calls for further investigations, and resignations. For instance, "Air New Zealand asked for their judicial review of the Inquiry's allegations and findings to be heard in the Court of Appeal rather than the High Court. Their request was initially rejected, but later accepted because of 'the magnitude of the disaster,' 'the public importance of the issues' and 'the conduct of an inquiry held by a high court judge.'" Similarly, "Justice Mahon resigned from the bench of the High Court in January 1982." See, for instance, "Court action following Erebus disaster inquiry: Cabinet accepts Judge Mahon's resignation," online at http://NZHistory.net.nz/media/photo/ongoing-debate-about-erebus-disaster (seen 21 October 2010).

2 Le Bon, *The Crowd*, 41.

the honour of the republic, the army, and the church.[3] Some people on both sides, perhaps exhausted by those arguments, when it came time to fight for Dreyfus's rehabilitation, decided the honour of the army and the security of the republic were more important than the honour or welfare of a single man, so that it did not matter at all whether he were guilty or innocent—due to expediency and reasons of state.

The more we examine the body of evidence adduced during the two courts martial against Alfred Dreyfus, the more it appears that Peter Mahon's expression is an apt way to describe the whole Dreyfus Affair: an orchestrated litany of lies. Almost all the books dealing with the affair are concerned with political and judicial questions, about the truth content of various documents and testimonies.[4] This book is also about evidence in a larger sense; about the nature of documents, testimony, and thus truth that can be articulated in a court of law and in the public media—that is, about the ways in which lawyers and judges, newspaper reporters and editors, construct illusions of truth in their arguments and, consequently, about the ways in which such spoken and written speeches are heard and understood by juries, other agents of the judicial and political systems, the readers of newspapers, and the spectators at various modes of conveying secondary reproductions of the courtroom drama on the stage, in films, printed on postcards, modelled into wax museums—in brief: a whole industry of propaganda developing at the time of the Dreyfus Affair.

Still another kind of evidence comes into focus in this book about Alfred Dreyfus, the man and the milieu, and the mentality and the *midrash*, for this study I have undertaken is not an attempt at biography or social history. It is primarily an examination of the surviving texts, especially those written at various times and under various conditions in his life during and after the affair by Alfred Dreyfus himself and by his wife. The examination uses the techniques of the history of mentalities and psychohistory but is not strictly or exclusively an exercise in either of those disciplines. I also examine Dreyfus's letters, journals, *carnets*, and *cahiers*

---

3 Romain Rolland: "Christophe asked Olivier: 'You have been lifted to the stars and hurled down to the depths of hell by your Dreyfus affair. Where is the poet in whose soul the height and depth of it were felt?'" (*Jean Christophe*, vol. II, 325).

4 Edmond Jabès wrote in *Du Désert au livre* (Paris: Belfond, 1980): "*Le Juif ne se pose pas seulement des questions; il est lui-même devenu question*" (The Jew not only asks questions; he himself becomes a question) cited by Ouaknin, *Le livre brûlé*, 262, n. 9.

as though they were texts of *midrash* and the midrashing of experience in themselves, and at the same time, I conduct the examination as though I were myself writing a *midrash* on Alfred Dreyfus.

In this last kind of study, there are three constitutive bodies of evidence that were composed by Captain Dreyfus during his years of imprisonment, exile, and forced isolation and silence and the twelve years that followed, during which he fought for his complete exoneration and the restoration of his good name. First, there are the personal letters, written between Alfred and Lucie Dreyfus for the most part, although there are occasional epistles between Alfred and his brother and the close allies he knew about before he was packed off into the oblivion of the French prison islands off the coast of northeastern South America. These letters shade off into printed collections, including edited versions of the original epistles, introductory remarks by the intimate parties, their relatives, their political supporters, and eventually academic students of the affair. Second, Alfred also kept workbooks or *cahiers* while he was in prison and journalistic notebooks or *carnets* during the second phase of his struggle when he returned to France.

As we shall see, he seems never to have intended the *cahiers* for anyone to see but himself, and actually destroyed at least half of them himself; they are remarkable therefore for two reasons: (a) because they are physical imprints of his experiences in isolation over an extended period of time; and (b) because they were read and reported on by his prison guards and political officials back in Paris. Third, the journals are evidence of a somewhat different kind, although they form an edited version of his feelings and opinions during the period of time they were written and, as reflected in later years, they can be seen as much more than a running record of his daily affairs, his immediate thoughts concerning the fight to rehabilitate his name after the second court-martial in Rennes, and the pardon he felt forced to accept because of his frail physical and psychological condition, along with copies of letters and conversations he and others had in that long period from 1899 to 1906.

Twelve Years of Lost Time

> *Cette animosité se dissimulait communément et cependant le juif intelligent la perçoit. Il sent une résistance devant lui,*

il a l'impression d'un mur que des adversaires ont dressé entre lui et ceux au milieu desquels il vit.

—Bernard Lazare[5]

In most of their lives before the affair and especially the five years of their marriage prior to that fateful Saturday morning in 1894, Lucie and Alfred Dreyfus pretended to themselves that they were assimilated, part of French society, and that anti-Semitism was something that did not impinge on their lives.[6] They refused to see the wall that had been set up between them and the rest of society, and when it was too late, they lost five years of their lives trying to find a way to dismantle that wall to free Alfred, and another seven to get him rehabilitated. Or so it would seem.[7] This book makes a somewhat different point. I argue that for the horrors of the incarceration, the shame of imprisonment, and the tortures, physical and psychological, that the couple endured, the wall never really came down. Yet, because of the false accusations, the judicial errors, the forgeries, and the purged testimonies, Alfred and Lucie in their letters to one another and in the journals that Alfred kept created something very important, and discovered and invented new aspects in themselves and their relationship. To a certain very limited degree, Lucie was able to start drawing out the reticent and shy young man who courted and then married her. As Michael Burns puts it, commenting on the first letters

5 "This animosity usually dissimulates itself and yet the intelligent Jew sees it. He senses a resistance before him, he has the impression of a wall that his adversaries have constructed between himself and those others in among whom he lives": Bernard Lazare, "Le nouveau ghetto," *La Justice* (17 November 1894), cited in Bloch-Dano, *Madame Proust*, 302.

6 As Eveylne Bloch-Dano says of Jeanne Proust, Marcel's mother, "*Comme des parents, elle est et restera une israélit, parfaitement intégrée à la société qui, autrefois accueillit ses ancêtres*" (Like her relatives she was and would remain an Israelite, perfectly integrated into the society which formerly had welcomes her ancestors), *Madame Proust*, 21. Jeanne never converted, and her husband, Dr. Adrien Proust, never demanded that she do so; the family Marcel grew up in what was nominally a Christian household, but he freely visited with his Jewish relatives and felt, particularly at the time of the Dreyfus Affair, a loyalty to the Jews (29). Like the Dreyfus family, the Weils had come from Alsace (32), but they had not only enriched themselves in Paris; as we see in Jeanne's life, they intermarried with the Christian political, professional, and intellectual elite (38), whereas Alfred and Lucie's background was more restricted to the comfortable manufacturing and professional Jewish community. Thanks to the affair, however, their two children, Pierre and Jeanne, moved into the circle of intellectuals, such as the Reinach brothers.

7 That even supposedly tolerant Frenchmen and women, supposedly supporters of the wrongly accused Dreyfus, could harbor anti-Semitic prejudices may be seen in regard, for instance, to Emile Zola's wife, who noted the predominance of Jews on the stock market and considered many professions as specifically Jewish (Bloch-Dano, *Madame Proust*, 60). Later in this book, I shall discuss different kinds and degrees of Judeophobia and their implications.

Alfred wrote to his intended while on manoeuvres:

> Lucie discovered her fiancé's mercurial moods, the abrupt shifts from lighthearted descriptions of standing watch on a frigid night with a horse whose whole purpose in life was "to return to the stable" to his obsession with work and a relentless perfectionism that made him appear selfish and insensitive. He admitted that it had always been difficult for him to share his private feelings, to "open up," and he agreed that Lucie had a right to know more about the man to whom she was "entrusting" her life.[8]

Foreshadowing the way they would learn to communicate in a kind of group therapeutical dialogue, Alfred responds to her questions and challenges, perhaps most of them implied by his own imagining of how she must see his flaws rather than actually present in her own cautious address to the older man she was soon to marry.

> He would try to express himself and to break his "disastrous habit: of taking everything seriously. But he pleaded with her not to interpret his reserved manner as insensitivity: "Surface insensitivity . . . I grant you," he wrote, using the *vous*, the formal address of a proper young suitor. "The real thing, no!" "I hope you'll come to realize," he added, "that however retiring I may be, I love you deeply."[9]

Then, a year later, in the spring of 1890, using one of those most prescient figures of speech that we will have to come back to deal with in the next volume, where we shall discuss Dreyfus's place in the artistic culture of the late nineteenth century, he tells Lucie,

> For two instruments to produce a harmonious sound to-

---

8 Burns, *Dreyfus: A Family Affair,* 83. It is a further frustration to realize that there are so many letters written between Lucie and Alfred from before his imprisonment that have yet to be transcribed, edited, and published.

9 Burns, *Dreyfus: A Family Affair,* 83.

> gether, they must be in tune, as in music. In physics, it's called "synchronic vibrations."[10]

There is no complete edition of all the letters written between Alfred and Lucie Dreyfus nor between Alfred and other members of his family and allies before or during his period of imprisonment, and none between Lucie and her family, friends, and government officials. Each book containing letters has a different, overlapping selection, and each is set in a different context with its own polemical or scholarly purpose. Nevertheless, given these constraints, I believe it is possible to analyze these letters and to draw a number of—one need not say preliminary but at least new kinds of—conclusions about the husband and the wife and their relationship to each other during the five years of separation between 1894 and 1899.

In 1901, already back in France and now pardoned, Dreyfus published *Cinq années de ma vie*,[11] a book dedicated to his children, in which he sets forth his ordeal as an unjustifiably accused and condemned Frenchman in order to establish his ethical (moral) credentials, seeks to evoke sympathy from any in the not-yet-convinced general public ready to support his cause, and appeals to his allies for their help in gaining full rehabilitation of his honour and rank. The letters are meshed into a text that includes an apologetic account of his life and the polemical argument for his innocence. At no point does he plead for mercy or pity, call attention to himself as an object of anti-Semitic prejudice, or cast aspersions on the army, the government, or the nation. What he does say is that he suffers physically and morally and has to make a special effort to avoid sliding into the depths of despair. He draws pictures of the island prison where he was sent into exile[12] and the hut, with its palisade blocking the sea, which kept him in solitary confinement and under the constant surveillance of guards who were under strict orders not to communicate with him.[13] This regimen of silence and isolation, along with poor food, sanitary conditions, and

10 Burns, *Dreyfus: A Family Affair,* 83.

11 Alfred Dreyfus, *Cinq années de ma vie* (1894–1899), with an introductory essay by Pierre Vidal-Naquet and an afterward by Jean-Louis Lévy (Paris: Editions la Découverte, 1994; this edition first published by Editions Francois Maspero, 1982).

12 *Cinq années de ma vie*, 100.

13 *Cinq années de ma vie*, 102.

insalubrious weather, increasingly wore him down.

He also inserts a journal that he kept for the first two years (1895 and 1896) to be sent eventually to his wife Lucie. Thus we know that on Sunday, 14 April, 1895, he wrote: "*Je commence aujourd'hui le journal de ma triste et épouvantable vie*" (Today I begin the journal of my sad and horrible life).[14] What he is concerned with is the tediousness and discomfort of his life in exile, his silence which keeps him at best in conversation with himself, and the failure of letters to arrive, the paucity of paper with which to write, and the lack of reading material.

Several little points come up, however, that seem to test his Jewish character and tastes. One, which Dreyfus makes no especial note of, is the fact that he was called in to confront the charge of treason on 13 October, 1894, barely two weeks after beginning his service in the Statistics Department (i.e., Intelligence Bureau) of the army in Paris; that day was a Saturday, the Jewish Sabbath, or *shabat*.[15] Although he as an assimilated Jew may have normally worked on this holy day, his accusers would have been aware of the irony—and the deliberate insult they were paying to this unwanted Semite in their midst. Dreyfus, however, does not react.

Day by day, week by week, Dreyfus notes in his prison journal and in his letters to Lucie sketchy, vague details of his feelings, very little of what is actually happening—there is no narrative in his life to be recorded—and, at most, only tantalizing hints of what he thinks about.[16] At times, both Alfred and Lucie refer to the ordeal as martyrdom or a calvary, using these very Christian reference words in a general, secularized form.[17] "Days are lugubrious. Everything is forbidden to me, the perpetual *tête-à-tête* with my own thoughts" (8 March, 1896).[18] He finds

---

14 *Cinq années de ma vie*, 103.

15 *Cinq années de ma vie*, page 51 at the start of his chapter 2.

16 It will be evident soon enough how the writing of such hints (*remez*, as the rabbis call them) are important, especially when they appear on the page inadvertently.

17 Or at least in a neutral sense. Ambiguity occasionally creeps in, though, as when Lucie reports that she and the children have gone to her family for dinner at *Pâques*, a term normally used for the Christian celebration of Easter, sometimes for Passover, but then usually presented as "the Jewish *Pâcque*" in the singular. Because it is more than likely that the family gathered for a Passover seder, not a vague and indeterminate Easter-holiday meal, those historians who translate the expression as "Passover meal" are correct up to a point, the point being that Lucie, like Alfred, aware of censorship, sought to avoid any direct indications of their Jewishness. Much later, Lucie makes reference to the eight days of Hanukkah, with the children happy as kings and excited with their presents (*Ecris-moi souvent, écris moi longuement*, 393).

18 "*Journées lugubres. Tout m'est interdit, le tête-à-tête perpétuel avec mes pensées*" Dreyfus, *Cinq années,*

himself crystallized in his own pains.[19] He suffers from nerves all night.[20] "A horrible night of fever and delirium."[21] These are not imaginary pains and anxieties: "I was put into irons last night! Why? I don't know why . . . . How can I not go mad through such long atrocious nights?"[22] He even draws a picture of the double manacles used to shackle him in the bed at night.[23] Only much later will Dreyfus find out the reason for this extra act of cruelty against him: in a ploy to force the issue of his wrongful imprisonment to the fore, Alfred's brother Mathieu arranged for a Welsh newspaper to report an attempted escape from Devil's Island, and when this false news reached France and the anti-Semitic press picked it up, the government reacted by imposing new conditions on Alfred's treatment in exile.[24]

Along the way, no matter what other matter he may write about in both the journals and the letters, Dreyfus complains of books and newspapers not reaching him or arriving very late, long after Lucie tells him that she had posted them to him. Most of the time, note, it is Lucie who chooses the titles, based on general hints given by Alfred, but also, as we have earlier suggested, titles selected from her knowledge of his tastes and interests and also probably on the shared conversations conducted in the first happy years of their marriage and courtship. In a supplement to his letter dated 12 September, 1896, Alfred recalls fireside chats with Lucie in the happier days of their marriage:

> *Je viens to causer encore, comme dans cet heureux temps, hélas déjà lointain, où nous bavardions tranquillement au coin de notre feu, en regardant jouer sur le tapis nos chers petits amours, nos enfants.*[25]

149.

19 1 September 1896: "*Je suis comme cristallisé dans ma douleur . . .*" *Cinq années de ma vie*, 152.

20 2 September 1896: "*Les nerfs m'ont fait horriblement souffrir toute la nuit . . .*" *Cinq années de ma vie*, 152.

21 3 September 1896: "*Nuit horrible de fièvre et de délire*" *Cinq années de ma vie*, 153.

22 7 September 1896: "*J' ai été mis aux fers hier au soir! Pourquoi? Je l'ignore . . . . Comment ne suis-he pas devenu fou dans la longueur de cette nuit atroce?*" *Cinq années de ma vie*, 155.

23 *Cinq années de ma vie*, 159.

24 A reader of this paragraph in manuscript shouted in anger and frustration, "Why on earth was Mathieu meddling in such a way? Couldn't he have imagined the consequences?" Alas, no he couldn't have. This was another failure of the imagination, another miscalculation in the strategy, driven by its own frustrations and rage.

25 *Ecris-moi souvent, écris moi longuement*, 315.

> I have just been speaking to you again, as in that happy time, alas so far distant, when we would chat peacefully in the corner by the fire, looking at our dear loves, our children, playing on the carpet.

A sentimental picture, to be sure, yet an idealized image of what must actually have been their custom at home. This is the time[26] when they could share feelings and ideas and thus lay the groundwork for the structure of the new kind of relationship and new kind of domestic language they would have to construct during the long ordeal ahead.[27] Alfred catches a hint of that preliminary labour in the same letter when he tells his wife, using long, involved syntax,

> *Vois-tu, chère Lucie, nous avons été tellement accablés par cet affreux destin—oh! l'affreux destin—oh! si horrible que l'on se demande à chaque instant comment nos cerveaux ont pu y résister—puis nous avons continué à nous entretenir de nos souffrances, de toutes nos douleurs, ne pouvant* [28]. . .

> Don't you see, dear Lucie, that we have been so crushed by this frightful destiny—oh! So horrible that we have to ask ourselves at every instant how our brains could be able to resist it—then we have carried on our mutual support through our sufferings, all our pains, only being able . . .

---

26 On time in Jewish thought, see Ouaknin, *Le livre brûlé*, 120.

27 Conversation in rabbinical writings involves mutual questions and answers, challenges, probing, and revelations through exploration of what one's master and student or between the study partners: what one asks and what one says in reply is never wrong but always in the process of becoming a part of the chain of a self-correcting and expanding tradition; this is called *mahloquet*, and as modern commentators like Ouaknin and Faur write, it creates an open dialectic. These, however, are not the set-piece dialogues between Socrates (Plato's master and his docile interlocutors who quickly accede to his higher wisdom and declare, "We knew nothing; we do not know what we are talking about." Above all, says Ouaknin, *mahloquet "est une façon de dire et de penser le réfus de la synthèse et du système; antidogmatisme qui, seul, rend possible une vérité vivante"* (is a way of speaking and thinking the refusal of synthesis and system; an anti-dogmatism which alone makes possible a living truth), *Le livre brûlé*, 134.

28 *Ecris-moi souvent, écris moi longuement*, 315.

These internal conversations in his mind are not only with himself but also, through his imagination, and through the force of mutual wills, in an imaginary space of textual union, for he speaks not only of his own cogitations but as though Lucie were also really and truly a party to these mental discussions and to the emotional and spiritual support they produce. But as the sentence meanders and the syntax falters,[29] Alfred begins to think that there is more to the case against him than merely an error of judgement by the courts, the military, and the government, something he cannot bring himself to say,[30] even to Lucie.

> *Que nos cœurs se sont aigris, à notre insu, malgré nous, et au lieu de ne penser qu'à une chose, ne voir qu'une chose, déchiffrer, faire déchiffrer le mystère de cet effroyable drame, au fur et à mesure que le temps passait, sans en amener l'êclairissement, nous avons fini par accuser d'un nouveau vouloir, veux mêmes qui font peut-être ce qu'ils peuvent pour cela . . . et à ce système, tout finirait par se délabrer en nous, et il ne faut pas, chérie, il faut voir plus haut.*[31]
>
> [So that only] our hearts are irritated, without our realizing it, despite ourselves, and instead of thinking of one thing only, of only seeing one thing, to decipher, [and] are led to this frightful drama [being] deciphered, more or less, as the time passes, without leading to any enlightenment, we finish by blaming even those who perhaps can wish for that . . . ill will and at this system, all will finish by falling apart on us, and this must not happen, darling, we must look higher.

29 According to Oaknin, "Dans la phrase hébraïque les mots ne sont pas subordonnées les uns aux autres par une logique grammaticale ou autre, ils 'coexistent', les uns auprès des autres et peuvent à [tout] l'instant signifier en dehors de leurs contextes ou être déplacé dans un autre contexte, tout en gardant les sens du premier contexte" (In a Hebrew phrase words are not subordinated to each other in one grammatical logic or another; they 'coexist' one alongside the other and may at any moment signify outside of their contexts or be displaced into another context, all the while keeping the sense of their first context), *Le livre brûlé*, 145. I do not mean that either Alfred or Lucie *mean to* write like this but that their education at its most basic level, in which the modalities of language are formed, *slip into* such constructs under sustained crisis conditions.

30 Not only is it difficult for him to conceive of these things, he finds it difficult, as we can see here in the confusing syntax, to put down in words.

31 *Ecris-moi souvent, écris moi longuement*, 315.

Thus, what began with a sentimental scene of domestic bliss reaches its conclusion in a despondent picture of moral collapse, and a frightful prospect of something he wants Lucie to reject with him by turning their inner gaze towards heaven—the scene of the infernal phantasmagoria projecting the worst anti-Semitic images over all of France.[32] Most of the time, however, at least in the letters and notebooks that have survived—or have been allowed to survive—Dreyfus maintains his appearance, keeps wearing the face of the loyal officer, and keeps the faith to Lucie, his muse and starlike guardian. The illusion he wants to hold on to is of their shared dreams and aspirations and of their mutual concern for each other and for the honour of their children.

After 1896, Lucie was told she could no longer pick and send books and magazines to her husband, but must instead remit funds for him to use to make his own orders through the penal system in French Guyana.[33] It would seem that this new policy served several purposes: first, it takes away from Lucie the opportunity to do something practical on behalf of Alfred, which like the actual tactile possession of letters written in the hand of each of the couple was interfered with to cause emotional distress; second, the authorities may have believed in their bigotry that Lucie's choice of books was some form of code, part of a Jewish, mystical conspiracy; and third, by channelling the book orders through the officials of the prison and colonial systems, these agents thought to add another layer of censorship over what the prisoner would be able to read. Only in the retrospective calm of his explanatory essays of *Five Years of my Life* does Dreyfus begin to name the specific titles. In chapter VIII, he outlines his programme of readings:

---

32 Romain Rolland, speaking of a M. Félix Weil: "He flung out ideas and created lines of thought: he would set great intellectual machines working, and would immediately grow disgusted with them. More than once he had scandalized people, who had been converted to a cause by his arguments, by producing the most incisive and discouraging criticism of the cause itself" (*Jean Christophe*, vol. II, 351).

33 18 July 1896: "*J'ai regret, mon chéri, de n'avoir plus la liberté de t'envoyer des livres. M. le ministre m'a fait savoir que tu étais autorisé dorénavant à faire toi-même ton choix*" (I regret, my darling, that I am no longer at liberty to send you books. The Minister has let me know that you are authorized from now on to make your own choices) *Ecris-moi souvent, écris moi longuement*, 307. This, of course, is a horrible, cynical joke played by the authorities. He was no more to do anything like ordering books than strolling around the compound to look at the sea or observe the flowers growing on the island.

> *Ce fonds comprenait, outré un certain nombre de revues littéraires et scientifiques, quelques livres de lecture courante, les* Etudes sur la littérature contemporare *de Schérer,* l'Histoire de la littérature *de Lanson, quelques oeuvres de Balzac, les* Mémoires *de Barras, la petite* Critique *de Janin, une* Histoire de la peinture, *l'*Histoire des Francs, *les* Récits des temps mérovingiens *d'Augustin Thierry, les tomes VII et VIII de l'*Histoire générale du IVe siècle jusqu'à nos jours *de Lavisse et Rambaud, les* Essais *de Montaigne, et surtout les oeuvres de Shakespeare.*[34]

Many of these titles and authors are commented upon in the *cahiers* of Devil's Island, while the others are hinted at by vague allusion. These books named here consist mostly of school texts, anthologies, and general introductions to history, literature, and painting. In a letter of 11 June, 1895, Alfred writes to Lucie about several magazines he has been able to obtain: "*On me remet la* Revue des Deux-Mondes, *la* Revue de Paris *et la* Revue Rose," and then adds the wish that she send him "*quelques romans de lecture facile*" (some easy-to-read novels).[35] It would be wonderful to know what he meant by this and what titles and authors she may have sent to him. Duclert claims that Alfred was allowed to receive twenty books each trimester, so that over the five-year period he might—had the jailers so permitted—have had access to at least three hundred titles.[36] The wide range of titles and writers in the *cahiers* indicates, as we shall see when we discuss the kind of intellectual he was, that Dreyfus not only read more extensively than he hints here but that he wished to read more extensively still. It is important to recall that for the first few years Lucie chose the books to send him, and that

---

34 *Cinq années de ma vie*, 165–166. "This collection consists of a certain number of literary and scientific journals, some books of current reading, some of [Edmund Henri Adolphe] Schérer's [1815-1889] *Studies on Contemporary Literature* (1886). Lanson's *History of Literature*, some works by Balzac, the *Memoirs* [1896] of [Paul, vicomte de] Barras [1755-1829] , [Jules Gabriel] Janin's (1804-1874) *Brief Critique (1886)*, a *History of Painting*, a *History of the Franks*, [Jacques Nicolas] Augustin Thierry's [1795-1856] *Tales of Merovingian Times* (1840). [Ernest] Lavisse and [Alfred Nicolas] Rambaud's [1842-1905] [Volumes VII and VIII of *General History of the Fourth Century to Our Own Times* (12 vols. 1893-1901)], [Michel de] Montaigne's [1533-1592] *Essays* [ed. 1877], and above all the *Works of Shakespeare*."

35 *Ecris-moi souvent, écris moi longuement*, 245.

36 Duclert, V, 1896, "*La detention, la double-boucle, l'enfermement*," *Ecris-moi souvent, écris moi longuement*, 283.

afterwards when the packets ceased to arrive Alfred drew more deeply from his memory. The complaints he makes show that many—most?—of what he hoped to receive never arrived at all. It is also likely that many of the authors, titles, and topics discoursed upon derived from memories of school study (from *lycée* through military college) and family discussions. Of Shakespeare, Dreyfus adds, "I had never understood this great writer so well as during this tragic period [of my own life]. I read and re-read him. *Hamlet* and *King Lear* appeared to me in all their dramatic power."[37]

Another list mentioned by Vincent Duclert is one of various journals, letters, and other papers supposedly returned to Dreyfus in 1900 after much effort, including most surprisingly: "*4 Bibles, 2 Nouveau Testament, 3 paquets contenant des brochures de Sermons.*"[38] The unexpected biblical material and sermons suggests, however, that these papers were not part of Dreyfus's personal readings during his stay on Devil's Island but materials sent to him by Christian missionary groups. This may have been normal for all prisoners, but for Dreyfus, such conversionary brochures and New Testaments would have seemed like gross insults, something confirmed by their absence from the captain's own list in his publications. Another document mentioned by Duclert but not found elsewhere is "*un cahier iconographique*,"[39] mysterious because all of the surviving *cahiers* contain large numbers of the doodles that could conceivably be called *iconographique*, unless this is a reference to the one very early notebook discovered by Maxime Préaud in Colonial Museum in Aix-en-Provence and called the *Cahier d'Aix*.[40] When we discuss Dreyfus's drawings in the next volume, we will examine the differences between these lost *cahiers* and the fifteen deposited by the captain in the Bibliothèque nationale. We will also consider in what sense these doodles may be considered iconographic—that is, having symbolic meanings individually and in clusters.

Interesting as the 1905 selection of letters and journal entries may

37 *"Je n'ai jamais aussi bien compris le grand écrivain que durant cette époque si tragique' je le lus et relus; Hamlet et le roi Lear m'apparurent avec toute leur puissance dramatique"* *Cinq années de ma vie*, 166.

38 Duclert, "Introduction," *Ecris-moi souvent, écris moi longuement souvent*, 55. This list is noted as coming from a *Lettre du ministre des Colonies à Alfred Dreyfus, 20 octobre 1900* (CAOM, 133 MIOM 5," 55, n.3).

39 Duclert, "Introduction," *Ecris-moi souvent, écris moi longuement souvent*, p 58.

40 Maxime Préaud, "Variations à perpétuité" in Alfred Dreyfus, *Cahiers de l'île du Diable*, ed. Pierrette Turlais (Paris; Editions Artulis, 2009), 251–255, including several pages of photoreproductions.

be in its own historical moment, since most of Lucie's have been excised and Alfred's own epistles carefully edited down, our emphasis now will be on the new edition of their mutual correspondence, because in this exchange over such a long period of time—although the latest editors have once again chosen not to put in all the letters, selecting mainly those by Lucie or Alfred that were stopped by the prison censors—because it is precisely in their repetitiousness and in their lack of direct coherence that many of the most interesting features of their individual personalities and of their mutual relationship are revealed.

The *Souvenirs et correspondance*[41] of his father, selected, edited, and commented upon by Pierre Dreyfus in 1936, adds several more letters than are to be found in *Cinq Années*, Alfred now being dead and the whole affair becoming an historical memory rather than a burning current issue. Divided into three sections, this new presentation of Alfred Dreyfus's life, career, and writings, while somewhat fuller than that of the earlier book, still frustrates in many ways. To begin with, the first part, "*La vie du Capitaine Dreyfus exposée par son fils, 1859–1899*," tells us virtually nothing about Pierre's own recollections of his father, mother, or family, either what he heard from his parents or other relatives or what he experienced as a child growing up in the midst of the affair and its aftermath.[42] The second part, "*Les souvenirs du Capitaine Dreyfus 1899–1896*," is mostly a reproduction of *Cinq Années*. However, the third part, "*Les dernières années 1906–1935*," brings in new information. The commentary that follows now concentrates, as does the rest of my book, not on the historical questions that still plague the student of the trials of Alfred Dreyfus and their impact on French society but on what these documents tell us about the man, his milieu, his mentality, and the *midrash* of his life.

In his *Préface*, Pierre Dreyfus (who never openly names himself except by the initials PD) gives a quick sketch of his father's personality, which I will gloss sentence by sentence:

---

41 P[ierre] D[reyfus], ed. Alfred Dreyfus, *Souvenirs er correspondance, publié par son fils* (Paris: Bernard Grasset, 1936).

42 Bloch-Dano: "*La cohésion du groupe vient de ce temps où, à l'écart de la société de ses institutions, les Juifs n'avaient d'autres ressources que celles du groupe familial. Plus ce groupe était puissant, plus l'individu était protégé*" (The cohesion of the group comes from a time when, kept apart from society and its institutions, Jews had no other resources than those of the family group. The more powerful was this group, the more the individual was protected) in *Madame Proust*, 105.

> *Mon père qui, par nature, n'était pas d'un caractère très expansif, avait été marqué encore par cinq années de tortures et de solitude absolue et s'était concentrée sur lui-même.*[43]
>
> My father, who was not by nature a very expressive character, had been marked by five years of torture and absolute solitary confinement and had drawn into himself.

By nature, that is, in essence, although as our discussions show, this quality of his personality is more complex than Pierre allows for and is partly a consequence of his upbringing as a Jewish refugee from Alsace separated from most of his family. These three qualities are significant in themselves and more intense through the conjunction in a young man suddenly subject to intense external pressures as the Jewish alien at a time of rising anti-Semitism, as well as being the deracinated youth growing up under tense personal and public pressures and perhaps also as the one male sibling brought up by older sisters when his brother was not. What did he do? He chose the most untypical profession for a Jew—a soldier; this was also the most masculine of professions, which that removed him from the female environment.

These choices, whether made freely or under family pressures, exacerbated his not very *expansif* character. The range of translations given for the word *expansif* includes *communicative*, *demonstrative*, *exuberant*, *confident*, *frank*, and *open*. In other words, from the range of antonyms, what his son Pierre says is that his father was reticent, reserved, and taciturn, although not timid or hesitant. Alfred Dreyfus was often perceived to be cold, withdrawn, unfeeling, lacking in both inner grace and external poise—and was called later by unsympathetic witnesses "the zinc marionette." I have suggested that this public perception, noted as much by friends and supporters of Alfred as by his political enemies, was a role of "delegated madman" in the *Grand Guignol* of the affair.[44]

---

43 Dreyfus, *Souvenirs*, 13.

44 It seems no accident that the theatre founded with this name to perform melodramatic horror shows should prove a success in Paris from 1897 on, the date of the height of the affair. *Guignol* had been the name of a popular local hand puppet in Lyons, and his name had become a common term for a type of fool who was involuntarily the object of ridicule because of his awkward movements and lack of social graces.

These characteristics may have been exaggerated, as the son explains, by the tortures undergone by his father, but also brought out some very minor symptoms of autism in young Alfred.[45]

> *Il vivait une vie intérieure intense, mais ne savait plus guère extérioriser ses sentiments.*[46]
>
> He lived an intensely interior life, but he hardly knew how to externalize his feelings.

This intense interior life that Pierre points to should be understood as marking the thoughtful, intellectual side of Alfred Dreyfus, a designation of his profound strength in being able to withstand so many years of physical and psychological torture by being able to withdraw into a world of philosophical ideas and discursive memories. If he was not able to express his feelings openly in such a way as to win the approval of the great public or even to evoke sympathy in his accusers and judges, he could maintain his dignity, as indicated by his proud proclamation of his innocence over and over again, not least when he was marched through the troops assembled to watch his degradation in 1894 or when he held himself erect and silent in the face of the hostile second court-martial in Rennes in 1898.

> *Il avait perdu l'habitude de les exprimer, et comme par ailleurs il répugnait à se plaindre, à exposer en public ses souffrances, il paraissait très distant à ceux qui les connaissaient peu.*[47]
>
> He had lost the habit of expressing them, and yet how he loathed to complain about himself, or to expose his sufferings in public; he seemed very distant to those who barely knew him.

---

45 This form of posttraumatic stress syndrome (PTSD) will someday have to be discussed, not only as it helps explain Dreyfus's behavior at the time of his arrest, trial, and condemnation, along with his lengthy period of imprisonment, exile, and isolation, but also the appearance he made upon his return to France and then his decision to retire from the army and lead a retired, private life.

46 Dreyfus, *Souvenirs*, 13.

47 Dreyfus, *Souvenirs*, 13.

He had lost his customary ability to express his feelings, writes Pierre, assuming that prior to his arrest and condemnation, his father had been more normal in the demonstration of his sentiments; yet close reading of the surviving documents, including those of friendly and bigoted prison officials, suggests that there were many moments, usually when he thought he was alone, or at least not under public scrutiny, when Alfred became enraged, threw himself against walls, and screamed in pain and frustration. Many of his letters also reveal a constant struggle to keep himself from losing all self-control, lapsing into wild tantrums, or falling into despondency and immobility. Alfred more than once writes to Lucie that she knows how fragile are his nerves and therefore how close to madness he has always felt himself to be. Aware too of the common slurs against Jews as nervous, weak, and timorous, Alfred has always done all he could to project a version of himself that is steady, strong, and brave. Almost never does he cry out in pain to anyone other than Lucie in what he hopes will be the privacy of their epistles, believing that showing such a reaction to his suffering will give comfort to his opponents and confirm in the eyes of the hostile public the unsuitability of a Jew to be a soldier-citizen of France. This is part of his honour, the duty he owes to the army and the republic, and the heritage he hands on to his children. However, Pierre knows that the coldness seen by those with little acquaintance with his father is not the true character of Alfred Dreyfus.

In his narrative of the accusation, arrest, and trial of his father, Pierre seems to pass over with barely a mention the most important factor, what he rightly—but without careful analysis of the words he uses and the phenomenon he refers to—"the virus of anti-Semitism," the monster that bores within the body politic and there picks out its scapegoat, "the abhorred Jew."[48] He can cite a letter of 28 October, 1894, from Colonel Joseph Henry to the anti-Semitic newspaper *Libre Parole* of Edouard Drumont announcing that "*Tout Israël est en mouvement*" (The whole of Israel is on the move)[49] and yet not take it as more than a minor annoyance, an incidental factor in the case against his father. These more neu-

48 *"Le virus antisémite . . . . le Juif abhorré"* Dreyfus, *Souvenirs*, 26.

49 Dreyfus, *Souvenirs*, 31.

trally termed "*haines religieuses*" (religious hatreds)[50] do not seem to him to constitute the very essence of the case. He does not see that an actual crime has not been proved, or at least not one of such significance as to warrant the charges laid against his father. Like others in the family and inner circle of their friends, he cannot imagine why the investigation to find the German spy terminated when a Jew was found to play the necessary role of scapegoat, thus satisfying petty jealousies amongst junior officers and the prejudices of officials in the high command and the Ministry of War. In outlining his father's life history, Pierre Dreyfus merely identifies Alfred as "of Israelite origins" (*d'origine israëlite*)[51] and does not even do as much with Alfred's chosen wife, "*Mlle Hadamard, fille d'un négociant en diamants, et petite-fille du capitaine Hatzfeld, ancien élève de l'Ecole Polytechnique* (promotion 1835)."[52]

Pierre, like his father, seems to assume that because religion is of minor importance in their lives—but this may not have been true for Lucie, as we shall see—it was not really important in the jealousies and arrogance roused by the affair.[53] Not even when Pierre cites an openly anti-Semitic remark made by one of the group involved in organizing the conspiracy does it strike him that such a calumny might be the driving force of the whole case against his father. Yet that conspiracy was not planned out step by step over many years or months but was rather an *ad hoc* arrogant response to the opportunity of finding a scapegoat, and then the manipulations became more and more byzantine when the opposition by the family and friends of Dreyfus was observed to challenge the authority and credibility of the army and the government; each new step taken took on the colouring of the latent anti-Semitism in the persons and the institutions involved in the cover-up. How could the system have responded to the initial lies and errors?

---

50 Dreyfus, *Souvenirs*, 34.

51 Dreyfus, *Souvenirs*, 40.

52 "Miss Lucie Hadamard, daughter of a diamond merchant, and granddaughter of Captain Hatzfeld, former student of the Ecole Polytechnique (commissioned in 1835)" Dreyfus, *Souvenirs*, 42.

53 David and Louise Hadamard brought their daughter Lucie Eugénie up to be a good Jewish wife. Burns writes: "As tall as Alfred, with thick dark hair parted in the middle and pulled back with a bandeau to control her curls, and with brown eyes, broad shoulders, and a slim waistline made slimmer by the tight lacing of the day, Lucie [she was nineteen when she met Alfred] had been raised at her family's country home at Châtou, near Paris." The information available concerning her education is spare and tantalizing: "She may have attended the private Ecole Monceau where one of her sisters had been a student, but tutors and family members directed much of her education" (Burns, *Dreyfus: A Family Affair*, 79).

Here, for instance, is how Colonel Picquart, himself no great friend of the Jews, but a man of honour, was handed an insult to his intelligence. After he pointed out to his superiors that the handwriting on the incriminating documents presented to bolster the case were similar to each other but not to Dreyfus's, and even that Dreyfus has been locked away for a year, he was confronted by this absurdity from his superior officer:

> *Et comme Picquart crut devoir faire remarquer qu'il s'agissait d'une correspondance récente, Bertillon répliqua sans sourciller: "Alors, c'est que les Juifs ont exercé quelqu'un depuis un an pour imiter l'écriture, ils sont arrivés à l'identité."*[54]
>
> And as Picquart believed it his duty to remark that it was a question of recent correspondence, Bertillon replied without flinching, "Well, it's the Jews who have over the year found someone to imitate the handwriting and now they've got it down pat."

Rather than a clash of cultures or religious apprehensions of reality, the confrontation is between prejudice and judiciousness, ignorance and common sense, and bigotry and tolerance. The choice, then, has to be whether the Dreyfus's opponents were stupid, naive, arrogant, or evil—that is, whether the misapprehensions and misprisions arose from an inability to comprehend the facts and circumstances, from an unwillingness to question authority and its official line of argument, from a resistance to giving any value to what was said or done by persons considered inferiors and interlopers, or from a sheer perverse wish to hurt or humiliate others. There probably were a few individuals who had secret agendas to work through and who took the opportunity of Dreyfus's presence in a sensitive position to deflect suspicion away from themselves or their allies, but that does not explain the length of the resistance to the truth nor the pervasiveness of the willingness to accept patently absurd claims as the truth.

This kind of misapprehension seen operating throughout the Dreyfus Affair arises through a false reduction of the concept of religion to a matter of personal beliefs and private feelings, one where theology and

---

54 Dreyfus, *Souvenirs*, 74.

religious practice are moved to the margins of modern, secular experience. Arguing or feeling this way creates a situation in which there is an epistemological impasse or crisis. How so? Well, on one side, there are those parties to the affair for whom religion is everything—a *Weltanschauung*, a mythical imagination, a racial quality separating every nationality, cultural group, language cohort, community, and regional culture—and, on the other, those for whom religion is so trivial that they try to avoid seeing its manifestations in themselves or in their neighbours or enemies. It is not a question of Pierre or Alfred Dreyfus not knowing that Judaism and anti-Semitism were relevant factors in the whole ordeal but that the intensity and seriousness of that relevance did not register fully. Hence, the two groups of partisans talked at cross-purposes, contended in politics and social rivalries without noticing the grid of blind spots between them, and misinterpreted their supposed victories and defeats. This is not just a matter of eviscerating religions of all their aesthetic, spiritual, and intellectual richness but of mistaking the motivations and consequences of their own mutual actions and achievements. Here is a passage that supposedly reveals another dialogue between some of the conspirators:

> *Du Paty, Henry et Gribelin s'y rendirent, mais Henry resta caché. Du Paty expliqua à Esterhazy les machinations des Juifs et l'assura qu'il pourrait compter sur des défenseurs résolus s'il était prêt à obéir aux instructions qui lui seraient données.*[55]
>
> Du Paty, Henry and Gribelin went to the place, but Henry remained hidden. Du Paty explained to Esterhazy the machinations of the Jews and assured him that he could count on resolute defenders, if he were prepared to obey the instructions which would be given to him.

It should be obvious that the conspirators are manipulating Esterhazy,[56] the real spy and traitor who is selling minor secrets to the

55 Dreyfus, *Souvenirs*, 93

56 Compare the satirical version of this manipulative and duplicitous action in Anatole France's short story *Emile*: "And here Zoé, we approach a scene in the comedy of life, the melancholy humor of which may one day be appreciated. During the Dreyfus Affair it occurred to Emile Vincent [i.e., Zola] to say that Esterhazy was a fraud and a traitor. He said it because he knew it was so

Germans because he needs the money to pay for his mistress and his gambling debts, and who actually hates the French—he writes in a letter later that he dreams of leading mounted Hungarian Uhlans into Paris to slaughter hundreds of thousands of French men and women.[57] So he was not motivated by simple, stupid greed or bribed by the dark forces lurking behind this petty intrigue. The others, the highly-placed military men, however, seized the occasion to get at Alfred Dreyfus because they resented him as a Jewish upstart, and then, once started in this plot, they are drawn by their own arrogance to elaborate upon the deception more and more, finding their own hatred of Jews the path of least resistance to gaining support in the rest of the army, the government, and French society. But this is not obvious to the writer of *Souvenirs et correspondance*: he sees the arrogance and the stupidity but not the endemic and persistent anti-Semitism. He knows that what is going on is a "simulacrum,"[58] but not how it works or what motivates it. Alfred goes further and writes on 23 January, 1895, from Devil's Island:

> *Il semble que je suis le jouet d'une terrible hallucination, que tout cela va se dissiper . . . mais hélas! la réalité est tout autour de moi.*[59]
>
> It seems that I am the plaything in a terrible hallucination, that all of that is going to fly off into nothingness . . . but, alas! reality is all around me.

He too, like his son and his other supporters, is so close and so far from understanding what is happening. Soon after, Alfred writes to "*Ma chère Lucie*" on 14 February, 1895, that he believes and hopes that in the future, "*quand on rancontera mon histoire, elle paraître invraisemblable,*"[60]

---

and because he was far too candid ever to conceal the truth. From that day he was regarded as the enemy of his country and of the army. He was treated as a traitor and an alien" (France, *Crainquebille Putois, Riquet and other Profitable Tales*, 126).

57 Remember that moment near the end of book IV of *Gulliver's Travels* when Swift's maniacal protagonist revels in the thought that thousands of Houhymhms will set sail for Europe to seek revenge on the madness of these talking Yahoos and confront their massed regiments and crush them into gelatinous putty, a mummy. Esterhazy was as mad as Lemuel Gulliver but for no good reasons.

58 Dreyfus, *Souvenirs*, 102.

59 Dreyfus, *Souvenirs*, 113.

60 Dreyfus, *Souvenirs*, 119.

when someone tells my story, it will seem unbelievable. However, these unbelievable nightmares and hallucinations are not a figment of Dreyfus's own mind but a mass delusion, a phantasmagoria, enveloping all of France and even the rest of Europe.

Three features of this process of deception and self-deception about Judaism and anti-Semitism can be seen in the letters that Lucie and Alfred write to one another that are published in their son Pierre's selective anthology. First, there are the casual and neutral uses of Christian terms, such as *martyrdom* (*martyre*), *sacrifice* (*sacrifice*), *calvary* (*calvaire*), and the stain of *sinfulness* (*tache*).[61] They can also write about "*une justice divine*,"[62] which they hope and pray will watch over them and solve the inscrutable enigma of the charges against Alfred. So far as the husband and wife seem concerned, these words are merely colorful expressions of their sense of pain and humiliation. They come with no sacramental, liturgical, or mythical resonance.[63] If there is a zone of allusiveness in this lexicon, it is to the principles and ideals of the French Revolution and republic, generally to abstract truth and justice. Similarly, when they occasionally use the word *God* (*Dieu*) or *faith* (*foi*), it is as an exclamation rather than an appeal to the deity or a prayerful statement. Words like *exile*, *saint*, or *martyr*, which could have a Jewish connotation or a Christian signification, tend again to be neutralized terms of intensification of the secular pains felt by the husband and wife. More specific references to Jewish customs and practices are subdued and virtually unnoticed.[64] For instance, Lucie writes on 30 December, 1894,

61 Benmozegh recalls "a principle of the Kabbalists, according to which 'all the foreign gods who are referred to in Scripture contain a spark of holiness'" (*Israel and Humanity*, 115).

62 Dreyfus, *Souvenirs*, 111.

63 "The philosophical study of the Hebrew language confirms in its own way this mystical explanation, by showing the genius of the language is to proceed directly to the fundamental idea without stopping at the verbal form, and that is one is perfectly entitled therefore to perceive the expression of divine qualities beneath the polytheistic names" (Benmozegh, *Israel and Humanity*, 115).

64 According to Michael Burns, who has examined the archives, personal and private, to discover all that seems possible to find out about the background of Alfred Dreyfus's mother and father and of the young boy's religious upbringing, "The Dreyfus family left no record of the children's religious instruction in Mulhouse; nor did the synagogue hold documentation of their formal schooling, if any. But if they learned the Hebrew required for the confirmation ceremony [bar mitzvah]—a ceremony of special significance for their observant parents—the children also had to learn the 'sacred declaration of patriotic loyalty' to France that accompanied the religious rite" (*Dreyfus: A Family Affair*, 39). Can we also assume that when a baby Alfred was circumcised and that he went to some sort of *cheder* for his earliest education in Jewish knowledge? As Burns sees, all such information remains conjectural and elusive, except that, as we are showing in our close reading of the letters and other documents extant of his life during the ordeal, Dreyfus has an implicit awareness of the basis

> *C'est ce soir l'anniversaire de la mort de ton père, nous irons tous au temple. Pauvre grand-papa, en mourant, il ne connaissait pas son bonheur.*[65]
>
> This evening is the anniversary of your father's death, we are all going to temple. Poor grandpa, in dying, he did not know his own happiness.

In a later letter, Lucie brings to the surface the equivalence of "*vérité = bonheur*"[66] (truth = happiness) This can be read in specifically Jewish terms: "Tonight is your father's *yahrzeit* [yearly memorial for him and his relatives] and we are all going to *shul* [synagogue] to pray. Poor *zayda* [grandfather] when he passed away didn't realize what *mazel* [luck] he had by not knowing of your arrest, conviction and exile." But the translation could render the terms in a less Hebraic way, without the inflections of Yiddish appropriate to Ashkenazi Jews: "This evening on the memorial day of your father's passing, the whole family will go to the temple (in the French sense of a non-Catholic house of worship) for a service. Poor Granddad, in dying before the events of your case became known, was saved private humiliations and public shame." On the thirtieth of December, 1894, Lucie again writes about this occasion but adds that she has gone to the temple with Mathieu to say *kaddish* (the prayer for the dead) for "*le triste anniversaire de la mort de ton pauvre père*" (the sad anniversary of your poor father's death), and then she adds still further, "*Que de soucis, que de chagrins nous avons eus en une année. Quels malheurs épuvantables et immérités peuvent s'abattre sur une famille en si peu de temps*"[67] (What cares, what grief we have had in one year. What horrible and unmerited miseries could beat down on one family in so little a time). It is as though she wants to cry out in words that Alfred will recognize from the Passover *haggadah* (book of traditional rabbinic tales and songs), "*Dayenu!* Enough for us!"

Another more specifically Jewish allusion appears in a postscript to Alfred's letter of 12 March, 1895, when he tells Lucie "*Quand tu auras une*

of Judaism and an occasional explicit ability to articulate those beliefs and patterns of belief.

65 Dreyfus, *Souvenirs*, 51.

66 12 August 1895. *Ecris-moi souvent, écris moi longuement*, 253

67 *Ecris-moi souvent, écris moi longuement*, 100.

bonne nouvelle á m'announcer, envoie-moi une dépêche, je l'attends chaque jour comme le Messie"[68] (When you have some good news to tell me, send me an urgent message, I am waiting for it every day as for the Messiah). Christians wait for the Second Coming, while Jews expect the *Moshiach* to appear at any moment—for the first time. Besides, the almost light-hearted and ironic mixture here shows the character of Dreyfus's *neshama* (his soul) more than any more ponderous or sanctimonious Christian expectation of the End of Days. Usually, as we shall discuss more fully when we deal with the latest edition of their letters, it is Lucie who lets slip the little Yiddishisms of her family, rather than Alfred, who, while not quite with the level of cynicism or bitterness against his background of Sigmund Freud arguing for his bride-to-be Martha Bernays to forgo her Jewish beliefs and practices, such as keeping kosher, has made an effort to assimilate himself to military life. Where her husband sees the forces ranged against him as part of some inexplicable enigma[69] that has caused a judicial error, it is the wife who speaks in more traditional rabbinical terms of their joint martyrdom, although she also is shaping remarks around supportive echoes of what Alfred writes:

> *Dieu qui nous a si cruellement éprouvés nous donnera la volonté d'accomplir jusqu'au bout notre de devoir, de relever notre nom de la tache qu'on lui a odieusement jetée, et nous accordera la réparation éclatante sans laquelle ni nous, ni nos enfants, nous ne pouvons nous résigner à vivre. J'ai la conviction qu'avec une volonté de fer, une énergie indomptable et une persévérance à toute épreuve, on peut surmonter toutes les difficultés, on peut sonder tous les mystères . . . .*[70]
>
> God who has so cruelly tested us will give us the will to reach the fullness of our duty, to remove from our name

68 Dreyfus, *Souvenirs*, 122.

69 Typical of his letters to Lucie, on 7 September 1895, Alfred writes: "Il faut avoir l'énigme de cette machination infernale qui nous a enlevé ce qui fait vivre et ce qu'il nous faut: notre honneur" (The enigma of this infernal machine must be found out so that we can live and have what we must: our honor); *Ecris-moi souvent, ecris moi longuement*, 258. Note how Dreyfus uses the "uncanny expression" (according to Norbert Col) rather than the more familiar idiom "*avoir l'énigme*"—uncanny because it indicates how Dreyfus is being twisted out of his normal ways of speaking and thinking, unless this is an error in the transcript by editor Vincent Duclert.

70 Dreyfus, *Souvenirs*, 128.

> the stain that has been so odiously thrown on it, and will grant to us a brilliant reparation without which we and our children, we cannot resign ourselves to live. I am convinced that with an iron will, [so that with] an indomitable energy and an unflinching perseverance [we can pass through] through all experience, we can surmount all difficulties, we can get to the bottom of all the mysteries . . .

Then, swept up by the power of her own enthusiasm and again echoing and reinforcing Alfred's own self-encouraging words and phrases, she states:

> *La vérité peut éclater aujourd'hui comme elle peut éclater demain ou après. Personne ne le sait, Dieu fasse que ce soit le plus vite possible. Je ne puis te dire qu'une chose, mon bon chéri, c'est que la lumière se fera et que nous l'aurons pleine et entière.*[71]

> The truth may flash out today as it may break forth tomorrow or [in the days] after. No one knows when God will make it happen [and may it be] as quickly as possible. I can only tell you this one thing, my dear good husband, it is that the light will shine forth and it will be full and whole for us.

Note here how Lucie, herself the light, the *Shekhina*, resonates with the kabbalistic terms found in nineteenth-century Jewish liturgy and hence familiar to herself and to Alfred, even if they have never thought of the sources or implications of such language. The truth is a light that flashes out like lightning (*zohar*) when God wills, and thus, while we cannot know when it will happen, the emergence of this *zoharistic* clarification of mysteries is not unexpected. It will be a Day of Redemption, messianic in its glorious light, may it happen, as the formula goes: "speedily in our days."[72] Then comes the *tikkun ha-olam*, the repair, the correction,

---

71 Dreyfus, *Souvenirs*, 128.

72 Ouaknin teaches: *"Le livre est donc le lieu d'un paradoxe—ou d'une rencontre; il recueille l'Infini*

and the reunification of God and his *Shekhina*, which is Israel.[73] It will prove the end of the *Galut*, exile, dispersion, suffering, and dishonour. In more plain and practical terms, as Alfred's brother writes on 25 September, two weeks later, "*Dieu ne permettra pas qu'un innocent paie pour des coupables*"[74] (God will not permit an innocent man to pay for [the crimes] of those who are culpable). But none of them seems fully aware of the "machination"[75] at work to keep the falsely accused exile locked away on Devil's Island).

Thanks to the lengthy delays between writing and receiving letters, it is only on 26 June, 1896, that Alfred answers the fervent hopes that Lucie has expressed of a divinely ordained release from torments:

> *Tu me dis aussi d'accepter la certitude que la lumière la plus complet serait faite sur ce lugubre drame. Non seulement, j'en accepte la certitude mais ma confiance, comme ma foi ont toujours été absolues; je connais trop bien les sentiments d'honneur qui animent tous les membres de nos deux familles pour avoir jamais pu en douter.*[76]
>
> You tell me to accept with certainty that the most complete light will shine on this lugubrious drama. Not only do I accept that with certainty, but my confidence, like my faith, has always been absolute, I know too well the sense of honor that animates all members of our

---

(Tsimtsoum), *mais il dévoile immédiatement son incapacité à cet accueil en montrant que l'Infini ne peut se laisser englober, ne peut se laisser enfermer en une présence sur laquelle on pourrait avoir une quelconque emprise. Il y a alors débordement, et plus, éclatement* (Chevira) *du Livre en trois livres*" (The book is thus a place of paradox—or of an encounter; it is gathers together the Infinite (*Tsimtsoum*), but it immediately reveals its incapacity in this welcome by showing that the Infinite cannot be englobed, cannot let itself be possessed by any act of domination or possession. There is then an overflowing, and more, the explosive shattering of light (*Shevira*) that shatters the Book into three books) in *Le livre brûlé*, 226.

73 According to Elijah Benamozegh, "Nowhere is God thought of as an isolated being which, having accomplished the work of creation, handed over control of the universe forever to the laws which He had established. These laws are regarded as the expression of an unending intercourse between cause and effect. They constitute the Divine as it exists here, the *Shekhina*, God inhabiting His creation," *Israel and Humanity*, 70.

74 Dreyfus, *Souvenirs*, 129.

75 Alfred speaks of "*cette machination dont nous sommes les malhereuses et épuvantables victims*" (this machination of which we are the unhappy and horrible victims): Dreyfus, *Souvenirs*, 130.

76 Dreyfus, *Souvenirs*, 137.

two families ever to have any doubts.

However, what Alfred has absolute confidence and faith in is not exactly that which Lucie has written about. She has been speaking, at least partly, about a spiritual expectation of divine intervention, albeit a concomitant enhancement of human strength of character, while he, to keep away from the doldrums of despair and defeatism, writes of his indomitable faith in the loyalty of the families. It is true that as much as husband and wife have been tested and proved in the fires of this iniquity, so too the Hadamard and Dreyfus families have rallied to support Alfred and to give comfort to one another, both actions being things that commentators have found remarkable, because too often in similar circumstances marriages have broken apart, families have disassociated themselves from members accused of high crimes and misdemeanours, and individuals have broken—sought divorce, changed their abodes and names, undergone mental breakdowns, or committed suicide.

The faith that Alfred writes about is also religious but in a different way than Lucie's. For him, ironically as for his bitterest enemies, France is the sacred country and thus duty to her and her institutions are sacramental acts.[77] He also sees France as the supreme judge to which he submits his fate, not to any biblical version of God but to this "*juge suprême*," his fatherland, "*la patrie*."[78] As a shocking corollary to that, it is Alfred's personal honour that is of supreme value. It seems as though Lucie is only echoing his sentiments as part of the therapy she is conducting for him, but she makes explicit a thought that Alfred would suppress—and that she, in her normal state of mind, would find horrifying: that they would rather that their children were dead than have to live in disgrace: "*J'aimerais mieux voir nos enfants morts que de penser que le nom qu'il portent est déshonoré*"[79] (I would rather see our children dead than think of the name they bear being dishonoured). This is his own horrible "*culte de l'honneur.*"[80] It seems Lucie, shaken by the violence of Alfred's treatment, attempts quietly to assuage his rattled nerves and help him turn towards

77 On 24 April 1897: "*Et la réalité, las voici, toujours la même: c'ést que dans cette horrible affaire, il y a un double intérêt en jeu, celui de la patrie, le nôtre, que l'un est aussi sacré que l'autre*" (And the reality here is always the same is that in this horrible affair there is a double interest in play, that of the nation, [and] our own, and that is as sacred as the other) Dreyfus, *Souvenirs*, 154.

78 Alfred to Lucie, 10 August 1897: Dreyfus, *Souvenirs*, 158.

79 Alfred to Lucie, 14 April 1895: Dreyfus, *Souvenirs*, 119.

80 Alfred to Lucie, 28 August 1898: Dreyfus, *Souvenirs*, 174.

a more peaceful resolution to the great mystery confronting them.[81]

Yet, knowing as only she knows—the true state of affairs back in France being still vigorously censored by colonial and prison officials—the need to keep this a secret is almost too much for her to bear. She fears that Alfred, with an already weakened body and mind, may not be able to withstand the new shock of positive news about a revision of his conviction. She knows his vulnerability because of the extreme statements he makes and also because, more than him, she has been observing from afar his mood swings and his detailed descriptions of the loss of sanity he fears.[82]

> *Moi, je ne vis que dans la pensée de la joie profonde à la pensé que tu auras en apprenant cette nouvelle, et je me souhaite des forces, un pouvoir surhumain pour te voir dans ce moment de satisfaction suprême. Pourvu, mon Dieu, que cet ébranlement si grand ne te soit pas funeste et que ton pauvre corps affaibli ne se ressente pas d'une telle secousse!*[83]
>
> I can only live [or rather: see] in this thought of profound joy the thoughts that you will have on learning this news, and I wish that I had the strength, a superhuman power to see you at the moment of supreme satisfaction. Provided, dear God, that this great shock does not prove fatal and that your poor weakened body does not suffer from such a great blow!

It has been Lucie's duty, she understands, to provide Alfred with

---

81 More disturbing is the resonance here of the temporary changes in Jewish sensibility that occurred at the time of the First and Second Crusades, when parents and whole communities took the decision to sacrifice their children rather than see them taken from them, forcibly baptized, and brought up as Christians to hate their former selves. At that time, during the eleventh through thirteenth centuries, there was a midrashic reconstruction of the *Akeda*, the Binding of Isaac, to show Abraham so willing to slay his son on the altar, that when God restored the youth unharmed from the ordeal, the father killed him again. At times, Sarah, who is usually kept away from the performance of the deed God has commanded Abraham because of her maternal sensibilities, emerges as an active participant in the *Kiddush ha-Shem*, the Sanctification of the Name.

82 She also knows his previous demonstrations of nervous irritability; she also has known since their days of courtship when Alfred's letters warned her of these tendencies and begged her to be patient and sympathetic with his appearance of coldness and rages. These matters will be discussed later in reference to the imposed autism seen in Alfred after his return to France in 1899.

83 Lucie to Alfred, 26 September 1898: Dreyfus, *Souvenirs*, 175.

the feedback he needs to keep up his strength and resolution, but also, insofar as she can in the midst of her own problems—her separation, her need to overcome the bourgeois Frenchwoman's reluctance to play a public role in politics, her shyness as a Jew to appeal to hostile government and legal officers, her need to hide from the children her fears and worries for their missing father (she tells them he is on a long trip as part of his soldier's duty), and her instinctive need to keep from exacerbating his sense of isolation or raising his hopes too high before any confirmation of social change can be addressed to him—to lead him gently toward a state of mind conformable to his own real character. This complex task becomes even more difficult in the final days of his imprisonment before his return to France, because the wheels of justice turn so slowly and the complete information on his current status is deliberately obscured by the same cruel and devious agents who have managed his whole experience on Devil's Island.[84]

The story of what happens to Alfred and Lucie just before, during, and immediately after the second conviction at Rennes will be integrated into discussions in further chapters of this book and those that follow, just as we will put off for the moment a close reading of their letters in the modern edition and the new edition of the journals Alfred kept between the time of his pardon and his rehabilitation. The focus, however, will be less on the political or judicial side of the story than on the personal. For even more than the strong active engagement by both Lucie and Mathieu in pursuing legal rectification of the judicial errors and later the crimes revealed, it is the special relationship that Captain and Madam Dreyfus established in their letters that amazes more than any other phenomenon in the whole affair. As we shall see in later volumes in this series, perhaps the most amazing thing of all is the intellectual reconceptualization of Alfred in his prison notebooks. Before that, more groundwork in preparation for those discussions has to be laid, or in midrashic terms: we have to look at the textures, contextures, antitex-

---

84 How cruel the jailers were is explained by Duclert in an introductory section to the last stages of Dreyfus's imprisonment on Devil's Island: "*Il n'imagine pas que tous ses appels ont été systématiquement ignore et qu'il a fallu une mobilization publique sans precedent pour que ceux de sa femme soient finalement entendus par le gouvernement*" (He did not imagine that all his appeals were systematically ignored and it would be necessary to mount a public mobilization without precedent by those [appeals] of his wife finally to be heard by the government) (*Ecris-moi souvent, écris moi longuement*, 401).

tures, and untextures of these two further bodies of evidence.[85]

PART 2: ALFRED AND LUCIE'S LOVE LETTERS

En Pologne, la mazoure devient souvent le lieu où le sort de toute une vie se décide, où les cœurs se pèsent, où les éternels dévouements se promettent, où la patrie recrute ses martyrs et ses héroïnes. En ces contrées, la mazoure n'est donc pas seulement une danse; elle est une poésie nationale, destinée, comme toutes les poésies des peuples vaincus, à transmettre le brûlant faisceau des sentiments patriotiques, sous le voile transparent d'une mélodie populaire. Aussi, n'y a-t-il rien de surprenant à ce que la plupart d'entre elles modulent dans leurs notes et dans les strophes qui y sont attachées, les deux tons dominants dans le cœur du Polonais moderne: le plaisir de l'amour et la mélancolie du danger.

—Franz Liszt[86]

But it is precisely in the space between the literal meaning and the legal ruling that the experience of Talmudism is to be found. After rudimentary explanation of words and concepts, after the judicial extrapolation of practices and regulations, the dance of reason begins.

—Leon Wieseltier[87]

This section of the chapter will argue that the letters between Alfred and

85 As [Ithamar] Gruenwald notes, the "midrashic condition" is a mental attitude that entails the creation of meaning rather than concern for the lexical or philological understanding of a text'" (Wolfson, *Through a Speculum that Shines*, 331, n. 19), and one might add of the historical or generic character of that same text.

86 F. Liszt, *F. Chopin*, 4th ed. (Leipzig: Breitkopf et Haertel, 1890). Chapter III. "In the mazurka the bold and vigorous colouring of the polonaise gives place to the most delicate, tender and evanescent shades; it is not the nation as a whole, in a united, single and characteristic impetus, which is brought before us, but the character and the impressions become purely personal and are always individualized and divided" (Franz Liszt, *Life of Chopin*, 2nd ed., trans. John Broadhouse (London: William Reeves), 86).

87 Leon Wieseltier, "Unlocking the Talmud's Secrets: Thoughts on the Steinsaltz Talmud in English" *The New York Times, Sunday Book Review* (17 December 1989), reprinted by David Sasha on *Sephardic Heritage Update* (11 November 2010) on the occasion of Steinsaltz's completion of his translation of the whole Talmud online at davidsasha@googlegroups.com (seen 11 November 2010).

Lucie Dreyfus are in themselves a kind of frenetic and, at the same time, subtle dance, an interchange and a mutually supportive sharing of ideas, feelings, and dreams.[88] Franz Liszt's romantic effusions on Chopin's life and music—they are one, in his mind—also provide interesting insights that can be applied, albeit with proper adjustments to the different times, places, characters, and intellectual and political contexts, to the interwoven and superimposed nature of the epistles between husband and wife. Although he was an anti-Semite, Liszt succeeded, as A. Z. Idelsohn points out, "in penetrating into Israel's spirit."[89] Taking the occasion of the mazurka in a metaphorical sense as both a figure of long-distance social relationships and longed-for emotional and intellectual encounters, what Liszt says in his own voice and that of other characters opens up the obscure region of the Dreyfus letters. For instance, when the older musician writes,

> Here chance may bring into contrast those who a few hours before were perfect strangers to each other. The ordeal of a single moment, a single word, may separate long united hearts; necessity often forces sudden confidences and invincible suspicions kept close in the mind.[90]

The reader of those desperate letters penned across the Atlantic Ocean, arriving out of order, held back for three or four months at a time, sees the correspondents forced by circumstances and intense longing to fear the worst, hope for the best, and seek to grasp some tangible echo or ghost of a remembered image to reassure the other and the self of their love, their loyalty, their courage to carry on, and their trust in an eventual resolution to the oppressive enigma that keeps them apart and in the darkness of doubts and fears.

Then Liszt cites an unnamed witty woman, who exclaims in regard to the dancers performing the mazurka: "They often play a comedy to avoid a tragedy!" He goes on:

> That which has never been spoken is yet often surmised

---

88 For a historical survey, social analysis, and pictures of the mazurka in action, see Maja Trochimcyzk, "Mazur (Mazurka)" online at http://www2/fiu.edu/~kneskij/mazurka (seen 14 November 2010).

89 Idelsohn, *Jewish Music*, 191.

90 Liszt, *Life of Chopin*, Broadhouse trans., 66.

> and understood. Vague generalities are often made use of to quicken interrogation, while hiding its drift, and evasive replies are closely listened to, like the ringing of a coin, as a test of quality. The suitor is often pleading his cause when he seems to be pleading for others, and the most graceful flattery is at times the veil which disguises exactions.[91]

To be sure, Alfred and Lucie were not courting or meeting for the first time; they had been married for five years, had two children, and found themselves in a state of shock and confusion by what had occurred when the arrest happened. But in this first major separation,[92] they had to find a way to communicate in letters across layers of obscurity,[93] knowing full well that everything they said to one another would be scrutinized by hostile censors, and thus they had to assume masks—how many, we shall be showing throughout this book, but not always masks of their own making—and then discovered that their own voices, intentions, and realities could not be seen or heard clearly by the other or by themselves.[94] They would ask each other questions and knew they could not answer directly for several reasons: it was too painful to speak the words, and they feared of alarming the other; it was forbidden to transmit such information under the conditions of their right to send letters at all; it was beyond their individual capacities to describe or even

91 Liszt, *Life of Chopin*, Broadhouse trans., 66–67.

92 Earlier separations, as we shall see in later letters that they write to one another, were part of the normal routine for army wives and their husbands, a matter of days or weeks on maneuvers; this long separation during the affair tested their love and loyalty to an extreme not imagined in romantic novels.

93 The figure of the *parokhet*, the curtain drawn across the Holy of Holies, the Ark of the Covenant, represents in kabbalistic thought a separation between the visible and the invisible, the literal words on the page of a text, and the interpretations that make the invisible visible; see Ouaknin, *Le livre brûlé*, 284. For Alfred and Lucy, however, as they stand on either side of a veil of metaphysical and geographical distance, of censorious regulations forbidding the communication of vital kinds of information, of anti-Semitic hatred that they know will punish any references thought to be treasonous and part of an international Jewish conspiracy, of anxiety about each other's abilities to write and read between the lines, and of fears that what they say will inadvertently offend the other and trigger uncontrollable mental disturbances. At the same time, the veil of ambiguity and hinting also creates a mystical covering or canopy under which they hope to find or must create a city of refuge.

94 Dreyfus only rarely uses the word "mask" himself, but when he does, it opens up the vision of the dreadful nightmare and phantasmagoria playing all around him during the affair; cp. His letter of 3 October 1896 (*Ecris-moi souvent, écris moi longuement*, 322).

imagine the full extent of their ordeals.[95] For these reasons, without becoming a lighthearted farce or a grotesque comedy, the irony of their crisscrossing epistles and mutually supportive language created texts that could not really sustain the generic capacity of the language they thought they were sharing.

For example, in no way, can one say that either Alfred or Lucie were lying in what they wrote to one another. They are quite frank at times about how difficult it is to keep news from the other, and so while they intuit that each has more to say about their suffering day and night, neither can really guess the extent of what is happening to the other, Lucie especially in regard to the increasing isolation and physical tortures Alfred is subjected to and Alfred in regard to the efforts Lucie is making on his behalf to win a retrial and eventual rehabilitation of the family name, and the mounting campaign throughout France and the rest of the world to effect these ends. Thus, we see a hint at how to describe these factors in what Liszt writes concerning Chopin's mazurkas:

> But the inimitable skill with which they are constantly able to interchange the garbs of truth and fiction (like touchstones, most certain when least suspected, the one always hidden under the cloak of the other) and the force which expends a great amount of intellect on the least important occasions (just as Gil Blas used up as much intelligence in finding the means of subsistence for one day as the King of Spain did to govern his whole dominions), at least make upon us an impression as painful as that produced by the jugglers of India and their exhibitions of wonderful skill, where sharp and deadly weapons fly glittering in the air, which the smallest error or the least lack of perfect mastery would convert into bright and swift messengers of instant death! Such skill is fraught with concealed terror, anxiety and anguish. From a complication of circumstances danger may lurk behind the

95 "L'essence de la question," writes Ouaknin, *"est d'ouvrir et laisser ouvertes [des] possibilités . . ."* (The essence of a question is to open and to leave open possibilities), and then *"La chose demandée doit rester en suspens . . . mise en suspens de façon que le çontre' équilibre le 'pour'"* (The thing asked must remain in suspense . . . put into suspense in such a way that the 'contra' balances the 'pro') in *Le livre brûlé*, 139.

> slightest inadvertence, in the smallest imprudence, in possible accidents, while on the other hand powerful help may be suddenly rendered by the most obscure and forgotten individual.[96]

Recognizing that not every single detail in this complicated statement bears pertinence to the Dreyfus letters, nevertheless I argue that Liszt's words set up a remarkable paradigm for arranging our analysis of those epistles. To begin with, however, we have to separate the rather complicated apparatus of analogues and allusions. In the first sentence, the two parenthetical remarks can be put aside for a moment, allowing us to see an allegorical narration of the dancers in the mazurka dressed alternatively in the costumes of truth and fiction and weaving in and out of contact with each other.

Then we see that the wearing of these "garbs" in the Polish dance is compared to the use of a touchstone, one of the four Stones of Wisdom can be shown to be metonymically related to each other, any one of which can stand for any one, two, three, or all four of the others, as a means of evaluating (the touchstone), sharpening (the whetstone), holding together (the keystone), and drawing into stronger contiguity (the lodestone) the others.[97] In each particular instance, the stone itself has little or no significance, but by its function becomes more powerful, influential, and essential to the operation of the whole phenomenon.[98]

---

96 Liszt, *Life of Chopin*, Broadhouse trans., 68–69.

97 In the second parenthetical comment, Liszt alludes to Le Sage's picaresque novel of the *Adventures of Gil Blas*. This literary allusion is followed by a sustained comparison of the mazurka dancers with Indian fakirs, emphasis placed as much on the showy, somewhat duplicitous quality of the performers and on the real dangers that obtain should there be any slip-up or loss of attention. Like all picaresque novels, *Gil Blas* is the somewhat cynical reflections of a man or woman who has made it through life, most of it "on the road," at all levels of society, secular and religious, in cities and towns, at courts and in slums, and revealing finally that it is wit alone and taking care of oneself that really matter.

98 Although Ferenc or Franz Liszt was at times a fairly rabid anti-Semite—much more so than Chopin—what he wrote about the mazurka can be taken as an interesting insight and approach to the Dreyfus letters. There is much we can learn from the Jew haters since in their very mental illness, they see and speak about things that nice, liberal, tolerant people do not like to talk about—or can perceive at all. See, for instance, Dan Damon, "Chasms of Perdition: How Ferenc Liszt tried to tame the divine essence of the Romani soul," *Central European Review* 3: 13 (2 April 2001) online as http://www/ce-review.org./01/13/damon13 (seen 14 November 2010). Considering the book on *The Gypsy in Music*, written under the influence of Wagnerian anti-Semitism, Damon argues, "Whatever the explanation for his anti-Semitism Ferenc Liszt made cynical use of the musical talent of the Roma to belittle whatever Jews had achieved. Liszt sought

Now back to the exchange of epistles between Lucie and Alfred. These letters, those that survive today—and we cannot be sure how many were lost, were never sent, did not arrive, or were destroyed by the prison censors—also constitute another kind of textual phenomenon, one that recalls, however distantly, the multiple layers and polyphonic voices of the Talmud. In the history of letter writing in the seventeenth and eighteenth centuries, a whole genre of fiction based on the exchange of epistles developed. These fictional letters make clear some of the more specific aspects of the Dreyfus Affair as a whole and the exchange of letters between Alfred and Lucie Dreyfus in particular. Although there were already telegrams and a few telephones available at the end of the nineteenth century, for the most part people still communicated by handwritten letters. In Marcel Proust's *A la recherche du temps perdu*, it is possible to see the progressive development of communication from handwritten notes, telegrams, and pneumatic letters to the use of telephones. Official documents were also beginning to appear in typewritten form.

Handwritten epistles have to be read as emerging from the midst of existential experiences, speaking privately to the person or persons they are addressed to in terms of ongoing events and urgent or contingent actions. Unlike the communications available to us a hundred years later, wherein electronic and digital information can be exchanged instantaneously, written letters require often rare and expensive physical equipment—sheets of paper, a supply of pens, sufficient ink, sturdy envelopes, postage stamps, and a delivery service of some sort—but above all, time: time to think about what to say, time to inscribe the message and usually a copy or a résumé for one's records, and time to send the letter across long distances by ship, train, automobile, or horse-driven carriage and eventually on foot by a postman.

In regard to those epistles sent between Captain and Madam Dreyfus, it is necessary to point out again that the time to think about what to write was, mildly put, constrained, stressed, and difficult because of

---

to prove that merely being persecuted and stateless was not enough to excuse the Jews for their material success and ambition. Liszt's thesis was: the gypsies glorified God through the creation of natural beauty in the form of music; the Jews could only manage the worldly creations of money and crafted goods." In other words: "Jews were too clever for their own good." Finally, says Damon, "Liszt's adoration was of little benefit to the Roma, just as his bigotry failed to bury the achievements of Jewish musicians." Unfortunately, the kind of bile spewed forth by such admirable musicians as Liszt and Chopin helped pave the road to the crematoria and other killing fields of the Nazi empire.

the conditions of Alfred's imprisonment: in particular his limited space; his confined quarters; the unpleasant, uncomfortable, and feverish heat; as well as the need to make his wishes for paper, pen, ink, and so forth known through the agency of prison guards who were meant to humiliate him and treat him as virtually a nonperson. It was consequently not only a matter of finding a time, a place, and a means for writing but of composing his mind, and that, most significantly, was something that was both the consequence of penning these letters to Lucie and the means by which such temporary "moral" equilibrium was achieved. Once he had found and made use of the time, the place, and the implements for composing his epistle, the situation was again out of his control: the letters he wrote, like those he received, were subject to strict censorship and might not be posted to Paris with any sense of urgency.

Similarly, Lucie Dreyfus also was constrained in what she could write by the knowledge that her messages would be scrutinized and subject to censorship, delay, or nondelivery. Yet her fortitude and forethought in inscribing letters were able to do several absolutely essential things: (1) not least, to meet the strict requirements of the regulations imposed by military and political officials, of which she was acutely aware—Lucie only slipped up on a few occasions, and those few were only because not even she could have imagined the cruelty operating against her and Alfred; (2) closest to the surface of what was being communicated, to use her cunning and intuition in composing letters that would provide some comfort to the prisoner, serve to forestall his depressive thoughts of suicide, engage him in a domestic relationship[99] neither of them could be sure would ever be returned to anything like normalcy, if at all, again, and providing subtle hints of a project to have his case reheard and the judicial error that he, she, and other close family members or friends always presumed had been made corrected. Perhaps there was also a third

99 Burns puts together from mostly unedited materials in the archives a typical routine for the young married couple raising two children in the days before Alfred's arrest when their whole world was turned topsy-turvy: "Rarely staying in his office later than 6:00 p.m., [Alfred] rejoined Lucie for a quiet dinner followed by an evening at the symphony or a rubber of bridge with the Hadamards and family members visiting from the provinces. Most of the time, however, the couple spent alone, taking short promenades through their *quartier* and returning to read by the fire. They were building a considerable library in the new apartment, with titles that reflected their varied interests—from six-volume sets of Napoleonic campaigns, cavalry tactics, and military fortifications to histories by Fustel [de Coulanges] and Ernest Lavisse. Balzac novels, Shakespeare plays (translated into French), and a broad range of literary magazines and Parisian periodicals" (Burns, *Dreyfus: A Family Affair*, 98).

subtle function in her letters to Alfred. Thus, more so than in his own desperate missives back to her, she reinforced his virtually never-mentioned Jewishness, directing in a very nuanced manner the direction of their private, intimate exchange of emotional signals, which lasted over a year or more, towards a sense of traditional, kabbalistic notions of *tikkun ha'olam*—restoration of primal order, repair of a fragmented existential reality, and revelation of a moral purpose and meaning in life.[100]

The exchange of letters between husband and wife was anything but an orderly or regular one, therefore, since there was no real natural or logical flow of question and answer, remark and reply, while letters from Paris could have words, sentences, paragraphs, or even the entire content between the salutation and the farewell blacked out by prison authorities. When Alfred remarked in one letter, for instance, on the comfort deriving from the very fact of holding in his hand a piece of paper Lucie had held and seeing her thoughts and feelings written in her own loving hand, the authorities decided to have her epistles typed out by some minor functionary and on neutral, prison paper, thus depriving the husband of the least physical contact with his wife. How hurtful this administrative procedure was to Alfred and Lucie may be seen in her letter of 20 February, 1896, in which she expresses her relief that a letter has arrived from him in his own handwriting rather than in the impersonal lettering of a prison official:

> *C'est toujours une grande satisfaction pour moi que de voir ton écriture, il me semble que je tiens aussi une parcelle de toi; une copie supprime tout le caractère intime de la lettre et vous [. . .] l'impression peut seul vous donner le travail machinal et tout personnel qui accompagne la pensée.*[101]
>
> It is always a great satisfaction for me to see your handwriting. It seems that I am holding on to a part of yourself. A copy suppresses all the intimate character of the letter and [gives] you [in the impersonal sense] the impression that only a mechanical piece of work gives and

100 Lucie had a more sustained and formidable knowledge of Judaism than Alfred, as we shall discuss in later volumes in which we consider Dreyfus in love and as a Jew.

101 *Ecris-moi souvent, écris moi longuement*, 350.

> [thus leaves out] everything personal that accompanies the thought.

Despite the awkwardness and fragmented nature of these remarks, we can see what she is trying to say. She recognizes the difference between a personal script, which can embody a writer's personality and circumstances, and a mere mechanical reproduction of the words. It is not only that the "impression" is different in each case but that the significant meaning is also different.

She then continues her little essay on the importance of handwritten epistles as a facet in their special, almost metaphysical relationship, generated under pressure in the letters they send to one another, a theme to be developed later in this chapter. For the letter, in the tradition of Jewish reading technology, has more than just a body of information that is communicated by the meanings of the words; the text and the words have a volume, a substantiality to them, in the way they fill the page they are written on, the size, the shape, the pressures of the hand on the paper, and the inner dimensions of language itself.

> *Même quand je te lis selon que ton écriture est plus ou moins ferme, je me forge toutes sortes de chimères, je te vois tantôt fatigue, tantôt énervé, ou courageux, ou déprimé.*[102]
>
> Even when I read according to whether your script is more or less firm, I create all sorts of phantoms. I see you sometimes fatigued, sometimes enervated, or courageous, or depressed.

Such a passage in her letters, when we read it after the passage of more than a century, resonates with historical ironies, not least of which is the connection to the nature of the crime committed against Alfred and his family through forged, suppressed, and pretended documents. But in this instant of her writing, Lucie is indicating the way she can interpret letters by extraverbal qualities in the physical object itself, and as we shall see later in this chapter, her own uncharacteristically formal tone points toward secondary levels of signification in her

102 *Ecris-moi souvent, écris moi longuement*, 350.

remarks—her own signal to Alfred that she understands more about his condition than she knows he is allowed to speak under the eyes of the censors and, furthermore, that she expects him to interpret her letters at deeper levels than she feels permitted to write, partly because of those same censorious eyes scrutinizing everything she sends to him and holding back or destroying anything that would bring him real comfort from knowledge of how far the Dreyfusard cause is progressing. Thus, still further in this same letter, with its misdating and its elided parts of sentences,

> *C'est cette impression qui me manque lorsque la lettre est copiée par une écriture indifférente et ce m'est l'une des choses les plus pénibles parmi tous les chagrins secondaires que j'ai eu à subir.*[103]
>
> It is this impression which is lacking when your letter is copied into an indifferent script and it is to me one of the most painful things among all the secondary chagrins to which I am forced to submit.

It should not be overlooked that "impression" is one of those words in the lexicon of late nineteenth-century Europe laden with aesthetic and intellectual weight, partly from the revolutionary changes in all the arts in regard to seeing, hearing, and shaping space and also in the views of the mind that give a new spin on the older mode of associationist psychology stemming from Descartes and Locke, there now emerging as a whole new concept of depth psychology, wherein the mind is not strictly under the supervision of the will, let alone the rational faculties (the superego), and deep memories, inexpressible passions, and anxieties (the id) act to create a consciousness (the ego) that is at best a phantasmagoric parody of the mind.

As in epistolary novels since the seventeenth and eighteenth centuries, such as Samuel Richardson's *Clarissa*, the recipient of letters could never be sure that what he or she held in their hands was an actual response to one of their own, and that answers were being given to their own questions and in the context of certain confessions or statements

---

103 *Ecris-moi souvent, écris moi longuement*, 350–351.

of fact, or even an actual message and not a major alteration or a total forgery. The entire case against the captain in the Dreyfus Affair itself can be seen as a series of manipulated documents, forgeries, out-of-sequence fabrications, and misconstrued or misapplied contexts.

Thus, the first body of evidence about Alfred Dreyfus the man, as opposed to the cipher used by others in an ideological battle that more or less obscures the real reasons for his being framed as a traitor, in his own words, comes in the five hundred or so letters that he and his wife Lucie wrote to one another. There are a few letters from his children and other members of his family, such as Mathieu, or friends, such as Joseph Reinach. These letters, while written under difficult circumstances for all concerned, (none, however, so much as Alfred's), were also composed with a consciousness that military and colonial censors would be scrutinizing every word for indications of Dreyfus's connections with the German government, suspicious markers of anti-government feeling or even conspiratorial machinations, and other evidence of alien thoughts and actions, not least of which would have been expressions of Jewish loyalty and beliefs, which in the heated anti-Semitic atmosphere of the times would have been tantamount to treason.

Nevertheless, Alfred and Lucie, in these letters over five years, managed to communicate deep feelings of mutual support and concern for each other and the children. Although Lucie could not let Alfred know about any of the efforts to gain a revision of the decision of the court-martial or reveal the extent of the support being built up amongst intellectuals, she could and did make him aware that he was not alone and that he should have hope. Alfred, on his part, in the way he repeated words and phrases from Lucie's letters, reiterated his own assertions of faith in the ultimate justice in the army and in France and of his affection for his wife and family, and—this is important—in what he did not write at all, in the choice of words he used, did more than communicate his private love for Lucie and the children and his profound faith in reason and in France, he also created a relationship that was, as we may see in many of the novels of the period, a new kind of very introspective domestic bond with Lucie, a very strong love based on trust and friendship without any of the traditional signs of masculine superiority or domination. These letters have been edited, selected, and printed several times in the past hundred years, sometimes to win support for Dreyfus in his call for a revision of the guilty verdict, sometimes to seek his rehabilitation as an honourable officer, and sometimes to provide a much fuller psychological or "intimate portrait" of the man and his wife.

The book called *Five Years of My Life*, published soon after his arrival back in France in 1898, contains a selection of those letters mostly between husband and wife, along with some introductory material and other things, such as sketches and photographs. Unlike the unedited, raw letters themselves, the book was designed, in all senses of the word, certainly with political intentions in order to garner support and sympathy for the cause of regaining the honour of his family name and his status in the army and yet as a means of creating a positive historical portrait of himself and thus hiding his weaknesses at the time of his arrest and during his long ordeal in prison and other aspects of his personality evident in the letters that he did not want made public. His weakness and feebleness were very real, and Alfred and Lucie both feared throughout the affair that he would not be able to make it through with his sanity intact. His hypersensitivity led him earlier in his life to assume a pose of aloofness, which was often taken as snobbery; he would not chat with his fellow young officers or drink with them, or even go riding with them. He was a shy, introspective and sometimes annoyingly withdrawn personality, preferring to spend time in the evenings with Lucie and the children, holidaying with her or his families, and studying.[104]

In addition, the very selecting and annotating of his letters, like the original act of writing them from his cell, provided Dreyfus with a means of trying to keep his mind focused and active in the endeavour he had undertaken to maintain his sanity and to avoid falling into despair, and committing suicide. Unlike the unedited letters, which demonstrate in their rhythmic repetition of key phrases and their private code of mutual affection the inwardness of Dreyfus's experiences, the edited collection does not emphasize this aspect of his circumstances. It misses out on the way he and Lucie helped each other create a special private Jewish space for their love.[105] The edited collection is presented after Alfred's return to France, his release from prison, and is part of the campaign he undertook, along

---

104 A number of extravagant lies were concocted at the time of his arrest and publicized in the popular, anti-Semitic press that he had been a womanizer and a gambler. Nothing could be further from the truth.

105 As Andrew Marvell told his reluctant lover, "The grave's a fine and private place/ But none do there embrace."

with his brother Mathieu and other friends and allies, to vindicate his name and punish the real culprits in the affair. The book presumes his own knowledge of how many supporters he has and how strong his case really is and therefore cannot be taken as a true context in which the painfulness of self-creation and self-discovery by Lucie and Alfred came about.

Dreyfus also kept a journal and added to it when he came back from Devil's Island. As he found out what had been done on his behalf, both by his family and by many strangers, he sought to understand the dynamics of the affair and to discover the truth of what had happened, who was really at fault, and who deserved punishment for this intricate and complex conspiracy to frame him and to protect the culprits who forged documents, perjured themselves in various trials, instigated the anti-Semitic riots, carried out assassinations, attempted murders, and put France into great danger from foreign enemies. While Mathieu Dreyfus had quickly transformed himself from an Alsatian manufacturer into a clever activist and legal agent on behalf of his brother, and dealt with politicians, social leaders, and cultural celebrities, Alfred—very much weakened in body and mind by his ordeal—nevertheless trained himself to join in the investigations into his case. He too became able to speak to the intellectual elite of France as an equal. His journals record his transformation from artillery officer well versed in technological knowledge to political scientist and, in a sense, moral philosopher.

The third body of evidence is much more difficult to deal with. It consists of his prison notebooks, the *cahiers*, kept while on Devil's Island. There were, it seems, at least thirty-five of these workbooks in all,[106] the first twenty of which were destroyed by their author, leaving fourteen, deposited in the Bibliothèque Nationale de France and now edited by Pierrette Turlais in a mixed facsimile-transcribed version. There may have been drafts of Alfred's letters in the first, now missing, notebooks. In addition to the mathematical formulae and drawings also probably evident in the lost volumes, the remaining *cahiers* contain in addition reading notes and exercises in translation of English.

106 Alfred Dreyfus, *Les Cahiers de l'Ile du Diable*, ed. Pierrette Turlais (Paris: Éditions Artulis, 2009), 44. See also Thomas Wieder, "Les exercices d'écriture du bagnard Alfred Dreyfus," *Le Monde des Livres* (17 Décembre 2009) online at http://www/lemonde.fr/web/imprimer_element/0,40-0@2-3260, 50-128 (seen 22 March 2010).

***Shekhina*, Lucidity, and Illumination**

> *If, therefore, he [Balzac] wrote chiefly to women it was not only, as he remarked scoffingly to Théophile Gautier, because "cela forme le style," but from a profound and perhaps partly subconscious desire to find the woman who would understand him.*
>
> —Stefan Zweig[107]

> *The divine woman is an "optical apparatus" that refracts the light and renders the veiled image visible, like the rainbow that is manifest in the coverings of the cloud.*
>
> —Elliot R. Wolfson[108]

Lucie Hadamard, young as she was during the whole Affair,[109] became the one person who found out who Alfred Dreyfus really was—that is, the real person inside the awkward, shy, and public cipher. Thus, she served as the virtual Jewish muse who inspired him with courage to explore his inner self and to stay alive as a thinking man. The woman of twenty-four at the time of his arrest discovered how, in the very act of understanding him as no one else did, neither at the time of the affair nor virtually since then, she could transform his love of herself, family, and nation into something more than romantic fantasy, sentimental piety, and patriotic fanaticism. Michelle Perrot correctly describes her character in this situation:

> *Elle connaît le pouvoir des mots, même différés. Elle est consciente de la situation épouvantable que vit son mari.*

---

107 Stefan Zweig, *Balzac*, trans. William and Dorothy Rose, 2nd ed. (London: Cassell & Co., 1948 [1947]), 113. This is the last book that Zweig wrote and posthumously edited from fragmentary manuscript pages by Richard Friedenthal in London in 1945.

108 Elliot R. Wolfson, *Through a Speculum that Shines: Vision and Imagination in Medieval Jewish Mysticism* (Princeton, NJ: Princeton University Press, 1994), 274. Wolfson, who is paraphrasing *Zohar* 1:18a, b, goes on to say most shockingly, "Here we come again upon the mechanics of vision, and the implied iconicity of the divine: what has form is invisible and what is visible has no form" (275).

109 When they were married on 21 April, 1890, by the Chief Rabbi, Zadok Kahn, she was twenty years old and Alfred was thirty. Cf. Michelle Perrot, "Lucie et Alfred: Avant-propos," Alfred and Lucie Dreyfus, *"Ecris-moi souvent, écris moi longuement souvent, écris-moi longuement . . ." Correspondeance de l'île du Diable* (1894–1899), ed. Vincent Duclert (Paris: Mille et Une Nuits, 2005), 9.

> *Elle sait la nervosité de cet être hypersensible, pénétré de l'importance du cerveau, organe phare du discours médical, qui lui confesse 'un état d'éréthisme cérébral et nerveux [. . .] terrible" (4 Novembre 1897).*[110]
>
> She knew the power of words, even [when] differed. She was conscious of the horrible situation in which her husband lived. She knew the nervousness of this overly-excitable being, who perceived the importance of the brain, the guiding organ of medical discourse, who confesses to her that he is in "a state of extreme cerebral irritability and [. . .] terrible nervousness" (4 November 1897).

How she grasped the psychological and psychiatric symptoms Dreyfus describes in his letters, which are only partly transferred from his journals written at the same time, indicates at least four factors in her personality which surprise and shock anyone familiar with the knowledge and understanding supposedly characteristic of middle-class women of the period. First, she must have had a particularly acute intuition, very much in harmony with her husband's mentality, and thus been able to extrapolate details and implications from his *cris du coeur* and attempts to articulate and hence to control his sense of *enervation*, the normal term for such irritability and unsteadiness. Second, well-read and intelligent, she was able to draw on her own formal education and memories of conversations at home with her parents, siblings, their spouses, and their intellectual friends, and coordinate it with recollected domestic discussions with Alfred during their first four years of marriage. Third, Lucie herself was going through a moral crisis—moral in the sense we have already shown as usual in the period as the term for what we would classify as both psychological and ethical—and thus could read out of her own painful experiences an analogy to Alfred's condition. Fourth, as the daughter of a religious Jewish household who imbibed the commonplaces and ritual patterns of rabbinical thought and who was educated in the essentials of liturgy, prayer, and argumentation accessible to intelligent women at the time, Lucie could fit the diagnosis she was intuiting of Alfred's mental illness with her knowledge of treatments implicit

110 Michelle Perrot, "Lucie et Alfred: Avant-propos," 15.

in many Hebrew proverbs, exemplary tales, and juridical rulings. While neither she herself nor her family were as *au fait* with intellectual developments in Parisian society as were Proust's mother and grandmother, the latter's formation in both French and Jewish cultures was probably not different in kind from that of Lucie Hadamard.[111] Each of these four qualities of her character will be discussed as we read our way through some of the hundreds of letters exchanged between 1894 and 1898.

Recent historians of the affair, like Michelle Perrot and Vincent Duclert, describe Lucie as the embodiment of truth, justice, and wisdom who was able to keep her husband sane and alive during the five-year ordeal of his imprisonment. More than that, she was to Alfred the incarnation or the imaging forth of *Emet*, *Daat*, *Hochma*, and *Shechina*, powerful, dynamic concepts in *Kabbalah*. We should be reminded that *Kabbalah* was becoming fashionable again amongst intellectuals at the turn of the century, and that unlike Eastern forms of mysticism to which it is often compared, it is, in Mel Alexenberg's words, "a down-to-earth mysticism to encounter everyday life."[112] More than that, I would argue, it is a brilliant exercise in mythical and mathematical thinking that coordinates rabbinical tradition with the most up-to-date science in its milieu, and hence the sort of thought-game that would have interested Alfred Dreyfus had he known about it. That he didn't know in any explicit way is obvious, but just as obvious, as I hope this book shows, was his implicit grasp of its essential principles.[113]

In *Ecris-moi souvent, écris moi longuement souvent*, the editors divide up the letters according to the historical periods of Alfred's incarceration, where he was located and how intense were the isolation and other forms of torture applied. The examination that follows, however, does not seek to read out of the epistles any historical narrative of their relationship or any coordination to events taking place in Paris at the same time. As we have said, the letters form a continuous process of recreating their mutual love and loyalty in terms virtually unknown elsewhere in nineteenth-century French or European literature, and they may be

111 Evelyne Bloch-Dano, *Madame Proust* (Paris: Grasset, 2004).

112 Menachem Wecker, "Interview: Mel Alexenberg" *Iconia* (31 January, 2007) online at http://iconia.canonist.com/2007/01/31/interview-mel-alexenberg (seen 20 December, 2010).

113 How such an implicit absorption or imitation of cultural factors can occur in a family group or small community is hinted at in Gabriel Tarde, *L'opinion et la foule* (Paris: PUF, 1989; orig. 1901), 66–67, insofar as he begins to use terms and concepts at the heart of contemporary psychohistory, such as group fantasy and collective unconscious.

seen as engaged in a kind of plural analysis.[114] It will be seen therefore that in the initial period of their communications, while Alfred was transferred to different military prisons in France and before the regimen of constant censorship, rewriting of letters, and delays or blockage of delivery was in place, husband and wife could probe each other's responses and teach themselves to read the subtexts in their epistles.

In these letters of late 1894 and early 1895, almost everything that will be found later is set out in a preliminary format. The first extant letter is the one of Tuesday, 4 December, 1894, that Alfred writes while still in the Cherche-Midi prison in Paris waiting for his court-martial. He says he finally has a moment in which to write to his dear Lucie.

> *Je ne peux pas te décrire tout ce que j'ai souffert, il n'y a pas au monde de termes assez saisissants pour cela.*[115]
>
> I cannot describe to you all that I have suffered; there are not words strong enough for that.

Although these statements are clichés common to all intimate letters and especially to lovers forced to be apart, they provide the establishment of a programme to overcome separation and the limits of normal language. Alfred will have to learn how to describe his sufferings—that is, to find a lexicon of words, phrases, and allusions that communicate his condition and his feelings—while Lucie will have to learn how to confirm his ordeal by expressing her understanding and her sympathetic suffering. Three aspects to the problem are (1) hitherto, the couple have not had to write letters to one another, except the normal notes back and forth when, during their courtship, Alfred was on manoeuvres, and so now both must learn how to translate their ordinary oral communications by fragmentary speech, gestures, and acts of endearment to one another into coherent written discourse; (2) as a respectable Pa-

114 The term is taken from the teachings of William Théaux, a French psychoanalyst who studied with Jacques Lacan in the 1960s and who developed in Paris and Lyons a form of relationship between analyst and analysands based on the group of patients making a contract with and monitoring the doctor in such a way as to interfere with the usual problems of transference: countertransference since it was the collective that had the power not the authoritative analyst. This mutuality of the Dreyfus couple also suggests other forms of lay analysis conducted by groups of individuals who alternatively play the roles of analyst and analysand.

115 *Ecris-moi souvent, écris moi longuement*, 70.

risian middle-class couple they suddenly have to override the norms and conventions of that respectability, with its built-in dominance by the husband, the reticence of the wife, and the coyness of both to articulate intimate desires, longings, and memories; and (3) as a mostly assimilated Jewish man and woman writing to each other in French, they have to devise some strategies for expressing deeper, more emotionally-laden and culturally-particular feelings and memories associated with their Jewishness.

Now a few lines later in the same letter, Alfred says,

> *Mais j'espère en Dieu en la justice, la vérité finira bien par se faire jour. Ma conscience est calme et tranquille, elle ne me reproche rien.*[116]
>
> But I hope for Justice in God, that the Truth will finally see the dawn of day. My conscience is calm and tranquil, and reproaches me in nothing.

For virtually the first and only time in all his letters, Alfred here explicitly expresses his belief in God; later he will allow Lucie to make those references, even obliquely, while he speaks, as he does in the next part of the sentence, of his secular faith in justice and truth. He is firm in his beliefs and is sure that ultimately the truth will out against all the calumnies brought against him. Yet by the next pasage, he is starting to describe a mental state that will trouble him throughout his entire five years of incarceration, one that Lucie will recognize as having been evident *in nuce* from the beginning of their relationship:

> *J'ai toujours fait mon devoir, jamais je n'ai fléchi la tête. J'ai été accablé, atterré dans ma prison sombre, en tête-à-tête avec mon cerveau, j'ai eu des moments de folie farouche, j'ai même divagué, mais ma conscience veillait.*[117]
>
> I have always done my duty, never have I bowed my head. I have been overwhelmed, thrown to the earth in

116 *Ecris-moi souvent, écris moi longuement*, 70.
117 *Ecris-moi souvent, écris moi longuement*, 70.

> my dark prison, in a conversation with my own brain, I have had moments of wild madness, I have been incoherent, but my conscience watched over me.

In what seems like a contradiction, he claims that he has never bowed down before adversity, like Mordechai in the book of Esther when asked to bow before the tyrant Haman, or like any Jews under pressure to bow to the idols of worldly power and corruption. The brute force brought against him has been overpowering, and he has been brought low, as he has, by implication in the metaphoric use of the same words that describe how he is actually—and will be even worse off as the time goes on, having been subjected to cruel treatment and torture. Nevertheless, in this state of physical and psychological defeat, he has entered into a dialogue with himself, a *tête à tête* with his brain, his mind, his intellect, and his inner self. Note how each of these clauses seems to relate to the others less as a developmental order of intensifying understanding or engagement but more as a string of *non sequiturs*, as though all were simultaneous, part of the knot of confused sensations and thoughts that assail him. Yet despite this confusion, he comes back to his faith, now in the form of his conscience that is the nurse, guide, and guardian of his sanity—his rational self. It is the guardian angel, the guiding spirit, this image of God in himself that he knows will protect him, but at the same time, given the context of all the subsequent letters, this conscience is also something else: it is Lucie herself, as he repeats more and more often, whose picture is in his mind[118] and whose constructed presence in his imagination keeps him healthy, alive, and sane—she is, in other words, his *Shekhina*, his *Hochma*, his embodiment of justice and truth.[119]

---

118 "Created in the image of divine reality, man is its realization in matter" (Benmozegh, *Israel and Humanity*, 155).

119 Wolfson shows that "Through the agency of the imagination one enters the *'ălam al-mithăl'* (*mundus imaginalis*), in Henry Corbin's telling phrase, which is not the imaginary world of subjective fantasy or psychotic hallucination, but is instead a realm where invisible realities become visible and corporeal entities are spiritualized. The world of the imaginal [*sic*] is an intermediary realm wherein the imaginative forms (or archetypal images) symbolize the intelligible in terms of the sensory. The primary function of the imagination is hermeneutical: rather than recalling past sense data or combining these data in some innovative and, technically speaking, unexperienced way, the imagination produces symbols of the spiritual entities that act as interpretive filtering screens through which these entities appear in human consciousness," (*Through a Speculum that Shines*, 61, 62.] As we shall subsequently show, in Dreyfus' special epistolary relationship with his

Then Alfred continues with his letter:

> *Elle [i.e., his rational inner self] me disait: "Haut la tête et regarde le monde en face! Fort de ta conscience, marche droite et relève-toi! C'est une épreuve épouvantable, mais il faut la subir."*[120]
>
> She spoke to me: "Hold your head up high and look the world in the face! Fortified by your conscience, march forward and free yourself! It is a horrible ordeal, but you must submit to it."

Preparing himself for the ceremony of disgrace when his military insignia will be stripped away and his sword broken and when he will be marched before the troops as a mark of his humiliation, Dreyfus girds up his loins with courage, rehearsing too his dignified refusal to accede to the charges against him by signalling to Lucie what he will do in the courtyard: he will shout out repeatedly, "I am innocent!" and "Vive la France!"

In a postscript to this letter, the husband warns his wife of the fact that from now on, they will have no moments and no place of intimacy, and that all their private messages will need to be oblique and secretive:

> *Ecris-moi souvent, écris moi longuement à la prison: tes lettres passeront comme les miennes, par M. le Commissaire du Gouvernement.*[121]
>
> Write to me in prison; your letters will pass like my own through the Government Superintendent

A more significant directive to Lucie than this reminder that from now on everything they say or write or do will be under strict censorship is

---

wife, neither the Sufi ideas nor the Jungian concept of archetype plays a part. However, Wolfson's most secret and shocking insights from medieval Jewish Kabbalah do touch on one of the most hidden of the torments Alfred experienced, the long separation from sexual relations with Lucie and the inability of his finding any relief because of his round-the-clock surveillance and because at times he was shackled to his bed throughout the night.

120 *Ecris-moi souvent, écris moi longuement*, 70.

121 *Ecris-moi souvent, écris moi longuement*, 71.

given in Alfred's letter of 10 December, wherein he tells her,

> *Nous aurons besoin tous deux de nous soigner réciproquement pour oublier cette terrible éprouve, la plus terrible que les forces humaines puissant supporter.*[122]
>
> We will both have need to take care of one another in order to forget this terrible ordeal, the most awful the human powers can sustain.

Here is a recognition of reciprocity in their ordeal and of the need for mutual endurance, and a dynamic and interactive process of communicating to create a place out of real space and a time out of real time where they can not only share their love and loyalty but also generate the power necessary to transform the *status quo*, a process that Lucie must undertake on her own, against all expectations of a young married woman, and with Alfred providing his own support and directions for her efforts. In the event, of course, he does not know and therefore cannot appreciate all that she is doing, both on her own and in collaboration with his brother, Mathieu, and other members of the family, along with a growing number of Dreyfusards who rally to the cause over the years.

Meanwhile, Lucie, through intuition and intelligent guesswork, tries to translate the clues and hints provided by her husband's letters at once to feed him back the strength he needs from his own words, by her confirmation in repetition of what he says or implies, and to avoid raising false expectations or generating suspicions in the censorious eyes always monitoring her letters.

We can see this happening in the first of her letters printed in *Ecris-moi souvent, écris moi longuement*, from 23 December, 1894. She begins with exclamations of sympathy and pathos:

> *Mon pauvre, pauvre Fred chéri,*
> *Quel malheur, qu'elle torture, quelle ignominie. Nous en sommes tous terrifies, anéantis. Je sais comme tu es courageux, je t'admire. Tu es un malheureux martyr.*[123]

---

122 *Ecris-moi souvent, écris moi longuement*, 74.
123 *Ecris-moi souvent, écris moi longuement*, 80.

> My poor, poor Fred darling,
> What unhappiness, what torture, what ignominy. We are all frightened, crushed. I know that you are courageous, and I admire you. You are an unhappy martyr.

Not Lucie alone but both her whole family and his are dumbfounded by what has happened, and no one believes the charges against him are possible. She has probably not received his letters yet, or if she has, they have not registered yet in their full import, so she speaks here on behalf of the whole extended family (the *mishpucha*) to reassure him that he is not forgotten or rejected. She also must begin to urge on him the importance of not giving in to despair, of not taking the soldier's way out—suicide—as hoped for by his brother officers in their initial search for confirmation of guilt, to avoid the tedious duties of preparing a case against him. She remains loyal. Unlike so many wives and families in similar circumstances, real and fictional, Lucie does not desert him in his time of need, having complete and utter faith in his innocence, nor will either of their families, no matter what public ridicule is poured over them and what social inconveniences are put in their way, such as servants leaving their employ, having to move into one large household together, and pooling their wealth to employ the best lawyers and detectives to defend him and get to the bottom of the mystery. Thus, she reassures Alfred:

> *Notre vie, notre fortune à tous sera sacrifiée à la recherche du coupable; nous le trouverons, il le faut. Tu seras réhabilité.*[124]

> Our life, our fortune, all will be sacrificed in the search for the guilty party, we will find him, we must. You will be rehabilitated.

By her second letter of 23 December, written in the evening, she begins to play off his words. She echoes his cries of pain and anguish, his fears of going mad, and his asseverations of innocence, and speaks now with a different form of "we" than in the earlier letter, where it seemed

124 *Ecris-moi souvent, écris moi longuement*, 80.

primarily to stand for all the people in his and her family; now it represents more clearly the couple itself, husband and wife, who must see themselves as together in this ordeal, each one's pains and humiliations, loneliness and torture, to be shared and thus made bearable.

> *Tu sais si je t'aime, si je t'adore, mon bien cher mari; notre immense malheur, l'horrible infamie dont nous sommes l'objecte ne font que resserrer encore les liens de mon affection.*[125]
>
> You must know that I love you so much, that I adore you so much, my dearly beloved husband, our immense unhappiness, the horrible infamy of which we are the object can only strengthen the ties of my affection.

Then she echoes the famous words of Ruth in the Bible[126] when she comes back with her mother-in-law Naomi to live with her as a dutiful daughter-in-law. For though a Moabite, the traditional enemy of the Israelites, she avers,

> *Où tu iras j'irai, où tu demeuras je demeurerai; ton peuple sera mon people, et ton Dieu sera mon Dieu; où tu mourras je mourrai, et j'y serai enterrée* (I.16–17)
>
> For whither thou goest, I shall go; whither thou lodgest I shall lodge. Thy people shall be my people, and thy God shall be my God; where thou diest, will I die, and there will I be buried.

This passage is a *locus classicus* of Jewish love and loyalty across all differences and distances.

> *Partout où tu iras, où l'on t'enverra, je te suivrai; à deux nous supporterons plus facilement l'expatriement, nous vivrons*

---

125 *Ecris-moi souvent, écris moi longuement*, 81.

126 As well as of the *Song of Songs*: "Set me as a seal upon thine heart, as a seal upon thine arm: for love is strong as death . . . ." (8.6).

> *l'un pour l'autre . . . ; nous élèverons nos enfants, nous leur donnerons une âme bien trempée contre les vicissitudes de la vie.*[127]
>
> Wherever you will go, wherever they will send you, I will follow you, we two together will support the expatriation more easily, we will live for one another . . . ; we will raise our children, we will give them a soul well-tempered against the vicissitudes of life.[128]

Although her words may echo romantic novels and other exaggerated and postured literature, in this letter, Lucie pushes herself beyond the boundaries of bourgeois convention to assert the mutuality of their love, not only a passionate sensual amour between lovers but a domestic bond transcending sentimental pieties. Later, to be sure, it will become clear that a special law has been passed in the assembly to keep Alfred from being sent to New Caledonia, where wives could follow their husbands and even bring their children to be raised in the colony. He will be sent to Cayenne, to the small former leper colony island known as the Ile du Diable, and there kept in isolation and subjected to unprecedented indignities. At the moment, however, when Lucie still believes there is a chance to go into exile with her husband, she is prepared to leave her comfortable life, her family, and her Jewish community to be with Alfred. When Alfred eventually hears of this, he will argue against her plans. Even before he knows of the destination of his exile, he does not want his wife to separate herself from her family and take the children away from their cousins and grandparents, and the opportunities for education possible only in Paris; most of all, to accomplish his deep wish to be reunited with her, he needs Lucie to stay in France and lead the fight on his behalf against the wrongful charges brought against him and the judicial error committed in the court-martial.

In making himself dependent on his wife in this way, Alfred departs

127 *Ecris-moi souvent, écris moi longuement*, 81.

128 A friend from France thought the words as well as the sentiments of the loving husband and wife "old-fashioned." But this reversion to a somewhat archaic diction and attitude certainly is the heart of the matter, especially as the passage echoes biblical Hebrew. The lovers *support* one another because they otherwise would fall, as a house collapses in a storm, as a wounded person needs the aid of another to stand straight. Their souls are well-tempered, in the sense of a musical instrument that stays in tune despite changes in the atmosphere.

from the normal continuities of domestic politics as understood in most of Europe at this time, which has men dominant and actors in the public sphere and women subordinate and at best active in the privacy of their homes or in small salon circles. Their love will be changed into one based on friendship, mutual trust, and negotiations of how to do and say things in public. Thus, in his letter of 24 December, 1894,[129] Alfred writes to Lucie:

> *Oui, ma chérie, tu es sublime de courage et de dévouement; tu vaux mieux que moi. Je t'aimais déjà de tout mon cœur et de toute mon âme; aujourd'hui, je fais plus, je t'admire. Tu es certes une des plus nobles femmes qui soient sur terre. Mon admiration pour toi est telle que, si j'arrive à boire le calice jusqu'au bout, ce sera pour être digne de ton héroïsme.*[130]
>
> Yes, my beloved, you are sublime in your courage and your devotion, you are worth more than I am. I loved you already with all my heart and all my soul; today I do more, I admire you. You are indeed one of the most noble women ever on earth. My admiration for you is such that if I reach the end and must drain the chalice to the dregs, it will be in honor of your heroism.

Here we can see the husband worshipping his wife, a sublime and noble woman, praising her for her courage and heroism, so much so that he would be honoured if he were called upon to sacrifice himself, as Jesus did before his Crucifixion, but such an explicit Christian concept might be given a less offensive tone by alluding obliquely to a classical instance, the point in his imprisonment when Socrates chose to drink the hemlock. Implicit in this confession of his faith in Lucie (*Pennina* or *Pn'ei Or*, meaning the Face of Light, divine illumination, or enlightenment) is recognition in her of the qualities associated in Jewish tradition with heroic figures such as Esther, Judith, or Ruth, females hypostatized in

129 They do not take notice of the fact that it is Christmas Eve. The normal calendar, Christian or Jewish, disappears before the existential time of their suffering and love. Holidays are only mentioned in reference to the children, both when Lucie speaks of their excitement and Alfred of the need to purchase them toys.

130 *Ecris-moi souvent, écris moi longuement*, 84.

kabbalistic tradition to the roles of Wisdom, Truth, and *Shekhina*, the shadow or presence of God in exile.

In response, not necessarily direct since letters were constantly delayed and crisscrossing each other, on 26 December, 1894, Lucie pens these words:

> *Pauvre cher Freddy, comme tu es courageux, quelles horribles tortures tu endures. Tu es bon, foncièrement bon, tu as toujours été pour moi le plus tendre, le plus attentionné des maris, tu m'as témoigné pendant ces quatre années de vie commune une affection, un dévouement dont je te sais reconnaissante et, mon pauvre trésor, ce qu'il y a de plus pénible c'est que tu n'es pas du tout au bout de tes souffrances. Je te demande un énorme sacrifice, celui de vivre pour moi, pour tes enfants, de lutter jusqu'à ta réhabilitation qui, j'en suis convaincue et nous le sommes tous, ne tardera pas à venir.*[131]
>
> Poor dear Freddy, how courageous you are, what horrible tortures you are enduring. You are good, thoroughly good, you have always been to me the most tender, the most attentive of husbands, you have vouchsafed to me over four years of our life together an affection, a devotion of which I am completely conscious and, my poor treasure, what is even more distressing is that you are not at the end of your sufferings. I ask of you an enormous sacrifice, that of living for me, for your children, of fighting on until your rehabilitation which, I am utterly convinced and so are all of us, will not be late in coming.

This mutual admiration society increases in intensity into a virtual cult of mutual worship, as when Alfred writes on 26 December, 1894:

> *Tu es sublime, mon adorée, et j'admire ton courage et ton héroïsme, Je t'aimais déjà; aujourd'hui, je me mets à deux genoux devant toi, car tu es une femme sublime.* [132]

131 *Ecris-moi souvent écris moi longuement*, 88.
132 *Ecris-moi souvent, écris moi longuement*, 89

> You are sublime, my adored one, and I admire your courage and your heroism. I loved you before already, but today I bend both my knees before you, for you are a sublime woman.

In one sense, the pattern of worship, adoration, and genuflection recalls the Marian worship popular in France during the second half of the nineteenth century, as seen in Emile Zola's *Lourdes*, the first novel in his trilogy, *Les Trois Villes*,[133] which describes the ecstatic fervour displayed at the shrine. It would have been difficult for a person to live in Paris in those years and not be affected by the intensity of the Catholic cult, even if, like Alfred and Lucie, as assimilated Jews, he or she found the whole idea of such popular mysticism bizarre and repugnant. Although the pair may have known something of Jewish mysticism, with its kabbalistic rituals and formulae, it would also have been foreign to their sensibilities. However, in times of extreme stress and anxiety, the language and iconography overcome these cultural filters, and the terms and concepts come streaming into their letters as a way of expressing the inexpressible and imagining the unimaginable. At one point, breaking the conventions of bourgeois French patriarchy, not in the manner of Romantic poets or even earlier troubadors from Provence, Alfred exclaims: "*Decidément, ma chère adorée, les femmes sont supérieures à nous; parmi elles, tu es des plus belles et des plus nobles figures que je connaisse*"[134] (Decidedly, my dearly adored, women are superior to us [men]; amongst them, you are the most beautiful and noble that I know). This hyperbolical language of love, is it sincere? Should we take it literally? In what sense is it metaphorical?

Without it, Alfred finds that he has no other way to tell Lucie about what he is going through: he can, he claims, resist the physical suffering—"*elles glissent sur ma peau*" (they slide off my skin). But what he

133 Emile Zola, *Trois Villes*, trans. as *Lourdes, Rome, Paris* by Ernest A. Vizatelly. It is especially in the crowd scenes of pilgrims processing up and around and then into the shrine of Our Lady of Lourdes—chapter after chapter of increasing ecstasy and bizarre behaviors—where Zola manifests the full power of the fanaticism in the pious Catholics of all ranks in society. This wild scene might also be compared to the religious excitement Zola describes in the second volume of the trilogy, *Rome*, where a papal ceremony nearly turns into a riot, and the Holy Father has to escape, though first trying to salvage the many coins that roll away.

134 Alfred to Lucie, 27 December, 1894: *Ecris-moi souvent, écris moi longuement*, 94.

cannot face is "*cette torture morale*" (this moral torture). As we pointed out already, the term *moral* plays a key role in the formation of the experiential basis of the affair and the way those closest to its centre respond to it: it refers to ethical, emotional, psychological, and spiritual states of being in the individual and the various collectivities involved, not least the husband-wife unit of Alfred and Lucie, their immediate families, and the inner circle of early Dreyfusards. This moral torture is also "*le drame le plus effroyable*" (the most horrible drama), a *calvaire* (a calvary) or *martyre* (a martyrdom). In other words, something inflicted by one group on another person who is himself less an individual than a metonymic representative for the group he or she belongs to. It is a festival of hate, pain, and humiliation against the central figure, who remains in the heart of the panopticon, where all can see him, although only a few, like Lucie, feel along with him because they are part of him.[135]

Alfred writes to his wife on the twenty-sixth of December—note how many letters are written in one or two days, as though writing is the only way for both of them to endure the torment of their separation and the knowledge of the other's sufferings:

> *Ah! ma chérie, si je ne t 'avais, comme je quitterais la vie avec délices! Ton amour me retient, lui seul me permet de supporter la haine de tout un people.*[136]
>
> Ah, my cherished one, if I did not have you, how I would quit this life with joy! Your love holds me back, the only thing that enables me to support the hatred of a whole people.

---

135 On what happens when the ritualized and licit Festival of Laughter and Blood gives way to the violent outbursts on the street of a new game called *Pasquino*, listen to Romain Rolland: "The more moral stringency paralyzed action and gagged speech, the bolder did action become and speech the more untrammeled during those few days. Everything that was secreted away in the lower depths of the soul, jealousy, secret hate, lewd curiosity, the malicious instincts inherent in the socials animal, would burst forth with all the vehemence and joy of revenge. Every man had the right to go into the streets, and, prudently masked, to nail to the pillory in full view of the public gaze, the object of his detestation, to lay before all and sundry all that he had found by a year of patient industry, his whole hoard of scandalous secrets gathered drop by drop" (*Jean Christophe*, vol. III, 305). In a sense, the Dreyfus Affair works in an analogous way, when France, afraid to speak the secret anxieties over modernization, projects its inner demons and empties the poison sack of its self-hatred on to the Jew and pretends it is all for reasons of state and the ideals of king, army, and church.

136 *Ecris-moi souvent, écris moi longuement*, 91.

The enormity of the humiliation and shame he feels is registered as the hatred of the whole nation, all of France, every single person outside of his own family, especially Lucie, and every institution and principle he once believed in with the fervour of a devotee.

The second section of *Ecris-moi souvent, écris moi longuement* is devoted to letters written from 5 to 17 January, 1895, while Alfred was kept in the Santé Prison awaiting deportation to Devil's Island. Reassuring his wife on 5 January, 1894, that the degradation having been passed through and the impending exile being imminent, "*Le moral tient*" (his moral being remains strong and firm, his inner courage); he nevertheless "*commence à être à bout de patience et de forces*" (begins to feel his patience and his strength running out).[137] He also fears the moral collapse of his mind, the plunge into a mad and painful confusion of his nervous structure: "*il me semblait que j'étais le jouet d'une hallucination*" (it seemed to me as though I were a plaything in an hallucination).[138]

Then on the evening of the same day, not finding any consolation, he cries out in near despair that all his ambitions, achievements, and honour, and his love and devotion to the fatherland are all "*perdues par une machination qui procède bien plus du fantastique que du réel*"[139] (lost in a machination—what we have decided to call the contraption—that is driven more by the fantastic than the real). In the letters that follow, Alfred and Lucie repeat the basic terms and images of the letters from Cherche-Midi, even with the constant warning that "*M. de Directuer de la prison . . . est obligé de lire toutes me lettres*"[140] (the Prison Warden is required to read all my letters). These writings, though, also advance the thoughts and feelings the husband and wife have about one another, something that shows them both learning, each in their own style, to operate within the straitened circumstances of distance and isolation, and the text thus confirms our earlier interpretations and also exposes the semantic zone allusion the Dreyfuses express, whether or not they are fully conscious of its implications.

Not all that they write indicates a realization of the need to maintain a secret code drawing on their shared Jewish background, but the

137 *Ecris-moi souvent, écris moi longuement*, 119.
138 *Ecris-moi souvent, écris moi longuement*, 120.
139 *Ecris-moi souvent, écris moi longuement*, 122.
140 *Ecris-moi souvent, écris moi longuement*, 131.

evidence does begin to mount that to a certain degree, they are indeed aware of something different and deeper in their minds emerging in these letters. Thus, on 8 January, 1895, in the same letter in which Alfred mentions the censorship operative all the time on his letters—meaning those he writes and those sent to him—he also says,

> *Tu me demandes aussi, ma chérie, ce que je fais du matin au soir, et du soir au matin. Je ne veux pas te communiquer mes tristes réflexions, ta douleur est déjà assez grande, et il est inutile de l'augmenter encoure. Ce que je t'ai dit plus haut suffit pour te faire comprendre ce que je désire en ce moment: l'exil en plein air avec toi, en attendant la réhabilitation, Quant au reste, je te le raconterai plus tard, quand nous serons réunis et heureux.*[141]
>
> You also ask me, my darling, what I do from sunrise to sunset and from sunset to sunrise. I do not want to tell you my sad reflections, your grief being already great enough, and it is useless to increase it further. What I told you above suffices for now to let you understand what I desire at this very moment: exile in the open air with you, waiting for the rehabilitation.
> As for the rest, I will tell you everything much later, when we are reunited and happy.

On the surface, Alfred says he will not give her details of his daily routine and thus fill his letters with a diary of the experiences and feelings of each day. He rejects the use of the letter as a journal of events and a narrative of his shifting emotions. What he has written already—a few brief descriptions of the conditions under which he is imprisoned—are all he will say on this matter. More profoundly, the dismissal of her request to share through letters his every moment of suffering indicates that the letters will be directed to a different level of experience and use language for a purpose other than conveying information.

In a letter from la Santé Prison written on 9 January, 1895, Alfred speaks to Lucie in one of his most explicitly Jewish confessions. He be-

141 *Ecris-moi souvent, écris moi longuement*, 132.

gins by telling her that he has just received a batch of belated letters from her and the rest of the family. In these circumstances, he tells her, "Il faut nous incliner et suffrir en silence"[142] (We must bow down and suffer in silence)—that is, accept the inevitable with resignation and make no cries of complaint or pain. Recalling the day of his degradation the previous Sabbath, he declares, "*Cette journée de Samedi reste dans mon esprit gravée en lettres de feu*"[143] (This day of the Sabbath/Saturday remains engraven on my heart in letters of fire), an image drawn from biblical and rabbinical writings, alluding to the tables of the law presented to Moses on Mount Sinai, and in kabbalistic terms, the flaming letters of the covenant between God and Israel. There may also be found a Christological resonance in these words, however, suggested further in his comment that "*[M]on coeur a saigné, il saigne encore, il ne vit qu'avec l'espoir qu'on lui rendra un jour ses gallons, qu'il a noblement gagnés et qu'il n'a jamais souillés*"[144] (My heart bled and bleeds yet, it cannot live without the hope that one day the stripes will be returned, those so nobly earned and never tainted). The image of the bleeding heart, however, does not allude to Jesus on the cross but to his own wrongful sacrifice in the ceremony of degradation, a dishonour he hopes will be reversed, the language now shifting from its religious aura to that of military rehabilitation, with his officer's braids returned and his rank and name restored.

The idea of purgation from the taint of the false charges of treason and espionage ambiguously sits between three points of reference: the ancient Jewish notion of sin-offerings, the Christian myth of salvation through the bleeding heart of Jesus, and the military code of honour and rehabilitation.[145] In another Sabbath letter, this one written on 12

---

142 *Ecris-moi souvent, écris moi longuement*, 133.

143 *Ecris-moi souvent, écris moi longuement*, 133.

144 *Ecris-moi souvent, écris moi longuement*, 133.

145 In his address to the First Zionist Congress in Basle on 20 August 1897, Max Nordau imagined the disappointments and disillusionments of the assimilated Western Jew when he or she discovers that their place in the society they believe to be home is questioned by those who dominate that nation, a realization that follows "recent tendencies," that is, the Dreyfus Affair: "The Western Jew has bread, but man does not live on bread alone. The life of the Western Jew is no longer endangered through the enmity of the mob; but bodily wounds are not the only wounds that cause pain, and from which one may bleed to death. The Western Jew meant emancipation to be real liberation, and hastened to draw the final conclusions therefrom. But the nations [i.e., the *goyim*,] made him fear that he erred in being so heedlessly logical. The magnanimous laws, magnanimously lay down the theory of equality of rights. But governments and society exercise the practice of equality of rights in a manner which renders it the same mockery as did the

January, 1895, Alfred wrestles with his belief in God and his trust in the law, also ambiguously rendered as having its primary focus on French republican principles and more covertly in Jewish notions of justice and truth:

> *S'il y a une justice en ce monde, il faut espérer que la vérité éclatera bientôt et nous dédommagera de tout ce que nous avons souffert.*[146]
>
> If there is justice in this world, we must hope that the truth will break through soon and compensate us for all that we have suffered.

Here again he speaks of the redeeming light that will shine through the darkness to solve the mystery of who the real culprit is in the case of treason and espionage, but also, more allusively, he thinks religiously and Jewishly of the divine power of the law to set the world straight on its path of righteousness again, the hope for messianic rescue from darkness and ignorance, with the pains and humiliations serving here as sin offerings—that is, his and Lucie's part in fulfilling the terms of the *brit*, the covenant entered into at Sinai. But this is not the humble, patient suffering of Christian schemes of salvation, where the help comes from outside, aided variously by faith and good works, but rather in Hebrew concepts of participation by the individual and drawing on the stock of merit (*zekhut*) built up by all of Israel and the *tikkun* (gathering up of lost and hidden sparks) of each person and each generation through the performance of *mitzvot* (obligatory acts of charity, ritual gestures, etc.). Only in this way, Alfred says, can "*cette énigme indéchifferable*"[147] (the indecipherable puzzle) be solved. A few days later he puts it this way:

---

appointment of Sancho Panza to the splendid position of Viceroy of the Island of Barataria. The Jew says naively: 'I am a human being, and I regard nothing human as alien,' the answer he meets is: 'Softly, your rights as a man must be enjoyed cautiously; you lack the right notion of honour, feeling for duty, morality, patriotism, idealism [everything, in fact, that Alfred Dreyfus lived and suffered for]. You must, therefore, hold aloof from all vocations which make possession of these qualifications as conditions [and when Alfred held himself aloof, he was mocked for having no feelings]." "Speech of Max Nordau at the First Zionist Congress, August 29, 1897," translated and reprinted on *Mideast Web* online at http://www.mideastweb.org (seen 12 December 2010).

146 *Ecris-moi souvent, écris moi longuement*, 141.

147 *Ecris-moi souvent, écris moi longuement*, 142.

> *Cette nuit, je ne me suis encore endormi qu'à 2 heures de matin. J'ai pensé à toi, à vous tous, à cette énigme épouvantable que je voudrais déchiffrer . . . J'ai roulé dans ma cervelle mille moyens plus violents, plus extravagants les uns que les autres à vous indiquer pour déchirer le voile derrière lequel s'abrite un monstre.*[148]
>
> Tonight I could not fall asleep until 2 a.m. I was thinking of you, of all of you, of this horrible enigma that I wish I could decipher . . . I turned over in my head a thousand violent ways, each one more violent and extravagant than the other, to show you how to tear the veil behind which hides a monster.

Again, looking at this passage, what seems fairly simple in the beginning—his sleepless tossing and turning all night worrying about the puzzle of his accusation and punishment and the need to find out the identity of the real spy and traitor who committed the horrible crime he was found guilty of—turns out to be much more complex. There are two different problems to solve that keep him awake: one is the mystery of who brought about the false charges against him—later this will come to include the need to understand the reasons why his brother officers and the institutions he had so much faith in turned against him—and the other, how to communicate to Lucie the need to see behind the veil of mystery that lies over their lives.

While he calls upon a variety of discourses well known in literature and scholarship about different kinds of love, what he does not mention here explicitly is the other figure of sacrifice for love and purification through suffering, Lucie, his dependence upon her as his superior, god-like guide and nurse who under the awful circumstances of their plight must speak and act on his behalf in Paris. It is this "*amour reciproque*"[149] that is at the heart of their new relationship, new for them, to be sure, but also new in literature, as it extends and transforms the Neoplatonic imagery of twelfth- and thirteenth-century troubador concepts of

148 *Ecris-moi souvent, écris moi longuement*, 146.
149 *Ecris-moi souvent, écris moi longuement*, 138.

fin'amor, phenomena hinted at but never fully developed in the theoretical-autobiographical essays of Stendhal, Michelet, and others in the course of the nineteenth century, as well as in the novels of Balzac, Flaubert, and Bourget. Not only do sensual or sexual relationships merge with ideas of hypostatized friendship, as in the courtly love treatises, with Ovidean realism impregnating Christian spirituality with real passions of the flesh, but Alfred and Lucie's letters raised the domestic love of parents for children and concern for their education and future development to a level of psychological bonding and social reformation. These ideas are hinted at in the epistles; they are developed more fully in the prison *cahiers*.

I hinted earlier that one of the ways Alfred and Lucie find to discuss deeper meanings in their relationship and in the circumstances they are trying to work their way through was through their discussions—and even, at times, arguments—about how to bring up their children, discipline them, educate them, and prepare them for their futures, which may be always tainted with the charges against Alfred. It is the "*gazouillement*"[150] (chirping or chattering) of the little ones that allows Lucie to act as a conduit, translator, and encoder of their and her own deepest feelings in letters she composes on their behalf.[151] Her intentions are the best, both to cheer her husband with reports on the progress of little Pierre and Jeanne, to confirm their innocent and unmitigated love and longing for their *pappa*, and to express longings of her own that exceed the proprieties of middle-class etiquette; they also serve to provide an alternative topic of conversation than that of Alfred's sufferings in prison, in that the upbringing of the little ones is a joint responsibility and Lucie claims to be turning for advice and support to the father in these matters. That these reports mirror Alfred's own may not be a conscious aspect of her writings, but it is all too clear to the outside observer, looking back long after the events, that the cou-

150 *Ecris-moi souvent, écris moi longuement*, 150, 151, etc.

151 Chaim Vital in *Sh'ar Ruah ha-Qodesh* 5d (The Gate of the Holy Spirit) speaks of *sifsufe 'ofot*, the chirping of birds: "Sometimes they can be explained in another manner, for the soul of some righteous person comes from the upper world and is clothed in that form and image; it is not an actual creature or bird, but only appears and is seen in this way, and he reveals the secrets of Torah" (cited by Wolfson, *Through a Speculum that Shines*, 320). For Alfred and Lucie, the children are the visual manifestation of their act of love that produced Jeanne and Pierre, as well as the showing forth of the innocent honor they must protect. As in Vital's explication, their chattering can be translated into the deepest secrets of their parents' hopes and fears.

ple's letters are also transcribed and their own intentions, whether fully known or not, have to be translated into terms appropriate to their social condition and to the special terms of the prison authorities.

But just as prison censors and politicians when asked to read the letters sympathetically could only find them tedious and vacuous, so Lucie—and sometimes Alfred himself—apologizes for the repetitiveness and clumsiness in expression.

> *Tu dois trouver mes lettres bien monotones, mon pauvre vieux, je me répète dans toutes, toujours je t'exhorte au courage. Je te vois te crisper en lisant ces lignes, mais je t'en conjure, maîtrise tes nerfs, pense moins à notre malheur. Je sais combine cela est difficile, car je passé moi-même par ces moments d'angoisse tels que je ne sais que deviner.*[152]
>
> You must find my letters very monotonous, my poor old fellow. I repeat myself in all of them, always exhorting you to courage. I can see you growing irritable in reading these lines, but I conjure you to control your nerves, think less of our misery. I know how hard that can be, for I too experience these moments of anguish, such that I only know will keep coming.[153]

The unusual term of endearment, "*mon pauvre vieux*," signals an odd tone to this apologetic. She already knows that Alfred craves her letters, receives them with ecstatic joy, and constantly rereads them, so her expressions of worry that he will be irritated by her repetitiveness are surely further indications of an encoded message between them. It is true, certainly, that she needs to keep saying over and over how much she admires his courage, just as she must remind him to avoid despair, to master his delicate nerves, and to remember that she shares with him all the anguish of the ordeal they are going through. But the repetitive-

---

152 *Ecris-moi souvent, écris moi longuement*, 151.

153 The syntax is obscure here, and Norbert Col suggests translating the last half of the last sentence: "for I too experience such moments of anguish that I can only make guesses." However, it is best that we simply recognize that Dreyfus is writing in pain and frustration. The amazing thing is how often, despite this, he breaks out of the doldrums and creates a virtual metaphysical conceit in praise of Lucie and of love.

ness in the letters also indicates that what the husband and wife are doing is fighting against the system that separates them physically and tries to interrupt the easy, intimate flow of information between them. Since they cannot present to each other a running and logical pattern of statement and response, following a relatively orderly chronological framework, because delivery of mail is awkward, haphazard, and deliberately constrained, as well as being subject to prying eyes ever vigilant to find either or both of them involved in some sort of Jewish conspiracy against the army or the republic, they need to remind themselves that the letters do not form a record of daily events, whose progress can be tracked through cause and effect, but a steady stream of confirmations and reassurances of their mutual love and loyalty. They also need to communicate something else about their relationship, which, while it breaches many codes of social and domestic propriety, never can be seen to overstep the boundaries of their respect for one another.

This is the state we find them in as they write in the third stage of Alfred's hallucinatory journey to Devil's Island.[154] From 18 January to 21 February, 1895, he is kept in the cells at Ile de Ré, the port of Saint-Martin, where an even more intense and humiliating regimen of body searches and incarceration is put in place. His letters are subject to greater scrutiny and delays, with all messages from other members of both the Hadamard and Dreyfus families forbidden.[155] Duclert[156] suggests that this harshness comes from an implicit wish by the authorities to drive Dreyfus to despair and eventually suicide. In the letters written during this period, the historian also opines, coming close to the inner dimensions of the husband and wife's communications, they seek "*de construire un espace que leur soit proper et que personne ne pourra leur retirer*"[157] (to construct a space all their own and from which no one can remove them).

---

154 This is how Paul Bourget describes the trip across the Atlantic from France to America in his travelogue *Outre-Mer*: "*Et dans la demi-hallucination que donne le bercement de la mer . . .*" (Vol. 1, subtitled "Notes sur l'Amerique" [Paris: Plon, nd], 15). But if the gently rocking motion of the large cruise liner gentled Bourget into a semitrance of luxury, with time seeming to disappear in a haze of fine foods, music, and luxurious appointments, for Alfred Dreyfus, the tense, cramped journey to Devil's Island was the culmination of transformation of his life from normality to the bizarre and on to the nightmare of his imprisonment, isolation, and torture.

155 Duclert, *Ecris-moi souvent, écris moi longuement*, III, "Au bagne de l'Ile de Ré," 155–161.

156 *Ecris-moi souvent, écris moi longuement*, "Au bagne," 158

157 *Ecris-moi souvent, écris moi longuement*, "Au bagne," 161.

Most of what they say to one another during this early period of their exchange of letters, if it can even be called that, remains similar in language, tone, and allusion to what has gone before. There are now and then, however, new points that strike us as different and consequently need to be discussed before we move into the main section of the letters, those written during the stay on Devil's Island itself.

For example, in a letter of 27 January, 1895, Lucie draws out the implications of earlier remarks on the mutuality of their love and loyalty by saying that, having passed through so much discouragement and worry already, they can only live in and through each other: "*Il faut que nous vivions tous deux.*"[158] She also realizes that words alone cannot release him from his atrocious sufferings ("*Je sais . . . que toutes ces paroles ne t'enlevent pas les atroces souffrances actuelles*") and that only his iron will and clear conscience will see him through, but even then, she adds, "*Il faut que nous résistions tous deux*" (We must be able to resist together, as a couple). How that can be done is hinted at in another of her close-to-articulate Jewish remarks, extremely rare according to Duclert, in an understatement of considerable interest.[159] She asks Alfred whether she should arrange for a rabbi to visit him and offer consolation, stating quite clearly that she could, if he wanted, call on the aid of the very rabbi who married them and who is likely to have been a friend at least of her family, if not of their combined family:

> *Ne serais-tu pas heureux et désireux de voir un ministre de notre culte: dans ce cas, les secours de la religion nous sont une grande consolation. Veux-tu, si tu penses comme moi, demander au grand rabbin de France de designer un de ces messieurs pour te consoler, te réconforter? Et si tu ne peux écrire toi-même, veux-tu prier Monsieur le Directeur d'être assez bon pour lui écrire?*[160]
>
> Would you not be happy and desirous to see a minister of our cult; in that case the support of religion would be a great consolation. Do you wish, if you think as I do,

158 *Ecris-moi souvent, écris moi longuement*, 177.
159 Duclert, Notes, *Ecris-moi souvent, écris moi longuement*, 481, n. 21.
160 *Ecris-moi souvent, écris moi longuement*, 177, 178.

> to ask the Chief Rabbi of France to delegate one of his ministers to console you, comfort you? And if you do not wish to write to him yourself, could you entreat the Warden to be so kind as to write to him?

The language Lucie uses here is rather complex and weaves around several of the key issues we have been discussing already in regard to the mutuality of their relationship, the need to discover an appropriate lexicon and imagery to transmit their deepest feelings, of a sort normally hidden in bourgeois families of the period, and, in addition, this letter's special circumstances, wherein she knows that it will be scrutinized by prison censors and realizes that reference to Jewish issues would be extremely suspicious. Perhaps, still further, it is likely that in previous discussions, long before the crisis of his arrest and imprisonment, Alfred had expressed the need to remain aloof from institutionalized Judaism, particularly in regard to their family friendship with Zadok Kahn, Chief Rabbi of France, who had performed their marriage. The expression "*un minister de notre culte*" is not only neutral, it is an official formula, one that made the members of the Israelite persuasion in France come under the same rights and obligations as Protestants of all types.[161] The syntax assumes a formality and indirection that is virtually absent in all her other letters, perhaps because, as we said, she is broaching very sensitive matters. Rather than speaking of their shared faith and the communal identity they share with their relatives and almost all of their friends, Lucie uses the virtually legalistic expression "minister of our cult." A meeting with a rabbi would, if he thinks as she does, offer consolation and comfort, and these terms, while certainly applicable in many instances to pastoral care offered by the Jewish ministry, are nontraditional expressions; more normally, the rabbi would come to pray with and help the despairing individual or family with ethical advice from modern or traditional books.

The oddest statement of all is the last sentence, wherein Lucie asks

161 Given the charged atmosphere of heightened anti-Semitism back in France, as well as elsewhere in Europe at this time, the word *rabbi* (other than in Zadok Kahn and *Jew* [*Yehidi* or *Yid*]) is laden with unsavory Eastern, Orientalistic and Semitic signals that neither Alfred nor Lucie would wish to trigger in the minds of their censors—or in the those of their non-Jewish supporters; similarly, a word like "*prêtre*" (priest), though specific to Catholic clergy, would not be appropriate to any form of post-Temple Judaism since the cult had fallen into desuetude and the role of priests (*kohanim*) had become at best honorific.

indirectly if Alfred wishes to write to Rabbi Kahn himself or request that Monsieur le Directeur do so on his behalf. Either she is extremely naive or disingenuous here, as any such request from either prison or colonial officials, or even the Chief Rabbi himself in this regard would be turned down flatly as something contrary to the special regulations sent from Paris or due to the already manifest prejudices of the prison authorities, or she has some ulterior motive. As it is unlikely that either she or any of her advisers, such as Mathieu Dreyfus, have any intention of forcing the government to show its anti-Semitic hand more openly than it already has, the only other reason for this kind of request to Alfred from his wife must be an attempt on her part to signal that her closeness to him goes beyond the kind of love, loyalty, courage, and hope they have spoken of before in their letters: she now wants him to know that she will be performing the role of spiritual adviser, giving him—in the role of a non-Christian Boethius in prison—the consolation of Jewish philosophy.[162]

Just like the *Shekhina*, the divine shadow and presence which separates itself from the Godhead during the crisis of creation, when the universe contracts in the *tsimtsum*, leaving in the otherwise vacuous space and time retreated from by the deity a mysterious aura of spirit, so Lucie, in the shared suffering and martyrdom of Alfred, becomes his active other in the world he has been forced to leave. Like the *Shekhina*, who is God's female consort and co-creator, Lady Wisdom or *Hochma*, Lucie plays the role of Israel, the Bride of scriptures, that extension of the divine—separated from the infinite *En-Sof* (world without end) by the cosmic energies of the *sephirot*—acting and suffering in this world, *ha-olam hazeh*. It is the duty of Israel embodied and unified in the *Shekhina* to gather up all the sparks of primal energy scattered and hidden after the breaking of the great vessels in the moment of separation—the Big Bang—the recollecting of these shells of light constituting the *tikkun ha-olam*, the repair and correction of the broken world, thus preparing for the moment when God and his *Shekhina* can join together again, inaugurating the messianic age.[163] The sparks

162 André Maurois recalls being at a Christmas party when he was five or six years old when "I learned from another child, who was beside me in the church, that my parents were Jews and that this was an astonishing fact" (*Call No Man Happy*, trans. Denver and Jane Lindley [London: Jonathan Cape, 1943], 11).

163 Ouaknin says, following Rabbi Nahman, "*Il s'agit de la* Chevira hakélim, *'la brisure des vases' . . . Après le* Tsimtsoum, *la lumière divine jaillit dans l'espace vide sous forme de rayon en ligne droite. Cette lumière se nomme* Adam Qadmon, *cést-à-dire l''Homme primordial*" (It is a question of the *Shevra*

that remain after millennia of regathering are now mostly those that emanate from the other side, *sitra achra*, which though malevolent, hostile, and pernicious nevertheless contain within them aspects of eternal energy and power. For Alfred and for Lucie, confronted by "*la machination infernale*,"[164] the task remains to soldier on bravely and stoically through all "*les tortures morales*,"[165] until the enigma is broken and the light of truth breaks forth again to free them.

Lo dibera Tora k'lechon bene adam[166]

> *Les Hébreux, en fait d'œuvres scéniques, ne paraissent point avoir atteint l'idée du drame complet, où l'on vise surtout à mettre l'action devant les yeux du spectateur, et où la vraisemblance, sous le rapport des changements de lieux doit être observée.*
>
> —Ernest Renan[167]

---

hakelim, 'the breaking of the vases or vessels' . . . After the *Tsimtsoum*, the divine light leaps forth into empty space in the form of a straight line. This light is called *Adam Qadmon*, that is, "Primordial Man"" (*Le livre brûlé*, 381).

164 *Ecris-moi souvent, écris moi longuement*, 181.

165 *Ecris-moi souvent, écris moi longuement*, 180.

166 Rabbi Nachom de Gamzo: "Torah does not speak in the language of man," a statement opposite to many Christian exegetes who say that the Bible speaks in the language of men and therefore must be read allegorically in order to read the language of God, and therefore says Ouaknin, "Everything is essential, each letters possesses a vital sense and importance, and everything needs to be interpreted, conjunctions and prepositions, punctuation marks and rhetorical markers, the size, thickness, and shape of letters, every jot and tittle" (*Le livre brûlé*, 116). In the case of Alfred and Lucie Dreyfus, we cannot go so far, but we will try to explode the text out of its linearity—little as there is of it left in the conditions they write in—to discover something of vital importance.

167 "The Hebrews, in regard to scenic plays, do not at all seem to have reached the idea of a complete drama where the chief aim was to put an action in front of the eyes of a spectator and where verisimilitude in regard to the changes in place was to be observed": Renan, *Le Cantique des cantiques*, 50. What Renan means here, typically in nineteenth-century terms, is that ancient peoples, especially the Jews, did not know how to mount a middle-class realistic play, with coherent actions performed before an audience with suspended disbelief in its artificiality and where the imitation of reality was to be complete. None of this, of course, would be seen in a Shakespearean play or theatre, not because neither he nor his audience was mature enough to conceive of such a performance but because the conventions of drama for the most part—in most times and in most places—operated on different principles than those developed eventually in the brief period of classical Greek tragedy and new comedy. Theatricality tended to be envisaged rather as ritual, ceremonial festivals, often with a transformative or shamanistic purpose—initiations, metamorphoses, conjuring forth of phantom ancestors—and consequently the emergence of monotheistic Judaism, with its abhorrence of idol worship and other forms of magic, recreated (midrashed) its own archaic cultural artifacts and the customs of neighboring civilizations, creating new inward dramas and performative rituals. See José Faur's forthcoming *The Gospel*

Because Lucie cannot write to her husband about any of the efforts being made on his behalf other than in vague hints, such as "*[c]omme on apprécie dans ces moments terribles les personnes dévouées et elles sont en nombre très grand*"[168] (as one comes to appreciate in these terrible times, there are many people devoted to you, a very great number), or even about who is making these efforts, and how many supporters there actually are beyond the family members he already knows about, she must return to the interchange of comments each makes on how they read and recall each other's letters. Alfred writes on 31 January, 1895, that he reads and rereads all her letters, finding in them "*un echo de vous tous*"[169] (an echo of all of you), this *all* meaning Lucie, the children she writes for from their supposed dictation, and other close relatives who have sent him epistles of their own. Then he describes the process more minutely:

> *Je relisais ta lettre quatre ou cinq fois, je m'imprégnais de chaque mot,—peu à peu les mots écrits se transformaient en paroles dites . . . il me semblait bientôt t'entendre me parler près de moi. Oh! musique délicieuse qui allait à mon âme! Puis depuis quatre jours, plus rien, la morne tristesse, l'épouvantable solitude.*[170]
>
> I reread your letter four or five times. I was impregnated by each word,—little by little written words transformed themselves into spoken statements . . . soon it seemed that I could hear you speaking close by me. Oh! what delicious music that came into my soul! Then for the four days, nothing more, the unbearable solitude.

According to the Jews, in section III of which he discusses the theatricality of Christianity and the rationality and legal disposition of Judaism; cp. my *Festivals of Laughter, Blood and Justice* (London, ON: Sussco, 2008). With the re-valuation of notions such as time, space, personhood, and reality, the rabbinical imagination passed on to men and women such as Alfred and Lucie Dreyfus an ability—and an anxiety—in playing out the roles that have been imposed on them by hostile and alien societies.

168 *Ecris-moi souvent, écris moi longuement*, 183.

169 *Ecris-moi souvent, écris moi longuement*, 184.

170 *Ecris-moi souvent, écris moi longuement*, 184.

The meditation on the epistle with its iterated reading[171] causes a metamorphosis in his perception of reality. As in kabbalistic exercises to achieve *devekut* (cleaving to the divine object), Alfred through intense focusing turns the inscribed letters on the paper into audible sounds, Lucie's own voice, standing close to him, speaking from within. It is a sacred music, a spiritual melody, like the heavenly choir of angels that sings around the enthroned Godhead. But harsh reality returns: because of the absence of further letters,[172] he experiences the closing down over him of solitude. In this metaphor of verbal impregnation, used again on 14 February,[173] when he speaks of being impregnated by her face ("*à m'imprégner de ton visage*"),[174] the reference is to at least two places. The first is quite Christian, deriving from the liturgical hymns and iconography associated with the Annunciation, wherein the angel Gabriel, on behalf of God the Father, impregnates Mary with the fecundating word to make her conceive Jesus in her womb in a spiritualized sexual act manifested in the passage of the *Verbum* into her womb as light passes through a glass, and often spoken of in the ingenious metaphysical conceits of the Baroque Era of the seventeenth century. The other source for this witty language of fertilization and conception through words as letter combinations, sound constructs, and thought containers appears in kabbalistic texts, especially those associated with the Song of Songs (*Shir ha-Shirim*).[175] Whether the mixing and matching of Christian, Jewish, and secular love imagery should be credited to some mystifying hybridity, philosophical ambiguity, or deliberate personal conflations,[176] the point is that Alfred and Lucie create a language of love far different from anything else to be found amongst their contemporaries.[177]

---

171 Leo Strauss explains that "the purpose of repeated conventional statements is to hide the disclosure, in the repetition, of the unconventional views" (Strauss, *Persecution and the Art of Writing*, 64).

172 On absence in a text as the demand for filling in, for something to be created in and through the silence of its apparent inanity; see Ouaknin, *Le livre brûlé*, 112.

173 Ironically, as we read this, it is St. Valentine's Day, but it is unlikely that anyone in France would have recognized this more American and British celebration until a hundred years later when commercial exigencies started to make it popular in the hexagon and elsewhere on the Continent.

174 *Ecris-moi souvent, écris moi longuement*, 200.

175 Alfred Dreyfus may have read about the Song of Songs in the commentary by one of his favourite authors published in 1860: Ernest Renan, trans. and commented, *Le Cantique des Cantiques* (Paris: Arléa, 2004).

176 These issues are discussed in Sandrick Le Maguer, *Portrait d'Israël en jeune fille: genèse de Marie* (Paris: NRF/Gallimard/L'Infini, 2008).

177 Faur cites the midrashic study of The Song of Solomon, *Shir ha-Shirim Rabba* VIII.1(2) 39b:

And of this solitary confinement, always with the silence of guards who do not speak to him, he feels his heart bleed and his nerves shiver with pain.

> *Toutes les fibres de la sensibilité tressaillir, l'une après l'autre . . . souffrir enfin le long martyre du cœur . . . Voilà ce qu'il y a de vraiment épouvantable!*[178]
>
> All the fibres of my sensibility shiver, one after the other . . . to suffer finally the long martyrdom of the heart . . . Here it is, what is truly unbearable!

Most remarkable here is the way Dreyfus describes his psychological and emotional condition, something we shall see him do with ever greater insistence and detail in the letters from Devil's Island. The term *sensibilité* can, in a general way, be matched to the English term *sensibility*, with its gamut of meanings from a positive notion of being intelligent and filled with common sense to the more negative connotations shown in Jane Austen's novel *Sense and Sensibility*, wherein the term is contrasted to common sense and reasonable behaviour; *sensibilité* thus covers the same ground as sentimentality in all its superficial qualities. But at its core, the word also can have a more technical sense, that of the *sensorium*, the body's nervous system and its processes of emotive responses to inner and outer stimuli. Not by chance, I would say, one of the exemplary citations in the *Petit Robert* dictionary comes from the son of Dreyfus's former teacher of mathematics and chemistry at *lycée*, the novelist and psychologist Paul Bourget:[179] "*un je ne sais pas quoi de frémissements qui trahissait une sensibilité restée vive et neuve*" (an indefinable something of quivering or trembling which betrayed a sensibility still alive and new).

More specifically, in this part of his letter, Dreyfus is referring to his nervous system, with each of his nerves being tortured by the long or-

---

"Borrowing from Song of Songs (8:2) the rabbis referred to [the revelation of the Law at] Sinai as 'my mother's house' because, they explained 'it was there where Israel was gestated, as a newly born baby'" (*The Horizontal Society*, Section IV, Introductory Remarks).

178 *Ecris-moi souvent, écris moi longuement*, 185.

179 Fuller discussion of the relationship between Alfred Dreyfus and these two Bourgets, father and son, will appear in the next book in this series.

deal. In the nineteenth century, we should recall, what we assign to mental states, hormonal imbalances, and other conditions of emotional instability were considered due to overly excitable nervous constitutions or the draining away of nervous energy, as in enervation.[180] Another word that Alfred uses in self-diagnosis of this long-term condition being exacerbated by the moral tortures in prison is *éréthisme*, from the Greek word *erethismos* (irritation), which takes on the medical sense of a violent exaltation, excessive tension, sometimes, and a state of extreme excitability and irritability associated with the heart as well as with the mind. Here, then, on 4 November, 1897, almost speaking of himself in the third person, Alfred self-diagnoses the ætiology of his mental illness:

> *Mais la trop longue souffrance, une situation épouvantable, le climat qui à lui seul embrase le cerveau, si tout cela ne m'a jamais fait oublier aucun de mes devoirs, tout cela fini par me mettre dans un état d'éréthisme cérébral et nerveux qui est terrible.*[181]
>
> But the excessive suffering, a terrifying situation, the climate which by itself is enough to set my brain on fire, which all by itself never made me forget any of my duties, all that finished by putting me into a state of cerebral and nervous erethism which is terrible.

The treatment he recommends for himself is silence—but how ironic, when his whole life on Devil's Island is one of enforced, obligatory silence on the part of all the twelve to fifteen guards who watch him day and night. The silence he needs is more than the absence of disturbing noise, confusing and irritating: it is the peaceful, warm home life with Lucie and the children. Without their quiet conversations by the fireside, the prognosis is dire, if not fatal. On 24 November, 1897, he tells Lucie, again withdrawing into the self-objectifying third person, that "*le corps, le cerveau, le coeur, tout est épuisé*" (the body, the brain, the heart, all are exhausted), and what remains is his soul: "*L'âme est restée intangi-*

180 This old psychiatry is still around in many common expressions, such as "to have a lot of nerve" or "to lose one's nerve," even in "to be nervous" and "to be nervy."

181 *Ecris-moi souvent, écris moi longuement*, 389.

ble, toujours aussi ardente, la volonté inébranable, forte du droit de tout être humain à la justice et à la verite, pour lui, pour les siens"[182] (The soul has remained untouched, as ardent ever, the will unshakeable, strong in the right of all human beings to have justice and the truth, for himself, for his own [family]).[183]

Alongside these descriptions of his painful and excitable nerves, which Lucie knows Alfred has always suffered from, there is also the question of the processes of reading and interpreting the letters, the language itself taken as an index of their inner and outer states. Their writings—and in Alfred's case there are also *journaux*, *carnets*, and *cahiers* to be considered—may be examined as external brains, as we will do in the next chapter.

In the same letter of 31 January, 1895, considered above, Alfred apologizes for his style, which he describes as "*baroque and décousu*"[184] (baroque and disconnected). Another way to speak of this conceited, baroque, witty way of writing and reading texts is to think of it in Jewish terms, as part of the invisible-visible dialectic of confronting words on the page with questions that challenge their status as linear and logical communication, that force the words on the page to have a substance and a volume, a volume which, as soon as perceived, spills out of the passage like water bursting from a dam, in an inexhaustible outflowing

---

182 *Ecris-moi souvent, écris moi longuement*, 392.

183 Faur cites Josephus, *Contra Apion*, I.60: "The result, then, of our thorough grounding in the laws from the first dawn of intelligence is that we have them, as it were, engraved on our souls" (*The Horizontal Society*, Section IV, Introductory Remarks). Note that this polemical defense of Judaism was edited by Théodore Reinach, with a French translation by Léon Blum in 1930, both leading Dreyfusards during the affair. Expounding on Josephus's metaphor of engraving the law on the soul, Faur calls it "a kind of ontogenetic intuition, continuously activated by Tora[h] learning and practices." Although Dreyfus did not continuously study the holy books, the deep impressions of rabbinical thought and practice were part of his mental makeup. The ordeal of his nightmare triggered archaic patterns of feeling, thinking, and writing inculcated in the ways he learned to speak and think at home, whether or not he was actually taught by his father or a Hebrew teacher. Those archaic memory patterns become the *sod*, the secret of his soul, although the precise and substantive knowledge was at best confused and at worst missing. Through the hints and the cryptograms (*remez*), he was able, in the depths of his soul, where the darkest secrets were hidden, "to dig up stems and innovative (doctrines) and corollaries [from the root principles]," but to have understood the laws and how to apply them, he would have had proper rabbinical training. "To accomplish this [Dreyfus would have needed] in depth analysis and judicial theory (*sebara*)" so that he could not condense or expand, only touch them theoretically and draw archaic strength, enough to survive. Cf. *The Horizontal Society*, Section IV, Section 4. One can know the truth but not necessarily the whole truth and nothing but the truth.

184 *Ecris-moi souvent, écris moi longuement*, 185.

of creative energies.[185] This overly intricate and uncoordinated writing, so far as Alfred sees it at first, is only a product of his mental or moral tortures. The conditions of his imprisonment have upset all his normal skills and intellectual talents.

> *Je ne sais plus écrite, les mots ne me viennent plus, tant mon cerveau est délabré. Il n'y a plus un point fixe dans ma tête: l'espoir de connaître un jour la vérité, de voir mon innocence reconnue et proclamée. C'est ce que je balbutie nuit et jour, dans mes rêves comme dans mon réveil.*[186]
>
> I no longer know how to write, words no longer come to me, so much is my brain torn to shreds. There is no longer just one fixed point in my head: the hope to know the truth one day, to see my innocence recognized and proclaimed. That's what I stammer night and day, in my dreams as in my waking.

The more he writes about what is going on in his head, and the more he tries to answer Lucie's questions and challenges in the letters that manage to arrive in his prison cell, the more the very act of repeating his words over and over with minor variations generates friction that ignites the charge inherent in the thoughts, so that for a few moments, now and then, the light flashes out and he—and Lucie—glimpse the inner truth of a transcendent experience.

On 10 February, 1895, somewhat more controlled, Alfred writes that he is going through something beyond the talents of any novelist to describe. "*Jamais romancier, si riche que soit son imagination, n'aurait*

---

185 Ouaknin tells us, "*Dans la conception talmudique de l interprétation, le Texte est indéfini, ouvert à des interprétations toujours nouvelles . . . . celui-ci demeure inépuisable et ouvert parce que sa structure est celle du 'visible-invisible'*" (In the talmudic conception of interprétation, the Text is indefinite, open to interpretations [which are] always new . . . this [Text] remains inexhaustible and open because its structure is that of the 'visible-invisible') in *Le livre brûlé*, 246. Ouaknin here cites Umberto Eco, *L'Œuvre ouverte* (Paris: Seuil, 1965) and Gershom Scholem, *La kabbale et son symbolisme* (Paris: Payot, 1975). The visible text has meaning only when it is interpreted, that is, when the hidden or invisible meaning is made manifest in the explosive act of questioning its very strictures. Ouaknin puts it this way in italics to emphasize the centrality of the idea: "*L'interprétation n'est pas seulement perception, elle est constitution du sens*" (Interpretation is not only perception; it is the constitution of sense) in *Le livre brûlé*, 247.

186 *Ecris-moi souvent, écris moi longuement*, 185.

pu écrire une historie plus tragique"[187] (Never would a novelist, however rich his imagination might be, have written a more tragic history than mine), a statement showing that he realizes how awkward and difficult it is to transmit a valid picture of his condition with the inadequate language, even if there were literary precedents, at his disposal. But not only rhetoric and novelistic discourses fail to provide the terms he so longs to find; it is also a failure of the imagination, his as much as that of his mentors and models.[188]

Then, on the same day, and thus with no chance of her having seen his letter, Lucie responds in similar terms, manifesting her capacity to anticipate as well as echo his complaints and cries of anguish when she says that she cannot understand why her letters do not arrive regularly, the rigor of the censorship seeming excruciatingly severe since all she does is write her true feelings to her beloved husband, and then says, in a passage previously edited from the published letters, "*Je m'imagine aisément les souffrances que tu as dû endurer étant ainsi sans nouvelles.*"[189] She has used the same word *imagination*, and says that through her own imaginative faculties, she can see and feel his sufferings—that is, that for all his fears of inadequacy of style and rhetoric, she has understood. She has picked up the hints, followed the allusions, rearranged the confused and baroque utterances, and created a forceful picture in her mind. Neither of them engage in a systematic process; they are not metaphysical poets or specialists in the occult, and the disorderly writing and arrival of letters ensures that what we finally see[190] can only be understood in hindsight when our own minds can *midrash* the collection.[191]

---

187 *Ecris-moi souvent, écris moi longuement*, 198.

188 Inadequacy and failure are not, however, absolute, not sins staining the soul of the feeble man crying out in despair. Benmozegh points out that "For the Kabbalah, just as imperfection is always mixed with holiness, so truth is perpetually mixed with error. The one is the husk or outer covering, the other the inner reality, the quickening spirit" (*Israel and Humanity*, 96).

189 *Ecris-moi souvent, écris moi longuement*, 199.

190 Until there is a complete edition of all the letters of Alfred and Lucie Dreyfus, including those written before the affair, everything we say has to be tentative, as well as speculative.

191 Faur: "There is a huge difference between rational idealism and Tora[h]. One exposes the basis of perfect demonstration (*apodeixis*), the other proposes. Rational idealism demonstrates; Hebrew Scripture persuades. Greek 'knowledge'(*episteme*) closes the subject; Hebrew 'wisdom' (חכמה [Hochma]) inaugurates a dialogue . . ." *The Horizontal Society*, Section IV, 46. Dreyfus tries to be assimilated perfectly to Greek knowledge, both *technē* and *episteme*, but he finds it constructive and uncomfortable and reaches out towards חכמה, Lady Wisdom, and *Shekhina*, his wife Lucie.

PART 3: INTERNAL PAINS AND EXTERNAL BRAINS

> Persecution . . . gives rise to a peculiar technique of writing, and therewith to a peculiar type of literature, in which the truth about all crucial things is presented exclusively between the lines. That literature is addressed, not to all readers, but to trustworthy and intelligent readers only. It has all the advantages of private communication without having its greatest disadvantage—that it reaches only the writer's acquaintances. It has all the advantages of public communication without having its greatest disadvantage—capital punishment for the author.
>
> —Leo Strauss[192]

> Study itself was viewed as a mode of "visual meditation"—a technique known in medieval Christian mysticism as well—in which there is an imaginative recreation of the prophetic vision within the mystic's own consciousness.
>
> —Elliot R. Wolfson[193]

The close to 250 pages of selected letters included in *Ecris-moi souvent, écris-moi longuement* can be seen to reiterate many of the same themes, images, rhetorical ploys, and *cris du coeur* registered already in the letters of the opening section of Vincent Duclert's book. My focus here is on a few key epistles wherein Alfred engages in sustained descriptions and self-examination of his fragile mental state and then Lucie mirrors his language, encourages him to talk out his pains and humiliations, and implicitly and quietly leads him towards resignation, reconciliation, and relief from the most acute of his fears and anxieties.

On 27 April, 1895, Alfred writes to Lucie from Iles du Salut (neither of them ever uses the term Ile du Diable)[194] that she should never ask on his behalf for the government to show grace or pity ("*que tu ne demandes pour moi ni grâce ni pitié*") but only that they carry out their investigations to the uttermost ("*à outrance*").[195] For no matter how awful his

192 Leo Strauss, *Persecution and the Art of Writing* (Glencoe, IL: The Free Press, 1952), 26.

193 Wolfson, *Through a Speculum that Shines*, 331

194 *Ecris-moi souvent, écris moi longuement*, 228.

195 *Ecris-moi souvent, écris moi longuement*, 229.

conditions are, he will not beg from them anything other than truth and justice. This is a very Jewish position, and appears in Amos Oz's work wherein a character says to his son after escaping the Holocaust, "Weakness is a sin." Nevertheless, Alfred knows that his situation is bleak and that Lucie, reading his letters, with their complaints and shattering cries of pain, will misunderstand him as asking for immediate release, no matter the nature of the conditions imposed on such a pardon or grace. Whatever his physical or moral torments, he pleads with her that she should only protest "*mon innocence jusqu'à mon dernier souffle*"[196] (my innocence down to my last breath). That leads to another confession of faith, expressed in muted Jewish terms:

> *Mais s'il y a une justice en ce monde, il me semble impossible, ma raison se refuse à y croire, que nous ne retrouvions le bonheur qui n'aurait jamais dû nous être enlevé.*[197]
>
> But if there is a justice in this world, it seems to me impossible, my reason refuses to believe that we will not regain our happiness which should never have been taken away from us.

The justice he seeks is on earth, if it is real, will be manifested in real historical terms and times, and he cannot believe otherwise—his unstated but implicit Jewish confidence in the almighty power of the law will not let him—than that he and Lucie will be happy again, the crime committed against them being totally unjustified. And yet, for all this faith and confidence, Alfred tells Lucie he is all too aware that the letters he writes are frightening to her and may convey the wrong impression of his firmness of heart and soul.

> *Je t'écris certes parfois des lettres exaltées, sous l'empire d'impressions nerveuses extrêmes ou de dépression physique considérable; mais qui n'aurait pas de ces coups de folie, de ces révoltes du cœur et de l'âme, dans une situation aussi*

196 *Ecris-moi souvent écris moi longuement*, 229.
197 *Ecris-moi souvent, écris moi longuement*, 229.

> *tragique, aussi émouvante que la nôtre?*[198]
>
> Certainly I sometimes write you excited letters, under the domination of extreme nervous impressions or of considerable physical depression, but who would not suffer acts of madness or rebellions in the heart, in a situation as tragic and horrible as ours?

He is trying desperately to ask her to read between the lines, or more accurately, inside the lines, to see that for all his agony and anxiety, he is not insane, and that she has to work with him in investigating the source of the charges against him.[199] He wants to live to take part in the public restoration of his good name, and to do this he needs her help, her support, and her understanding. She cannot fall into the trap of thinking he has gone mad or dismissing his extreme statements as marks of folly or despair. He therefore again asks,

> *Et puis, toujours seul, en tête-à-tête avec moi-même, livré à mes tristes pensées, sans nouvelles de toi, des enfants, de tous ceux qui me sont chers depuis plus de deux mois, à qui confierais-je les souffrances de mon cœur, si ce n'est à toi, confidente de toutes mes pensées?*[200]
>
> And then, always alone, in conversation with myself, given over to my sad thoughts, without news of you, the children and all those who have been dear to me for more than two months, to whom can I entrust my heart's sufferings, if not to you, confidant of all my thoughts?

Alfred then moves to a realization, implicit earlier, as we have seen, that it is not he alone who suffers or Lucie who suffers in her own way because of his condition, but that they suffer together, within one an-

---

198 *Ecris-moi souvent, écris moi longuement*, 229.

199 Strauss, *Persecution and the Art of Writing*, 26. "Another axiom: 'a careful writer of normal intelligence is more intelligent than the most intelligent censor. For the burden of proof rests with the censor.'"

200 *Ecris-moi souvent, écris moi longuement*, 229.

other, a metaphysical and psychical process expressed in his concern for the future of their two children:[201]

> *Je souffre non seulement pour moi, mais bien plus encore pour toi, pour nos chers enfants. C'est en ces derniers, ma chérie, qui tu dois puiser cette force morale, cette énergie surhumaine qui te sont nécessaire pour aboutir à tout prix à ce que notre honneur apparaisse de nouveau, à tous sans exception, ce qu'il a toujours été, pur et sans tache.*[202]
>
> I suffer not only for myself, but indeed much more for you, for our dear children. It is from them that you, my darling, must draw out the moral force, the superhuman energy that you must have to bring this about at any price that are indispensable to you, so that at all costs our honor will be visible again, to everyone with exception, as it has always been, pure and unsullied.

The designations of moral strength and superhuman energy can, of course, be registered simply as exaggerated rhetoric to impress on Lucie the urgency of the situation.[203] In context, in the pattern of allusions this study is uncovering, the expressions also describe a more kabbalistic power that derives from the performance of the mitzvot. Suffering is not the passive phenomenon it is in Christian mysticism, where it prepares the faithful soul for the reception of a heavenly grace, either after

---

201 Compare this mode of indirection and deference of communications with what Strauss sees in Maimonides's *Guide of the Perplexed*. There, Rambam calls his book both a treatise (*ma'amar*) and also something spoken in conversation, part of fleeting, passing speech. "If the *Guide* is, in a sense, not a book at all, if it is merely a substitute for conversations or speeches, then it cannot be read in the way we may read, for instance, Ibn Sina's *Al-Shifâ*, or Thomas Aquinas's *Summa Theologica*" (Strauss, *Persecution and the Art of Writing*, 47, 48). How then is the *Guide* written, and how do we read it? In the same way, I suggest, as we do the letters of Alfred and Lucie Dreyfus. "The *Guide* is written in the form of letters addressed to a friend and favorite pupil, Joseph. By addressing his book to one man, Maimonides made sure that he did not transgress the prohibition against explaining *ma'aseh merkebah* [esoteric discussions on the description of the Heavenly Chariot in Ezekiel] to more than one man. [He mentions too that] Joseph possessed all the qualities required of a student of the secret lore and explains the necessity of written communication by his pupil's departure . . . [and] Joseph's departure . . . was the consequence of his being a Jew in the Diaspora . . . . Only the necessity of saving the law can have caused him to break the law" (49).

202 *Ecris-moi souvent, écris moi longuement*, 229.

203 Strauss, *Persecution and the Art of Writing*, 26.

life or perhaps within it. In rabbinical thought, suffering is an active process of struggling to attain justice, to fulfil the commandments of the law. By drawing on the innocence of their son and daughter, Alfred says, Lucie can carry out the tasks Alfred is unable to do, and her actions will further energize the husband to endure his tortures and survive until the mission is accomplished: the charges dismissed, the verdict overturned, and the sullied family name returned to its former glory

By late April and early May 1895, Lucie writes a series of letters that she holds back until she can send them all at once, thus creating, as Duclert suggests, a virtual diary or journal of her own. In these letters, amongst other matters, she tells of the birthday of her father, David Hadamard, a happy occasion marred by sad thoughts and worries about Alfred, indeed of a collective grieving. Again, rather than an actual narrative or list of events that occur from day to day, Lucie's letters speak in more general terms of feelings and aspirations, sadness and frustrations. On 4 May, 1895, for example, she writes:

> *La bizarrerie de l'existence fait que le corps vit indifféremment de toutes les souffrances morales, c'est une sorte de machine qui [sait]*[204] *de routine et accomplit machinalement les exigences de la vie.*[205]
>
> The bizarre nature of existence makes the body live regardless of all moral or psychical sufferings; it is a sort of machine that knows the routine and performs all the exigencies of life mechanically.

Those details of act, emotion and situation that constitute the normal content of a diary or a personal letter are not dealt with because, for her, life is a mechanical process wherein actions seem almost to perform themselves, normal feelings are numbed or felt at a level of virtual unconsciousness, and people, places, and events simply pass unnoticed. Like Alfred, she finds more reality in the writing and reading of letters than in the physical existence of things and persons around her. While

---

204 The suggested missing word is from Duclert. The whole letter is printed here for the first time. *Ecris-moi souvent, écris moi longuement*, 231.

205 *Ecris-moi souvent, écris moi longuement*, 231.

this is not strictly true, the statement does describe one whole aspect of her life. The reality is more complex: on the one hand, because she is well attuned to the needs of her children and her parents' home, where she has now moved and, on the other, because in a substantial part of her daily life she is devoted to Alfred's release and working diligently with his brother Mathieu and others to lobby the government and to supervise detectives hired to investigate what the police or other agents refuse to look into. If read sequentially as a record of cause and effect or logically as a rational argument, her letters collapse under the weight of contradiction and *non sequitur*.[206] They need to be perceived in the way of Talmudic midrashing, where events are replaced by figurative, encoded anecdotes (*aggadot*), chronological sequencing of time by intertextual associations,[207] and coherence of expression by suspensions and fragmentation that come together only occasionally in the text itself but much more often in the minds of the students learning.[208]

---

206 On the use of contradictions and *non sequiturs*, Strauss says, "To speak of the same subject in a contradictory means on pages far apart from each other; to make one of the two contradictory statements in passing . . . incidental . . . not directly to contradict but to deny the first statement's implications, to seem to repeat the first statement but to add or omit an apparently negligible expression . . . to be introduced between the two contradictory statements an intermediary assertion which, by itself not contradictory to the first statement, becomes a contradictory to it by the addition, or the omission, of an apparently negligible expression; the contradictory statement creeps in as a repetition of the intermediary statement" (Strauss, *Persecution and the Art of Writing*, 70, 71). But at the same time, we should recall what Wolfson points out, "We must be aware of the fact that any given culture fosters divergent views that are not always logicially consistent. Indeed, different impulses can be operative within a culture at the same time without necessitating a resolution that adopts one alternative to the exclusion of the others" (*Through a Speculum that Shines*, 27).

207 Following his rabbinical authorities, Ouaknin argues that at a certain point in reading "*histoire et interprétation sont deux termed inseparable l'un de l'autre*" (history and interpretation are two terms that cannot be separated) in *Le livre brûlé*, 258. Time being in man and man being in time, history cannot be measured only by one, making the individual dependent upon the chronological passage of years and centuries flowing forward from the past through the present into the future; instead, by acts of interpretation—midrashing of memory, experience and action—time reveals its meanings in regard to eternity and infinity. The Jew can reach back into the past and draw forth strength and courage, as well as the honor and loyalty won by good deeds of ancestors, just as each small mitzvah, even when performed only through intention when the circumstances do not permit otherwise, still adds to the patrimony (*zekhut*) to be passed on to future generations. In this sense, time is reversible and can transform the outcome of actions and decisions taken.

208 "But how does he proceed," asks Strauss following Rambam's argument in the *Guide of the Perplexed*, "if the pupil fails to understand the hint? He will simply stop. This does not mean that he will stop talking. On the contrary, since by suddenly becoming silent he would perplex the pupil without being of any help to him, he will continue talking by giving the first, rather revealing sentence a more conventional meaning and thus gradually lead him back to the safe region of accepted views" (Strauss, *Persecution and the Art of Writing*, 53).

At that point, Lucie turns from her concern for the relationship between herself and her husband as though they reached an impasse, and so to avoid provoking an epistemological crisis that might harm the two of them or open their conversation to abuse by the scrutinizing censors who read and assess all their communications, she begins to speak of their innocent children.[209] Such maternal concerns and the recording of infantile prattle are, as we have already remarked, hints of something beyond, which at the moment Lucie dares not express openly, both because she fears the reaction by the military censors and because she intuits the need to tread very slowly and softly on issues that would upset her husband.[210]

On 8 May, 1895, Alfred writes one of the letters which contain his lament for the physical distance between them, but also his realization that, thanks to the sacred mission they have each undertaken to accomplish, "*nous nous réfugerions dans notre affection mutuelle, dans notre amour grandi par des événements aussi tragiques*"[211] (we would take refuge in our mutual affection, in our love enlarged by such tragic events). On 11 May, Lucie writes—one can hardly say responds, since letters cross and arrive out of sequence—"*Tu sais que mes pensées sont les tiennes et que nos souffrances sont communes*"[212] (You know that my thoughts are yours and that our sufferings are common)—that is, that she occupies the same textual space Alfred does, a locus of refuge created by love and an area of understanding that needs only the barest of hints to spark off understanding in the other. "I spend hours in reading and re-reading your fine letters," writes Lucie on 7 June, 1895;[213] "they are my consolation, waiting until I will have the joy of seeing you return." Then she adds, showing her part in the exchange: "I will tell you what I think, that which I cannot stop writing to you: I have hope, a great deal of hope. I have the conviction that all will come out well,

209 "But a good writer will never submit to the ordeal of indulging in insignificant talk. Consequently, after having given a hint which refers to a certain chapter of the secret teaching, he will write some sentences which at first glance seem to be conventional but which on closer examination prove to contain a new hint, referring to another chapter of the secret teaching" (Strauss, *Persecution and the Art of Writing*, 54).

210 A saying by Ibn Ezra: "He who understands should be silent" (cited by Leo *Persecution and the Art of Writing*, 184).

211 *Ecris-moi souvent, écris moi longuement*. 232.

212 *Ecris-moi souvent, écris moi longuement*. 235.

213 *Ecris-moi souvent, écris moi longuement*. 243.

that your rehabilitation will be a brilliant explosion of light and life will preserve you again in goodness."[214]

The allusion to the explosive, lightning flashes that characterize kabbalistic reading services here are by now familiar to their letters, as much so as the highly intimate, perhaps repressed innuendos in their description of their way of transmogrifying the reading itself into a sexual encounter:[215] "*Il me semble,*" Lucie writes on 8 July, 1895, "*que je t'entendais parler, que ta voix chérie résonnait à mes oreilles; il me parvenait enfin quelque chose de toi, tes pensées si nobles et si belles venaient se refléter dans mon esprit*"[216] (It seems to me that I hear you speak, that your beloved voice resonates in my ears; there enters into me finally something of yourself, your noble and beautiful thoughts come to be reflected in my soul).[217] Surely, behind her passionate language there are these familiar verses from the Song of Songs, *Le Cantique des Cantiques*:

---

214 "*Je passé des heures à lire et relire tes bonnes lettres: elles sont ma consolation, en attendant que j'aie le bonheur de venir te retrouver. Je te dirai ce que je pense, ce que je ne cesse de t'écrire: j'ai de l'espoir, beaucoup d'espoir. J'ai la conviction que tout ira bien, que ta réhabilitation sera éclatante et que la vie te réserve encore du bonheur* [. . .]"

215 Marc-Alain Ouaknin writes: "*Eclatement d'un espace littéraire: le texte ne sera plus abordé dans sa linearité, mais dans sa spatialité, son volume. Ou peut-être doit-on dire que l'éclatement du texte est ce qui va permettre le passage du Texte-ligne au texte-volume*" (An explosion of literary space: the text will no longer be approached in its linearity but in the spatiality of its volume. Or perhaps on ought to say that the explosion of the text is what permits the passage from linear Text to volume-text) in *Le livre brûlé: Philosophie du Talmud* (Paris: Leiu Commun/Sagesse, 1993), 103.

216 *Ecris-moi souvent, écris moi longuement*, 248.

217 Gabriel Tarde describes the fullness of conversation as a speech act and social event and consequently as a civilizing phenomenon: "*Les interlocuteurs agissent les uns sur les autres, de très près, par le timbre de voix, le regard, la physionomie, les passes magnétique des gestes, et non pas selulement par le langage*" (The interlocutors would act on one another, [standing] very close to each other, by the timbre of their voices, the look [they give one another], the physiognomy, the magnetic passes of their gestures, and not only by the [spoken words of their] language) *L'opinion et la foule*, 88. Although he mentions some of the facets of conversation lost in a telephonic version, as Proust does in greater detail (perhaps referring to this section of Tarde), the attempt of novelists (rather than dramatists and actors on the stage) to reproduce the fullness of the occasion become acute in the development of fiction in the nineteenth century when rhetoric *per se* is suppressed in such writing. For Lucie and Alfred, the process of inscribing their letters surpasses both the efforts of orators, playwrights, novelists and others because this couple is compelled to create in letters subject to excruciating censorship across vast distances of geographical and epistemological space and in a time-scheme that lacks order, coherence or control by themselves. Note too in Tarde's expression about magnetic passes in the gestures of the speakers in a conversation, that he thinks they hypnotize each other and themselves, forming imitative shape and boundaries to their communication. In a sense, too, Alfred and Lucie also create a magnetic relationship of this kind in their letters, and when they tell each other they read and reread these epistles in the silent, lonely days and nights, they recognize part of the phenomenon.

> *C'est la voix de mon bien-aimé!*
> *Le voici, il vient,*
> *Sautant sur les montagnes,*
> *Bondissant sur les collines,*
> *Mon bien-aimé est semblable à la gazelle . . . .*
> *Mon bien-aimé est à moi, et je suis à lui . . . .*
> (CC 1:8, 9, 16)

These lines not only resonate through liturgies of both Jewish and Catholic worship but echo through secular courtly love songs long afterwards, brought closer to general knowledge in the nineteenth century through a host of biblical plays, music performances, and pseudo-medieval histories. The figurative language of resonance of sound and projection of light, psychic entry of one soul into another and transformation of the spirit, all this also plays its part in the metaphysical discourses that Alfred and Lucie seem to recreate for each other, almost without being aware of it, inadvertently. Another metaphor used by Lucie is that of resonating in harmony with one another, as in her letter of 9 December, 1895:

> *Lorsque je lis ces lignes toutes pleines de volonté et d'énergie, je sens que mon être tout entière vibre avec toi, ton activité morale entretint mes forces et il me semble qu'elles sont doubles par la puissance de ta volonté.*[218]
>
> When I read these lines full of will and energy, I feel that my entire being vibrates with you, your psychic activity supports and repairs my strength and it seems to me that it is doubled by the power of your will.

Although there might be echoes here of Nietzsche's and other nineteenth-century philosophers' theories of the will to power and the force of destiny, the imagery in Lucie's and Alfred's letters vibrates rather within a zone of allusions derived from kabbalistic writings and seventeenth-century erotic poetry. However, this language has much more

218 *Ecris-moi souvent, écris moi longuement*, 267.

than a rhetorical wit to it: it is their only way of expressing the violent passions within them. Unlike even the most subtle or naturalistic descriptions of conjugal desires in the novels of the period, the letters of Lucie and Alfred break out of all conventional bonds of propriety. More than that, Lucie's images and concepts come close to the secret heart of Kabbalah as expounded by Wolfson.[219]

Just before the last letter discussed above, Lucie writes on 28 November, 1895, that the letters she puts in the mail to be transported across the sea are "*lignes inanimées et froides*" (inanimate and cold) and it is a "*déchirement*" (a rending to pieces) to send them out,[220] as though someone had ripped a foetus from her womb. How can he respond to the tenderness and affection of her feelings when the words once inscribed and sent into the world are like a horrible abortion?[221] Each epistle is consequently like a still birth: "*Le sentiment est trop violent pour que je puisse le décrire*" (The passion is too strong for me to describe).[222]

Before he ever receives such a letter, Alfred is still writing on 27 December, 1895, that he is in anguish over the failure of mail to arrive. Yet in another sense, they have already established such a powerful bond between them through the writing of letters that each can intuit what the other would write or has written on pages that are lost in the

219 Wolfson: " . . . according to kabbalistic phallocentrism, the feminine is ontologically localized in the male organ. Thus, the engendering mythic structure of kabbalistic symbolism may be referred to as the androgynous phallus. The unification of masculine and feminine symbolically signifies the ontological reintegration of the female to the male. Representations of the *Shekhina* as an autonomous feminine persona are characteristic of the state of exile and fragmentation. Even the image of the *Shekhina* as a bride adorned for her wedding is a transition between exile and redemption. The latter is fully represented when the bride enters the nuptial chamber and is transformed therein into the crown of the bridegroom. This transformation represents the final restoration of the female to the male, for the bride becomes the corona of the penis" (*Through a Speculum that Shines*, 275, n. 14).

220 *Ecris-moi souvent, écris moi longuement*, 266.

221 André Maurois: "In a child's mind words are not well defined; they designate zones of emotion more or less extensive and not clearly bounded; in this respect many adults remain children all their lives" (*Call No Man Happy*, 15).

222 Wolfson cites Elijah Solomon Zalman, the Gaon of Vilna: " 'It is known that all union is dependent on sight, as it is written, '[When the {rain}bow is in the cloud] I will see it and remember the everlasting covenant . . . .[the sign of the] covenant that I have established' (Gen. 9:16–17) It is known that the establishment of a covenant (*haqamat berit*) is in [sexual] copulation.'" Then Wolfson says in his own voice: "The biblical idiom *haqamat ha-berit* is here understood as signifying the erection of the penis that is necessary for sexual intercourse, and that is dependent on the vision of the bow in the cloud: the union of the masculine in the feminine. In the phenomenal plane of kabbalistic ritual and myth, eros and vision are harnessed in an inseparable bond" (Wolfson, *Through a Speculum that Shines*, 286–287).

dark and empty space between them.

> *Nos pensées sont communs, nos cœurs ont toujours battu à l'unisson, nos âmes vibrent aujourd'hui ensemble et veulent leur honneur avec l'ardeur brulante d'êtres honnêtes frappés dans ce qu'ils ont plus précieux.*[223]
>
> Our thoughts are common, our hearts are always beating in unison, our souls vibrate today together and wish for their honor with the burning ardor of truthful creatures beaten down in what they hold most precious.

Again on 31 December, 1895, as the New Year comes in, Alfred moans that he can only live with and because of Lucie; everything in himself is dependent upon her. Out of the depths of the tomb, of the excruciating silence of his cell, *de profundis*:

> *J'exhale des cris de douleur, cris de souffrance, de quelques noms qu'ils se nomment, le cœur est toujours vaillant s'il ne sait pas toujours se taire.*[224]
>
> I breathe out cries of grief, cries of suffering, of several names which it names, my heart is always valiant if it does not always know how to keep its silence.

The plea is not towards God the Unnamed and Unnamable, but to the three names always in his heart and on his lips—Lucie, Pierre, and Jeanne. It is this most blasphemous of religions that keeps Alfred alive, much more so than his cult of reason and truth, his belief in justice and in France.[225]

By 26 March, 1896, the conditions under which Alfred lives on Devil's Island have become worse than ever. The more efforts are made in

---

223 *Ecris-moi souvent, écris-moi longuement*, 269–270.

224 *Ecris-moi souvent, écris moi longuement*, 272.

225 Eleazar of Worms: "The Creator has no body, physical stature, image of form at all . . . . The glory is an appearance of the resplendent light which is called *Shekhina,* and the will of the Creator shows and images that very light to the prophets, according to the hour, to this one as that [form] and to the other as that . . . . The appearance of His splendor, which is His glory, is like a consuming fire, and is called *Shekhina*" (cited in Wolfson, *Through a Speculum that Shines*, 214).

Paris to call for a revision of the trial he had undergone two years earlier, the more the authorities in Cayenne are told to make life so uncomfortable for the single and singular prisoner on Ile du Diable that he will do something desperate. If he dies, the instructions go, his body should quickly be disposed of at sea for the sharks to take care of, rather than risk a returning a martyr's corpse to France. Yet Alfred tries to keep the information of his condition from Lucie, and the letters continue to manifest a timeless and placeless existence of separations, loneliness, hope, and encouragement. Thus, he writes with exquisite understatement and painful irony:

> *Je suis un peu comme le malade sur son lit de torture qui souffre le martyre, qui vit parce que son devoir l'y oblige et qui demande toujours à son médecin: "Quand finiront mes tortures?"*[226]

> I am a little like the sick man on his bed of torture who suffers martyrdom, who lives because his duty obligates him to and who always asks his doctor: "When will my tortures come to an end?"

The new regimen means that Alfred is shackled to his bed every night, his view of the sea blocked by a palisade built around his tiny hut, the fresh air cut off as well as the light, and the number of guards observing but never speaking to him round the clock increased. Letters are withheld more often, and the arrival of books and magazines is continuously delayed. Yet could Lucie read past the effort to make her think his language merely exaggerates his daily life in prison? It would only take reading past the insignificant phrase "*un peu comme la malade*" to grasp the reality. He has always suggested strongly that his tortures were physical as well as "*morales*" and that "*cet infernal supplice*"[227] (this infernal agony) has two objective essences: the pressure on his delicate and excitable nervous system and the threat to his very physical existence. But can she believe that *supplice* and *torture* are not figurative constructs and are actual cruel and excessive punishments, acts of sadistic

226 *Ecris-moi souvent, écris moi longuement*, 294.
227 *Ecris-moi souvent, écris moi longuement*, 298.

violence? The "*abominable cauchemar dans lequel nous vivons*"[228] (this horrible nightmare we live in) must be the literal reality in which they find themselves. The phantasmagoria does not blow away when the wind dissipates the clouds of smoke and the magic lantern is switched off.

> *Je viens jeter dans mes lettres les cris d'angoisse et d'impatience de mon âme, et j'en souffre ensuite tout un long mois, en pensant à l'émotion que tu vas avoir, et j'en suis plus malheureux encore,*
>
> I have thrown my cries of anguish and the impatience of my soul into my letters, and I have suffered from that for a whole month in thinking of the emotion which you will have, and I am even more unhappy.

For he knows that his missives are not neutral reports or merely rhetorical *cris du coeur*; they are part of himself, and part of the agony that crosses the sea and becomes part of Lucie, and when they enter into her soul they are doubled, not diminished. On those increasingly infrequent times when her letters do arrive and he can read her words, drawing their content—and the physical embodiment of her longing and suffering—into himself, it is only partly a consolation and a relief to him. He feels like a madman full of grief, and his head blows up, ready to explode and unable to understand anything, like the man with the exploding head in Georges Méliès's film: "*Je suis comme fou de chagrin, ma tête gonflée ne comprend plus.*"[229]

However, in what seems like a less stressful day, 3 September, 1896, when he can write one his longest letters to Lucie, he hints at how she should interpret his words, using directions that seem as though they were lifted directly from Maimonides's council to his pupil in *The Guide of the Perplexed*:

> *Tu pardonneras le décousu de cette lettre; je t'écris, comme je te le disais, sous le coup d'une émotion profonde, ne cherchant même pas à rassembler mes idées, m'en sentant même*

228 *Ecris-moi souvent, écris moi longuement*, 302.
229 *Ecris-moi souvent, écris moi longuement*, 304.

> *incapable, me disant avec effroi que je vais passer tout un mois n'ayant comme lecture que tes pauvres lignes, si courtes, où me parles des enfants, où je n'aurai rien enfin à lire de toi; cependant, je vais tout de même essayer de résumer.*[230]
>
> You must pardon the disconnected nature of this letter; I write to you, as though I were speaking to you, under the pressure of a profound emotion, not seeking to collect my ideas, feeling myself incapable, speaking to myself afraid that I am going to pass a whole month with nothing to read other than these poor lines, so short, where the children speak to me, where I will have nothing finally to read from you; however, I am going to try all the same to sum up.

It seems at first as though he were speaking only about his own difficulty in writing a coherent letter to Lucie and cautioning her not to try to make sense out of what is only an outburst of emotion. However, the more carefully we examine the words, the more it emerges that he is also talking about how all letters should be read, and using negative and fragmentary hints—as the Rambam advised—he outlines a more subtle method of analysis, a midrashic exercise. The difference between written and spoken discourse is elided. The words that come out under the pressure of intense emotional stress do not just mirror the disconnected and illogical words that flow out. They also embody the deepest, most secret passions of their soul, the tortuous conditions of both their lives having sensitized each to a degree of intuitive comprehension never before experienced in their marriage. It will indeed be necessary to collect his apparently random and scattered thought to make sense of what he—and she—are trying to say to one another. But the secret meaning is not a veiled allegorical discourse that needs to be decoded and spread out in the sunlight. Instead, it is the very supernal superverbal love and loyalty of their relationship that needs to be manifested mutually in their souls, a kind of affection and trust that lies outside all confines of bourgeois domesticity or romantic love in literary tradition.

230 *Ecris-moi souvent, écris moi longuement*, 313.

It is something akin to the mystical intention and cleaving of Kabbalah, yet outside the norms of those mystical exercises as well, because it is part of an attempt to rectify the world of French justice and truth. The closest analogue is the letters of the children, innocent of the intentions of their parents and transcribed for ostensible reasons other than being part of the mutually longed-for paternal sensuous embrace. When Lucie pens the letters from Pierre and Jeanne, adjusting their childish words to the written mode, she seems to disappear from the letters she writes to Alfred. Yet it is this selfless withdrawal from the handwritten pages of her epistles that mimics the *tsimtsum*, the contraction of the Godhead into His own mysterious and ineffable otherness (*En-Sof*), that leaves a created and creating space (*makom)* for the *Shekhina* to take shape, to enter into this world (*ha-olam hazeh*), and to dwell with Israel in exile and accompany the children of Israel on their long exodus from the lands of darkness, idolatry, and superstition—indeed, to be with and in Israel, each and every individual.

Did or could Alfred and Lucie Dreyfus know enough to be aware of what their letters are saying in the interpretations we have shown, or are our midrashings too far-fetched to be sustained by the documentary facts in the historical record? I think that Alfred goes in and out of such an awareness, as does Lucie, and only under pressure, when their epistles seem to give them each mutual reassurance strong enough to maintain the illusions they wish so intently to maintain, do they believe—and know—what they are saying. There is no explicit proof that either of them actually did read, hear lectures or sermons on, or think about rabbinical and kabbalistic ways of thought, but had they been so inclined, as we know from studies of what Marcel Proust was reading at about the same time, the information was available in French translations of classical Jewish volumes and in articles being published in reviews of the Jewish Consistory.

Furthermore, with his fluency in German and his connections in German-speaking lands, Alfred could have gone further in his readings, as well as attended lectures and seminars on his travels into Alsace and Switzerland. Nevertheless, the proof is in the pudding, and when one or the other of the couple—or both together—creates little disquisitions and poetic conceits or *midrashim* that conform more or less to rabbinical precedent, then our own readings require us to make explicit what is implicit in their texts.

These impressions and illusions she wishes she could actualise are fully Jewish in their import, without, however, necessitating either Alfred or Lucie to know or say that they are. On 5 March, 1897, the wife tells her husband,

> *Quand je t'écris, au moins, j'ai quelques instants d'illusion, la plume, l'imagination, la tension de la volonté me transportèrent près de toi, là, tout près, comme je voudrais être, te soutenant, te consolant, te rassurant sur l'avenir, et t'apportant tout l'espoir que mon cœur contient renfermé et que je voudrais tant te communiquer.*[231]
>
> When I write to you, at least, I have several instants of illusion, the pen, the imagination, the tension of my will would carry me close to you, there, so close, just where I would like to be, supporting you, consoling you, reassuring you of the future, and carrying to you all the hope that is wrapped up in my heart and that I would so much want to communicate to you.

Yet the terms of this metaphysical conceit that both letter writers try to generate by force of will cannot be equated with kabbalistic ecstasy. The momentary instants of feeling that make them believe they have transcended the vast ocean between them or crossed over into a realm of experience already at peace and governed by justice and truth cannot be sustained, only hoped for—sometimes to the point of hallucination. In the supplement to the letter of 12 September, 1896, discussed earlier in this chapter, Alfred remarks,

> *On dit que la douleur était la grande éducatrice du cœur humain; eh bien, c'est faux, archi-faux; le malheur, autant on ne l'a pas mérité, révolte, rend mauvais, injuste.*[232]
>
> They say that pain was the great teacher of the human heart; oh well, that is false, hugely false, unhappiness

231 *Ecris-moi souvent, écris moi longuement*, 353.
232 *Ecris-moi souvent, écris moi longuement*, 316.

rather that is unmerited, rebellion, makes one evil and unjust.

Cynically put, Dreyfus rejects the Christian idea that suffering is salutary, that it teaches the soul to be wise and forbearing, and that it prepares the believer to receive the grace of God. Not at all, he says: unhappiness arises from the experience of injustice in the world, the signs of rebellion against truth and honour, and one feels only bitterness and anger as a consequence. But once he spits this out, he tells Lucie that although he may be crushed under the weight of physical tortures and stretched to the limits of his sanity by the pressures of his rage, he, with her help, must ceaselessly labour to find the truth, to expose the perpetrators of the criminal acts against him, and to achieve their goal of a new trial and thus acquittal and rehabilitation. He reiterates, "*Qu'il faut redevirir ce que nous étions, ce que nous sommes, des êtres humains, qui souffrent horriblement, atrocement, victims de la plus effroyable machination qu'on puisse rêver*"[233] (We must become again what we were, what we are, human beings, who suffer horribly, atrociously, victims of the most frightful machinations one could ever dream of).

In Jewish tradition, the victim of injustice must never give in, but struggle on in heart and soul, by reason and through faith, waiting for but not dependent upon a divine sign, and the goal is to become fully and truly human, a *mensch*, a willing partner in the covenant of the law. Dreyfus acts and thinks and feels not on his own behalf in some private inner relationship with an absent God, but through and with the support of his wife and on behalf of their children.[234] Thus this supplement

233 *Ecris-moi souvent, écris moi longuement*, 316.

234 A brief letter from Jeanne on 10 October 1896 permits us to see what Lucie is teaching the children in Alfred's absence, and we must assume that she would not instruct them in any beliefs contrary to his own or what they have already decided should be taught to the little ones: "*Papa chéri,/ Je voudrais que tu reviennes bientôt, il faut que tu le demandes au bon Dieu, moi je lui demande tous les jours./Je t'embrasse beaucoup beaucoup./Ta petite Jeanne*" (Dear Papa, I wish that you come back soon, you must ask the good God, I ask him everyday. I kiss you lots and lots. Your little Jeanne" (*Ecris-moi souvent, écris moi longuement*, 324). Similarly on 25 December 1896, Pierrot writes to his Dear Papa that he often writes "*au bon Dieu*" for the return of his father (*Ecris-moi souvent, écris moi longuement*, 332). Both children, it would seem, have been taught their prayers and a belief in God, as well as Bible stories; what these prayers, beliefs and stories consisted of, however, remains lost in the mists of time. Remember that Lucie transcribes the letters on behalf of the children and probably coaches them in what to say as well. She uses a Catholic expression, "*le bon Dieu,*" a formulaic not to be found in Protestant cultures, and perhaps here, a little like Proust's mother, she felt closer to the majority French culture than the minority Christians. It

to this epistle concludes with a statement of faith suppressed in previous editions of the letters:

> *Nous devrons avoir cette foi qui nous fait accepter les plus dures situations, pour arriver à rendre à nos enfants un nom sans taches, un nom respecté.*
> *Oui chère Lucie, cette foi, il faut que tu l'aies, il faut que vous l'ayez tous; elle doit planer au-dessus de toutes les souffrances, de toutes les douleurs humaines.*[235]

> We must have this faith, so that we can accept the most difficult situations, in order to be able to render to our children a name without stains, a respected name.
> Yes, dear Lucie, this faith, you must have it, all of you must have it, it must soar above all sufferings, all human pains.

This is an intellectual faith, not a vague spirituality; it is a commitment of the heart in all knowledge of its implications and consequences. This time, Alfred calls on not only Lucie to pledge herself to the duty they have before them but to all the others in their two families. The clearing of his name of all infamy includes all of them, all generations, backwards and forwards in time, for it is not an individual matter; it belongs to the family, and to all of Israel. More than that, to see that Alfred has the proper titles, rank, and honour restored to his name is also to ensure that the dignity and reputation of the God of Israel in the world is restored.

This comes close to being, but always remains just below the surface of his text, and there is no doubt also of his consciousness, an admission that the key causal factor in his horrible nightmare is anti-Semitism. Yet despite such a "*long examen de conscience*," as he calls it, the long dark night of suffering ("*cette nuit atroce que je viens de passer*") continues to pass into a day that merely precedes the next. This meditation ("*réflexion*") that comes from his hallucinating brain ("*mon cerveau halluciné*")

---

may seem to her a more endearing and personal term to speak of a Jewish deity who in Yiddish can be called *Gottenyu*, my dear little God.

235 *Ecris-moi souvent, écris moi longuement*, 316–317.

continues his dreadful nightmare ("*ce lugubre cauchemar*").[236] But to what end these meditations, he does not know, and he cannot understand himself when Lucie is there in his dreams or in her letters to help him out.[237] Only in her letters does he find a calm moment and place. Yet "*je comprenais, sous le calme apparent de vos lettres, quelle douleur atroce se cachait*" (I understand under the apparent calm of all your letters what an unbearable pain was hiding). [238]

There are moments like this when Alfred feels despondent because he does not believe the family back home appreciates fully what he is going through on Devil's Island. Because Lucie cannot report on the progress of efforts for a revision of the trial or the extent to which new evidence has been piling up of the perfidy of the officers and court officials, as well as politicians, in their collusion against him from the very beginning of the case, he doubts sufficient measures have been taken on his behalf. He also finds that Lucie's letters seem to miss out on the directions he has given her or that she has misread the feelings he has expressed. It is sometimes as though someone were to wake up in the night and find himself blind and deaf, unable to know what has happened to him, unaware that anyone is trying to help, frightened that the world has disappeared into a vast, impenetrable, and silent darkness.

> *Je relisais aussi, comme chaque mois, les lettres que j'ai de toi, les compagnons de ma profonde solitude, les lettres de tous, et je crois que tu n'a pas saisi entièrement ma pensée, un peu confuse forcément dans les nombreuses lettres que je t'ai écrites.*[239]
>
> I was also rereading, as I do every month, the letters I have had from you, the companions of my profound solitude, the letters from all of you, and I believe that you have not fully grasped my thought, inevitably a little confused in the numerous letters I have written to you.

He wants to excuse her, take some of the blame on himself for not

236 *Ecris-moi souvent, écris moi longuement*, 317.
237 *Ecris-moi souvent, écris moi longuement*, 318.
238 *Ecris-moi souvent, écris moi longuement*, 319.
239 *Ecris-moi souvent, écris moi longuement*, 329.

writing clearly enough and for having written too much in a confused and disorderly way. He doesn't want to blame her, become angry with her, and risk alienating his own and only support throughout the whole ordeal. So when he speaks to her about avoiding rancor or bitterness against any individuals who might be behind the crimes against him—that is, to maintain a dignified and calm posture in all her dealings with the outside world, especially the persons responsible for seeing his appeals through to their justifiable conclusion, he is also speaking to himself, to quieten his frustration and his impatience—and his doubts about her loyalty and determination. "*J'ajoute qu'il ne s'agit d'apporter dans cette horrible affaire ni acrimonie, ni amertume contre les personnes. Il faut viser plus haut*" (I must add that it is not a matter of bearing acrimony nor bitterness against individuals in this horrible affair. One must aim much higher). Perhaps also, ironically, when he tells her to aim higher—higher than, in the immediate import of the sentence, the underlings in the whole sorry affair, and look to God for help, support, and understanding—he might be also saying, "Watch out for the persons in the most responsible positions in the army and the government." Although it is most unlikely that Dreyfus could think such a thing at this time in the affair, because of his idealism and the limits on his knowledge of what is happening back in Paris, nevertheless this caution and hint to seek out the culprits in the highest offices in the republic will be all too true in retrospect.

On New Year's Day of 1897, Lucie begins her letter to her dearly beloved Alfred with the usual mixture of hopes and encouragements for a peaceful future through the resolution of their problems. Then, in a passage suppressed in the earliest editions of the letters, she says, "*Que Dieu enfin ait pitié de nous*"[240] (May God have pity on us!), thus seeming to break the taboo against crying out for pity and mercy, as though the couple were Christians; but to push these common expressions, embedded in French life and culture, though indeed imbued with Christian overtones as though they could mean more than the context allows them to resonate, would be to expect far too much of Lucie and Alfred as theologians. Her plaintive letters continues: "*Qu'il nous permettre de vivre le repos, qu'il mette un terme à nos angoisses, aux blessures de notre coeur et de notre âme*" (May He permit us to live in repose, may He put an

240 *Ecris-moi souvent, écris moi longuement*, 341.

end to our anguish, to the wounds in our heart and in our soul), formulaic demands for release from intense pain in the cruel and unmerited catastrophe of their lives.

At the end of the letter, in an appended statement, Lucie returns to the more familiar language of their interprenetrative experience of one another, where they regarded one another's letters as reflections of each other's souls ("*un reflet de ton âme, de ta pensée*") and as a mystical space in which they converse, their usually tightened nerves relaxed ("*ce qui m'a détendu les nerfs et reposée un peu*").[241] In response, as it were, on 6 January, 1897, Alfred writes something quite similar, though in the language of his own more masculine sensibility, affirming that the goal is always the same—the rehabilitation of the family name:

> *Mais, hélas! si l'on peut être stoïque devant la mort, il est difficile de l'être devant la douleur de chaque jour, devant cette pensée lancinante de se demander quand finira cet horrible cauchemar dans lequel nous vivons depuis si longtemps, si cela peut s'appeler vivre que de souffrir sans répit.*[242]
>
> But, alas! if one can be stoical before death, it is difficult to be [so] before daily pains, before this penetrating thought of asking oneself when will it ever end, this horrible nightmare in which we have lived so long, if it can be called living to suffer without respite.

The specific terms may be more classical and impersonal, but the anguish is the same, and the same cry for relief binds Alfred's letter to Lucie's. Yet Lucie has another strategy to make manifest the deepest, virtually unspeakable anguish in her heart: the projection of her feelings into the voice, person, and condition of the children. Thus, on 1 February, 1897, she tells her husband about little Jeanne's illness and how it has been passed on to Pierrot. The girl had a mild case of chickenpox and now the boy has it, both desiring to be pampered and fondled ("*d'être dorloté et câliné*").[243] To show this otherwise repressed longing, the wife

241 *Ecris-moi souvent, écris moi longuement*, 342.

242 *Ecris-moi souvent, écris moi longuement*, 345.

243 In a section of the letters previously unpublished: *Ecris-moi souvent, écris moi longuement*, 348.

and mother signs her letter with a never-before-used phrase: "*Ton affectionnée Lucie*" (Your affectionate Lucie).

It is possible to see Alfred moving, by the force of his will, into self-analysis, while at the same time, under the pressures of the physical and moral tortures he is undergoing, slipping back into black despair. In his letter of 24 April, 1897, he starts by saying that it is utterly painful to keep waiting for her letters, and because he has no letters from her to answer, his own are filled with repetitions of what he has written too often already. Repetition warms his heart, as though he were generating heat to make a spark, or as though he were in sexual congress with her, and yet for all that, the constant iteration of words and phrases does not relieve him. The agony is inexpressible, and the inexpressible does not go away through a one-sided expression, even if he were to howl like a beast.[244] When he attempts to pull himself together and transform this personal pain into a statement of idealism, his love and loyalty to the nation,[245] when, indeed, he sees himself a martyr to Lucie and to France, he becomes detached, as he often says, from the essential core of his self, his Jewishness:

> *Et la réalité, la voici, toujours la même: c'est que dans cette horrible affaire il y a un double intérêt en jeu, celui de la patrie, le nôtre, que l'un est aussi sacré que l'autre.*[246]
>
> In reality, the here and now, [is] always the same: it is that in this horrible affair there is a double interest in play, that of the nation, and our own, which is as sacred as the other.

The words are cryptic, cramped, ambiguous at best: the double interest at play is on the one side, clearly that of France, "our nation," his and Lucie's and their children's; he also says, "*[M]a vie est à mon pays*" (my life belongs to my country), but on the other, the interest is in his

244 *Ecris-moi souvent, écris moi longuement*, 359.

245 Romain Rolland's Olivier remarks of the Jews: "The best of them . . . make the mistake, in all sincerity, of identifying the destiny of France with their Jewish dreams . . ." (*Jean Christophe*, vol. II, 385) and then a little later: "The Jews are well off in France: I am glad of it: but they must not think of turning France into Judea!" (II, 386).

246 *Ecris-moi souvent, écris moi longuement*, 360.

honour, his integrity, and his innocence. He owes it to Lucie to stay alive and healthy and sane. He owes it to his children to fight against the machinations of the state, the army, and the judiciary to clear his name of all taints. What he owes to the family and to and through his love to Lucie is his Jewish self. In another sense, behind or inside this paradox, "*le nôtre*" refers to the interest he has in honouring the name of the God of Israel, insofar as Lucie has come to embody that concept of the sacred. When he speaks of *name* and *country* and *patrimony*, each word can reverberate with Jewish meanings, the *Shem* of the God who blesses all things, the *Makom*, the place which is infinite and eternal and which is also the *Eretz Yisroel*, the Promised Land of Israel, and the *Zekhut*, the legacy of obligations of the deity accumulated by all of Israel by the righteous of all generations and to which all of Israel is entitled to a portion in times of need and despair.

Most of the time Alfred speaks outside the explicit language of religion and tries to secularise and Frenchify his hopes and dreams, to juxtapose rather than oppose or prioritise his love of Lucie and of France. Thus, in his letter of 5 July, 1897, he tells his wife:

> *Je joins les mains dans une prière suprême, que j'adresse encore à tous ceux [à qui] j'ai fait appel, pour qu'ils t'apportent un concours plus ardent, plus généreux que jamais dans la découverte de la vérité.*[247]
>
> I join my hands in a supreme prayer which I address to all those to whom I have appealed for them to bring to you a more burning unity, more generous than ever for the discovery of the truth.

An ardent prayer, with joined hands—anything but a Jewish gesture, but a commonplace of French Catholic culture so deeply embedded in the ordinary language that the significance is totally neutralized—directed not at God but at his family and their allies, for them to double their efforts on his behalf.[248] The news from home is totally inadequate

247 *Ecris-moi souvent, écris moi longuement*, 367.

248 On 22 July 1897, Alfred writes in the same figurative gesture of joined hands in prayer: *Ecris-moi souvent, écris moi longuement*, 370.

to his emotional needs. He does not realize—how could he?—what has already been accomplished and how close the nation is to the idea of his rehabilitation. Yet he is also correct, insofar as it will not be until Emile Zola forces the issue with his public *J'Accuse* that the most spectacular stage of the affair is set off. As the censored passages in Lucie's letter of 15 July, 1897, show, the truth was on the march—"*Cette fois je m'avancerai avec plus de certitude encore et je t'affirmerai d'une façon absolument catégorique que ton nom sera lavé de cette horrible souffrance, que la certitude de ta rehabilitation est absolue en moi*"[249] (This time I will be advancing with even more certitude and I can affirm to you in a fashion absolutely categorical that your name will be cleansed of this horrible suffering, that certainty of your rehabilitation is absolute in me)—yet there was no way he could know it.[250] Whatever truths he could read out of her letters that did arrive were oblique, fragmentary, and understated. The point at issue here, though, is that whenever Dreyfus wants to make a statement that could be read by the public—even if that public is only himself, Lucie, and the censors who read their letters—his language is vague, pompous, and secular. When he is crushed by circumstances, crying out in pain, appealing to Lucie for moral and emotional support, he reveals the hidden core of his being, obliquely, to be sure, but profoundly true in his Jewishness.

Alfred writes what he calls "*mon testament moral*" on 20 August, 1897,[251] a letter stopped by the censors from being sent to Lucie, and existing only in fragments. Although he speaks insistently of "*l'extrême franchise, la franchise brutale même*" (the extreme frankness, brutal

---

249 *Ecris-moi souvent, écris moi longuement*, 369.

250 Further explicating *mahloquet*, Ouaknin draws on Emmanuel Lévinas' *De Dieu qui vient à l'idée* (Paris: Vrin, 1982, 166): "*la parole de question est 'la première fissure visible dans le psychisme de la satisfaction'. Le refus de la satisfaction, du contentement où, en d'autres termes, de la totalité est un des traits essentiels de la* Mahloquet. *La question brise la totalité, le concept, elle est l'ouverture et chemin de (et vers) la transcendance, elle est source de* Hidouch, *de savoir transcendant*" (The word of the question is "the first visible fissure in the psychism of satisfaction." The refusal of satisfaction, of contentment or, in other words, of the totality is one of the essential characteristics of *Hidoush*, of transcendant knowledge" (*Le livre brûlé*, 233). The purpose of the questionings and challenges of authority is to "make it new", new in the sense of a continuous, dynamic overflowing of meaning, never stuck into a fixed iconic statement or of what is true, since such a truth is false, is an idol. "*L'importance du* Hidouch," writes Ouaknin, "*réside dans le fait qu'il introduit une discontinuité dans le rhythme de la conscience et dans le train de l'être, qu íl brise le bloc de l'être*" (The importance of *Hidoush* resides in the fact that it introduces a discontinuity in the rhythm of consciousness and in the train of being, that it breaks the [solid] block of being") in *Le livre brûlé*, 243).

251 *Ecris-moi souvent, écris moi longuement*, 375.

frankness even), it is difficult to see in what survives of this letter what goaded the prison authorities into stopping the epistle from going to its destined reader. In contradiction to this assertion, he tells Lucie on 2 October, 1897,

> *Comme je te l'ai dit, mes longues lettres sont trop l'expression intime et profonde aussi bien de mes sentiments que de mon immuable volonté, pour qu'il soit utile d'y revenir; elles sont comme mon testament moral.*[252]
>
> As I have told you, my long letters are too much the intimate and profound expression of my sentiments as of my immutable will, so that it would be useful to return to them, they are like my moral testament.

In other words, this time around, what he calls his moral testament is not brutally frank, but carefully considered, an edited version of his hopes and aspirations. But a testament of this sort, common to Jewish tradition as a means for fathers to set out the principles by which they hope their children will live after their demise, sometimes appended to and sometimes substituted for an actual disposition of worldly goods, would normally be written in Hebrew, weaving together in *melitza* format many scriptural and Talmudic phrases and concepts, and would become a family treasure in itself.[253] For Alfred Dreyfus, however, aside from citing Shakespeare—he speaks of Banco's (i.e., Banquo's)[254] ghost from *Macbeth*—the legacy to his children will be the good name he hopes to be restored and the example of his own endurance under terrible duress during the whole of the ordeal of imprisonment.

This citation from Shakespeare or any other literary source, including the historians and philosophers he so extensively comments on in the *cahiers*, is rare, the language of Alfred remaining close to the neutral,

---

252 *Ecris-moi souvent, écris moi longuement*, 382.

253 One thinks here of the famous inscription Sigmund Freud's father wrote on the flyleaf of the Bible in modern edition and translation he had read to his son from when he was a boy and now passes on with hope that the grown man, already successful as a neurologist, would return to the Law for inspiration and guidance.

254 *Ecris-moi souvent, écris moi longuement*, 383. See also Duclert's lengthy note on this error and Dreyfus' love for Shakespeare, 492, n. 56. We will discuss these matters more closely when we consider the prison *cahiers* from Devil's Island in the second volume of this series.

secular ideals of mid-nineteenth-century French patriotism, or, as we have been trying to show, occasionally slipping into the rhythms, tones, rhetorical tropes, and words of biblical prophecy and poetry, Jewish liturgy, Talmudic debate and sometimes kabbalistic fantasy, this slippage brought on by the extremes of torment, physical and moral, he lived through for five years of his life. Although at times Lucie picks up his lead, echoes his rhythms and words, and occasionally takes the directing role in moving through this exalted discourse, she is usually anchored to domestic matters and care of the children. She is also forced to suppress her wish to enlighten her husband as to the state of play in the project to rehabilitate him, with a few exceptions, at which time, of course, her letters are censored or stopped altogether.

In this last phase of their epistolary communications, whether intentionally or not, she begins to mimic the ringing polemics of Zola and other Dreyfusards. This can be seen in the previously unpublished letter of 20 January, 1898, as pointed out by Duclert.[255] It is unlikely that Alfred was able to recognize these clues as to the advanced state of the affair, which was reaching its climax in Paris. But the closer the end comes to his sufferings, the less can he see the clues in the erratic behaviour of his jailers. Sometimes they relax their guard a little, then they increase it cruelly and sadistically. Lucie's letters, as we can now see, begin to drop their guard and speak enthusiastically about the coming resolution, but since these are the very letters held back from him, Alfred begins to doubt her commitment and assumes the worst in his legal and political position. Sensing a crisis rising again in his mental state, Lucie begs him on 6 March, 1898, to give her a detailed account of his health: "*Dis-moi longuement comment tu es, comment tu te portes. Dis-le moi en toute franchise*"[256] (Tell me at length what is the matter with you. Speak to me in all frankness). Later still, on 7 April, 1898, she tries to explain away a misunderstanding on his part, that she is not annoyed by his repeated descriptions of his poor mental health, that she understands his position exactly and admires his courage and fortitude, and that she herself is glad to suffer along with him, to share his burdens.[257] She is

255 *Ecris-moi souvent, écris moi longuement*, 408–409 ; see also 494, n. 7. She is insistent that the great burden is finally being lifted in her letter of 17 March 1898: *Ecris-moi souvent, écris moi longuement*, 415.

256 *Ecris-moi souvent, écris moi longuement*, 413.

257 *Ecris-moi souvent, écris moi longuement*, 417.

even more insistent on 16 August, 1898, when she writes, "*Je désire si ardemment te pénétrer de ma pleine confiance en un bon avenir prochain que j'ai peut-être manqué de clarté dans l'expression de ce sentiment. Dorénavant je tâcherai d'être plus nette*"[258] (I desire so ardently to penetrate you with my full confidence in a favourable outcome soon that perhaps I missed being clear in my expression of this sentiment. From now on I will attempt to be plain).

Although Lucie can see everything coming right at last, still the weeks drag by, the months pass without an official decision, and no news she can send to him which will be confirmed by documents and newspapers. What encouraging words she does write, as on 14 July, 1898, Bastille Day, ironically are prevented from coming to him because the political factions against him, and the prison authorities, absolutely convinced of his guilt and of a Jewish plot against France, resist to the very last moment.

In late July of that last year of his imprisonment and exile, his letters change markedly. They suddenly take on the character of little essays on topics such as the education of the children or on the nature of language, as though the boundary between the epistles and the *cahiers* was breached. Nevertheless, just as about at the same time, in his last workbooks, the facade of intellectual objectivity and distance from his own sufferings begins to break down, here too he lets cries of pain and frustration seep into these little disquisitions:

> *Et si je n'écoutais que mon cœur, je t'écrirais plus souvent, car il me semble ainsi—pure illusion, je le sais, mais qui soulage néanmoins—qu'au même instant, à la même minute, tu me sentiras à travers la distance que nous sépare battre un cœur qui ne vit que pour toi, pour nos enfants, un cœur qui t'aime . . .*[259]
>
> And if I had only listened to my own heart, I would have written more often, for it seems to me thus—a pure illusion, I know, but which nevertheless comforts me—that at the same moment, in the same minute, across

258 *Ecris-moi souvent, écris moi longuement*, 431.
259 *Ecris-moi souvent, écris moi longuement*, 428–429.

> the distance which separates us you feel a heart beating that only lives for you, for our children, a heart that loves you . . .

Again, the more hopeless things seem, the more he expresses himself in these metaphysical terms, creating the conceit of the two hearts beating in unison or one heart in two distant places. He need not write because they are closer together than geography or the physical delivery of pieces of paper with words inscribed on them. But never have they been caught up so much in a crisis of communication, when, right on the cusp of success, their physical letters fail to arrive or are misread because of the lack of coherence, and because, at least on Lucie's side, with the confidence she has in the expected resolution to all their problems, she falls away from that sense of shared crisis that made the metaphysical union possible.

By 26 September, 1898, she writes a totally new kind of letter to Alfred, one filled with a catalogue of actions taken on his behalf: "*Je veux te raconter très brièvement la succession des faits.*" [260] Such a letter, however, she should have known, would be held back, and when it did arrive without a proper historical context and not backed up by confirming documents, it would be misunderstood by her husband. Matters reach such a point of confusion that in her letter of 22 November, 1898, she signs herself "L. Dreyfus,"[261] the driest, most impersonal way possible. Salutation and inner greetings are less formal, so why this strange signing off? Could it be that, so hopeful is she of an immediate release from his prison, she expects the letter to be stopped before it reaches Alfred and either held by the officials or posted back to her?

Unfortunately, nothing happens for many more weeks and months, and their letters slip back into the old routine, perhaps tinged with an even greater despair and frustration than before. In the letter of 6 March, 1898,[262] again filled with demands for him to send all the details possible of his health and mental condition, as well as her apologies for the tediousness of her repeated words and phrases from previous letters over all these years, she diagnoses her moral condition as "*cette obsession,*" manifest in the fixation on rehabilitating his honour.

---

260 *Ecris-moi souvent, écris moi longuement*, 433.

261 *Ecris-moi souvent, écris moi longuement*, 439.

262 *Ecris-moi souvent, écris moi longuement*, 412–413.

Just as she intuits the need to make him talk through his pains and humiliations in order to draw him up out of his black hole of despair, so too she makes her treatment consist of self-abasing comments about her own lack of skill in writing and her weak intellect. Her attempts to reassure him of the light that is already breaking forth into the darkness of the mysterious case against him, Alfred does not comprehend in a way that makes her confident of his mental condition: she knows, in a way, that her letters may not be getting through; she confesses to her inadequacy in expressing herself clearly and cogently, and she fears that her husband may be too far gone in his illness to recover even after a judicial revision and rehabilitation. For example, in her letter of 7 April, 1898, she writes that they should be habituated to suffering *"l'irrégularité des couriers,"*[263] but everything is much worse than that. In a previously unpublished part of this letter,

> *Je me souviens quelquefois de tristesse combine je me sentais isolée, malheureuse quand je me devais de me séparer de toi pendant quelques jours, j'aurais donné beaucoup pour que ces moments envisagés avec tant d'anxiété, soient passes. Qu'aurais-je dit si j'avais pu prévoir une chose pareille, que toi mon mari bien-aimé tu me serais arraché pendant près de quatre ans, et que pendant ces quatre années, j'aurais le supplice de vivre, s'assister à la torture et d'être impuissante à la soulager, à adoucir tes souffrances.*[264]
>
> I sometimes recall with sadness how I felt isolated, unhappy, when I had to be separated from you for four days [during military manoeuvres]. I would have given anything for those moments I dream of in anxiety to be over. What could I have said if I had been able to foresee such a thing as you, my beloved husband, wrenched away from me for close to four years, during which I found life an agony, of being with you in your torture and being powerless to comfort you, to soften your sufferings.

---

263 *Ecris-moi souvent, écris moi longuement*, 416.

264 *Ecris-moi souvent, écris moi longuement*, 417.

She had been prepared to take the normal difficulties of being a soldier's wife, of having him away from home for days at a time on official duties, but she could never have imagined this horrible fate of not only enduring more than four years of separation but of knowing intimately his terrible pains in exile, in isolation, and in torture, and of not being able to offer the right kind of relief through her letters. More than a distant witness of his misery and agony, she tells him she has been sharing every moment of his torment. Is this merely a figurative statement? She has to convince Alfred now that she has not resigned herself to his fate, accepting it all as a given, beyond remedy, as she thinks he is now accusing her of doing, but to show him that she is painfully aware of the terrible burden of responsibilities destiny has put on her to accomplish things beyond the capacity of a woman, beyond the conventional restraints put on a middle-class wife by a sexist society, and beyond the range of public sympathy a Jewish wife and mother could elicit from an essentially anti-Semitic culture. And yet this confession of inadequacies is not all true; she has accomplished much, transformed herself into something Alfred dreamed she could be—and was already, in his conceit of the *Shekhina*—and something, if he did know, as he will come to know, he will hesitate in speaking of because he is not all that different from other men in France at that time.

As we shall see, when we consider the *carnets* and journals, Alfred barely mentions Lucie and what she did for him, just as he shades from public view all his own intellectual accomplishments and interests. Partly this relapse into patriarchal and cultural conventionality is a consequence of the broken body and soul he brings back from Devil's Island and partly a result of social pressures, probably as true in his Jewish families as it is in the wider community. Nevertheless, nothing should obscure what the two writers created during the five years of the ordeal and across "perilous seas forlorn" nor, as we will argue in detail soon, the outstanding intellectual creation in the fifteen remaining prison workbooks.

Chapter Three: The Phantasmagoria of a Secular *Midrash*

INTRODUCTION

> *Mais il ne fallait pas oublier que toutes les folies avaient reçu droit de cité dans mon affaire et s'y étaient donné libre carrière. Il fallait donc pénétrer résolurent dans les arcanes de toute cette fantasmagorie.*
>
> —Alfred Dreyfus[1]

The prison workbooks or *cahiers* tell quite another story than that seen in the various collections of letters alone or in the selected and commentated editions discussed already, and these compendia of jottings and drawings expand aspects of what we find in the journals following Dreyfus's return to France.[2] But why have fewer than half survived? It is not so much because the tropical heat and humidity destroyed them, or because the prison authorities confiscated them, but because Alfred Dreyfus did not wish their contents to be made public.[3] Yet, as Pierrette Turlais suggests, "If it quickly seems that the correspondence with his wife Lucie and the writing of his journal opened up a source of life, it also

---

1 "It should not be forgotten that all the madmen were given the keys to the city in my affair and they had a free run. It should therefore be necessary to penetrate resolutely into all the secret passageways of this phantasmagoria." Alfred Dreyfus, *Carnets (1899-1907): Après le process de Rennes*, ed. Philippe Oriol (Paris: Calmann-Lévy, 1998), 215.

2 Speaking of the Goncourt Brothers *Journal,* Anatole France defines the genre in this way: "A journal [is] a memorial, a volume of reminiscences [that] escapes all the fashions, all the conventions that are imposed on the works of the mind" ("The Journal of the Goncourts" in *On Life & Letters*, first series, trans. A. W. Evans [London: John Lane/The Bodley Head, 1924 (1910)] 74). Though the *cahiers* do not form themselves into a journal, we could say there are at least two aspects of Dreyfus's personality at work in their composition, one consciously attempting to stave off madness by deliberate intellectual, mathematical, and repetitive exercises, the other unconsciously revealing his pains, his often manic idealism, and his probably little understood Jewish heritage; and these various components of his jotting escape conventions under the outrageous conditions of his treatment on Devil's Island.

3 The fifteen remaining books were donated to the Bibliothèque Nationale in Paris in 1923. The latest discussions on the state of the missing and surviving *cahiers* can be found in Pierrette Turlais's new limited edition and the fine essays included therein, including her fine "Foreward."

appears that the unknown part of his writing permitted him to communicate with that same source."[4] What this "source of life" now appears to be is an inner world of intellectual ferment, an expanding and critical ocean of memories—expanding because the more Dreyfus began to write down his thoughts, the more he remembered, and the more he remembered, the more he could compare, weigh, and extrapolate new ideas from these remembered texts. To again cite Turlais, whose critical judgements are sensitive, rich with provocative implications that I will be trying to draw out, and contextualized in a midrashic way:

> Whereas the letters and the journal authorized an intimate gushing forth of life and construct, letter by letter, an unfalsifiable memory, the *cahiers* permit an opening into the world that extends and probably relieves the strict limitations to his self.[5]

The *cahiers* that survive are those that Alfred Dreyfus wanted to survive, and it is now possible to study them in Turlais's mixed facsimile and transcribed version. Aside from a few, usually scratched-out, beginnings of letters to Lucie or government officials, occasional lists of food and personal items the prisoner wished to request from his guards, and some exercises in learning English, the pages in these workbooks are a mix of doodles, mathematical formulae, reading notes, and translations of the books he was thinking about studying during the nearly five years of incarceration, and finally, perhaps most important of all, Dreyfus's short essays on a wide variety of topics. As Turlais points out, "The inner world of Capt. Dreyfus's exile rests in these notebooks,"[6] and therefore it is important for us to begin to take a measure of how large that inner world really was—or rather, we need to assess its volume, shape, and power of resonance. Most historians of the Dreyfus Affair to date have assumed that it was rather small, restricted not only by the harsh conditions of his imprisonment but by the limited horizons he had as a middle-class provincial from Alsace, an artillery officer, and a Jew.

Therefore, with only some of the *cahiers* available, everything I have

4 Turlais, "Foreward," 44. All translations from this and other documents in her edition of the *cahiers* are my own, unless otherwise stated.

5 Turlais, "Foreward," 44.

6 Turlais, "Foreward," 44.

to say in this book must remain tentative and incomplete. However, even those speculative and fragmentary conclusions that can now be offered will destabilize all previous generalizations about the man, his experience of the milieu in which he found himself by destiny and by choice, the mentalities he shared with those in the various concentric and interweaving circles in which he moved, and the midrashic universe he had inherited, only very small parts of which he knew about or realized he was participating in. These intersecting, overlapping, and sometimes wholly unperceived and imperceptible worlds within worlds are not all composed of his natural languages, mostly French, of course, but also the English he was learning so he could read Shakespeare in the original and also perhaps because he was beginning to think of migrating to North America or the British colonies in the South Pacific,[7] as well German, Italian, Scandinavian, and Russian languages. These circles within circles were also made of mathematical and chemical symbols and equations, geometrical forms, and line drawings of machines and natural objects. Next to this rational and abstract world of science and technology there lies that far more mysterious realm of his obsessive doodling. In Turlais's words:

> And then . . . and then an element—what can we call it?—a strange design, abstract, born from an identical structure but ever-changing, comes in to punctuate or mark the stresses of the manuscript hundreds of times. The patterning suggests, over and over again, arabesques, cerebral lobes, demonic rictus, masks or indecipherable heraldic devices.[8]

There are suggestions that these apparently endless drawings represent Dreyfus's attempt to fill time and space and to create a visual correlative of the horrifyingly heavy cloud of silence he lived under night

7 See also Dreyfus's interesting comments on the British colonization of North America and its confrontation with French efforts in the same region, his fascination with Paul Bourget's travel account of a visit to New York City, Newport, and other parts of the United States, and the details of contemporary Australian and New Zealand politics and economy. Was he perhaps thinking of leaving the civilization of France after he was eventually released and going to the Anglo-American culture that seemed to offer more tolerance and freedom?

8 Turlais, "Foreward," *Cahiers*, 44. See also Comte-Sponville "La leçon d'Alfred Dreyfus" in Turlais, *Cahiers*, 242.

and day for all those years. His prison guards, required to examine carefully all his journals and notebooks, as well as letters, were stupefied by these doodles; they could make no real sense of them but suspected that they were kabbalistic signs or secret messages of some Judaic plot or another. As we will keep arguing, the Jew haters of the time—of any time!—may not always be as wrong as we would like to think, not because they are total ignoramuses and blinded by their bigotry and inanity but because they are prepared by these social, moral, faults to notice what "normal" and "liberal" minds do not want to deal with.

So what are these doodles or drawings or cryptic messages? First of all, they are not so much a sign of madness as a deliberate attempt to avoid insanity. In the last several years, unfortunately, we have learned from hostages held by terrorists for long periods of time that worse than physical torment is the mental anguish of being forced to do nothing, to receive no news about the outside world, to experience no sympathy or empathy from one's captors, and to find consciousness shrinking down to almost nothing. It then becomes important, as Dreyfus seems to have discovered, to organize what time and space there is in one's mind on the empty pages of notebooks one is allowed to scribble in and thus to gain a modicum of control over the psychological environment.

Perhaps at the same time, this was an attempt to envisage, embody, and participate in time and space, expanding it beyond the debilitating confines of a bed to which he was shackled for long hours of the night, of a tiny cabin—and one that was replaced by one even smaller in the course of the confinement—poorly ventilated and sparsely furnished, a very small rocky island whose domains he was soon forbidden access to, with even the comforting sight of the sea cut off by the construction of a palisade. Perhaps this psychological (moral) expansion was also aesthetic, metaphysical, intellectual, and spiritual; it was certainly desperate. As Jean-Louis Lévy puts in his preface to Turlais's edition of the *cahiers*, "For the exiled Dreyfus, automatic drawing is nothing more nor less than strategy for survival." Then he adds, "It is up to us to respect the mystery."[9]

A typical page from the notebook, if we dare suggest such a thing, has the whole surface of textual space filled with hundreds of relentlessly repeated drawings, sometimes fitted around, under, or over the writing

9 Jean-Louis Lévy, "Préface," *Cahiers*, 49.

of words, and all these doodles look alike at first insofar as they emerge from an X or an א, sometimes from a Y or a ץ, but each one distinct in size, shape, and elaboration. In one sense, they correlate with the mathematical formulations; they abstract from the environment, the outer world of hatred and loneliness, the formal patterns of rationality and design. They also correlate to the literary and philosophical texts and intellectual speculations on other pages, especially where Dreyfus engages with his two favourite writers, Montaigne and Shakespeare, and argues with the key nineteenth-century thinkers Michelet, Taine, and Renan.[10] The drawings affirm that there can be order and reason even in the midst of chaos, and that chaos bows to pattern and order. He argues through his doodles that each individual entity has its own integrity and value, whereas the state, the government, the press, the public, and his prison guards seek to crush him, grind him down into nothingness. I will come back to the problem of these drawings in a later volume, where I will integrate them into Jewish art and aesthetics.

The earlier, now missing, *cahiers* probably could have revealed how intensely despondent or even suicidal Dreyfus was. That is not quite all guesswork, however, since one atypical journal from the earliest period has survived, inadvertently, in the Colonial Museum at Aix, and has now been discussed and a few pages reproduced in Turlais's volume.[11] But

10 Turlais, "Foreward," 44. It will be shown in later parts of this book and in subsequent studies of the authors, both creative and historical, that Alfred Dreyfus felt most intellectually drawn to, one of the characteristics he searched for was a commitment to practical applications of scientific and moral ideas. This is also a very Jewish attitude, as we shall show. Although he tried to remain upbeat in his prison notebooks, nevertheless Dreyfus would have agreed with Anatole France that "M. Renan is distinguished by a special feeling of resigned mistrust. He has never had illusions regarding the irremediable uncertainty of human testimony" ("The Errors of History" in *On Life and Letters*, second series, trans. A. W. Evans (London: John Lane/The Bodley Head, 1923. 1914), 110). Surely one of the great lessons learned from his ordeal, even before he became aware of the full dimensions of the affair that was occurring whilst he was in exile on Devil's Island, is that documents and witnesses, along with experts and judges, cannot be trusted implicitly. For this reason, we may have to reevaluate Dreyfus's attractions to beauty (poetic and natural) over dispassionate discourses of naturalistic fiction or supposedly objective science, when we read Anatole France saying, "For my own part, if I had to choose between beauty and truth, I should not hesitate either: it is beauty that I should keep, certain that it has in it a higher and deeper truth than truth itself" (113). However, as we will give a preliminary report in the final chapter of this book, in Dreyfus's case at least, the argument would need to be contextualized by Jewish concepts of both beauty and truth. One might want all to compare, as France does, this very nineteenth-century Romantic idealism with what Ernest Renan writes in *Histoire du peuple d'Israël*; cp. Anatole France's review essay, "The History of the People of Israel" in *On Life and Letters*, second series, trans. A. W. Evans (London: John Lane/Bodley Head, 1923/1914), 293–299.

11 Maxime Préaud, "Variations à perpetuité" in Turlais, *Cahiers*, 251–255. This so-called Aix

although it seems to derive from the very first weeks or months of his exile and there is a gap of about four years between it and the workbooks we do have, it is not easy to determine what the intermediate versions might have looked like or contained, if indeed there were any. Because this somewhat anomalous workbook contains many schoolboy drawings of geometrical figures, some attempts at caricatured faces, and a jumble of plays on the letters of Alfred Dreyfus's name, initials, monogrammatic elaborations, and mathematical equations, Maxime Préaud speculates on a transitional series of developments in the missing *cahiers*—those that Dreyfus himself suppressed and probably destroyed. But that information cannot be verified, and the very idea of some gradual shifting from the kind of page in Aix *Cahier* No. 60 to the BNF *Cahier* 1 dated 3 August, 1898, seems highly unlikely, for we do not know whether the *cahiers* that Dreyfus destroyed were regularly or irregularly written over the years before 1898 and 1899—or whether he kept any at all. The evidence from letters and journals suggests otherwise, that is, that the prisoner was too disheartened, depressed, and "detached" to write—that is, that this was some manner of warding off evil spirits from within, as he says,[12] or that the scribbles, including the drawing of repeated variations on the flowering X/א and Y/ץ were, as the prison reports suggest, "*cabalistiques*" and "*architecturales*," meant to engage in the kind of creative intellectual activities the workbooks demonstrate.[13]

What we do know from the extant journals is that Alfred was reading quite a bit, although the kinds of scholarly journals and literature he could receive was limited, both by his own tastes and what Lucie felt she could safely send to him.[14] There was also a period in which, after new regulations from the Minister of the Colonies in Paris, his wife had

---

Cahiers is marked as No. 60, and there are two other partial copies made from it listed as No. 63 and No. 64.

12 Anatole France reminds his readers that "it is not from magicians and spirits but from novelists and poets that we must ask the way to the unknown world" ("Hypnotism in Literature," a review of *Marfa: Le Palimpseste* by Gilbert-Augustin Thièrry in *Of Life & Letters*, vol. I, 106). We should add to poets and novelists letter writers, and keepers of *cahiers* and also remind ourselves of the palimpsest of midrashic writing, whereby rabbinical writers present their arguments in the name and through the words of predecessors and keep occupying the same textual space as the scriptures they claim to explicate and renew.

13 Préaud, "Variations à perpetuité," *Cahiers*, 253.

14 We have collated various lists and discussed these journals, as well as the known books Dreyfus had in his possession on Devil's Island, in chapter II. There could have been up to three hundred or more actual texts in his personal library, perhaps not at any one time; there would certainly not have been room for them, at best two or three at a time.

to stop sending him books and journals, and therefore Alfred had to depend on what was available from the prison library in Cayenne. This man, whose Jewish culture elevated books to the highest category of intellectual pleasures, felt the deprivation of reading matter deeply. The receipt of packets from Lucie or from the local library was vital to his sense of self and sanity.[15] Given the hundreds and hundreds of titles and authors he refers to, it also is more than likely that the bulk of the books, authors, and themes he writes about derive from his memory of what he had read and studied as a boy, from the literature he and Lucie discussed in their fireside chats in the evenings, and from phrases, images, and ideas sparked off by references in the various magazines he could receive from time to time. Certainly, his beloved Montaigne's *Essais* was a rich anthology of quotations and paraphrases.

The pages of these fourteen remaining *cahiers* contain more than just the reading notes and exercises in translation that Turlais and others have noted. There are also a few prose poems, lists of aphorisms and apothegms of his own composition, technical discussions on bicycles, photography, economics and meteorology, and speculative mini-essays on politics, aesthetics, rhetoric, historiography, and education.[16] I have

---

15 Bloch-Dano: "*Les livres font partie de son univers mental, et reflètent une culture, vivante qui n'a rien à voir avec une occupation mondaine. Jeanne [Proust] est bien représentative de ce milieu israélite pour lequel la vie intellectuelle est primordiale, et jugé supérieure à toute autre activité*" (Books were a part of her mental universe, and reflected a living culture which had nothing to do with a worldly occupation. Jeanne Proust is a good representative of this Jewish milieu for whom intellectual life is primordial and judged to be superior to all other activities), *Madame Proust,* 156.

16 Perhaps the shape and contents of Alfred Dreyfus's workbooks recalls the Talmudic commentaries created over generations by the rabbis. Important to this conception was the institution of the *kalla*, which according to José Faur, was "a month-long convention, during which students and sages from all over the Jewish world gathered to study a Talmudic tractate . . . . There were two *Kalla* meetings per year, one in the month of Afar (winter) and another in month of Elul (summer). In addition...the *Kalla* was attended by outside students and sages, as well as by the magistrates and highest judicial and political officials of the nation." Then Faur draws the important analogy, which we extend to Dreyfus's *cahiers*, comparing larger to smaller things: "Just as the Synagogue is a virtual experience of the Temple, and the liturgy of the sacramental services, so the Talmud is a virtual *Kalla* experience. Through the Babylonian Talmud, students and sages from the fragmented Israel have unfettered access to the *Kalla* world and hear the voices of Jews from Tiberias and Caesarea, from Lydia and from Sippore, from Nehar De'a, from Fum be-Dita [sic] and from Sura, and from countless other seats of learning and as one, pupil and teacher, learned and common, disciple and sage, brilliant and mediocre, share in their discussions, reflect on their ideas, and renew their bonds with an *integral Jewish society*. This is why the Talmud is much more than a book or a landscape of things lost; it is a virtual *Kalla,* a holistic experience . . . . Hence the folklore, exegesis, psychological insights, esoteric and metaphysical meditations, stories and tales, crisscrossing the legal principles and doctrines taught by the sages" (*The Horizontal Society*, Section IV, 46).

compiled three indices in the Appendix in the next book in this series to show (a) the books and authors Dreyfus refers to, (b) the topics he writes about, and (c) the mathematical and scientific notions he names in relation to the formulae and equations he plays with in the *cahiers*.[17] Given that we only have the notebooks of 1898 and 1899, the range of reading is nothing but amazing, particularly as these were the last frustrating and painful years of his horrible nightmare.

What were the books Dreyfus was reading and thinking about? Montaigne and Shakespeare, to be sure, as Turlais points out[18]—and as everyone who has glanced at the manuscripts has recognized, he taught himself English so as to read the great Renaissance playwright in the original. Yet there is much, much more. He also read and commented on nineteenth-century authors such as Hippolyte Taine and Ernest Renan, Jules Michelet, and Paul Bourget. He calls the first three amongst the most important of his century and points to the fourth as his teacher from lycée, with whom he had maintained contact. Taine, Renan, and Michelet are, for the compiler of these *cahiers*, more than just historians; they are great stylists, teachers, and poets, while Paul Bourget is a popular novelist but also a psychologist.

Although Marcel Proust did not like his style of psychological fiction—he thought Bourget explained too much, according to Anatole France[19]— Bourget belongs to the school of Hippolyte Taine, and this makes Dreyfus doubly within that tradition as well. Literature, in the sense of *belles-lettres* rather than a more strict construction of creative writing or even fiction, should be morally and psychologically true; instead of the self-indulgence and introspective tendencies that became

17 I have also added a brief comment on the nature of the mathematical, chemical, and physics formulae in the workbooks prepared by Ken MCNeil, a former colleague in the Department of Humanities, University of Waikato.

18 Turlais, "Foreward," *Cahiers*, 44.

19 Dreyfus is not alone in such tastes and evaluations, as we can see in a remark made by Anatole France, "Science and Morals: M. Paul Bourget" trans. Bernard Mill, *On Life and Letters*, Third Series (London: John Lane, The Bodley Head, 1924): "By his method and general bent of mind he [Bourget] belongs to the school of M. Taine, for whom he professes a legitimate admiration, and he is not without intellectual affinity with M. Sully Prudhomme, his senior as a poet" (53). (Prud'homme was another poet Dreyfus admires in the *cahiers*.) In this essay, France discusses Bourget's latest novel *Le Disciple*. Most significant is the fact that although Dreyfus gained the support of and often became friendly with writers in the Naturalist School, such as Emile Zola, his own predilections belonged to a more conservative group of writers concerned, as France entitles this essay, with Science and Morals. See also France's discussion of *Un Coeur de Femme* in "Paul Bourget," *On Life and Letters*, 4th series (London: John Lane/Bodley head, 1924, 1925), 21–28.

prevalent in the 1890s and beyond, this form of discourse serves society and the individual reader through its ability to express its liberal ethic through clarity of style. It is a literature of wit and scepticism, intellectual and fluent.[20]

20 Cp. The witty ironies in Anatole France, *The Amythst Ring*, trans. B Drillien (London: The Library Press, 1899), where one of the characters, the Duc de Brécé, explains to a gathering of important friends in his rural chateau: "I am convinced . . . that the fuss made over this affair is, and can only be, some abominable plot instigated by the enemies of France" (17). And when the Abbé Guitrel says who these enemies might be—"free-thinkers, and freemasons . . . Protestants," Brécé adds pointedly. "And Jews . . . Jews and Germans. What unheard of audacity to question the decision of a court martial! For, when all is said and done, it is quite impossible for seven French officers to have made a mistake" (18). Still further, the Duke continues, ominously foreshadowing events forty years later under the Nazi regime: "the Jews will bring misfortune upon France. Why don't we get rid of them? Nothing could be easier" (20). The fear he and his friends express was all too common during the affair, even among those clever and honest enough to see through the smoke screen to Dreyfus's innocence: "For when all's said and done, the Army is all that is left us . . . . That is why I insist that to meddle with it is nothing short of sacrilege" (49). Many of these good Frenchmen in Anatole France's novel are not slobbering racists but fervent conservative patriots. Thus, speaking of the Baronne de Bomont, a converted Jew, the curate explains, "What I mean is that she has been converted and baptized, and is therefore a Christian. She is a good Christian, I might add, and gives largely to our charities . . ." However, Brécé interrupts his friend and reveals himself as an anti-Semite of a more racist and rabid variety: "To me a converted Jew remains a Jew; I cannot make any distinction between them" (62) The abbé tries to wriggle out of this problem by arguing "that the curse pronounced against the Jews was inspired by their crime, and not their race and that therefore . . ." but the duke diverts the conversation to something else. Only later does the novel return to the subject of Jews and a discussion on "anti-Jewish frenzies" (82). In another anecdote, concerning a duel fought between Raoul and Isidore Mayer, the issue was the fact that the true Frenchman refused to allow the Jew to touch a book containing a list of military officers because "It is sacred to the French Army!" Mayer asks why Raoul is so upset, and the answer is: "Because you are of the same religion as the traitor!" (89). In other words, while exposing the graft and pettifogging nature of small town elites, France weaves in and out of their stupid conversation allusions to the Dreyfus Affair and attitudes that run the gamut of rabid to mild anti-Semitism. Some of the characters, like M. Letterier and M. Bergeret, express a more liberal, tolerant view of both the case against and the person of Dreyfus, but they are basically ineffective and comical persons. Outside in the streets, the mobs march, shouting, *"Mort à Zola! Mort à Leterrier! Mort à Bergeret! Mort aux juifs!"* (148). In another place, another cry is added: "Conspuez Leterrier!" or "Conspuez Bergeret!" (190), that is, "Spit on them!" For most people, then, the Dreyfusards are a "syndicate of treachery" (168) and anyone who expresses sympathy for or belief in Dreyfus's innocence is himself "a Jew, a Prussian, an 'Intellectual' . . ." and their opinion "was bought" (187). Greater scorn is heaped on such stupidity by Bergeret, a favorite and repeating character in France's stories and novels, when he confronts M. de Terremonde and tries to convince him that Jews are assimilable. But the self-proclaimed anti-Semite will not be moved. Prof. Bergeret then warns him to be careful of Jehovah: "If I were in your place, I would beware of Him. He was a Jew at heart, and who knows whether He has not always remained a Jew? Who knows whether at this moment He is not avenging His people?" (258) As Terremonde rides away from the professor of Latin, the spokesman for the author shouted "Beware! . . . Do not keep their God" (259). The novel closes at about the time of Colonel Henry's suicide, an event that forced all but the most die-hard anti-Dreyfusards to give up their cause, and they, rather than own up to their error, simply slink away into the darkness (278–279).

At the same time, always in solitary confinement, always at the confluence of rage, despair, nostalgia, and madness[21]—indeed, at times, he veers away from his stated topic, with a *cri du coeur* or a long-repressed memory of infancy or schooldays—Dreyfus was working through and learning from the technical journals he was sent, exercising his professional skills, attempting to keep up with advances in science, and maintaining his grip on secularism and sanity. Recall that he was by profession and training, after all, a military engineer. While he writes little essays on the technical problem of inclines on the curves of railway lines or the way to improve the recoil in rifles and cannons, his mathematical formulae seem to be most concerned with abstract geometrical forms. At times, too, he writes out chemical equations, sometimes connected to an understanding of the human body as an organism and sometimes to changes in the weather. In a way, he is reassuring himself that the natural world—kept apart by all sorts of physical and moral barriers—was rational, orderly, and sane, no matter how absurd and hostile the political and juridical realms might have become for him.

In addition to his literary, historical, and scientific essays and notes—and we also need to point to the several descriptive passages that seem effectively to be nothing less than prose poems—there are the many pages of various drawings.[22] These drawings perhaps are the most unusual and fascinating feature of the prison notebooks. Yet my argument is that they should not be treated as separate from all the other modes of composition and speculation in the *cahiers*.

The modern biographers of Dreyfus, if they touch on his intellectual formation at all—and some even saw the notebooks in the Bibliothèque Nationale before they were made public at the end of 2009—at best seem to ask why he spent so much time with classical texts such as Homer and Cicero or Renaissance authors such as Montaigne and Shakespeare, or Racine and Corneille. Their reading is superficial and inadequate. Look at the appendix of the next book and you will see a much longer list and a much wider range of authors, with Dreyfus citing

21 One can justly compare Dreyfus's prison notebooks therefore with not only Job's complaints from the dung heap or Boethius's search for a consolation of philosophy from his cell in Ravenna but also various nineteenth-century exemplars we will discuss anon, as well as comparing Dreyfus's imposed isolation with the self-chosen experiences of Gauguin in his tropical dreamland and Proust in his cork-lined bedroom.

22 It is estimated Dreyfus drew more than 25,000 of these "*petits desseins*."

many eighteenth- and nineteenth-century writers in French, English, Latin, and sometimes in Italian. Most of the time, as we examine the list, it is clear that the closer he comes down to discussing his own time and place (that is, France in the *fin de siècle*), he not only talks about philosophers, historians, psychologists, and scientists but also discusses painters, musicians, poets, dramatists, and novelists. Sometimes he is quite up to date, as when he refers to Eugene Brieux's play *Les Bienfaiteurs* published in 1896. Although he does not mention all or even a few of the avant-garde cultural figures, he knows enough to have opinions,[23] and his tastes and predilections are for more traditional, more bourgeois, and, one might say, more *practical* authors and artists, practical in the sense that they were concerned with the world more than with themselves. Hence his admiration of Michelet, Renan, Taine, and Bourget.

However, it is not enough to ask how many authors and texts he read or recollected during the years on Devil's Island, nor just to set them out in columns by period, language, and topic. Such exercises certainly enhance our view of Dreyfus's wide reading, but they do not express all his interests in European culture. After all, as we have observed, he seems not to be concerned with any of the avant-garde movements in the arts or the most radical advances in mathematics, psychiatry, or philosophy, and in fact, when he approaches them, he backs off with *boutades* against the art for art's sake programmes and rejects the inherent absolutism and racism in many of the so-called philosophical ideas of the *fin de siècle*. It is therefore important to go beyond those lists and explicit statements of taste and opinion. Who appears most often, both explicitly by name and by implication in the preferences and likes Dreyfus expresses? When he does comment on books and authors, which passages does he focus on or choose to translate? And does he develop a kind of theory of literary or historiographical criticism that blurs the distinction between genres, because he believes that a moralized aesthetic should obtain in all cases? At times that seems to be the conclu-

23 On the importance and uniqueness of "opinions" in the nineteenth century, see Tarde, *L'opinion et la foule*, esp. 73ff. Rather than well-crafted traditional statements of belief and philosophical or political ideology that could be taught in schools, as well as preached in churches and other institutions of public faith, the new bourgeois individual of the modern age was forming "opinions" of his or her own based on private experience, and crowds were coerced or seduced into "public opinion" by the emergent mass media, such as newspapers, magazines, and best-selling books.

sion one must reach, and yet Dreyfus is too often questioning himself as well as his authorities to arrive at any one fixed point. Perhaps, while he was in prison under his onerous conditions of exile and solitary confinement, he was allowed—or rather, allowed himself, dare we say?—the luxury of thinking through matters that he had never had the time or opportunity to deal with before.

In his commentaries on the more recent authors of the eighteenth and nineteenth centuries, while he often considers their moral and political positions, he does keep turning the argument towards—or has sudden slides into—consideration of aesthetics and the artistic temperament or personality. And yet, while he pays close attention to matters of style and form, he rejects the notion of art for art's sake. What also comes through in these choices and ways of questioning and challenging the books and persons he deals with is his rabbinical attitude and method, again something as evident in the product of his musings as absent in any direct way of allusion or citation.

PART 1: MIDRASHING THE *CAHIERS*

> *He [Hillel] used to say: If I am not for myself, who will be for me? And being for my own self, what am I? And if not now, when?*
>
> —*Pirqe Avot,* 1:14

> *My memory, even my involuntary memory, had lost all recollection of the love of Albertine, But it seems that there is also an involuntary memory of the limbs, a pale and fruitless imitation of the other kind, which lives on longer, rather as none non-intelligent animals or vegetables live on longer than man.*
>
> —Marcel Proust[24]

The very first little essay in the prison notebooks appears on folio 2. Let me cite it in full to give some idea of what it is all about and how Dreyfus works:

24 Marcel Proust, *Finding Time Again* (1927), vol. 6 of *A la recherché du temps perdu*, trans. Ian Patterson (London: Penguin Classics, 2004), 5.

> "The Virtues are lost in self-interest as rivers in the sea"—from La Rochefoucauld
>
> The idea is reiterated by D'Annuzio in *The Triumph of Death* I believe, and it is admirably developed in a poetic form. It struck me when I read it, but I could only recall the germ of the thought, resting on the maxim of La Rochefoucauld, It is so true that ideas that guide human nature remain eternal; one can only rearrange them or modify their form, the better to appropriate the expression.[25]

Self-interest is, of course, the common term for egotism and greed in the world before our own, when it has come, if anything, to mean the goal and essence of one's life. Dreyfus belongs to a traditional world of moral values, and he recognizes a commonplace in the contemporary Italian's poem, assigning its clearest expression to the French aphorist of the seventeenth century. He draws the analogy from memory, not an available encyclopaedia of citations. He then states the rhetorical principle that the truest ideas are those that form part of the universal tradition, rhetoric here meaning not only a school discipline or a technique of formal argumentation, but a body of knowledge: what is known is knowable and memorable precisely because it has already been shaped into memorable sentences and mental images. This grounds Dreyfus firmly in his own civilization and, at the same time, as we will be showing, permits him to express his own Jewishness in modes of argument and thought that overlap with the secular and Christian heritage of French education.[26] If the virtues are lost in self-interest and run into the vast sea of confused and meaningless experience, it is because this ideal of an ethical life must keep orienting itself to both the social world of human relationships (including politics) and a more transcendent world of religious and philosophical ideas.

On the same folio page of the first extant *cahier*, Dreyfus places a

---

25 *Cahiers*, 52.

26 Faur: "Since times of yore, Jews have been absorbing ideas and values from other civilizations—that is a fact. What is significant is *what* they chose to absorb and *what* they chose to reject" (*The Horizontal Society*, Section V, 56). Hence, we need to examine what Dreyfus chose to read and comment about, what he puts aside as relevant and what he chooses to question and challenge.

short crucial essay on Pierre Loti. To understand it as typical of the prison notebooks, the whole text needs to be cited and analysed closely:

> *The Dust, Galilee*, Jerusalem by Pierre Loti
>
> Very inferior to his earlier works. No psychology. A great intensity of picturesque sentiment, perception and melancholy things, fugitive and vague images, an incurable delusion. A very correct and vibrant notation of vague and changeable states of nature, a piercing acuteness of perceptions and sensations, but without arriving at any moral conclusion. All that one can say about these books is that Loti has fixed the most mobile and strange aspects of nature with a surprising justness, and that is all. *Raimundo* by Loti. Quite superior to and distant from these travel books describing the stages towards Jerusalem. He disengages his personality to write a simple and natural human work. Admirable descriptions of Basque life.[27]

In the telegraphic prose of this critical essay, Dreyfus measures and compares books by the very popular Pierre Loti. They may have been among the "easy little books" he had first asked Lucie to send him when he knew he was being transported to Devil's Island. Of the first three travel books about a journey to the Holy Land, Dreyfus sees how superficial and facile they are, yet he is also aware of the reason for their popularity: they are slickly written and pander to popular tastes for the exotic, the picturesque, and the sentimental. Without psychology, that is, with no consideration of the way the mind receives, processes, and evaluates the scenes Loti so aptly describes, there is no lasting value in the books. The best one can say about them is that they reproduce static pictures, postcard views of what was then still called Palestine. However, in *Raimundo*, Loti succeeds in delving into the character of the lead character in order to arrive at the essence of the Basque people and culture. Although he does not mention it, the first three books come close to evoking the Land of Israel, the older Jewish settlements, and

27 *Cahiers*, 52. This critical essay about Loti is separated from the opening essay on D'Anunzio and La Rochefoucauld by several mathematical equations.

what was beginning in the last two decades of the nineteenth century, the new *Yeshuv*, the return of Jews to their ancestral homeland and the beginnings of political Zionism. It may be said, on the basis of what we uncovered in our long analyses of the letters between Alfred and Lucie, that this period of martyrdom on Devil's Island was the beginning, albeit aborted or at least deferred to unconscious workings-out, of his own moral journey to Jerusalem.

Following this literary excursion, Dreyfus writes down, seemingly at random, some verses in Latin from Virgil:

> *Ah! miseram Eurydicen! anime fugiente vocabat:*
> *Eurdicen toto referebant flumine ripae.*[28]

> . . . with fleeting breath, called Eurydice—ah, hapless
> Eurydice!
> "Eurydice" the banks re-echoed, all down the stream.[29]

These two lines are taken, whether from some passage in Montaigne or from his own schoolboy memories, from Virgil's *Georgics*, Book IV, lines 526 and 527. They describe how Orpheus, ever lamenting the loss of his wife, whom he was forced to leave in the underworld because she had broken the regulations on looking back once her husband had rescued her from the clutches of Dis, Death, was torn apart by the frenzied maenads, and his head was thrown into the river Hebrus. As it is swept down the rushing current, the severed head sings the name of his wife over and over again, with the banks echoing his lament. Aside from the sheer beauty of these poetic lines by Virgil, one must ask why Dreyfus cites these lines and why here?[30] In the first place, the prisoner feels cut off and helplessly separated from his beloved wife Lucie. Invisible and mysterious forces that seem to have broken apart his domestic life and his professional career are sweeping him along. Second, it is not only a madness that rips up apart his life, but a madness within himself, the

28 *Cahiers*, 52.

29 Trans. H. Rushton Fairclough, Virgil, *Aeneid and the Minor Poems*, vol. I, Loeb Classics (London: William Heinemann and Cambridge, MA: Harvard University Press, 1966 [rev. ed. 1934, orig. 1918]), 233.

30 Hillel the Elder: "Moreover he once saw a skull floating on the face of the waters. He said to it: For drowning others thou was drowned; and they that drowned thee shall be drowned" (*Pirqe Avot* 2:7).

frustrations and rage that he can barely contain arising from his long-standing hypersensitive disposition and enervation exacerbated by the tortures of the prison authorities.

Still on this second folio page, Dreyfus cites in English Shakespeare's *Othello,* III.iii, the speech by Iago:

> Who steals my purse steals trash; 'tis something, nothing;
> 'Twas mine, 'tis his, and has been slave to thousands:
> But he that filches from me my good name
> Robs me of that which not enriches him
> And makes me poor indeed.

Although a modern literary scholar would see the words of this arch-villain as darkly ironic, given Iago's evil and Machiavellian intentions against the tragic Moor, and as much a tissue of commonplaces as Polonius's rodomontades in *Hamlet*, for Dreyfus it is these very time-worn expressions that encapsulate his own feelings, otherwise almost inarticulate in his nervous condition. Throughout the letters, we have seen Lucie and Alfred repeating their frenetic need to clear the honour of the family name, and this compulsive impulse drives virtually everything Alfred reads, thinks, and writes about.[31]

Thus, it is not out of nothing that Virgil's lines or this speech from Shakespeare appear on the pages of the workbooks. They are deeply constitutive concepts of his whole project in writing out and so creating an intellectual refuge from the terrible machine grinding him down every day and every night. Dreyfus does not seek refuge in great books and ideas only to escape from the tortures he is undergoing: he works hard to create this alternate space and to draw out of his deepest memories aspects of his own personality he was not normally engaged in developing, and he wrestles with the angel of his own intellect to make his self viable in the harsh, agonizing environment he cannot deny. Like with Jacob, though, it takes more than just enduring a whole long night to emerge victorious in the morning with a new

31 "For Judaism, the world is like a great family, where the father lives in immediate contact with his children, who are the different peoples of the earth . . . . In heaven a single God, father of all men alike; on earth a family of peoples, among whom Israel is the 'first born, charged with teaching and administering the true religion of mankind, of which he is priest.'" Elijah Benamozegh, *Israel and Humanity*, trans. and ed. Maxwell Luri (New York and Mahwah: Paulist Press, 1994), 53–54.

name; it also means being wounded and realizing that the victory is far from complete. Jacob gains a new name, Israel, and a new determination in his life, while for Dreyfus the return to his ancestral identity is more complex and subtle.

In the very next little essay, he attempts, on the verso of folio 6, to confront one of his favourite authors, Ernest Renan, and begins to wrestle with a theme that bothers him many times throughout the surviving *cahiers*:

> From Renan: "The study of literary history will replace in great part the direct reading of works of the human mind." I am grieved to find myself in absolute disagreement with Renan. The study of literary history can only complete direct reading of works of the human mind.[32]

Having decided in some sort of conscious way to fill his *cahiers* with intellectual matters of various kinds, as we have noted before, Dreyfus now has to rationalize what he is doing, that is, justify to himself the project according to his circumstances—he does not have a large library to draw on or colleagues to consult; he has limited space, time, and energy, and even further, limited emotional focus in which to contemplate the ideas he wishes to write out. So here for the first time, we can see him starting to engage with his intellectual masters; he confesses that he disagrees with Renan—absolutely. As though prescient with foresight into the postmodernist obsession with theory over substance and the death of an author in a mode of criticism that "privileges" the critic over the creative artist, Renan laments that direct experience of works of the human mind will have to give way to secondary texts.[33] In a sense, this is the old Platonic problem of *mimesis*, of art as an imitation of reality, and so less perfect, if not a mere hollow and shallow shadow of the original, and then critical essays or histories of the imitations as even more distorted and inane compositions, divorcing each new generation

32 *Cahiers*, 53.

33 Compare that to another of Dreyfus's favourite authors, Hippolyte Taine: "The modern method which I strive to pursue, and which is beginning to be introduced in all the moral sciences, consists in considering human productions, and particularly works of art, as facts and productions of which it is essential to mark the characteristics and seek the causes, and nothing more" (*The Philosophy of Art*, trans. John Durand. [New York: Holt & Williams, 1873] 37). Dreyfus does not limit his method to such a positivistic science and seeks something more than physical facts.

from its ability to enter into a living dialogue with the products of human cogitation and speculation.[34]

Such questions, though, seem appropriate within a culture formed on Hellenistic ideas of art as imitation and texts as arguments whose basis is in historical facts and testimonials shaped by tendentious drives, while a Jewish point of view argues in a different way altogether, stating that mankind, formed in the image of God, seeks to enhance and develop that image so as to participate more fully in the divine creativity and that textuality moves in and out of direct contact with the earliest intellectual voices, enlivening them at the same time as making them enhance the individuality of the latest and future voices.

Consequently, at a seemingly mundane level, Dreyfus begins to advance his thought by proposing *contra* Renan that "the study of literary history can only complete direct reading of works of the human mind," for this kind of secondary approach to direct experience of another mind than one's own,

> [which] coordinates the elements, minimizes the obscurities, makes comprehensible the transformations, the influence exercised by the surrounding milieu and current ideas.

These criteria for conducting and evaluating the critical programme would undermine the wall set up by Renan between direct access to an author's creative energy and excitement and the student, who he fears will only encounter the lesser mind of the historian or reviewer. Dreyfus sets out the parameters of a critical theory that uses the developing

---

34 According to Ouaknin, there are three steps in *mahloquet*, the rabbinic manner of questioning and challenging a text in pairs: study and thought are the necessary preparations for entering into such a dialogue of learning; it is not a simple exchange of ideas through question and answer, as in a Socratic dialogue, with its maieutic of recalling what was what once known and has been forgotten but a constant process of *sheylot-ou-t'shouvot*, questions and challenging responses, and finally the dialogue does not take place on the same level of thought—it creates a new dimension of thought (*Tsimtsoum*, 111). This new level of understanding where truth is constructed is a shared interiority, shared by the interlocutors themselves and with God who is always a participant as well (112). This is what Lucie and Alfred believe they are constructing in their letters, a language—world at a different level of experience than they have ever known and that is beyond the understanding of the censors reading their epistles. He also believes he is creating something of the same sort in the various workbooks he fills out, in dialogue with himself, with the authors he reads and recollects, and with the man he hopes to become through the whole exercise.

secondary texts to create an approach that directs the student through a well-shaped course of study towards contact with ancestral minds, shadow voices that would otherwise recede into obscurity by the passage of time. History conceived as both the accumulation of differences and the loss of points of direct contact can also be reconstructed in this way to become a roadmap that takes advantage of hindsight, each advance into the future at the same time being a clarification of what happened in the past and how its meaningfulness has become more evident with the realization of its potentialities. The reason Dreyfus prefers Renan, Michelet, and Taine, for instance, rather than say Sainte-Beuve or Thiers,[35] is because these moral teachers take into account the transformations, the influence of surrounding milieu, and the current of ideas. To find out how they do this takes up much of his mental energy.

But first he needs to affirm for himself that "never will anything be able to replace direct reading of great works of the human mind." By this he means more than reading old authors in their original languages, or more recent philosophers and historians in their pristine texts, rather than a schoolbook *résumé* and dumbed-down popular paraphrase; these original readings require introductory essays, generous annotations and glossaries, and translations into contemporary languages. For what purpose?

> A moral or intellectual emotion will never be produced except by direct reading of great works; the ideas they stimulate, that they arouse in passing in the consciousness and then the unconscious provokes in the mind a form of elevated character.[36]

---

35 Although he is critical of these authors, Dreyfus came to them because, as Anatole France put it in terms of one: "The 'Histoire de la Révolution' and the 'Histoire du Consulat et de l'Empire,' by M. Thiers, were, for more than thirty years, the books most read in France, if we except 'Les Trois Mousquetaires,' which it will be admitted, does not belong to the same class" ("M. Thiers as Historian," on the occasion of the inauguration of the monument to him at Père-Lachaise in *On Life & Letters*, I, 209). Dreyfus would therefore have read Thiers and Sainte-Beuve in school and he can now, with a more mature mind and a sensibility honed by the nightmare, reflect more wisely on the tasks of a historiographer.

36 Note that my translations attempt to follow Dreyfus's own often halting syntax, hesitations, and repetitions. Instead of crossing out and rewriting to polish his style, he starts again in several places to write new versions of these essays that are so important to him. Sometimes, though, he starts and then crosses out and moves on to something else, and even, rarely, he starts his essay, then is diverted to something else—and when that something else is highly personal, such as a memory of his childhood or a *cri du coeur* in reaction to current torture, frustration, and

The purpose of reading, he argues here, is to come into direct contact with another human mind through its intellectual and artistic productions, and that contact is stimulating, inspiring, and creative in itself. The purpose is to create a character of a high moral kind. These developments should happen both to the conscious and the unconscious mind—but what can Dreyfus mean by "unconscious" in 1898 when he is writing these notebooks? This is the time when Sigmund Freud was only beginning to develop his theories of the mind as overwhelmingly composed of drives, passions, impulses, memories, and anxieties mostly below or outside the range of volitional control or awareness. Poets and philosophers throughout the nineteenth century had been probing the limits of the conscious mind, and some, following Rousseau, had already been asserting the primacy of secret inner realms over distorting socially-constructed paradigms of personality, thus seeking out primitive, folk, and exotic models and experiences. Others, like Nietzsche, sang the praises of violent emotions and actions over peaceful and contemplative lives.

In rabbinical writings, however, the unconscious was what was either forgotten and could be learned through study under careful guidance or what was not yet articulated and realized, so that an interpretation of a text would be measured by how far it enhanced, clarified, and made relevant ancient pronouncements and narrative exemplars, and ethical life always sought to adjust and thus advance the applications of the law in such ways as were most just and compassionate.[37] For Dreyfus, too, reading to be inspired and challenged by great works of the human mind was a moral act with the purpose of making himself and other students wiser and better able to cope with adversity. He would certainly have agreed with most of what is in *Pirqe Avot*, the Ethics of the Fathers, the highly *aggadic* book of the Mishna traditionally read aloud in the synagogue during Sabbath services between the end of Passover and the start of the New Year, through the northern hemisphere summer. For example, Simeon, the son of Rabbi Gamliel, is quoted as saying,

---

loneliness, we shall take special note of those moments.

37 In an ambiguous and perhaps teasing tone, see Romain Rolland: "Kindness is not a rare quality with the Jews: of all the virtues it is the most readily admitted among them, even when they do not practice it" (*Jean Christophe,* Vol. II, 379).

> All my days I have grown up among the wise, and I have found naught of better service than silence; not learning but doing is the chief thing; and he who speaks profusely causes sin . . . By three things is the world preserved: by truth, by judgment, and by peace . . .[38]

Whether Alfred Dreyfus ever read these words himself or heard them recited in synagogue during the summer months,[39] they nevertheless resonate within his own objections to Renan,[40] a teacher he respects but whose pronouncements he cannot accept without question or challenge:

> The study of literary history is the domain of criticism, the realm of purely subjective science. The reading of great works is the domain of the objective, preserved in the light of awakening wise and intellectual ideas. One must therefore see in Renan's phrase a mere whim [*une boutade*] or, more likely, his mind was tending towards the same criticism, philology . . .

Look at what he says here: literary criticism is the zone of the subjective whereas direct reading of those texts is objective. This is what we now call "counterintuitive." It is a witty paradox, an overturning of the expected, commonsense judgement. He seems to dismiss Renan's remark as a joke or a whim and calls such criticism philology. But what Dreyfus actually meant to say here we cannot tell, because the final four lines are rubbed out.

What he wishes to say, though, is suggested by a second version of this same essay, which he wrote on the verso of folio 11.[41] Skipping over

38 *Pirqe Avot*, 1: 17–18.

39 Idelsohn: "One of Judaism's chief features is its staunch adherence to and fearless proclamation of the truth, however painful to personal vanity that truth may be" (*Jewish Music*, 78); or put another way, no matter how painful and dangerous it may be to the individual or community forced to live in a hostile society.

40 Cf. Anatole France: "It seems that the true image of the past has been revealed to us by the great historical school of our own age . . . . we have created the comparative history of humanity. Fresh sciences such as ethnography, archaeology, and philology had had a great share in doing this . . . . And this sense of origins, this divination of a lost past, this knowledge of the childhood of humanity, is possessed in the highest degree by M. Renan," in "M. Ernest Renan, Historian of Origins," *Of Life & Letters*, 286).

41 *Cahiers*, 55.

his little essay on the writings of "great northern writers, Bjornson, Ibsen, Tolstoy, Dostoivesky,"[42] and two versions of the essay "On Religious Faith"[43] that we will deal with at length presently, let us turn for a moment to this rewriting of the response to Renan's dictum. It is virtually the same word for word until the last two paragraphs. These modify what he said on the previous page:

> The study of literary history is the domain of criticism, the domain of science; the reading of great works is the domain of sentiment, of the awakening of impressions of beauty of all kinds.

Rather than making the rhetorical balance of subjective/objective, Dreyfus here speaks of science and sentiment, expanding on that last term into impressions of beauty. The contrast is less strong and shades into complementarity, the only problem occurring when Renan draws the contrast himself. For Dreyfus, in the lines he was presumably not satisfied with before and crossed out, the solution is one of trying for a reconciliation, a compromise, a making of peace, and so he withdraws his own denigration of Renan's comment as a *boutade*, a toss-off line:

> One must not see in this idea expressed by this great mind who calls himself Renan only a simple whim [*une boutade*] at a moment when he himself plunged into the study of pure criticism, into philological studies that totally absorbed him. The study of literary history makes one see the evolution of the human mind and, under this name, it is instructive and interesting.

Although Renan, for reasons of his own, turned his attention in a

---

42 *Cahiers*, 54. This determination of northern writers includes Russians and Scandinavians and also Nietzsche from Germany and Switzerland, whom he also mentions, or rather, having pointed out the "humane" quality of the writers mentioned and taken their side against detractors, he slides into a discussion of the importance of putting literature into its context, chronological and geographical, which concern for the "temperament, climate, ambient influences" leads him to watch how the individual escapes from "Cartesian oppression" wherein the mind exists in a purely abstract vacuum, with Nietzsche being a primary example of someone who has "broken from himself."

43 *Cahiers*, 54–55, *Cahier* I, F°8 and *Cahier* F°10.

more strictly philological (scientific) direction,[44] Dreyfus appreciates the great man's previous openness to the humanist approach to literary studies and explains his own belief in the evolution of the human mind—a mind that grows, changes, and adjusts to its environment, and is not oppressed by the Cartesian split between an abstract inner world and the confused sensations on the outside. What Dreyfus must fight against in his own life are the horrible external tortures, the physical shackles of his exile on Devil's Island, with its loneliness and despair, and the moral disintegration of his own mind, already hypersensitive and now likely to slip into madness through the shame and humiliation of the charges against him. It would be all too easy to plunge himself into a kind of philology, a universe made up only of words that rattle about in a vast and empty space. The important thing to do is to face up to the real problems of the hostile and dangerous world, and to wrestle with them like a good Jew, guided by the ethics of the fathers and the long tradition of questioning and mutual challenging. Neither one nor the other, not withdrawal from reality into sterile intellectualism and not total engagement with pain, humiliation, and suffering, but as

> Rabban Gamaliel, the son of Rabbi Judah the Prince, said, An excellent thing is the study of the Torah combined with some worldly occupation, for the labor demanded by them both makes sin to be forgotten. All study of the Torah without work must in the end be futile and become the cause of sin. Let all who are employed with the congregation act with them for Heaven's sake, for then the merit of their fathers sustains them, and their righteousness endures forever.[45]

Intellectual work (Torah in the widest understanding of the term[46])

---

44 For Renan and for Dreyfus, the immediate sense of philology would be the scientific study of literary texts, that is, seeing each as a type produced by the measurable qualities of nationality, race, and economic class, but this kind of avoidance of dealing directly with the imaginative, poetic quality of the texts as works of art would conform to the rabbinical procedures of *pilpul*, where the immediate contexts, implications, and legal application of the scripture being studied are made subordinate to exegetical acrobatics.

45 *Pirqe Avot*, 2:2.

46 "The word *Torah* is left untranslated. It is variously used for the Pentateuch, the scriptures, the Oral Law, as well as for the whole body of religious truth, study and practice," *Siddur Sephath Emeth*

and real-world labor (*avoda*), which is the work both of serving God in liturgical and ritual duties and also earning a living through service to the community, go together to help one forget sin, and through working with society (the congregation) one can draw on the "merit of the fathers" (*zekhut avot*) and inherit the rewards of piety and ethical life: "All Israel has a portion in the world to come," according to the headnote of the *Chapters of the Fathers*. So too we hope for Alfred Dreyfus.

But would he have known or cared?[47] In this same *cahier*, between the two versions of the Renan essay, he writes two versions of an untitled essay I call "Religious Faith." Let us see what he has to say. The difference between the two is not large, but shows how their author is thinking through and refining his ideas. On both folio 8 and folio 10, he begins in the same way with the same words:

> *Religious Faith*
>
> We need to reduce the question to two essential terms: to choose between determinism and revelation; and this choice is not a matter of reason—it is a question of faith. Against such faith, no criticism prevails; it is admirable and I envy those who possess it . . .

This is Dreyfus's religious credo and his philosophical position. One either is or is not religious, and that means one is either: a determinist, since some god or other has created the world, limits where one is and what one can do, and thus sets out the basic parameters of life; or one is a rationalist, who sees the world as subject not to an arbitrary will but to laws of nature that can be understood by reason and science and, with that understanding, has the freedom to make adjustments in one's life to secure advantages, subject to the realities of nature. But the type of person one is is not open to a totally free choice; it is a matter of faith, but what he means by *foi* needs to be found out. To begin with, accord-

---

(Speech of Truth) Order of Prayers for the Whole Year, Hebrew and English, no editor or translator named (New York: Hebrew Publishing Co. 1953), 229, note.

47 Compare the words of André Maurois, who like Alfred Dreyfus came from a Jewish family of Alsatian manufacturers displaced after 1870, in his autobiography: "To sustain me in this premature crisis of adolescence I had no religious faith whatever. I did not know (and even to-day do not know exactly) the doctrine of the religion which by birth should be mine" (*Call No Man Happy*, 30). Thanks at least to Lucie and her family, Dreyfus would not have been so ignorant of his own background.

ing to Dreyfus, placing himself within the large camp of secularists and rationalists of the nineteenth century, but not completely and dogmatically, faith is a frame of mind. He envies those who have it, finds it enviable, and yet cannot will himself by logical argument into its possession. At this point, the two versions of the essay begin to diverge. The first version continues in this way:

> But since one doesn't believe, not even as a child, since criticism, the spirit of reason, was melded into me—it is useless to break your head, to get all tipsy with aesthetic reasons, to search in nature, in the universal conscience etc. for reasons to believe—with the affirmations—with the affirmations of reason, of science, leave the dissolution of religions . . .

Before the syntax breaks down altogether, notice how Dreyfus finds himself unable to follow the various schools of rationalism, idealism, mysticism, and romantic naturalism available around him. He laments the fact that he cannot have faith because he was brought up with too much of a critical sensibility, and he says, speaking more to himself than to any objective imaginary audience, that there is no use getting yourself into a state of confusion through Romantic aesthetics or German idealism or some imperative will to believe, all of which would attempt to break down the structures of organized religion. It would be so much easier to bear his own pains and humiliations if he could believe, but he doesn't and he can't, so why should he pound his head on a brick wall?

In the second little essay on folio 10, he says something similar but not quite the same:

> Against faith, no criticism prevails, and I envy those who posses it. But since one doesn't believe, like a small child, without reason, and true science does not meddle with it—despite the bankruptcy of science—it is useless to break your head, to get all tipsy with a so-called rational aesthetics—to search for it in nature, in the universal consciousness . . . or for reasons to believe in: of an affirmation of reason in science, a kind of dissolution of all religions.

Once again, he begins by stating that he envies those who have faith, who were born with it, or at least were born into an environment where faith was impressed into their personality. The failure of science and rational philosophy on their own to help him out of his despair exposes their bankruptcy: true science, in fact, steps away from the most important questions of all in life, and consequently, there is no use chasing the phantasm in any form of Rousseau's back-to-nature primitivism or more contemporary pseudomystical aestheticism in search of the egotistical sublime or Hegelian hunt for the universal Time Spirit.[48] He doesn't see traditional religions as the great enemy, and wants no Voltaire to scream in his ears, "*Ecrassez l'infame!*"

In both versions, then, Dreyfus wishes he had faith to believe in religion, but he also cries out in pain at the inadequacies of all the apparent alternatives propounded by his favourite authors and the supposed bedrock of his civilization. Therefore, he tries to explore the alternative more closely. In the first essay he writes:

> To those who don't believe, reason furnishes a contrary explanation to the phenomenon of belief. God enters the category of the ideal, in the dream that we all share of humanity where all will become noble, good and just. Religion is the beauty in the moral order and that is all. For purely philosophical idealism is only available to the highest intelligences, while purely religious idealism is only accessible to the most humble minds.

This seems to set out a paraphrase of the latest secular, moral religion for the nineteenth century. The old religious systems can be rationalized away as variations on a shared human deism, wherein everything essentially good, noble, just, and tends towards a perfect ideal eventually. God is the ideal of beauty of a moral universe.[49] But without considering

48 Proust, *Finding Time Again*: "Dreyfusisme was now integrated into a range of respectable and normal things" (33–34).

49 Benmozegh cites Renan: "Enamored of beauty, nature soars towards her with an unceasing impulse, and approaches closer and closer to her in its forms. The universe is thus an immense being which rises relentlessly toward a higher end which it has prepared though all its previous efforts, proving at once its enormous desire for the good and its marvelous ingenuity," and adds that in Kabbalah, this concept is carried out in a way that makes the enhancement of natural beauty come about

the absurdity of such time- and culture-bound categories of thought, Dreyfus sees their weakness in the social limitations they enforce: one must be rich and comfortable, well educated, and arrogant to believe in the ideals, but the primitive and poor, the uneducated and unsophisticated alone have access, not to a lesser faith or set of popular superstitions, but to religious idealism—to the longed-for faith of other times and other places.[50] In a sense, Dreyfus mocks both science and religion as failed ideals and at the same time regrets that he cannot have faith in either.

He makes this even clearer in the second version of the essay *On Religious Faith*:

> To those who don't believe, however, reason furnishes an explanation of the phenomenon of all beliefs, the innate need in all beings to come out of brutal realities, of plunging oneself into the domain of dreams, of the ideal, of a humanity which will be supremely beautiful, noble and just. A religion whichever it may be, is the beauty of the moral order, that is all. For a purely philosophical idealism is not intended for use by all intelligences, while the purely religious idealism is meant for more humble spirits.

The modern authors, such as Michelet, Renan, and Taine, whom

---

through man's intimate participation in the creative processes themselves, through nourishment, sexuality, and performance of the mitzvot (Benmozegh, *Israel and Humanity*, 188).

50 Faur: "'superstititon' and 'superstitious' are terms associated with 'dread and belief in the irrational.' In the original Latin, however, *superstito* and *superstitious* had a different meaning. 'Superstition' was knowledge of a past event, and '*superstitiosus*' was that individual who had the peculiar gift to 'testify' about an event in which he was not present" (*The Horizontal Society*, Section IV, Introductory Remarks). We could go further in this etymological game that opens up whole new ways of breaking into the hidden meanings of Dreyfus's text. For instance, *to testify* was a legal term related to *to theorize*, which described the particular mission of delegated representatives of one city state (polis) to visit, participate in, and report back on the power of another city's rituals; hence, it was the special ability to bring home a charged testimony a speech filled with *enargaeia* that infused the home state with the "truths" of their enemies or rivals. Dreyfus looks backwards to his life before he was charged with crimes and foreward to the day he will be rehabilitated, regaining his name and honor, and the purity of soul for himself and his family, that is all important to his sense of self and identity. His critical readings and commentaries give him a theoretical power to testify to his own innocence. Cp. discussions of *melitza* throughout this book.

Dreyfus reads intensely, or those writing at around this very time, such as Freud and the Reinach brothers, whom he as yet does not know about, offer ways of rationalizing revealed religions based on faith; of explaining away mysteriousness and spirituality by recourse to analysis of dreams, myths, and archaic rituals; and of smoothing away all the specificities of different times and cultures in order to envisage a utopian ideology of one sort or another, and it all depends on class and other circumstances to determine in which category of belief you fall.

Then, at this point in both versions of the essay, he makes his formal statement of belief. In the first he writes:

> I am neither a believer not hostile to belief—I am a sympathetic witness, on the contrary, to those who believe, since I am conscious of the moral good of those who do believe, on condition always that this belief does not become a narrow idea, an abstract formula, or that reduces itself to an airy idealism. In conclusion, philosophical idealism for high intelligences, religious idealism for humble minds: this is what will become of the summing up of the beauty and the moral good in our beliefs.

Is Dreyfus, then, an agnostic or an atheist or merely confused and despondent? He seems to want to take a neutral stand, neither for nor against religion per se, inclined by disposition towards science and rationalism but all too aware of their inadequacies to deal with the situation he is in or the surging sense of meaninglessness in his life. He observes from afar, a not quite dispassionate witness to those with faith who can find the moral strength to withstand the forces of oppression and evil in the world, who can, as he seems unable to, understand the conspiracy of arrogance ranged against him. He ought, by his own calculations, to belong to the superior intellects who can be satisfied—find a consolation of philosophy—in the higher ideals; he wishes he could have a simpler faith, perhaps like those of women and children or of his rabbinical ancestors.

The second version of this final statement follows exactly the words of the first, until the final sentence, where it diverges with a subtle new expression:

> In conclusion, philosophical idealism for high intelligences, religious idealism for humble spirits; this is what we should reduce beauty and moral good in our beliefs.

It is the difference between "*à quoi devraient se resumer*" and "*à quoi doivent se reduire*," between what should be summed up into a belief system and what must be reduced into that desired system of beliefs. In the first, there is a sense of fulfilling a future duty and collecting together of diverse ideas; in the second, a subjunctive hope and speculative doubt about the consequences of reducing the diverse ideas into one faith.

On folio 10, after those last words shared with the first essay, Dreyfus draws a line across the manuscript and adds nine of his doodles. He then writes:

> Human thought in all its power, in all its [illegible word] can only use that force with a moral value which is imprinted, or else it is as abstract and as dry as a mathematical problem can be [illegible word].[51]

If not conceived as a part of the essay on faith, these lines supplement it in a striking if ambiguous and frustrating way. The two unreadable words in the manuscript prevent any complete understanding of what it is that Dreyfus wishes to say here. Just as he argued that a person cannot reason his way into faith if he has been brought up to be critical and believe in science, even after he has realized that rationalism itself and science are inadequate to provide him with consolation or a way of understanding the horrible ordeal he is going through, just so *la pensée humaine* with all its *puissance* can only achieve its ends by the moral value (*la valeur morale*) it has imprinted (*est empreinte*) in it—but what

51 Compare the words of Max Nordau, as he ironically and scathingly excoriates the French attitude towards Jews: "I must utter the painful word. The nations which emancipated the Jews have mistaken their own feelings. In order to produce its full effect, emancipation should first have been completed in sentiment before it was declared law. But this was not the case . . . . The emancipation of the Jews was not the consequence of the conviction that grave injury had been done to a race, that it has been treated most terribly, and it was time to atone for the injustice of a thousand years; it was solely the result of the geometrical mode of thought of French rationalism of the 18th century. This rationalism was constructed by the aid of pure logic, without taking into account livings sentiments and the principles of the certainty of mathematical action; and it insisted upon trying to introduce these creations of pure intellect into the world of reality." Nordau, "Address at the First Zionist Congress" (1897), *MidEastWeb*.

the additional quality in such thoughts is that makes it effective we can only guess. Without that power of moral suasion, however it is come by, reason by itself is as dry and abstract as the mathematical equations Dreyfus scribbles up and down his pages, along with the obsessive little drawings.

Nothing explicit, it seems, is said about Judaism in either of these essays. Nor, it would seem, about Christianity, since the debate in his mind is between scientific rationalism and a kind of poetic, philosophical religion on the other. It may be that Dreyfus has couched his terms in a vague, occluded language that recalls Maimonides in his lengthy instructions to his pupil, *The Guide of the Perplexed*, in which someone who has trained himself in Greek knowledge—philosophy and mathematics, for the most part—finds himself perplexed by the mythical and mysterious language of the revealed scriptures, as well as by the crabbed, oblique midrashic style of the rabbis. The Rambam does not aim to enforce a faith on his student, to force a dogmatic interpretation on that divine text, or to reject reason and science; instead, he teaches, in his own midrashic style, with all its mixture of tones, its fragmentation and seemingly disordered presentation of the argument, how to read the sacred books so that they conform to Aristotelian principles of logic, grammar, and science.

On folio 12 of the first *cahier*,[52] Dreyfus then offers a critical reading of Tolstoy. It will be of interest, in light of his statements about religion and science, to see what Dreyfus has to say about *The Gospels Translated, Compared, and Harmonised*, which was published in Russian between 1880 and 1882 and translated by Wizewa and G. Art. He begins by paraphrasing what these two translators say in their introductory remarks, noting that the Russian thinker is using his study of the New Testament to advance his own "new Christianity." For them, this innovative reading is peculiar.

> The translators find that Tolstoy is at home in the sacred text. Discourse and parable, thought and imagery, all are taken in a new sense.

But then, as so often happens, Dreyfus intrudes into the paraphrase

52 *Cahiers*, 56.

to speak in his own voice, to raise his own objections to what Wizewa and Art have written, and to question Tolstoy's ideas as well.

> This should not astonish us. The text of the Four Gospels are not in agreement in all interpretations!

Dreyfus takes a sceptical position in regard to these Christian documents, establishing first of all that the Four Gospels do not agree with one another and that they are a composite of diverse kinds of discourse whose meanings interpreters have not agreed on. If Tolstoy offers a unique approach to interpretation, Dreyfus is not surprised: everyone in rabbinical tradition, and certainly anyone who has read or heard of Maimonides, should be prepared to see in discourse, parable, thought, and imagery a dynamic and multilayered textuality; this category naturally includes the Gospels.[53]

The two translators of Tolstoy express another surprise, that the Russian, "having proclaimed the divinity of Jesus's doctrine, refuses then to recognize the divinity of his person." For Dreyfus, that in itself seems a rational distinction, the revealed word having a divine nature that does not necessarily pass on to the deliverer of the Word, as with the law given to Moses on Sinai and Moses himself who is always a man, albeit the best of the prophets. What surprises Dreyfus, in the sense that his own Jewish sensibilities cannot follow Wizewa and Art in their Christian faith, is that "Tolstoy is simply incomplete" because "neither the person nor the doctrines are divine, they are simply human." This is the position of a nineteenth-century secular, assimilated Jew, and one that he shares with many secularised Christians of his day, whether they call themselves atheists, agnostics, or nothing at all.

In the final sentences of this brief critical essay, Dreyfus becomes more complex and more obscure to us—because he has crossed out too much and his handwriting becomes undecipherable to the modern editors:

> It would have been better for the translators to grasp simply these words [illegible word] of Alexandria, that

53 Marcel Mergui and his *Champs du Midrash* group will be discussed later. One of their most interesting characteristics, as they seek to explain Christian scriptures as the result of primitive misunderstandings of Hebrew *midrashim* as the core of Gospel thinking, is that they stress the visualized *midrash* in iconography and art.

> it was not so well to examine all the matters of religion, that it would be better for each one of us to remain in his own beliefs. [This whole text has been crossed out.]

Which writer of Antiquity he refers to is not clear, but the import of his statement is, let everyone remain in the beliefs he was born to and make the best of it, since conversion under duress or in crisis means nothing, and those who did become something new, presumably Christian, have not really benefited. In a way, this accords with Dreyfus's own statement of tolerance and envy of anyone with a true belief, any departure from what one grew up into being a form of drunken lurch.

Then, with the passage obliterated, in place of the rejected text, Dreyfus draws a horizontal line, and writes, "Let us enter this subject"—and nothing follows but a drawing of two hyperbolas and a long series of numerical equations. Hopefully, these mathematical games are not the dry and abstract formulation of another inadequate state of mind.

From now on, rather than attempting to give a close reading of each of Dreyfus's critical or speculative essays,[54] we shall only focus on a few that demonstrate some special feature in his personality or situation that breaks through the surface of the text. But first a brief interlude and series of digressions.

Dreyfus's Doodles, Iconography, and Kabbalistic Signs

> *That is what Bacon called the principle of our eternal ignorance, the ignorance to which the conditions of man condemns us, walled in as we are within a rock, solitary and deceived in the midst of the world.*
>
> —Anatole France[55]

In the various studies of Dreyfus's drawings in French, the common term used for them is *dessins*, drawings, sketches, or designs, there apparently being no French equivalent to the English word *doodle*.[56] To

54 In a future book, we will deal more extensively with Dreyfus's readings, tastes, and opinions in matters of literature, historiography, culture and science.

55 France, "Goerge Sand," *On Life & Letters*, I, 300.

56 It is possible that folk-etymology projects back into "doodle" some of the qualities associated with a similar-sounding word *dawdle*, to linger, to temporize, to wander about aimlessly.

speak of these line drawings as scribbles or scratchings misses the point of the nonverbal quality of the work. Another French word, *gaspiller*, comes to mind, in that it matches with the etymological root of doodle (to play on a "doodle-fife" or bagpipe and hence to make annoying, tedious, and meaningless sounds or, by metaphoric extension, to make obsessive, pointless, empty drawings while listening or speaking to someone else), but if the closest French equivalent to doodling is *gaspillage*, in the sense of wasting time, squandering energy, and lavishing effort better spent on something important, it seems never to have been used in regard to Alfred's drawing.

Although many (though hardly all) of the drawings begin with an X (or *aleph* א) or a Y (or *tsadeh* ץ), these do not serve as letters or abbreviations for words. They might be compared to the bizarre imagery to be found in Glozel, and the connections between the whole Dreyfus Affair and this controversial archaeological site in central France, near Vichy, may be seen both in terms of the actual objects collected between 1924 and 1932 and the newspaper articles, scientific studies, and popular imagination that swirled about in what came to be known as the War of the Bricks or the Second Dreyfus Affair. A key figure connecting the two affairs is Salomon Reinach, a strong Dreyfusard in the 1890s and a major supporter of the legitimacy and importance of Glozel during the 1920s.

It is also possible to see in these drawings a kind of childish game, such as Elias Canetti imagines in his early memories when he saw people inside the wallpaper designs of his bedroom, but in regard to Alfred's doodles, we could rather see projections of his anxieties, fears, desires, and hallucinations caused by isolation, sensory deprivation, and illness. They might be nightmare images, distortions of the once-familiar faces, flowers, and buildings he is now deprived of.

The constant iteration of these pictures, each one drawn to a basic X/א or Y/ץ pattern with endless variations of efflorescence of curvilinear designs, may also suggest a kind of series of animated cartoons, not in the sense of comic strips or books, with either satiric or heroic purpose, but rather a manifestation of the need Dreyfus felt to make order out of his disorderly life, to find the mobility his incarceration denied to him, and to generate a kind of free creativity otherwise impossible in the circumstances in which he found himself.

The prison guards assigned to watch all of Dreyfus's activities and to collect and either recopy them or write a report on their contents described the doodles in three ways: sometimes they called them architectural shapes, and we now know that in the missing *cahiers*, there may have been some transitional movement away from the cones and other geometrical drawings, along with shaded outlines of various structures that could well be construed as "architectural." At other times, they called them "*desseins cabbalistiques*" by which they probably meant nothing more than tediously, esoterically, and exotically Semitic, without seeing any specific secret significance in them. To them Kabbalah might not even have alluded to any historical school of medieval or Renaissance mystical traditions. If it did, then they would surely have sought expert advice, even if perversely anti-Semitic, since the constant surveillance of the prisoner's behaviour and the censorship of his writings was meant precisely to uncover evidence of any treasonous intentions, such as clues as to his non-French, that is, Jewish, tendencies and attitudes or beliefs.[57]

On a very few occasions, the scrutinizing guards recorded the doodles as not only kabbalistic but as "*desseins cabbalistiques ordinaires*," this second adjective suggesting either some further knowledge they had obtained or subtle inferences they were making as to a particular system of Jewish conspiratorial system or code, with *ordinaires* pointing towards an official, regular purpose in the drawings.

But while again it is likely that the government agents assigned to check up on the deportee's secret thoughts and feelings did not really have anything more in mind here than a vague allusion to the kind of absurdities contained in *The Protocols of the Elders of Zion* or at least spoken of in irrational terms by anti-Semites such as Edouard Drumont, the argument made in this book is that we cannot dismiss the nonsense of the Jew-haters out of hand because this nonsense forms the matrix of the affair and of the society of irrationality in which the Holocaust would crystallize over the subsequent half-century. In other words, here as in other places, these anti-Semites did not merely misinterpret Jewish practices, traditions, and beliefs. They did see and feel something

57 As a matter of fact, while at this same period the School of Jewish Science (*Jüdisscheswissenschaft*) in Germany was spreading amongst rationalist reformers in France and other progressive countries, there was a countervailing body of opinion, usually centered around Sephardic and Italian rabbis, such as Elijah Benmozegh, who would argue that in many, though hardly all, instances that Kabbalah "is a faithful exponent of rabbinic thought" (Benmozegh, *Israel and Humanity*, 188).

that academic historians of the affair then and now overlook, much as they fail to recognize certain aspects of the whole crazy conspiracy of arrogance. The central characters in the affair, such as Dreyfus himself and his closest supporters always tried to deny the anti-Semitism out there, and the Jewishness in the prison writings and the letters, as if the noise in the streets and the slurs in the press meant nothing. One has only to look at the writings of Marcel Proust to see how deeply the feelings and prejudiced thoughts of anti-Semitism went in French society during the whole period of the affair and afterwards, when people forgot what they had been so excited about.[58]

Instruments for Hearing, Seeing, Thinking, and Feeling

> *However, for religious reasons the idea was conceived by the Ashkenazic rabbis, to express the significance of every holy day by distinctive tunes, and to consecrate special melodies to each occasion in order to create the distinctive atmosphere for that day. . . . Upon entering the house of worship on one of these days, the Jew was inspired by the dominating mode or melody which reminded him of the purpose of the day.*
>
> —A. Z. Idelsohn[59]

According to the Belgian artist Emile Verhaeren, what distinguished the Parisian art scene at the end of the nineteenth century was its seething diversity of schools of painters, groups which were, he says, forever dividing up, regrouping, and splitting again.[60] In a sense, this might also be a way of describing the political dynamics in the capital of France, and Paris was, as many come to think of it now, the capital of the nineteenth century in many other ways. But these competing, hostile and coalescing factions were not so much unstable and incoherent, that is, chaotic or anarchic, random or mindless, as they were exploratory and

58 Proust, *Finding Time Again*: "For the rest, to conclude the topic of the duchesses who now frequented mme Verdurin's, they came there, though this never occurred to them, in search of exactly the same thing as the Dreyfusards had once done, that is to say a social pleasure constituted in such a way that its enjoyment both assuaged political curiosity and satisfied the need to discuss among themselves the incidents they read about in the newspapers" (37).

59 Idelsohn, *Jewish Music*, 134–135.

60 Cited in Ingo F. Walther and Rasiner Metzger, *Van Gogh: The Complete Paintings* (Koln, London, etc.: Taschen, 2006 (original German edition 1990), 272.

creative. Thus, Verhaeren goes on to say

> The diverse tendencies remind one of movable geometrical patterns, as in a kaleidoscope, one moment opposed and the next united, merging then separating again, and then crumbling, but nonetheless moving within a constant circle, that of modern art.[61]

It will pay to look more closely at this metaphor and then to explore its implications in regard to two other complex conceits that I use in this book to try to see and understand Alfred Dreyfus and the Dreyfus Affair—and use more than as just a touchstone by which to measure and test the constituency of its elements, but much more as a whetstone to sharpen our comprehension of what was going on in the minds of involved individuals and groups and their milieu; as well as a lens.

The word *kaleidoscope* came into use in French on the model of the term invented by Sir David Brewster in 1817, built on the Greek roots *kalos* (beauty), *eidor* (aspect or form), and *skopein* (to see), to denominate a long tube, like a microscope or telescope, but with a lens through which are seen, against a background of curved or angular mirrors, an array of small pieces of coloured glass or beads; when the tube is rotated, the particles of tinted glass are reflected and refracted in the mirrors as ever-changing symmetrical patterns. Although it was quickly popularized as a toy for children or a device for adult entertainment, with the kaleidoscope Brewster was seriously working in the investigation of polarized light, and he imagined uses for architects, painters, jewellers, and other craftsmen seeking new design patterns and colour combinations. According to the specifications in his patent document,

> The kaleidoscope . . . is an instrument for creating and exhibiting an infinite variety of beautiful forms, and is constructed in such a manner as either to please the eye by an ever-varying succession of splendid tints and symmetrical forms, or to enable the observer to render permanent such as may appear most appropriate for any of

61 Cited in Walther and Metzger, *Van Gogh*, 272.

> the numerous branches of the ornamental arts.[62]

Before it became either a mere toy or an interesting metaphor in aesthetic discourse, Brewster was thinking,

> if any object, however ugly or irregular in itself, is placed before the aperture . . . the part that can be seen though the aperture will be seen also in every sector, and every image of the object will be seen also in every sector, and every image of the object will coalesce into a form mathematically symmetrical and highly pleasing to the eye. If the object is put in motion, the combination of images will likewise be put in motion, and new forms perfectly different but equally symmetrical will successively present themselves, sometimes vanishing in the center, sometimes emerging from it, and sometimes playing around in double and opposite oscillations.

Thus, more than the Newtonian prism used to break up a ray of light into its constituent rainbow of colours, the kaleidoscope now creates new forms, tints, and—this is very important as a forerunner of animated motion pictures—movements. This way of thinking about the nature of sight and what can be done to create various illusions sought, by the play of mirrors and lenses, to foreshadow developments in painting and other arts that eventually come into focus under the names of impressionism, post-impressionism, cubism, fauvism, and so forth.

In regard to the mysterious designs or doodles that fill whole folios and the empty spaces on pages in Dreyfus's workbooks from Devil's Island, we can perhaps suggest that he is himself playing with configurations of light, lines, space, and movement. As we have already discussed in reference to Taine's theories of intelligence and Tarde's notions of imitation as the driving force of social behaviour and collective thought, the scientific ambit of Brewster's new invention takes part in the impetus of the nineteenth century's break with the previous age's rationality and classical concept of symmetry.

---

62 "Brewster's Patent, A.D, 1817, No. 4136, Kaleidoscopes, Brewster's Specifications."

> The partial polarization of the light by successive reflexions occasions a partial analysis of the transmitted light; but in order to develop the tints with brilliancy, the analysis of the light must precede its admission into the aperture. Instead of looking thro' the extremity . . . of the tube, the effects which have been described may be exhibited to many persons at once, upon the principle of the solar microscope or magic lanthorn, and in this way, or by the application of the camera lucida, the figures may be accurately delineated.

Significantly, as a metaphoric reference point, this instrument does not introduce new materials or colours but generates new combinations and patterns and hence new responses in the viewer's eyes. It moves into a realm of dynamic, moving imagery and perceptions that can be shared between many viewers, thus creating collective experiences of polarized light shows and illusionary visions of nonnatural phenomena. Moreover, in his final comments in the patent document, Brewster sees a further application which would correct the faults in previous attempts to visualize sound:

> When Custillon proposed the construction of an ocular harpsichord, he was mistaken in supposing that any combination of harmonic colours could afford the pleasure to the person who viewed them, for it is only when these colours are connected with regular and beautiful forms that the eye is gratified by the combination. The kaleidoscope, therefore, seems to realize the idea of an ocular harpsichord.

This ideal of a mechanized synesthesia looks forward, not so much to the realistic or documentary style of motion pictures ("talkies") that someone like Proust objected to on the ground that it would limit the imaginative play of the eye on reality that is the essence of poetic creation, but rather to the kind of fantasia and phantasmagoria filmed by Georges Méliès—including coordinated speaking and music—at the time of the Dreyfus Affair.

It was an advance on the many optical instruments invented during the preceding century and would culminate in the 1890s with what we now call motion pictures. To understand the metaphorical and rhetorical uses we are putting together in this book on Dreyfus, then, we need to be aware of the shifts in imagination that were occurring during his lifetime.[63] Whether he had ever attended an entertainment or scientific performance involving these fantasy-producing machines is not more relevant, in a sense, than whether he attended an art exhibition or visited museums such as the Louvre in Paris displaying works from the various impressionistic and post-impressionistic schools during this period of the late nineteenth century. What is relevant is that these transformations in perceptual and aesthetic mentality were happening around him and that he himself shows an interest in the psychological, scientific, and aesthetic ideas that were driving these developments.

The phantasmagoria, which we have alluded to several times in earlier chapters, was developed in France during the period of the Great Revolution and thus at about the same time as the kaleidoscope. Rather than a single instrument, the phantasmagoria was often a sustained, lengthy, and complex performance using optical projections, music and auditory effects, as well as tactile and olfactory elements. It was part of the popular entertainment industry that grew up in Western Europe over the nineteenth century, sometimes in ad hoc street performances and sometimes in fairgrounds, circuses, and theatres of magic and illusion, and then on film. But there are two other manifestations of the phantasmagoria that we need to look at in order to understand how it can help us understand the Dreyfus Affair, this frenzied obsession that tore at the heart of France for at least seven long years.[64]

One is the way, partly touched upon earlier, in which, following Taine's psychological discussions of intelligence, the double and triple play of simulacra and memory images form themselves into what is

63 In Bourget's discussion of Flaubert's imagination, a discussion Dreyfus shows that he read, there are two forms of this mental faculty and thus two constitutive collections of images registered from experience and created in the mind from the interplay of the individual's own cognitive processes. Unlike Taine, but more like Proust and Flaubert, as Bourget indicates, Dreyfus saw the spirit of man engaged in a dynamic dialectic, constantly making and unmaking himself and struggling against deterministic tendencies in society and nature; cf. Bourget, *Essais de psychologie contemporaine*, 165–167.

64 Romain Rolland: "Both man and wife had been bowled over by the storm of the Dreyfus affair: both of them had taken the affair passionately to heart, and, like thousands of French people, they had suffered from the frenzy brought on by the turbulent wind of that exalted fit of hysteria which lasted for seven years" (*Jean Christophe*, Vol. II, 340).

called an inner phantasmagoria of the mind. The other, apparently limited to the period of the Revolution and the First Empire, is how tacticians and strategic operators projected spectral images into foggy night battles in order to disorient, frighten, and cause panic in the enemy; such a practical military usage suggests, moreover, that the devices developed by magicians and theatrical entertainers for popular audiences were available for propagandistic purposes—a kind of manipulation of crowds into mass trances that culminated in Nazi rallies in Nuremberg during the 1930s.[65]

Zekhut

> *All Israel have a portion in the world to come, as it said (Isaiah lx.21). And thy people shall be righteous; they shall inherit the land for ever, the branch of my planting, the work of my hands, that I may be glorified.*
>
> —*Pirqe Avot*

It has already been mentioned several times that one of the underlying secret principles behind Dreyfus's self-concept as a Jew was that of intergenerational merit.[66] This idea of *zekhut* was surely one of the most revolutionary ideas in the development of rabbinical Judaism after the fall of Jerusalem and the end of Jewish autonomy in the Land of Israel, after the destruction of the Temple and the impossibility of maintaining the cult of sacrifices by priests and Levites, and after the burning of the *morasha* or National Archives, where the statutes of the law were kept. Before the fourth century CE, *zekhut* usually had a simple meaning "merit" or "reward." Individuals, usually the famous forefathers and foremothers of Israel, performed meritorious deeds. Abraham, Isaac, Jacob, Moses, Sarah, Rebecca, Leah, Rachel, and Ruth, as well as many others, were included in this group. They were all honoured by Israel and by God for their great acts of generosity, goodness, bravery, and daring. They were remembered for their goodness, and the rest of Israel could remember them with pleasure and pride, and thus, because God also shared these

65 Further discussion on this and related matter will appear in the next volume of this series.

66 Jacob Neusner, *Theological and Philosophical Premises of Judaism* (Boston, MA: Academic Studies Press, 2008); this is my primary authority on the concept and history of *zekhut*. Other authorities will be brought in later in this book.

feelings of pleasure and pride, all of Israel could feel close to God.

But the radical shift in meaning and usage of *zekhut* was quite different, shockingly so.[67] In the first place, as Jacob Neusner points out, "the Mishnah's philosophers reject prophetic and charismatic authority and deem critical authority exercised by the sage's disciple who has been carefully nurtured in rules, not in gifts of the spirit,"[68] but also that the heavenly court gives its judgements and favours on the status of the whole community and is therefore not the sole determining authority; indeed, one is the concomitant of the other, forming "a single system of power."[69] Without the mediation of the temple, where the priestly cult of atonement sacrifices took place, the rabbinical courts could call on heavenly power to supplement or replace their own through submission. This submission takes the place of charismatic or heroic deeds, precisely because it involves acts that involve what the covenantal law grants to each individual and which God cannot demand from him or her—free will, life, and love of family and self. As Neusner puts it,

> What we cannot accomplish through coercion, we can achieve through submission. God will do for us what we cannot do for ourselves, when we do for God what God cannot make us do. In a wholly concrete and tangible sense, love God with all the heart, the soul, the might, we have.[70]

Thus, not only did the great men and women, our forefathers and foremothers of blessed memory, gain spiritual merits that have been

---

67 One of the translations offered for *zekhut* is the Christian term *supererogation*, where it refers to the overflowing of grace attained by Jesus on behalf of sinners and saints whose individual and collective good works are not sufficient for salvation. Using this term as a heading for his tale, S. Felix Mendelssohn recalls that "[d]uring the High Holiday services in a Brownsville Synagogue [a suburb of New York City] a bearded young man chanted the introductory prayers. When the services were over an elderly gentleman walked up to the young fellow and congratulated him, 'May I ask how much you are being paid for your services?' 'Nothing at all,' replied the young man, 'This represents my contribution to the congregation.' The other thought a moment and said: 'That's very nice of you. If one is unable and is yet a willing contributor, his conduct is certainly praiseworthy'" (*The Jew Laughs*, 180). The joke works on the disguised insult of the old gentlemen (damning the younger with faint praise) and exposing a moral truth (that even a faulty public prayer well-intended earns merit in the world to come).

68 Neusner, *Theological Premises*, 167.

69 Neusner, *Theological Premises*, 168.

70 Neusner, *Theological Premises*, 176.

credited in the national heritage—often in the sense of honour and sometimes material or political rewards—for their heroic acts, but now the post-Fall rabbis began to teach that this *zekhut* is stored up in such an overwhelming abundance that God, when he remembers their good deeds, would reward their children's children, all of Israel, even if the people of today are unable to carry out the mitzvot. God's grace and love would come to all men and women just because they were Jews, even if, because of the terrible circumstances they lived in, they could neither perform meritorious deeds nor remain Jews and had converted against their will. So on the one hand, this new concept of *zekhut* constructed a cosmos in which Israel had inherited a vast stock of former merits and God would distribute them wherever they were needed. On the other hand, *zekhut* was something that ordinary individuals could earn for themselves and for their families; one need not be a priest, a patriarch, a prophet, a king, or a hero. Neusner then makes an even more astounding claim:

> It must follow that *zekhut*, not Torah, in a single word defines the generative myth, the critical symbol of the Judaism in the documents of which that symbol figures. A single case amplifies the claim that ordinary folk, not disciples of sages, have access to *zekhut* entirely outside of study of the Torah. In stories told about the rabbis, a single remarkable deed, exemplary for its deep humanity, sufficed to win for an ordinary person the *zekhut*—"the heritage of virtue and its consequent entitlements"—that elicits the same marks of supernatural favour enjoyed by some rabbis on account of their lifelong, perpetual Torah-study.[71]

In other words, this new kind of meritorious deed was precisely the sort of action, whether active or passive, that God could never force a person to do; it was not among the commandments or mitzvot already mandated by scriptures as part of the original covenant between God and Israel. Above all the God of Israel, blessed be He, could not interfere with an individual's free will, for that freedom of conscience is the one

71 Neusner, *Theological Premises*, 179.

lasting aspect of humanity that each one of us possesses—and shares in a profound universal way—with the deity; it is what makes us fundamentally created in the image, the *tzelem* of God: like the Holy One Himself, we each have free will, moral choice, a determination outside of all prescribed formulations of the law. Who and what we are is not determined by arbitrary rules or laws: we are who and what we are to a limited degree because of our parents and the education they give us, just as we are shaped by the evolution of our species and the geography and environment in which we are born and developed.

But these aspects of our existence, while they can condition what we experience in life, do not determine how we think or feel or see the world. Thus, the God of the Covenant could not ask a father to sacrifice his son or a son to sacrifice himself for his father, or a mother to give her last piece of bread to her son or daughter, or a person to help a stranger at the cost of his own well-being or life. But in the new interpretation of Jewish tradition and writings that developed at the time when Israel went into the world outside of the Holy Land without a priesthood or a temple to perform sacrifices, without a national territory under its control, and without an assured legal right to believe whatever it wished, the new dispersed people needed an ideology or a myth or a faith to live as a nation in exile. What Israel could not do for itself had to be done in another way, so that the accumulated merits of the ancestors could be put into effect in extreme circumstances.

These kind of ethical acts, often secret, usually very humble, always private and probably painful to perform, earned *zekhut*—rewards in the form of rain on a parched field, recovery of an infant after a horrid illness, relief from taxes in hard years, a sense of meaningfulness in an otherwise empty or evil world. Note that the people who are singled out for *zekhut* now are neither the priests, kings, or prophets of Israel nor the great rabbinical scholars of the Talmudic Age but rather simple, lowly folk. They are ordinary men and women, like Alfred and Lucie Dreyfus, and by their submission to their ordeal on behalf of truth and justice, not by any specific religious acts or Talmudic knowledge, they draw on the heritage of Israel and gain a portion in the world to come.

Zekhut was, when the new belief system began to develop in the centuries following the *churban* (destruction) of 70 CE, a revolutionary epistemological response to the unexpected and shocking rise of Christianity as a rival religion, one that, having assumed the powers of the Roman Empire, challenged the very existence of Judaism in late Antiquity. It was an extraordinary and unexpected mythical answer to the myth of a Father-God who sends His only begotten Son to earth to give His life on the cross for the sake of all who believe in Him. In the Christian soteriological narrative, no individual, by himself or collectively, can effect this salvation, whether by works or faith. Saints and martyrs can imitate Christ and win salvation only because Jesus had already done it, their lives reducing their individuality and condensing their historical specificity to the sacred *imitatio christi*. Faith and good works, depending on the mode of Christianity, flow from God's grace, and only those who accept Jesus as their Messiah are entitled to these gifts earned by the Saviour.

In the rabbinical concept of *zekhut*, however, Israel collectively in the past and individually in the present creates the signs of merit that stir God's heart, remind Him of His obligations under the covenant, and cause Him to pour forth His favours—but always in small, oblique, and unspectacular ways. World and national history do not change, but individual lives are experienced in different ways, experienced as midrashic assuagement, correctives, and consolations. Faith or belief is moreover not the determinant value: deeds that were outside the range of Jewish law and Roman censorship and were often unperceived by both the Gentile and Jewish communities were what counted most. To the individual who felt he or she could not endure another moment of history's pain and humiliation, there came a moment of peace and rest, a small relief from agony and despair. So it seemed that there was order, so there was justice in the world, and there was a law still operative, but the law no longer needed a cult centre, a national government, or a body of esoteric rabbinical knowledge.

Were the answers to the two major crises at the formative period of Rabbinic or Talmudic Judaism still relevant in France at the time of the Dreyfus Affair? And were they pertinent to the specific historical case of Alfred and Lucie Dreyfus? Yes, I think, but not because they can be seen directly in the circumstances the Dreyfus family and other Jews were put through for close to two decades—and which closed with only an illusion of respite or resolution. The Great War that followed in 1914 and the rise of Nazism in the 1930s and the Holocaust of the 1940s showed that the dominant negative forces of history had been grinding on relentlessly, even after Alfred was pardoned and seemed to regain his honour. The false security of the Jewish community in nineteenth-century France came to an end. The fervent belief in the principles of the Enlightenment and the Republic proved fatuous. Besides, just as there were already other forms of Judaism at the time of the fall of the temple and Jerusalem—among the followers of Philo Judeus in Alexandria or Flavius Josephus in Rome, for instance, and the writers of the Book of Jubilees or the book of Esther—and different alternatives would be developed throughout the later ages, such as various *Kabbalot*, the *Haskallah*, and secularised philosophies, as with Spinoza, so too, as Dreyfus saw, there were alternatives in reason and science or in poetic idealism and primitivist mysticism. But these alternatives could not be sustained in the face of what the state could do to all individuals, and especially to the Jewish people. In the letters he and his wife wrote, as in his prison notebooks, the Dreyfuses endured moral and physical tortures and in the process created something new for themselves—through these writings, minor as they are in regard to world literature or history, they created a new kind of love and a new kind of loyalty, a new kind of intellectual critique, and a new kind of poetry.[72] Thus, Neusner's comments strike to the heart of the matter of how to read and evaluate the letters between husband and wife and their powerful love of family and the prison workbooks filled by Alfred Dreyfus with an abundance of topics from science to art, mathematics to literature, and philosophy and psychology:

> *Zekhut* integrates what has been differentiated. It holds together learning, virtue, and supernatural standing, by explaining how Torah-study transforms the learning man. Hierarchical classification, with its demonstration of the upward-reaching unity of all being, gives way to a different, and more compelling proposition: the unity of all being written within the heritage of *zekhu*t, to be attained equally and without differentiation in all the

72 My own temptation is to spend hundreds of pages in close reading and discussion of all the topics in the *cahiers*, but that sort of extensive analysis must be put off to the next book in this series on Dreyfus, tentatively entitled *Alfred Dreyfus: Essayist, Historian, Poet and Jew*. From now on I will begin to deal only with a few of the topics, choosing those in which long-lost aspects of his personality and character reach the surface, obliquely in other people's words and images or explicitly in cries of agony.

principal parts of the social order. The definition of *zekhut* therefore carries us to the heart of the integrating and integrated religious system of Judaism.[73]

PART 2: MORE ESSAYS AND EXCURSIONS

Ils perçoivent les choses et non les idées des choses. . . .[74] *Un esprit se trompe. Un esprit ignore—Jamais une machine à penser.*[75]

—Paul Bourget

The fragmentariness or distortion of the human image in Jewish art is in effect not a reduction but an expansion of the human form. The negative commandment prohibiting the depiction of the complete man is in substance a positive commandment to introduce the human spirit into the human form. In short, the slashed nose is the symbol of the soul.

—Steven S. Schwarzchild[76]

It is time now to turn back to the intellectual excursions in the prison workbooks from Devil's Island. After leaving his discussion of a new translation of Tolstoy's book on the Gospels, wherein he took issue with the comments of the translators on the need to focus on the odd ways the Russian idealist had dealt with the modes of narrating, appropriateness of genres, mixing of styles and other peculiarities of presentation, without actually drawing his analogies to Maimonides, Dreyfus leaves off by asserting his unstated Jewish scepticism and rejection of the sanctity either of the New Testament or of Jesus. The first *cahier* continues for a while then with fragments of letters begun to Lucie, with

73 Neusner, *Theological Premises*, 183.

74 Bourget, *Outre-Mer,* I, 87. Although he is talking about the new mind of Americans created in their vast and open land, the thought can be recontextualized to the situation of Dreyfus, who is forced to think and see and read all over again in a new way.

75 Bourget, *Outre-Mer,* I, 129. This passage can be translated as: "They see things but not the idea… of things.The mind fools itself. The mind knows nothing—there can never be a thinking machine."

76 Stervn S. Schwarzchild, "The Legal Foundation of Jewish Aesthetics," *The Journal of Aesthetic Education* 9:1 (1978) 35.

lines recollected from the Latin, such as Ovid's *Mens interna sus ne siet usque melis* (Of fear that my soul be not always occupied with its own flaws),[77] introduced with a notice that "I could apply these lines of Ovid to myself" or simply set down on the page with no attribution or contextualization, as with *Semper veritas* (The truth forever).[78]

There are also clusters of citations, from the ancient classics through to Renaissance writers, such as Montaigne and Shakespeare, constituting a small anthology of aphorisms and commonplaces. But then he has an outburst of personal feelings that trails off into silence and then bursts forth suddenly into an ambiguous Latin tag:

> I am always on guard in my obstinate soul. The memory of these long and mournful days where I go, my head empty, body exhausted. In the empty future, dreaming of my destiny . . .
>
> *Fortis imagination generat casum*
>
> [A powerful imagination produces results][79]

This *cri du coeur* laments the tedious, empty days he lives through, which he can only endure thanks to his obstinate, obdurate determination. The motto, however, suggests a resolution to this impasse through the imagination, a word loaded with both classical and romantic resonance and beginning to gain increasing power in the new depth psychology of the 1890s. It will be not just an act of the will based on ideological commitment to the cause of justice and truth, but the creative act of imagining—whatever Dreyfus and his age will come to make this word mean, as they go beyond the classical sense of a faculty of the mind to store images, to generate vivid and persuasive pictures in the mind that can reshape those memories, and then the legal or political decisions taken because they overpower other people's recollections and modes of perception.

By adding the dimension of scientific investigations into public

77 *Cahier* 1, Folio 13, *Cahiers*, 56.
78 *Cahier* 1, Folio 18, *Cahiers*, 57.
79 *Cahier* 1, Folio 31, *Cahiers*, 59.

myths, private dreams, and culturally constructed paradigms of seeing (e.g., phantasmagoria, kaleidoscopes, photography, and x-rays), Dreyfus approaches the more dynamic, generative notions of midrashic visualization. The imagination, in brief, becomes more powerful and productive than the poets or novelists—whether Baudelaire, Mallarmé, or Flaubert—claim because it becomes a faculty through which the mind speculates on historical forces hidden within positive (determinable, measurable) facts and creates previously unperceived insights into itself as a complex, evolving organ of consciousness.[80]

In one rare instance, Dreyfus puts down a line that comes from what the modern editors vaguely designate as the Vulgate: *Mori lucrum*.[81] This is seemingly a second unit in the longer passage from the New Testament: *Vivere Christus est, et mori lucrum.*

> It is my eager expectation and hope that I shall not be at all ashamed, but with full courage now as always Christ will be honoured in my body, whether by life or death.
>
> —Phil. I:20

However, while it might perhaps function within this Christian zone of meanings that Dreyfus is thinking of at this time, more likely, from the context and the whole drift of the intellectual content of the prison *cahiers*, he would be casting such a statement into an ironic or skeptical light, making "To die is to gain" a paradoxical aphorism, reading *lucrum* less as financial gains or profit than the honor or merit suggested by the New Testament translators, and resonant with anti-Semitic slanders against the miserly and shylockean meanness of money lenders. He thus twists the bigoted connotations around into something like "Through my death I will gain victory over your cruelty and superstitions."

---

80 Bourget is here talking about the novelist Gustave Flaubert: "*Chacun de nous aperçoit non pas l'univers, mais son univers; non pas la réalité, mais, de cette réalité, ce que son tempérament lui permet de s'approprier. Nous ne racontons que note songe de la vie humaine, et, en un certain sens, tout ouvrage d'imagination est une autobiographie, sinon strictement matérielle, du moins intimement exacte et profondément significative des arrière-fonds de notre nature*" (Each us perceives not the universe but his *own* universe, not reality but *this* reality only what his temperment allows him to appropriate. We only recount our dream of human life, and, in a certain sense, the whole work of the human imagination is an autobiography, if not strictly material, at least intimately exact and proudly significant of the background of our nature) *Essais de psychologie contemporaine*, 115.

81 *Cahiers* 1, Folio 34, *Cahiers*, 59.

This difficult aphorism is followed by the first of a series of little essays on Nature that appear many times in this and the subsequent prison notebooks.[82] These meditations take into themselves themes that include the nature of intelligence and reason, the nature of child-like apprehension of the world and scientific investigations, the nature of observing the landscape with the eyes of a poet or an agronomist, and then the powers of the mind through those various eyes to rest passively and muse on the impressions of what is or recollected as what was seen or then to act to change the physical world and thereby also to effect changes in the inner world of thought and feelings. At the close of this first essay on nature, Dreyfus writes:

> The law of nature is love. The moral grandeur of the human heart measures itself by this need for, by its capacity to love, the power of a man's mind, in some order which the spirit (or kind) examines in pure science, philosophy, literature, etc., resides in the power to love that in which it is occupies. The law of nature is thus love.

The periodic sentence rolls on through a series of sorites, interlinked and incrementally repeated, enclosed by the same dictum that the law of nature is love. This makes for an attempt to synthesize and reconcile competing attitudes towards the natural world prevalent in the late nineteenth century. But the dictum and the synthesis are too facile, and later versions of the essay begin to explore other ways of approaching the problems inherent in the conjunction of ideologies. For though Dreyfus always tried to be the great peacemaker and resolver of contradictions, he knows that merely wishing for irreconcilable forces to disappear in a lukewarm bowl of chicken soup is not enough; the rabbinical tradition of continuous question, challenge, and dialogue draws him out of these classical and Christian dreams of unrealistic harmony.

In the second essay of the series that follows immediately,[83] he writes instead that the law of nature is love.

> Moral guardian of the human heart, it measures itself

82 *Cahiers* 1, Folio 34, *Cahiers*, 59.
83 *Cahiers* 1, Folio 36, *Cahiers*, 60.

> by the need, by the capacity to love, in whatever order of ides this love exercises itself. The law of nature is love.

Stripped to a less complex structure and focused on nature rather than on the contemplating mind, this essay allows Dreyfus to save himself from some of the enthusiastic excesses of the previous piece, but still comes out with an unsatisfactory poetic statement. It is just too facile to equate love and nature as though this were a popular music hall song. He will have to wrestle with this cantankerous problem many times before he reaches a less superficial resolution.

If love stands for the moral guardian of the human heart, then what morality is has to be pulled apart and examined carefully, no more to be assumed a given than nature or love. Dreyfus finds it dangerous to think in these allegorical personifications, although at the same time he finds it all too easy to slide into such essentialist categories of thought when he is suffering from all the woes of his exile and incarceration.

Then in another surprise statement, when he starts a brief critical review of Henrick Ibsen's *John Gabriel Borkman*,[84] a play only published in 1896 and thus contemporaneous with his own ordeal, Dreyfus announces that he has just reread the play, "the last work" of this author, and

> I can hardly understand the moral worth of this work
> and it seems to be a weakness in this great man.
> What is there in this play?

After a cursory outline of the plot and a sketch of the main characters, Dreyfus asks, "What does the author want to tell us?"

> There is only the great foolishness of Erhart who speaks the sentence: "One must live." But what does he mean by "live"? Is it to have fun with Mrs. Wilton? I can't understand?

In one sense, it seems very strange that Dreyfus cannot understand

84 *Cahier* 1, Folio 38, Verso, *Cahiers*, 61. The English translation (with no translator named) may be found in *Eleven Plays of Henrik Ibsen*, intro. H. L. Mencken (New York: Random House. The Modern Library, n.d.), originally from the Everyman Edition.

this tragedy since it is about a man who suffers from his illusions and a crime committed that he should not have let himself fall into and returns home to a self-inflicted isolation, an exile from the world and the consequences of his incarceration, the two imprisonments both, as it were, the result of what the essayist calls here "the great foolishness" and a little earlier "his great dream." In another sense, everything about the play is based on matters that go against Dreyfus's high ideals and his Jewish perspective on life, both in the confusion of financial and sexual ambitions and in the morbid, relentless self-blinding that overwhelms the protagonist who gives his name to the drama.

Moreover, Dreyfus has gone back to Ibsen because he expects to find a different kind of modern tragedy, a different kind of morality, and the play disappoints on both scores. On the one hand, literature should be moral and possess a social theme, showing how misunderstandings and personal weaknesses lead to crimes and thus to a profound sense of guilt; on the other, Dreyfus wants great authors to probe into the complexities of human character and to reveal the contradictions and paradoxes in well-intentioned people who are driven beyond the limits of their capacity to deal with pain and humiliations through no real fault of their own. Borkman's ideal of creating a financial empire seems paltry to Dreyfus, just as his relationship to the two women he has loved—one truly and deeply but sacrificed to his ambitions and the other less intensely and foolishly, only for wealth and social position—strike Dreyfus as stupid and obnoxious. Although his own great dream of rehabilitating his honor might seem a foolishness to a more practical or hard-headed realist, for Dreyfus it is precisely the thing that gives both meaning and substance to his life, his family's future, and his relationship to the historical state to which he has pledged his loyalty. Thus, of Ibsen's problematic play, he writes:

> I can see no moral thesis. I only see the baseness of mankind in all its depravity, which Ibsen demonstrated in his previous work. But I don't see it here, that which he did in those earlier works: no effort at all for these beings to disengage their senses from their impure complications, the noble effort of humanity to do good.

Because he himself is suffering a terrible injustice and finds the outside world—outside of Lucie and his children, her family and his own, so far as he knows—depraved and both cold and indifferent to his plight and collusive in his torments, now Ibsen is hollow, superficial, and flaccid. True, he was neither a professional drama critic nor a trained philosopher or psychologist, but we cannot deny that Dreyfus had the potential to become a great thinker in the coming century had he not been crushed by his experiences.

Hard on the heels of this little essay, Dreyfus cites two little Latin tags, one of which we already dealt with:

> *De natura reurum* and above all *Mori lucrum.*[85]

This linking of the classical to the biblical suggests a new fermenting of ideas in his mind, and one is driven to cite, as Dreyfus does not, these lines from Lucretius, always echoing through his notebooks.[86]

In terms of number of references, Alfred de Vigny seems to be Dreyfus's favourite poet, and one can see why in the first little essay of *cahier* 2,[87] where he says of him, "The basis of de Vigny is solitude and bitter distress that accompany the sentiment of solitude." These are the leading qualities of Dreyfus's own conditions on the Ile du Diable. The assessment of the poet thus continues:

> He has no other resource than flight into dreams like Chateaubriand and lacks in imagination and egotism. He is alone and feels indifferent or hostile to humanity,

---

85 *Cahier* 1, Folio 41, Verso, *Cahiers*, 61.

86 Lucretius, "Fear of Death," *On the Nature of Things*: "True, men often declare that disease and a life of disgrace are more to be feared than the pit of death. And they may say that they know the soul is made of blood—or else of wind, if by chance their whim so wills it—and therefore that they have no need at all of our philosophy. Yet, you may be sure that this is nothing but idle boasting to win praise, and not their true belief. These same men, exiled from their country and banished far from the sight of their countrymen, stained with some foul crime, beset with disease heralding approaching death, keep going all the same. To whatever situation they come in their misery, in spite all their talk, they sacrifice to the dead, slaughter black cattle, and lay out offerings to the gods of the dead. In their bitter plight, they far more keenly turn their hearts to religion.

"That is why it is more fitting to judge the quality of a man when he is in doubt and danger, and to observe his manner in adversity; for then at last an honest cry is wrung from the bottom of his heart: the mask is torn off, and the truth stands exposed." It will be evident in many of the essays on nature, the mind, and moral philosophy that Dreyfus has read deeply in Lucretius, although he would not agree with all the aspects of such an atomist and epicurean, an *epikoros*.

87 *Cahiers* 2, Folio 2, *Cahiers*, 64.

> impressive and beautiful nature, those empty skies, and God, if he exists, is dead to the cries of the miserable.

> *Le juste opposera le dédain à l'absence*
> *Il ne répondra plus que par un froid silence*
> *Au silence eternel de la divinité.*[88]

Whatever merits or demerits there may be in the prisoner's literary criticism, clearly he finds himself able to express his otherwise inarticulate pains and humiliations through this description of de Vigny's character and the citation of these chosen verses.

The next important insight into his character appears in a set of comments given without title[89] on the power and psychological discourses of literature and history. The first sentence, however, is almost unreadable: "It is curious [two words illegible] in reading writers however famous and of an unprecedented [*inoüie*] intellectual power [two words illegible] in many of them, the psychological sense is weak, even absolutely missing." This is to be a *leitmotif* of his own criticism, the necessity of evaluating authors by a combination of their rhetorical strengths, their poetic insights, and their moral (i.e., their psychological) acuity, for these are characteristics he hopes to find in himself and which he looks to create in his own writings, whether in the letters to Lucie, as we have already noted, or here, through a more oblique suite of modalities, in the prison workbooks. Of these modern novelists, he says,

> They speak very learnedly in order to use all the language of Rabelais on this or that case of morbidity, on such and such a social situation, accusing them of vices and faults, with a clarity that is often remarkable, without the ability to sense how everything is dependent on man, on his soul—in a word, on his psychology.

The missing words in the opening sentence might help focus on the authors or the type of literary and philosophical movements in the late

88 "The just man will oppose the disdain of absence/he will no longer reply except with an icy silence/ in the eternal silence of divinity" (my translation).

89 *Cahier* 2, Folio 7, Verso, *Cahiers*, 65.

nineteenth century he is reading and subjecting to this sensitive critique. The discourses of these writers are grounded in a low and mixed language, categorized here as Rabelaisian, but without satire or wit. This new species of literature has turned its focus on to the morbid themes and images of lowlife, crime, depravity, and madness, features of a hostile and confused world that Dreyfus himself keeps fighting against and which he dreams great works of the human mind can help fortify him against and understand. But the poets, the novelists, and the psychologists of his own day disappoint Dreyfus because they wallow in the worst qualities of the human condition.

> Such a fact would appear peremptory in a certain class of ideas, when one only considers that the idea will be formally denied when one studies man and the determinant causes of this idea.

Why should such an idea of morbidity seem *péremptoire* to him? The destructive and limited factor must lie in the narrow focus of authors who only seek out the worst qualities in man to write about and who develop methods of research that narrow down this moral field. In his own experience, Dreyfus has a daily struggle to keep a wider perspective open, and hence he searches for texts that can both guide him through the present tortures and soften their blows until the nightmare of his life comes to a favourable resolution. Above all, he asserts as much to himself as to the authors he is arguing with, it is necessary that one not become obsessed by these *idées fixes* but seek a higher moral ground of objectivity and dispassionate observation.

> Otherwise there are few men so detached from their own ideas as not to be astonished when they no longer serve those to whom they are dear. In all discussions of ideas, each one brings this unconscious false consciousness which is the fact of mankind. And it is this more than anything which must be avoided if one wished to bring to a study, of whatever order it might be, plain impartiality.

The fixation on man's disgusting nature, like all other obsessions, must be overcome by a more objective, scientific approach, and yet, as we have already seen hinted in earlier essays and as will become more evident in those that are to come, Dreyfus also looks for poetic insights and imaginative speculations.[90] Before that, however, he must read his chosen models carefully and keep questioning and challenging them, in accordance with his rabbinical propensities, whether or not he himself is conscious of the paradigm he works within:

> No one ever felt this more than Fustel de Coulanges when he said in [one of] his books that before one undertakes any subject in history, it is necessary to disengage from all private interests, from all one's foundations, from all one's own ideas, to study this history in its own milieu where it was elaborated—in a word, in the human context. And that which is true for history is true for everything. And this is one of Fustel de Coulange's highest qualities, this higher impartiality that he brings to his historical studies.

To be sure, such an absolute objectivity is not only impossible to achieve—no one divorces himself from who he or she is and how that character was created by nature and nurture—but even as an ideal goal, it is questionable, as Dreyfus himself comes to remark. In the short run, had such an objectivity and dispassionate approach to evidence been operative in the military courts of Paris, the captain would not be sitting in a lonely prison cell penning these words. The mysteries of what prejudices and distortions of reason were manipulated against him remain to be solved, and the easy casting of blame onto human perversity must be resisted or madness ensues.

As though it is logically appropriate after this praise of Fustel de Coulanges and his ideal of objectivity, Dreyfus takes up a critique of Cesare Lombroso's writings on the relationship between the criminal mind,

---

90 Cf. Anatole France: "Beauty depends upon ourselves; it is the sensible form of all that we love. It is a mistake to contrast the realist novelists with the idealists. People oppose the real to the ideal as if the ideal were not the only form of the real which we can grasp. The truth is, the realists want to render life odious, while the idealists seek to beautify it" in "George Sand and Idealism in Art," a review of E. Caro's *George Sand, On Life & Letters*, I, 303.

insanity, and genius.[91] The Italian Jew's work would seem to fit the category of those authors obsessed by the morbid and unable to achieve a detached position from which to measure these qualities, either in his scientific method or in his style of composition. For Dreyfus to find the solution to such theoretical problems, he must wrestle with the authors who most attract him and yet who expose the very faults he sees within himself, for we discover facts about his own character through the choices he makes in what to write about, the places he enters to make his critical comments, and the attitudes he refines as he moves along through the whole of the remaining fourteen prison *cahiers*.

> M. Lombroso's *Theory of the Man of Genius*
>
> The celebrated Mr. Lombroso spent his life in searching to find out cruel truths and those which always charmed. He asked himself, whatever the facts might be—and they came often and, at the same time, they always gave him a formal denial—well, under which latitudes, in what conditions of the ambient milieu are alcoholics, criminals, idiots, deaf-mutes born? In his latest book, he discovered that some great men, belonging to a family of epileptics, have near cousins whose genius is a sort of degenerative psychosis!

Here is an author whose scientific penchant and personal obsession take him again and again to investigate the most degenerate members of the human race. Wherever he looks, he finds these morbid types, and then, of course, he only looks where he will find them. Even when he looks where others have found men of genius, heroes, and supermen, Lombroso finds the defectives and the deviants. In fact, because he looks in this way, the Italian scientist can now claim that degenerates and geniuses are cousins germane.[92]

---

91 *Cahier* 2, Folio 8, *Cahiers,* 65.

92 Cp. Shel Kimen, "The Power of Genius" *Concepts of Culture* (Spring 2003) online at http://www.klever.org/wrdz/world/genius (seen 1 September 2007). From its classical sense of "guiding spirit" of a person or place, the word came by the 1700s to designate the importance or influence of a person in society and eventually to mark the inner spirit of creativity or understanding; from thence, it took over the old sense of "virtuouso" as an outstanding performer to become an artist out of the ordinary and above all normal rules of conduct and morality. For Dreyfus, genius is still

What fascinates Dreyfus here is less the discovery itself than the way of finding it, and the way Lombroso claims to have resisted and denied what he was seeing before his very eyes. Like a good, objective scientist, however, the Italian doctor had to accept his own findings, first resigning himself to the facts and then finally proclaiming the consequences of these facts. "But the facts appeared so manifest to Mr. Lombroso," Dreyfus writes, with his own wit shining through, "that he had to accept them as proof, he tells us with a childish naïveté." The problem, Dreyfus adds, is that

> Mr. Lombroso had forgotten that genius is nothing without that which gave it value and which, alone, puts into relief the highest moral values. Worker in thought or worker by hand, all those who have produced great works have a high moral conscience of their duty and of the goal they are pursuing.

What is at stake here in Dreyfus's evaluation of this morbid theory of the close alliance between genius and idiocy is his own sanity and his own need to fight against everything in his circumstances that has been set up to break him, to drive him mad, to make him do as Job was urged by his so-called comforters to do, and accept appearances for reality, rhetoric for evidence, and guilt for innocence. For a man to stand up to adversity, he may have to appear mad to those who want to see him degenerate into their bigoted caricature of what a traitor or a Jew looks like. A high moral conscience, resisting for all it is worth the inner and outer demons of his existence, may finally look like anything at all, but it retains its honour to the very end. A proper scientist should not be taken in by illusions shaped by his own prejudices.

When Dreyfus reads Lombroso's new book, he is, first of all, repelled by the conclusions reached. However, he is not convinced by the facts presented and not sure they are facts at all.

> *Mais moi qui suis d'humeur difficile et rétive en ces sortes de matières, j'estime que M. Lombroso se contente de peu.*

---

somewhere between an external guiding power and an internal source of energy and imagination.

"But to me," the prisoner writes, "with a difficult and stubborn humor in these sorts of things, I reckon that Mr. Lombroso contents himself with too little." It is important to catch here especially, as from the opening sentences of this little essay, Dreyfus's wit at work, his defensive Jewish humour in his treatment of a fellow Jew—though he never acknowledges that relationship between them. In his darkest hours on Devil's Island, tortured, deprived of all human contact, and without tactile support for his hypersensitive nerves, the captain maintains his dignity through his writing, and his style is not plodding or repetitive so much as it is exploratory, self-analytical, and probing. Here is a respected man of science, a fellow Jew, telling him that great men are virtually the same as idiots on the most basic level of their moral characters and personalities. Dreyfus must reject that. But he himself has to give reasons and not just shout out his defiance in a cry of pain.

He does so in a long paragraph[93] we must cite and analyze because it is so filled with the ideas we have found important for overturning the previous judgements of Dreyfus's character and personality, as much among those who admire him and his stand as among those who despise him and wish him the worst, as well as those who believe they are merely objective reporters of the facts. But facts in themselves do not constitute truth:

> The alienist-physician, who has made the greatest reputation more by his paradoxes than by his books, is a laborious compiler of anecdotes and he gives them to us as unassailable proofs.

Such proofs prove to be mere anecdotes, some curious, some suspect, and this leads Dreyfus to an even sharper criticism, not only of Lombroso but of many others who are mesmerized by their own voices and the illusion of reason where there is only delusion, for the captain is no passive recipient of other people's opinions and he reads carefully and critically.

> He affirms that Hegel, in an access of megalomania, had begun one of his lectures with these words: "I may say with Christ that not only do I teach the truth, but I am

93 *Cahiers*, 66.

> myself the Truth." Whoever knows a little about Hegel will doubt this little story strongly. If Poisson said that it does a man good to know mathematics, would one conclude that Poisson was deranged? Why, one day Ampère, in the heat of a mathematical discussion—and this anecdote is true—took hold of the bonnet of a vehicle and used it for a blackboard so as to re-do his demonstrations, and must we therefore conclude that Ampère was crazy!! . . . All that is naïve and puerile.

These anecdotes may prove that some great men can be occasionally eccentric and even touched in a more acute way, but it doesn't mean that genius itself is kin to insanity or degeneration, nor does it mean that readers should accept every personal report on faith.

> I do not wish to follow with the citation of a great number of anecdotes which swarm through Lombroso's work to affirm his theory. I have shown their value sufficiently.

Thus, it is not the theory or the extrapolation of facts that is really at fault but the method of affirming or asserting one's own personal biases without taking into account either the provenance of the anecdotes or the circumstances of the acts or words reported, as well as the tendency to confuse anecdotes with statistics. Hoping that Lombroso or those readers sympathetic to him will not think Dreyfus has an axe to grind (or a whip to lash), the only conclusion he can reach is "The author of these books is himself alienated," a statement perhaps teasingly reflexive, as Dreyfus fears he will be found insane.

Next comes an attempt by Dreyfus to give an English translation of Hume's *The Miser*, which he must have had in a French version.[94] A kind of Meneppian satire, the exemplary tale describes a miser who refuses to pay the fee to Charon to ferry him into the Underworld, for which Minos decides as a just punishment to send him back to the upper world "to see what use his heirs are making of his riches." Not satisfied with his grammatical mistakes, Dreyfus attempts the translation again and then leaves it unfinished.

---

94 *Cahier* 2, Folio 10, *Cahiers,* 66.

More significant than this momentary view into Dreyfus's intellectual efforts is his essay on another two of his favourite historians, Jules Michelet and Augustin Thierry, and his discussion of the best way for a writer to make use of evidence.[95] It is Michelet he admires most as a sensitive model for his own writings, but Thierry who is recalled nostalgically as a school text, despite all his faults and failings as a Romantic. What is so special about Michelet is that "he had the patience and the labor of an historian and the pen of an artist." Going much further than Thierry, who was able to assemble vast numbers of facts from his archival documents, Michelet

> had recourse to the chroniclers, he interrogated the works of literature and art; a piece of some proceedings, a book of devotions, a monument, a form of architecture often more than the falsified testimonies of historiography.

History therefore is not merely facts and figures, royal decrees and laws, or any other official version of events and persons. Michelet closely studies all works of human genius, including art, spirituality, and political aspiration, not what great men and their lackeys wanted to be known, but what an age really felt that it was experiencing, an age made up of people at all levels and in all walks of life, public and private.

> Michelet in all his history is [of the] people and a poet. He had vibrant soul which loved everywhere, sensed everything everywhere, and put his life everywhere. The expression [in his writing] is intense and solid, and he fixes the character of the epoch and draws out of it its beauty. Michelet protests against the Romantics, [but] in reality his history is a masterpiece of Romantic art.

There are inconveniences to this method, Dreyfus knows; he has already commented on the futility of attempting to be objective or to assume that one is implicitly and intuitively in touch with the essence of what one studies and thus does not need to give proofs or demonstrate as valid a technique of interpretation. Although a Romantic in his

95 *Cahier* 2, Folio 12, Verso, *Cahiers*, 67.

enthusiasms, nevertheless, to Dreyfus, his approach to history breaks the boundaries of formal documentation and opens the research to the study of aesthetics and psychology, along with religious experiences; history belongs to all the people, not just the elite. In Jewish tradition, especially considering the Sephardic sympathies and sense of toleration for the defeated and the downtrodden, history belongs to those who have been beaten down, sent into exile, and made to wander in poverty and despair.[96]

A discussion and a paraphrase of Montaigne comes next, with Dreyfus translating the original Renaissance text into a form of modern French and paring down the text and sometimes recasting what remains to compensate for the missing passages. Like Shakespeare, to whom Dreyfus returns often and leans on as a major intellectual and moral support, and Montaigne, both of whom belong to the tradition of Crypto-Jewish literature,[97] Dreyfus implies more than he knows he is writing. It is not that Dreyfus does not know he is Jewish or thinks he can hide his religious identity, nor is it a question of whether on certain occasions he would keep some of the traditions at home with Lucie, but that he does not know in a deep way the rabbinical ways of thinking and feeling. More importantly, for strategic reasons, both before and after

---

96 A rather distorted and toxic version of this view was written by that champion anti-anti-Semite of all time, as his biographer Curtis Cate, put it once, Friedrich Nietzsche, in *Beyond Good and Evil*: "All that has been done on earth against 'the nobles,' the 'mighty', 'overlords'. . . is as nothing compared to what the Jews did against them: the Jews, that priestly people who were only able to obtain satisfaction against their enemies and conquerors through a radical revaluation of the latter's values, that is, by an act of the most spiritual revenge . . . . It was the Jews who...dared to invert the aristocratic value-equation . . . saying 'the wretched alone are the good ones, the poor, the helpless, the lowly . . . . You who are powerful and noble are to all eternity the evil ones . . ." cited in Barry Rubin, "The Strangest Antisemite of them All: The Bizarre Case of Friedrich Nietzsche," *Gloria Center: Global Research in International Affairs* (12 December 2010) at http://www.gloria-center.org/gloria/2010/1w2/astrangest-antisemite-of-them-all-friedrich-nietzsche (seen 13 December 2010). What Nietzsche was saying was that by inventing Christianity, the Jews committed an unintentional error of cosmic importance. In themselves, Rubin says of Nietzsche views, Jews are a strong and proud people, to be admired and not despised, but the Nazis rendered those philosophical words absurd, putting the blame for all of Europe's woes on the Children of Israel. Thus, the danger of using a rhetoric of exaggeration and irony where feckless, ignorant ideologues can transform them into apologies for genocide.

97 See Norman Simms and Charles Meyers, eds., *Troubled Souls: Conversos, Crypto-Jews and Other Confused Jewish Intellectuals from the Fourteenth through the Eighteenth Centuries* (Hamilton: Outrigger, 2001). Though Shakespeare's background is a bit speculative still, and the connections are probably through the so-called Dark Lady who was his mistress, an Italian *conversa* he met through musical performers in London, there is no doubt that Montaigne is the son of a *conversa* mother—and his scepticism and curiosity are typically converse themes.

his arrest he feels the need to keep any overt signs or statements of his Judaism under wraps. At work in the army headquarters, he was known to be unsocial and to avoid personal conversations with his fellow officers whom he justifiably mistrusted. After the accusation, arrest, and court-martial, he knew more than ever that censors would be looking for any excuse to increase the harshness of his treatment in prison, and the mere mention of Jewish ideas, images, or acts would sound alarm bells.[98]

The essay by Montaigne he has selected to talk about comes from the *Essais,* Book III, chapter 5, "Upon some Verses of Virgil."[99] The essay Dreyfus writes is introduced by two general statements, one on Montaigne's book in general, and one on this particular meditation on the relationship between classical style, epitomized in Virgil, in relation to French style in the Renaissance. When Dreyfus describes Montaigne's whole book of essays as "easy and simple" in style but "with no unity, no composition," he could be speaking of his own *cahiers*. When he moves on to the particular essay "On the Verses of Virgil," however, he describes it as engaging "in some unknown way," with its topic, presenting "a citation from Lucretius . . . right in the middle of the most scabrous reflections that Montaigne parades before us." Because Dreyfus's own bourgeois sensibilities are offended by the frankness of the language Montaigne uses—and which he elsewhere labels Rabelaisian, that is, earthy and concerned with bodily functions—"I cannot resist

98 According to Max Nordau at the First Zionist Congress, "The emancipated Jew is insecure in his relations with his fellow-beings, timid with strangers, suspicious even toward the secret feeling of his friends. His best powers are exhausted in the suppression, or at least in the difficult concealment of his own real character. For he fears that this character might be recognized as Jewish, and he has never the satisfaction of knowing himself as he is in all his thought and sentiments. He becomes an inner cripple, and eternally unreal, and thereby always ridiculous and hateful to all higher feeling men, as in everything that is unreal. All the better Jews in Western Europe groan under this, or seek for alleviation. They no longer possess the belief which gives the patience necessary to bear sufferings, because it sees in them the will of a punishing but not a living God" (*MiddleEastWeb*). Although Dreyfus would never have considered himself one of those New Marranos, as Nordau calls them, who try to flee Judaism, while being unable to escape from themselves, he does seem to work out a temporary *modus vivendi* through his writings, first in the letters to Lucie, where they jointly create a new kind of metaphysical love and a new kind of space for their domestic hopes, and then in the prison *cahiers*, where he forges a temporary pseudo-Talmud in which he can speak in a traditional rabbinic way, even though the specific subjects are alien to *midrash*.

99 This little essay on Montaigne is not all that little insofar as it contains Dreyfus's lengthy paraphrase, and runs over several folios of the workbook. *Cahier* 2, Folio 13, 13 Verso, and 14, *Cahiers,* 68–69.

the temptation of reproducing this exquisite chapter, except perhaps in passing over several of the facetious remarks which Montaigne permitted himself to make." To our own twenty-first century sensibilities, it seems most odd that a man who is living in squalor and under atrocious conditions, who has been subject to physical and moral indignities day and night for four years already, should find himself unable to set down in his own words equivalents to Montaigne's sixteenth-century vocabulary in matters of this kind. Yet this is what Dreyfus says and what he actually does in producing his abbreviated version of the essay.

What attracts Dreyfus to this exquisite essay on style despite its scabrous remarks are Montaigne's reflections on training oneself to be healthy and sane from childhood onwards in order to prepare oneself, as Virgil did, for the moral life necessary to becoming a great poet. By making oneself strong and gaining self-control over one's bodily needs, Montaigne reflects that it is possible to achieve the strength of character that can resist all the temptations of maturity and prepares oneself to confront the coming of old age when the decline of those physical abilities mocks the desires to still perform them. At such a time, arrived at an age when one feels oneself "[a]ll dried up and weighed down" by the burdens of life, poetry provides both a comfort and a channel through which the remaining passions can run their course. "Venus," writes Montaigne in Dreyfus's paraphrase, "is not so beautiful all naked, nor so alive and breathless, as she is in the verses of Virgil."

Through citations from Virgil and Tasso, the Renaissance essayist expresses his longings and explains his appreciation for style, arguing that art becomes consolation and a mode of creation when physical relief has become impossible and the days of reproduction are over. Can it be that here, squeamish as he appears and yet fascinated both by the Old French language and Montaigne's citations from sensuous poetry, Dreyfus is indulging in erotic fantasies, dreaming of the most intimate of moments with his wife, Lucie, which he could not even bring himself to think of, let alone inscribe, in his letters home? It would certainly be remarkable if, through all the years of separation, and yet under constant scrutiny by guards—including through the nights when he was sometimes shackled to his bed by iron chains—a still young, though hardly at this point vigorous, man, did not seek some physical outlet for his frustrated desires. Dreyfus distances himself from these unperformable deeds and unthinkable thoughts, first through reading Montaigne's essay and choosing this particular one for such an extended discussion, and then modernizing the language into his own and therefore controllable terms, editing out the most intense locutions, thus allowing Montaigne, Virgil, and Tasso to express what he cannot admit to imagining for himself.

At the point at which Montaigne begins to follow Virgil's descriptions, mythologically and pastorally, of the affairs of Venus and Mars, he comes to a line from the *Georgics*, III, 137f:

> *Quo rapiet steins Venrem interiusque recondut* . . .[100]

At this point, Dreyfus stops and leaves a large gap in the text of Montaigne before he picks up his paraphrase again, but, even then finds himself entwined in a style of verbalized sensuousness he must have found as fascinating as troublesome. Yet it is Montaigne himself and supposedly not Dreyfus who says,

> I am vexed [bothered, frustrated] at the same small points and verbal allusions that have been born since. To these good people, one must not encounter [embrace, be intimate with] them with sharp and subtle words. Their language is firm and right and great with [pregnant with] a natural vigor and contrast—they are all epigramme, not by tail alone, but by head, stomach and feet. . . .

The sensuousness of the sentences slip by, barely subject to Dreyfus's sense of propriety and his strenuous efforts to censor his own improper thoughts, until Montaigne cites, "It is sinewy and solid eloquence which does not so much please as it fills and ravishes." Montaigne keeps going, citing Quintillion, Gallus, and other classical and later authors; Dreyfus trails off into longer or shorter ellipses until he concludes, in Montaigne's words:

> It also happens in my writing, as in a wild country, where no one either aids me or relieves me, when I ordinarily hear men who understand neither Latin nor French. I

100 "It is thus that the [thirsty female] seizes Venus and becomes most deeply impregnated."

> would have done my works elsewhere, but it would have been less my own, and its principal end and perfection is to be me.

With almost no adjustments necessary, these also could be Dreyfus's deepest sentiments. For those historians who still say we know almost nothing and cannot know anything about the inner man of Dreyfus, surely it is time to read and to listen to what remains of the evidence in these *cahiers*, as in the letters. His wild country was a deserted and insalubrious prison island. Although there were guards constantly observing and manhandling him, he was locked into a silence and solitude beyond the limits of almost any other prisoner in modern history.[101] Paradoxically, however, it is unlikely that Dreyfus would have ever permitted himself the time and energy needed to compose the essays he did had he not been held in an extended period of torment and humiliation. We search—so far in vain—for evidence in any later documents created after his return to France of the articulation of so many literary, philosophical, psychological, and religious ideas.

What he writes about next after this discussion of Virgil's style, by which is meant nothing less than the capacity of a writer to subsume his own sensual urges into beautiful poetry, is one of the strangest books about prison life in the nineteenth century, Xavier de Maîstre's *Voyage Around My Room*.[102] As Sainte-Beuve points out in his introduction to the 1862 edition of de Maistre's *Ouevres Completes*, the younger brother to the more famous novelist Joseph composed this lighthearted and sentimental idyll inadvertently as a *joi d'esprit*, adopting the tones and often the phraseology of Lawrence Sterne's *Sentimental Journey*, itself more popular in France than the more impressive and profound *Life and Opinions of Tristram Shandy*.

In forty-three chapters, de Maîstre records his imaginary excursions around the room where he is kept under house arrest in Turin at the time of the Napoleonic Wars, each short chapter consisting of a musing on some object, portrait, or moment of memory in his confinement.

---

101 Except perhaps those exemplars in allegorical fictions, such as *Robinson Crusoe*, or in romantic novels, *The Man in the Iron Mask*, *The Prisoner of Zenda*, and so forth.

102 *Cahier* 2, Folio 16, *Cahiers,* 70. The *Oeuvres Completes du Comte Xavier de Maistre* were published with Sainte-Beuve's "Notice sur Xavier de Maîstre" in Paris by Garnier Frères in 1862, including drawings by Staal and engraved by several hands.

Dreyfus says he is attracted by the "soft, amiable figure of Count Xavier," but although he cites some of the poetic lines from the text, surely it is the very condition of imprisonment that he identifies with, although, of course, the differences between what the nobleman underwent and his own circumstances are striking. De Maîstre had a manservant, lived in a well-appointed apartment in the middle of Turin, whose streets, parks, and crowds he could observe through his windows, and his house arrest lasted barely a month and a half. Dreyfus could only envy the author of this "soft" book and its poetic dreams.

The next little essay returns his attention to more serious matters. This discussion of the Abbé Félicité Robert de Lamennais (1782–1854) reflects on the questions of religion, strength of character, and the relationship of faith to science. The standard view of him is that he "*fit un effort pour adapter le catholicisme à une société plus humaine*" (made an effort to adapt Catholicism to a more humane society).[103] His theories have been summed up in this epigraph from the newspaper *Avenir* (Future): "*Dieu et Liberté*" (God and Liberty). He also argued in his *Essai sur l'indifférence* that the greatest danger to the Church comes not from its enemies without but from the indifferent members of its congregation. Dreyfus may have agreed in general to some of the principles here but would not have been interested particularly in theological or pastoral matters within the Roman Catholic Church. Was there, rather, anything particular in Lamennais's character or career[104] to attract Dreyfus? When the young critic Sainte-Beuve went to visit him in May 1830, he found him "a drab, dusty little man, who looked like a village sacristan."[105] According to Harold Nicolson, he was also "a melancholy man who took a pessimistic view of the century . . . by nature timid and irresolute,"[106]

103 E. Abry, C. Audic and P. Crouzet, *Histoire illustrée de la littérature française* (Paris: Henri Didier and Toulouse: Edouard Privat, 1942; originally 1912), 475. This revision of an old school textbook under war-time censorship gives a noncontroversial view of French literary history, the new editor declaring it "*un acte de reconnaissance et un acte de foi*" (an act of gratitude and of faith), gratitude for being able to present to the reading public an up-to-date version of this book with four new chapters on the major authors from 1900 to 1938 and of faith in the integrity and viability of French civilization after the defeat by Germany. There is, of course, no mention of the Dreyfus Affair, the facts of either Nazi occupation nor of Vichy rule in the southern zone, and the few authors with Jewish background not noted as such.

104 A sort of biography is given in the entry on Lamennais in *The Oxford Dictionary of the Christian Church*, [ODCC] ed. F. K. Cross (London: Oxford University Press, 1963 [1958]), 781b–782b.

105 Harold Nicolson, *Sainte-Beuve* (New York and London: Constable, 1957), 45.

106 Abry, Audic, and Crouzet characterize him as already in his childhood displaying "*une âme inquiète et indépendante*" (an agitated and independent soul) in *Histoire illustrée de la litérature française*, 475.

and yet he was "inspired by a fervent conviction that man was too weak to be accorded the right of private judgment." What could possibly have appealed to Dreyfus, who, unlike Sainte-Beuve, was at once "fortified and perplexed" by his encounter with Lamennais?[107]

The life of this Catholic rebel begins with him losing faith at an early age (through the reading of Rousseau, it was said) and then being led back to the fold by his more pious brother, Jean-Marie Robert (1780–1860), then taking orders at the age of twenty-two and eventually becoming a professor of mathematics at the episcopal college of his birthplace, Saint-Malo, in 1804.[108] When we look at the trajectory of his life, we see that he was a troublemaker from the beginning, asking too many questions and challenging the authority of the church. His first book, *Réflexions sur l'état de l'église* (1808), was suppressed by Napoleon. Though an apologist for Ultramontaine Catholicism, he appealed to royalists and conservatives, but his repeated calls for religious freedom made him always suspicious to the hierarchy.

In *Essai sur l'indfférence en matière de religion* (1818–1824),[109] Lamennais "reproached the upper classes of his time with infidelity, and with giving all their aspirations to temporal matters."[110] For his liberal Fideist views,[111] including an appeal in *Paroles d'un croyant* (1834),[112] in which he called upon the Holy See to accept democracy, he was denounced as a subversive and castigated by Pope Gregory XVI in 1832[113] and then, as Nicolson puts it, "spent the rest of his life attacking the Vatican,"[114] with a tendency in his writings towards a humanitarian socialism and mysticism. "Active in the 1848 revolution, he sat in the Assembly until

107 Nicolson, *Sainte-Beuve*, 43.

108 ODCC, 781b.

109 *Chambers Biographical Dictionary* [CBD] calls this book "a magnificent, if paradoxical denunciation of private judgment and toleration, which was favorably received at Rome," ed. Magnus Magnuson (Edinburgh: Chambers Harrap, 1995; based on the original 1897 edition), 853b.

110 S. Reinach, *Orpheus*, 407–408.

111 For background on these movements and the personalities involved in early nineteenth-century France, see Salomon Reinach, *Orpheus: A History of Religions*, trans. Florence Simmonds (New York: Liveright Publishing, 1930; orig. 1924), Chapter XII, "Christianity: From the Encyclopædia to the Condemnation of Modernism," esp. 94–95, 433–434.

112 One bishop called these *Words of a Believer* an "Apocalypse of the devil" (S. Reinach, *Orpheus*, 407). CBD describes it as the book "that brought about complete rupture with the church" and resulted in one year's imprisonment (854a).

113 S. Reinach, *Orpheus*, 407.

114 Nicolson, *Sainte-Beuve*, 46.

the *coup d'état.*"[115] According to Frank Paul Bowman, after the *coup* in December 1851, "He retired to private life . . . and, as he had requested, was given a pauper's burial."[116]

If it is not possible to see any continuity or a clear development in Lamennais's themes, it might be possible to credit him for working with two sets of ideas that in other thinkers might have been too contradictory to be sustained, but although these inconsistencies infuriated others, even his friends and admirers, they nevertheless marked him as one of the great if quirky philosophers of the first half of the nineteenth century.[117] On the one hand, Lamennais proposed,

> The principle of authority, which he equated with the "raison générale" or "sens commun." He maintained that the individual is dependent on the community for his knowledge of the truth; to isolate oneself is to doubt; and toleration is evil.[118]

Thus, at the same time as he challenged the moral authority of the pope and the church hierarchy, stating that they were not above reproach, he also argued that ordinary men and women were incapable of making decisions of faith on their own and should yield to the spiritual powers of the church as guardian of traditional beliefs. But he also

> equated Catholic Christianity with the religion of all mankind, denied the supernatural and proclaimed subjects freed from loyalty to their temporal sovereigns

---

115 CBD, 854a.

116 Bowman, Lamennais, *Oxford Companion to French Literature* online at http://www.answers.com/topic/lamennais-f-licit-robert de (seen 01 January 2011).

117 CBD calls remarkable his *Esquisse d'une philosophie* (1840–1846). Of this four-volume treatise, *The Catholic Encyclopedia* writes: "It comprises a treatise on metaphysics in which God, man, and nature are studied by the light of reason only. Many of the opinions maintained in this book remind one that it was begun when its author was a Catholic, but there are many others which betray his later evolution; he denies in formal terms the fall of man, the Divinity of Christ, eternal punishment, and the supernatural order. The portions of the work devoted to æsthetics are among the finest that Lamennais ever wrote, while the general tone breathes a spirit of serenity and calm" online at http://www.newadvent.org/cathen/08762a (seen 01 January 2011). Frank Paul Bowman in his entry on Lamennais in the *Oxford Companion to French Literature* calls it "an ambitious synthesis of Romantic aesthetics, German transcendental philosophy, Christianity, and dreams of a new faith yet to come."

118 ODCC, 782a.

> when rulers refused to conform their conduct to Christian ideals.[119]

If these controversies were merely squabbles within the Roman Church, they would have no interest for Dreyfus, but what attracted him was the intellectual struggle itself. Perhaps, then, he would be interested in the ideas discussed, especially Lamennais's drift towards a more tolerant and liberal modernity, albeit with a strict sense of the weakness of ordinary people and the power of the church as an embodiment of traditional truths. Raphael Ledos de Beaufort sums up the key matters after the Revolution of 1830 in this way:

> Lamennais was no longer the defender of Catholicism or the champion of the Restoration. Times had changed since the Breton *abbé* in his "*Essai sur l'indifference en matière de religion*" endeavoured to restore public faith in the principle of authority, thereby causing quite a sensation, and winning from the enthusiastic gratitude of the supporters of the Church the proud name of "*Bossuet Moderne*". In 1831, he had already in various articles which he contributed to the newspaper *L'Avenir* [The Future], placed himself in opposition to the past. In these he had tried his democratic strength, and stood up in the contest as the powerful and gifted advocate of Christian brotherhood and freedom, which, when released from its subjection to princes, should unfold itself under the banner of the Church.[120]

Beaufort also explains why this modern Bossuet was attractive to fiery young men like Franz Liszt in this late Romantic period:

> Lamennais's true piety, his democratic principles, his

---

119 ODCC, 782a.

120 Raphael Ledos de Beaufort, *Franz Liszt: The Story of his Life* (Boston: Oliver Ditson & Co., 1887); because this book is reproduced in the Project Gutenberg, it can only be annotated by chapter number: Chapter XIV. (It will be noted that, except for the insertion of my own contemporaries' remarks on the nature of anti-Semitism and attitudes towards Judaism, I prefer to cite texts close in time to Dreyfus. This is part of the midrashic method of challenging and questioning the text.)

> views on life, imbued with love of freedom and humanity, and which led him boldly and violently to break off with the Church and with his glorious past, found an echo in the generous and impulsive soul of the young artist, and ripened the Christian ideal views of art already awakened by the doctrines of the Saint-Simonians, and which were to give foundation to his artistic career and productions.

Sainte-Beuve, who was disappointed by the way Lamennais broke with the Church, wondered whether this once admirable writer had become neither a priest nor a philosopher: "Was he nothing more than a fine but ambulating artist? . . . It is a misfortune to possess a mind that never ripened."[121] Can something similar be said about Dreyfus? He seems attracted to this contentious and melancholy Catholic writer a little over sixty years later, not by his specific ideas or faith, which would not interest him at all, but by what happened to him when the pope attacked him and how he reacted; that example might be attractive—up to a point.

Dreyfus begins his own little essay by saying,

> Certain men are interesting by the unity of their doctrine, by the force of their character, the logic of their system, their general intelligence which permits them to embrace in one ensemble everything in a vast system of ideas and to bring in all secondary ideas which circumstances, reflections, facts are caused to stand before their mind to create a synthesis, in a word, a doctrine.

This opening by way of a truism (a *sententia*) indicates that there are more ways than one to attain greatness as a thinker, whether in religion or in any other field; consistency and constancy are not necessary, which is a comfort to Dreyfus, who finds himself, under the duress of his imprisonment, forced to rethink his ideals and his attitudes, while at the same time asserting over and over again his steadfastness in regard to his loyalty to France, the love he has for Lucie and their families, and

121 Cited by Nicolson, *Sainte-Beuve*, 46.

the honour that he must regain at all costs. In Lamennais, he sees a man who seemed to vacillate, to shift and change his views under the pressures of theological authoritarianism and in the context of revolutionary transformations of French society.

Hence, the second paragraph balances the first statement, offering an alternative way to greatness, that of Lamennais and perhaps of Dreyfus himself.

> Others, on the contrary, are interesting by the variation of their thoughts. Above all and, at best, it is on recognizing that they were not the result of powerlessness, but rather the unintended logical development of a living idea, one that changes and transforms itself.

Since thinkers cannot always, from the beginning, know the full context or the hidden forces at work in the circumstances they must work in, a doctrine may develop out of the logic of its own engagement with the world and not merely by the intentions of its author. These divergences come about out of strength instead of weakness, the writer—Lamennais or Dreyfus—proving in adversity that he can follow where the truth leads him, not where others wish to direct his career.

The next sentence loses itself in a smudged word or two, but shows the importance of that very defiance of external power, whether of the state in all its mysterious machinations or of sadistic individuals who revel in treating a prisoner with contempt:

> On the other hand [illegible words] . . . Considered from the one or the other point of view, the thought and work of a man becomes, following the very expression of Lamennais, his memoirs serve as a history of human thought. They show in one such man, as happens so often in the history of humanity, a doctrine, the steps or questions of which are all logical, or all at least having their own profound reasons being, touching on the contrary.

After this point Dreyfus reaches a conclusion about the relation of science and religion which does not come down on either side but seeks a reconciliation, a harmony, and a balance to make peace in the house (*shalom ba'bayit*).

> All religion is the explanation of things by the supernatural, all science excludes the supernatural in its research, and all scientific philosophy, even the most elementary kind, eliminates the supernatural, at the same time at the point of departure and at its goal.

By this he argues that religion and science are different, to be sure, but difference does not make one more correct or apt than the other. Both are intellectual systems of thought. Two out of the three clauses in the sentence come down on the side of science over religion and do not cancel out the first.[122]

In his next essay on Shakespeare's *King Lear*,[123] it is likely that Dreyfus is talking at least as much about his condition and feelings as he is about the characters in the tragedy. The essay is not an example of literary criticism in any objective or historical sense but an exercise in confessional inner dialogue,[124] an exposure and expression of his own secret pains, his repressed grief and sorrow, as well as his rage against the injustices of the world and his doubts about the firmly-held beliefs and ideals he is suffering for. Although he seems to focus on Shakespeare's text, his own syntax trembles and falters. He fumbles for words, he repeats himself awkwardly, and he gets lost in the convolutions of his grammar, so the little essay becomes, as it were, a mirror held up to his own mind, an embodiment of the deepest agony within his own soul.

There are two ostensible points of self-identification in the tragedy: first, he grieves with and for Cordelia, expressing a sense of anguish and outrage he elsewhere attempts vigorously to keep under control, fearing at every moment the bursting forth of sheer madness; second, he sympathizes with the old king, and yet the scene he chooses to concentrate on is one between Lear and Kent. In reading those lines of the play, he goes over the questions of justice, loyalty, and self-sacrifice that are not

---

122 The little essay on Lamennais ends with a mysterious line: "I have pushed towards F too slowly." At this point, I will not venture a wild guess as to the meaning of this.

123 *Cahier* 2, Folio 20 and 21, *Cahiers,* 71–72.

124 "*Mahloquet* is a way of speaking and of thinking the refusal of synthesis and of system: an anti-dogmatism that, alone, makes possible the living truth" (Ouaknin, *Tsmimtsoum,* 110).

only pertinent to his own situation but form the repeated motifs in his letters to Lucie. It is possible to extrapolate from this essay some of the key phrases and sentences that expose the elusive inner world of Alfred Dreyfus:

> The excess of misfortune and the black anguish of the heart makes this piece of drama the most . . . grievous that was ever written . . . I believe that there is not one which wounds the heart more grievously than that of King Lear; for there is no other which shows more profoundly the unbelievable feebleness of human nature. In order to destroy the happiest of conditions, it takes only one word, one remark—such is human judgement, where prejudices and passions are involved—it is feeble, it staggers. . . . Our sentiments are less certain than those of most honest beasts. . . . they are so trusting, that they do not know how to distinguish true sentiments from [illegible words] and threaten them. . . . But, alas, how many men at all times and in all countries do we not see . . . with their high-flown notions of responsibility . . . fooled previously by the over-confidence they have in their own power. . . . The unbelievable blindness of human nature creates the sombre sadness of Shakespeare's drama. . . .

Grief, weakness, and blindness are the key factors in his identification with the tragedy, the main elements in his own tragic life.

After a brief stanza by Hegisippe Moreau,[125] Dreyfus begins two long essays, one on art[126] and the other on beauty in Michelet,[127] to be followed themselves, strikingly for our purposes, by a discussion of photographic equipment.[128] While we shall have much more to say about

---

125 *Cahier* 2, Folio 28, 72. Perhaps in this little poem, Dreyfus finds a dreamy image of his horrible torment when shackled to his bed. "On the cot [*grabat*], hot in my agony, /For the pity I still find in tears, / For a perfume of glory and of genius/ Is spread on this bed of pains [*ce lit de douleurs*];/ It is that what comes, widow of hopes/ To sing again, then to pray and die."

126 *Cahier* 2, Folio 29 and Folio 29, Verso, *Cahiers,* 73.

127 *Cahier* 2, Folio 30, *Cahiers,* 74.

128 *Cahier* 2, Folio 35, Verso, *Cahiers*, 75. This essay is preceded by a few brief remarks on *Henry IV* and an aphorism: "No one is great to his *valet de chamber*."

Dreyfus's attitude towards art, aesthetics, and the psychology of seeing in the next book in this series, when we return to a long discussion on his many drawings or doodles in the *cahiers*, it will be important to run through the key ideas he presents in these three essays. It is sufficient here to notice that the psychological bent to his critical remarks on literature, philosophy, and history is also relevant to the way he considers painters, musicians, and other artists. He knew what Paul Bourget wrote in his *Essays on Contemporary Psychology*: that there is a theory that considers our "ego" to be "a bundle of phenomena ceaselessly in the act of making and unmaking itself."[129]

The essay on art starts with general statements, truisms, which as we will see can belong to the general cultural milieu around Dreyfus but also can be seen to have peculiar aspects that derive from his own mentality and also from a more specific tradition of rabbinical visual midrashing of beauty as both service to God and creating an aesthetic of the law. Not all these aspects of the topic will be contained in this first of many little essays to be found in almost every one of the remaining *cahiers*, and not each essay will handle the topic clearly or coherently, but the ideas are working through Dreyfus's mind whenever he can find the moments of sanity and calmness to let them:

Of Art

> Art has in its hands all the power of creation, all that the poetry can do, the passion, the grandeur of a human period; all the aspiration, towards the Ideal, all the pantheistic images, all which falls from the sky or all which lifts itself from the earth.

The human labour that produces this category of externalisation of beauty participates in a vaster, divine project of creation. It is a process generated—and generating itself, as one can see from the personifica-

129 Bourget, *Essais de psychologie contemporaine*, 157: *"la théorie psychoogique qui considère notre 'moi'comme un fasiceau de phénomènes sans cesse en train de se faire et de se défaire."* This *"collection de petits faits"* (collection of small facts) constituting the "moi" (ego) accords with both Taine and Flaubert but lacks the dynamics and moral direction that Dreyfus considers as essential to the individual struggling to maintain his personality under the most desperate of circumstances (cf. Bourget, *Essais de psychologie contemporaine*, 163).

tion of art in the first clause—by mental and manual labor (*avodah*), work that is a necessary duty and a voluntary service—and that leads the maker towards the ideal, the perfection, and thus within human experience and history towards the process of perfecting of what is imperfect. The labor of art reflects itself into poetic, passionate, and pantheistic images, merging both what has fallen from the heavens like manna and what is produced on earth and seeks to rise above it, each after its own kind by natural growth. While some of these statements can be set within rabbinical discussions about beauty and truth, the words and phrases here are vague and confused in themselves. Can Dreyfus clarify what he means to say?

> Here is what art reflects (*reflète*), art; here is the chaos in which art kneads or moulds (*pétrit*) the life of thought, in order to represent all its manifestations.

The juxtaposition of two different metaphors to describe art is at first disconcerting: as a process of reflecting, such as in optics and its modern developments into photography and x-rays, and as either in a baker kneading dough in preparation for baking bread or a potter moulding clay in preparation for placing it in a kiln.[130] In either of these views, what is without form is given form through human effort, and the world of *tohu v'bohu*, the original chaos, becomes in an orderly, thoughtful sequence of actions the world of order and harmony.

> Art has its doctrines as religions have their rules or laws, not that these doctrines must be immutable—to hear the heart beating, to set thoughts free to flow, to give life an energy to all human aspirations: here is the doctrine of art that must rule over the odious hairshirt (*cilice*),

130 "At times, the reliance of the artist on specific photographs done by others may border on slavish imitation. This accurate rendition of a photograph was, of course, precisely what was demanded from an engraving artist concerning a photograph into an engraving. This was the only viable way for publishing photographs before the introduction of photo-mechanical printing later in the [nineteenth] century . . . However, especially in the case of landscapes, the engravings were often modified slightly; an imaginary reality was introduced to accommodate some pictorial convention that was not necessarily commensurable with the original photograph," Haim Finkelstein, "Lilien and Zionism," *Assaph: Studies in Art History*: 3 (1998), 208; online at http://www.tau.ac.il/arts/projects; http://www.melalexenberg.com/paper.php?id=2.

> that is to say, the rule of Aristotle, Longinus's *On the Sublime* and Boileau's *Art poétique*. Method *(la méthode)* is a refuge for the sterile (*stériles);* for the others, she is a guide, a preparation for the hand of the sublime worker (*ouvrier sublime*).

The typical nineteenth-century notion that art is itself a religion developed to compensate for the secularisation of society and the breakdown of formal religions. If art is not to be seen as a religion for people who have lost faith in the old myths and truisms, it can at least be taken as a starting point for Dreyfus's critique of classical and enlightenment rationalism. It is not that this new religion has no rules, but that they are not constrictive and deadening: they are the laws of following the impulses of nature and the release of ideas to grow and develop as they will. Method in itself is not wrong: it is a refuge, an excuse or a subterfuge, for the sterile soul, while for the sublime worker, it is a preparation or a training for the exalted tasks ahead. Again we watch Dreyfus trying for a compromise, a harmonization of seemingly incompatible views, and see that this is a man who thinks, perhaps without knowing it, within Jewish patterns of thought—even though, to be sure, those rabbinical themes can be found elsewhere and can be expressed often in a language Judaism shares with (if not bequeathed) to Christianity and the modern secular world coming into being.

In this little essay, for the most part, Dreyfus writes in a language of romantic idealism, using excessive superlatives and absolutes, so that as he writes he must keep adjusting his perspective, modifying his terminology, and not always succeeding in this endeavour, so that he comes back many times to try to write the same thoughts from a slightly different angle. This kind of style—he has no thoughts of publication in mind, nor does he have any partner with whom he can try out his ideas in conversation—is the manifestation of the inner dialogue with himself that he writes to Lucie about in their letters.

> Art in its supreme mission must ceaselessly aspire to the infinite, such as to ascend the bleak and rough (*âpre*) mountain, where the Ideal flourishes. But if art sometimes lacks stamina, if, in certain epochs, it is incapable of reaching the highest summits, for art is the reflection

> of each era's soul; it always follows the truth that emerges from the depths, completely naked and continuously shimmering.

The goal of art, its quest in some romantic mission, is to climb the highest mountain and retrieve the magical flower growing at its peak; this is a fairy tale, in which the young aspirant to marry the king's daughter—here it is art personified in each era as a different youthful candidate—does not have the strength to succeed; nevertheless, in every age, the ideal is always the same, Truth, in all her naked and glorious beauty.

The Ideal and the Truth here are the two supreme characteristics of Art: those that unite the two radiant faces of Beauty, and thus able to produce a masterpiece. Without, however, arriving at this supreme expression of art, each one may be permitted to use his talents according to the nature of his own means, allowing one to be a scholar, the other an original, one a poet sure of his form, the other a pantheist who loves all that is alive, with no concern for higher thoughts or the mystery of creation.

These abstract hypostatised personifications do not necessarily require that each and every artist be perfected in his or her skills, and each may choose his or her own particular way of approaching the idealized goal. Just how the artist goes about the specific duty set by his own mind depends on many factors:

> But before the hand executes [the work of art], it must always [be put in] place the thought that inspires it; the eyes and the soul fly in advance of all the others. Thought, this is the genius of all activity in which the order of art, which this thought exercises itself; thought, that is, God, though has no limits at all, like Jupiter's eagle soaring above the world.

While this sounds like a paraphrase of a poem by Keats or Shelley or almost any other Romantic poet, there is also something peculiar, not just in the awkwardness of Dreyfus's syntax as he attempts to soar in his own enthusiasm but also in his hesitations about dwelling too long in these platonic categories, not least the notion that God is merely the name for our own idealized thought (*la pensée*). Then the allegory continues to unfold:

> Execution, the daughter of Study, is material art, submitting to certain laws, chained to certain modalities. Genius is not the work (*oeuvre*) of chance, but the work (*oeuvre*) of thought.

The key word here is *œuvre*, which may mean a range of things, such as a product, a pew (seat in a church), or a setting (on a ring for a precious stone), or even an action (in a performance or staging of a play or choreographing of a ballet). As for *la Génie*, it is not so much either the Genii of the *Arabian Nights* or the brilliance of a unique mind so much as the manifestation of the power of creation, the thing produced, along with the force that creates and its guiding principle. It is something intellectual rather than an irrational burst of external energy. This rational, intellectual, and controlled operation in the process of art is something Dreyfus makes the otherwise hackneyed iteration of the Romantic dream mean.

Then comes an exemplary tale to animate the personifications introduced and identified above.

> Timanthes wished to paint a storm, He went to the seashore on a stormy day; he observed but he didn't think. He believed that he knew how to paint a storm. He made a work that had neither soul nor life and broke his brushes. Another day, this same Timanthes entered a school of rhetoric; he heard them reading Homer, he felt his heart beating, his imagination was inflamed, he ran to his studio, he took out his work and painted a tempest which astonished [even] him (*l'épouvanta lui-même*).

This is a traditional exemplar on the power of art to astound through rational schooling of the senses and the skills of the craft. An ancient Greek painter, Timanthes, learns how to become an artist not when he studies the techniques (*technē*) of his craft but when he hears how to read—that is, to listen intelligently in a school of rhetoric—the classical verses of Homeric epic. He does not need to paint *en pleine aire*, as many of the nineteenth-century Impressionists believed, or by copying old masters as the teachers in the École des Beaux-Arts insisted, but by doing both, by learning to order his thoughts through the discipline of the schools. He could then return home, take up the plank of wood upon which he was attempting to put down his impressions of the storm he had experienced on the beach, and now create a work of art, a product of the human mind.

On the second folio of this essay on art,[131] Dreyfus moves back to a discussion of artistic theory, aesthetics, saying,

> The search for the beautiful has occupied all philosophers, as it has all artists. They are thus one or the other guided by genius, the ray which lights up the soul as the sun lights up the world.

Unlike the artist proper, who seeks to produce his *objet d'art* by using the material means available to him in his own time and place, the philosopher searched in theory for the ideal, yet both of them are directed in their search by their own genius, a ray of light from some higher realm. Dreyfus then turns to the debates between the various schools of artists and theoreticians active in his own period of history.

> Also, how often do we see this in the battle of the schools—those of the idealists and of the realists. Idealism, as I have said, would speak of Beauty in its two conceptions, the Ideal and the Truth. Take the example of a realist's painting of a domestic interior, man in all his material reality; we can neither scent the perfume of the soul nor see the spirit of the home. The same picture, inspired by a thought will give us the soul do the interior scene, will give us mankind and not a man.

Instead of speaking, say, of the Impressionists and the Naturalists, or of the official painters rewarded by the Salons and those new movements forced to set up their own private exhibitions to win public approval and sales, Dreyfus chooses these two more traditional ways of looking at art. For him, the realist painters are those who copy nature, who see as the ideal of art the ancient concept of *mimesis*, with all the

131 *Cahier* 2, Folio 29, Verso, *Cahiers*, 73.

mixed feelings that the classical thinkers roused in their discussions: whether the best painter was the one who could so reproduce the appearance of flowers or grapes that flying creatures would be fooled and crash into the walls upon which they were depicted, or even, like the Dutch and Belgian old masters, create realistic paintings of domestic interiors that seem to be virtual photographs of their genre scenes, or whether the ideal to be aimed at was that exemplified in the tale of Timanthes, who had to train himself in the power of rhetoric—learn the art of imitation in terms of *enargaeia*, vivid illusions of reality based on conventional patterns of thought. The mere illusion of reality, the photographic reproduction, lacks the soul that true art aims for and sometimes achieves.[132] Otherwise the viewer cannot smell the perfume of the living soul nor feel the spirit of the home. The goal is not the individual and the instant—the impression of the artist's neutralized sensorium, his or her "negative capability," as Keats would have said—but the universal and the eternal.[133]

> Idealism and Truth in its sublime concept of a humanity which progresses, in its Beauty; Realism is the truth of a single point of detail which cannot interpret humanity and which is false because it is only of an instant.

Although somewhat crabbed and awkwardly expressed, this contrast between idealism and realism continues Dreyfus's main argument. Idealism contains as a complement the sublime concept of humanity which progresses both according to its moral development and its natural evolution towards beauty. Opposed to this view of art there stands realism, which lacks the ability to interpret humanity and insofar as it captures at best an instant in time and in the existential experience of an individual can only be false to the ideal of beauty it claims to pursue as well. From this, Dreyfus draws, in a separate paragraph, the maxim that he underlines:

132 As Taine put it: "Photography is the art which completely reproduces with lines and tints on a flat surface, without possible mistake, the forms and modeling of the object imitated," *The Philosophy of* Art, 52). It is important to note that Dreyfus does not take such a naive position, and as we shall see argues that the very "accuracy" of the camera is what makes it distort reality, and the human imagination must interfere in this false reproduction to provide both perspective and meaning.

133 Or as Dr Johnson would say, the goal was not to count the number of stripes on the petals of a rose but to create the essence of the rose.

> *Pour voir, il faut les yeux, pour comprendre, il faut l'intelligence.*
>
> To see, one must have eyes, to understand, one must have intelligence.

Just as a natural, innocent, and unsophisticated sensory perception contrasts with a moral and aesthetic understanding, so do the eyes and the trained cognitive faculties of the mind. This leads him to explicate on the contrasts between approaches to seeing and understanding, recording impressions and working towards interpretation:

> It is only given to a few men, [this ability] to reveal through the phenomenon of visible beauty to invisible beauty, of man to humanity.

In a sense, Dreyfus is an elitist; he believes that not all people are created equal, that there are some born with superior talents and mental faculties, but these differences are neither racial nor national nor social in the sense of fixed classes. Men and women of genius must, having been given superior capacities, use them in whatever ways are open to them by their own personal preferences and according to the cultural discourses provided by the times and the places they live in, seek to express through the imitation of physical nature and its beauty the secret, hidden dimension of supernal beauty, a beauty that, moreover, is moral and spiritual, raising individuals from their historical matrix into the purer domain of humanity—from the fallen Adam back to the original Adam, *ha'adam hakadmon*. This perfectibility of perception to moral vision provides the model for all other forms of *tikkun ha'alom*, kabbalistic rectification of the created universe: "And that is true for all those orders of ideas in which human thought exercises itself.

But then where we might expect, under other circumstances, the argument to follow through into the Talmudic and mystical ideas they seem to be working towards, despite the secular, classical, and sometimes even Christian terminology Dreyfus writes in, he picks up the model he wrote about a few pages earlier in this second *cahier*:

> It is for this reason that I already said a few days ago in the study of Michelet: The facts have provided material to Michelet, to be shaped by the form of his intelligence, his thought, he knew how to give life back to (*reviver*) the before us, to give a soul (*donner l'âme*) to a people, to an epoch.

It is this historian who shows Dreyfus how beauty is produced and how to write history in a way that shapes the facts into an image of the meaningful life of a people and an epoch, so that what is produced has within it the soul that is otherwise missed in impressionistic copies and photographic reproduction. Beauty has nothing to do with proportionate harmonies or pleasing exteriors: it is in the perceived truth that is expressed through a just interpretation of a higher truth.

> That which is true for History is true for Literature, for Painting, for every order of ideas where human thought exercises itself. It is not sufficient to see; one must comprehend with the eyes of the heart, with those of the soul.

To place this principle of beauty and truth into a Jewish context, we need to consider the Hebrew terminology that lies behind Dreyfus's praise of Michelet—and two other names he adds in a final short paragraph, Michelangelo in painting and Leonardo da Vinci in goldwork. This special word is *hadar,* הדר, a form of beauty associated with splendour and glory. For example, according to Shlomo Riskin,

> *hiddur mitzvah* is the term used to describe the performance of a commandment on the highest possible level, which includes searching out the most beautiful objects required, as well as expending extra time, effort and money.[134]

This way of understanding beauty goes back into Talmudic authorities, such as R. Abahu, who interprets

134 Shlomo Riskin, "Beauty Lasts," Sabbath Sermon in *The Jerusalem Post* (24 September 1999), 23.

> *hadar* to also mean (in addition) to beauty the one who inhabits, literally referring to that particular fruit which lives on the branch from "generation to generation"(season to season) without suffering the natural calamities of wind, storm and rain.

Riskin extrapolates from this, along with the rabbinical tradition, that "true beauty is expressed by the citron's ability to overcome the blasts of the elements," meaning that it is not an appearance in this *ethrog* or any other thing that is beautiful; it is a hardiness, a capacity to endure in love, loyalty, and life—in other words, it is inner strength and character. Moreover, "*hadar* rises from the core of a person's being." For this reason, the Jewish notion of beauty differs radically from that set of principles coming from Hellenistic civilization, including both Christianity and the secular European cultures that derive from it.

> The difference between Hellenism and Hebraism is that the former worshipped at the altar which claimed beauty was truth, while Hebrews affirmed the exact opposite, that "truth is beautiful."

Continuing his discussion of Michelet and Beauty onto the next page of his workbook, Dreyfus writes:

> Michelet had radiant thoughts, the concern for truth, the pen of an artist, so as to render this truth. Michelangelo had the palette of a great artist, the thoughts of a great genius which directed his hand. What more marvellous than the birth of the human thought by the hand submitting to intelligence than the frescoes in the Sistine Chapel in Rome?

These lines embody in two different and specific artists the principles laid out on the previous pages of the essay on art. Whether Dreyfus ever himself visited Rome and saw the Sistine Chapel is unlikely, but he probably saw pictures of it in a book, and what is most important is the idea of the perfected idea as the work of art.

Then Dreyfus repeats his argument on the limitations and deficiencies of Impressionist art, which he now identifies with realism in the philosophical sense:

> The Realist violates Truth by submitting to us only a point of detail, staring into the sun with his naked eye, without a soul to comprehend and grasp. It is the Ideal which enlightens the Truth.

A passive art, in which the painter, poet, or musician acts only as a vehicle through which the external world passes, makes its impression, and then projects that impression into the work of art, is a hollow, superficial thing, an idol. This action, however, does more than set itself up to be a sounding board to resonate with external stimulus or a wind chime through which inspiration wafts to create a pleasant melody; it is a sexual violation of the naked truth. Paradoxically, this violation is itself passive, allowing oneself to engage in a self-blinding enterprise, staring with the naked eye into the sun. The lack of a soul, here standing for the active intellect well trained in the arts of the humanities, makes the artist more than a suicidal fool; by violating the truth, such an artist is a terrorist who destroys the basis of civilization. The idealist, on the other hand, the true artist, enlightens, actively interprets experience and casts the radiant beams of what is produced into the world.

Incrementally repeating what he said earlier about genius not working to dogmatic beliefs, Dreyfus mimics Lamennais's shift from strict obedience of Catholic doctrine to a call for freedom, a liberal interpretation of theology, and a tolerance of other ways to the truth:

> Genius does not recognize doctrines, it only recognizes tools (*outils*) to give a form to its own thought. Let us salute free spirits who go in search of their inspiration in the poetry of Homer, even in the mysterious pages of the Bible, those above all who seek inspiration in the radiant book which is *called Nature*.

Rules and regulations serve to train the hands and the eyes of the artist, whereas set rules for what constitutes a pretty or a pleasing picture or musical composition or some other work of art would stultify genius. But *libres esprits*, like Timanthes, are inspired by rhetoric of great poetry, by the deep mysteries of Scripture, and mostly by the Book of Nature, the last two words in that paragraph being underlined in the manuscript. By this concept of nature, surely he does not mean the rural scenes and cityscapes that the painters of the late nineteenth century went out into to find their subjects, unencumbered by neoclassical rules, and Dreyfus could not have been so naive about contemporary art as to pass over their dependence on the masters of the previous generations and the models they copied in museums in Paris and Rome to train themselves, even when they rejected the strictures of the Salon juries and official patrons of the state. Yet there is something bizarre and troubling in his conclusions here, something that makes his argument ring hollow, even when it has the resonance of rabbinical themes. Thus, the final paragraphs, beginning with this odd paean to pantheists and deists, is hardly comprehensible either in import or in tone, given the fragmented state of the words:

> Pantheists or deists [three words illegible] all those who adhere to the cult of Beauty in these two concepts the Ideal and the [illegible word] Truth.

This would be a positive statement by the writer of the *cahier*, but does he really favour these forms of religious thought, pantheists perhaps finding their most authoritative model in someone like Spinoza in the seventeenth century and deists in the followers of Locke in the eighteenth? The next sentence, separated into a new paragraph, either repeats or attempts to advance that thought:

> Thus, pantheists or deists, it matters little, let us salute those who adhere to the cult of Beauty, in these two concepts, the Ideal and the Truth.

Does it matter whether we call such persons pantheists or deists, or are they of little significance themselves, and the call to praise them ironic, self-mocking, because although they exalt the concepts of the ideal and the truth they do not have the mental or spiritual capacities to interpret what they see and try to reproduce in their works? What was Dreyfus trying to say in the words that are now illegible in the first version of this statement? We will probably never know. Yet he gives a slight hint in the short citation from the Vulgate that follows:

> *Post tenebras spero lucem.*
> After the shadows, I hope or seek for the light.

This has been taken by Calvin and others within Protestantism to stand for a saying such as "After the Darkness, the Light," referring to Christ. The fuller text is found in Job 17:11–13, which in the Vulgate reads:

> *Dies mei transierunt cogitationes meae dissipatae sunt torquentes cor meum noctem verterunt in diem et rursum post tenebras spero lucem si sustinuero infernus domus mea est in tenebris stravi lectulum meum*

The Authorized Version in the Knox edition translates this, emphasizing the Protestant interpretation of the text:

> My days are past, my purposes are broken off, even the thoughts of my heart;
> They change the night into day: the light is short because of darkness.
> If I wait, the grave is mine house: I have made my bed in the darkness.

The translation into French by Louis Segond, first published in 1873, from both the Hebrew and the Greek Septuaguint and thus likely to have been seen by Dreyfus, reads:

> *Quoi! Mes jours sont passés, mes projets sont anéantis,*
> *Les projets qui remplissaient mon cœur . . .*
> *Et ils prétendent que la nuit c'est le jour,*
> *Que la lumière est proche quand les ténèbres sont là!*
> *C'est le séjour des morts que j'attends pour demeure,*
> *C'est dans les ténèbres que je dresserai ma couche . . .*

Would Dreyfus have recognized these differences in translation and in religious perspective, or would he only have seized upon the most obvious metaphorical meaning of the text as a saying? On the one hand, it would be interesting to examine very closely the original context in the Book of Job, which we have studied in the past,[135] and show, in collaboration with Israel David, that this Book of Wisdom has a special concern with breaking apart the dogmatic readings of both scriptural and liturgical imagery in order to forge a version of Judaism which, along with Ecclesiastes and the Song of Songs, for instance, is nonmythical and that calls for philosophical as well as legal interpretations of the language through a pre-Maimonidean rationalism. On the other hand, paying more attention to the context of the essay on art, it would be useful to accept the metaphors of light and darkness in their non-Jewish acceptations, with only slight modifications to follow the argument of Dreyfus. Nevertheless, given that in this citation Dreyfus authorizes us to confirm his knowledge of the Bible—that mysterious book he places second after Homer and behind the Book of Nature, unless the lines quoted above were ironically conceived—it is possible to take the analogy between his condition on Devil's Island and Job's on the dung heap as more than an imposed juxtaposition; it can be a conscious identification he makes with the great man suddenly and unfairly brought low, despondent but roused to rage against his erstwhile friends who take his losses and afflictions as proof positive of his guilt, since the God of their religion would never do an injustice, and his denials of any slight confirmation of their position as further evidence of why he deserves to be ruined for his arrogance and pride—and eventually alienated from God.

At first the deity seems to confirm the case against Job until, remarkably, the voice from the whirlwind returns to proclaim that Job was correct to rail against his friends and young Elihu, and that, indeed, a man must demand accountability from the justice of Heaven and not accept the apparent punishment as a given. In this sense, the darkness would be the deaths, the losses, the illnesses, and the rejection by his friends, and the light would be, not Jesus coming into the world as Light

135 Norman Simms and Israel David, "God's Answer to Job: Revelation and Confession," Simms, ed., *In a Season of Hate: Selection of Papers from the Proceedings of the Tenth Biennial Waikato Jewish Studies Seminar* (Hamilton: Outrigger Publishers, 2002), 52–56. See also "Theodicy and Job in Three Eighteenth-Century Novels," Serge Soupel, ed., *Crime et Châtiment dans les îles britaniques au dix-huitième siècle* (Paris: RBC, 2001), 201–222 and "The Alienated Woman: or, Mrs. Job Suffered Too," Vladimir M. Bychenkov, ed., *Anonymity, Impersonality, Virtuality* (Moscow: Russian and British Cathedra, 2002), 280–297.

or Truth incarnate, but the very reason that interprets the illusions and delusions the friends and Elihu recite uncritically and irrationally. Job the man and *Job* the long dramatic or rhetorical poem are each works of art, beautiful because they manifest truth and truth is beautiful. That truth is what interpretation creates, not what is given, to be taken passively and on faith. Alfred Dreyfus is also still waiting and hoping for the truth to emerge, and although he and Lucie have said that such enlightenment will break into the world unexpectedly, they also know that such an event will happen only because they have, each in their own way, remained steadfast in their love and loyalty, endured the pains and humiliations thrown upon them by a hostile and bigoted world, and worked hard to produce the change in interpretation of the facts and the exposure of the forgeries.

The essay on art, however, concludes lamely, with a statement that Leonardo da Vinci "gives the supreme example" of how a great artist has "revealed the soul in painting the body, in chiselling the material." More irony through understatement or overstatement? Indirection, as the rabbis often counsel, to put the censors off balance? Who knows? But after a brief reading of a poem by Vienne on King John,[136] in which Queen Isabelle's plea is rebuffed because "you are only a woman," Dreyfus adds a word on *Henry IV*:

> However brave he was, when one came to say to him, "Here are the enemies," it was always taken as a kind of canting (*dévoiment*), and he shut him off in raillery and said, "I am going to do something good for them."

This leads into another aphorism that might come from La Rouchefoucauld or some other cynical thinker of the past:

> *Personne n'est grand pour son valet de chambre.*
> No one is great to his personal servant.

All three of these little comments can be seen to show that what you say has its effect more because of who you are than through the value of the remark itself. Truth is normally a social construct and

---

136 *Cahier* 2, Folio 34, *Cahiers*, 74.

does not shape words into things of beauty.

The next significant essay in *cahier* 2 is the one on photographic equipment.[137] Yet having said that, the reader must not expect a highly technical disquisition on the mechanics of optics and the latest developments in the construction of the machinery used to fix images on plates or the advance towards motion pictures occurring at the time Dreyfus was writing this short piece. Rather, two features make it significant: one is that the essay concerns itself, at least in the opening paragraph, with the implications of this technical method of reproducing and storing images, already available for at least fifty years and known to a wide public, with many artists coming to understand its potential as an art form in itself, and the second is that for the first time in his *cahiers*, Dreyfus, under the same underlined title, swerves to a seemingly very different topic altogether.

Thus, of the five paragraphs in this little essay on folio 35, actually only two concern themselves with photography. The first announces the theme, perhaps taking as a starting point some article he has read in one of the magazines sent to him:

> It is one thing amateur photographers fail to take account of. In photographic equipment, one has, according to circumstances, copied the fashion (*la façon*) of making man and most animals, or the fashion (*la façon*) of making a fish in order to make an objective point.

In the repetition of *façon*, he introduces the primary ambiguity in his thought. Amateur photographers, who now have at their disposal smaller, less unwieldy apparatus that makes it possible to take their own pictures for whatever purposes they may choose, do not act as though they had total freedom to follow their own inclinations but “follow the fashion,” in the sense both of selecting objects to take pictures of and deciding how to arrange the object in a setting and in the sense of already perceiving the final product according to current styles and modes they have seen in galleries and illustrated magazines, that is, fashion in the sense of being *à la mode*.

The third and fourth paragraphs deal with the organic chemistry of

137 See also the essay “*Amplification des épreuves photographiques*” on *Cahier* 2, Folio 46.

fat and the implications for human health, and the fifth with a great chemist calling on his students at the polytechnic to apply their learning to public health issues. The essay therefore allows us to watch Dreyfus's mind working by word associations as he slides from the original topic, with its theoretical base and moves towards implications to another subject where the same thing happens, his concern being both for the science that fascinates him and for the application of this technical knowledge in the real world for social and moral ends, his real concern throughout all the prison workbooks.

For most people, the amateurs, the circumstances in which they live have unconsciously turned the fashion, the manner in which they learn to operate the equipment and utilize to make pictures that they will enjoy looking at, showing to others, and keeping in their personal archives, into a style or mode of predetermined paradigms of perception, reception, and memorial value. What could be a mechanism for scientific exploration or artistic creation has become just another way for the powers who control the society to impose their tastes and social agenda over the broad public. These photographs of men, most animals, and fish confirm what the amateurs believe, because they have been so conditioned, man, most animals, and fish look like.

On the other hand, as the second paragraph begins to conjecture, what the objects in the outside world look like is beginning to change because the photograph does not exactly reproduce the optical mechanism of the eye, and so the use of the photographic equipment has begun to change the way in which we all see, think about, and recollect the world we live in.

> When one uses spectacles, one modifies the focus of the lens; one does like a man and most animals do who, adjusting their eyes to diverse planes, vary the focal distance by changing the curvature. When, on the contrary, one focuses with a ratcheting device to vary distances between the ground-glass and the lens, which is the general case for most equipment, one operates like fish who lack the facility to change the curvature of their eyes, but can advance or return their retina to make the focus.

This seems to be pure mechanics, the science of optics: to accommodate the eye's focus to objects at various distances, the mechanism can either change the focal point of the lens or move the retina back and forth, one is the usual form in mammalian eyes and the other in fish. The latest equipment for a *camera oscura* uses both means, what is natural for a human being and what is not. Dreyfus does not at all seem aware here of the two implications of his topic, neither of the social and aesthetic opportunities provided by the invention of the camera nor of the deeper philosophical and political implications. They are, however, implicit in his essay, because we may see them being opened in the essays already examined and will see even more in the folios to come in the remaining thirteen *cahiers*.

That is why the segue into the discussion of chemistry and health should be seen as significant and not merely as a random loss of attention.

> Up to now, the question of organic chemistry, to know the transformation of fat in an organism, has remained more than obscure (*plus qu'obscure*). We certainly knew how we get fat, thanks to starches, but we hardly had any doubts about the phenomenon of getting thin. They used to believe that fats oxidize under the influence of oxygen in the air; that is false—oxygen does not oxidize fats. However. . . .

Before following Dreyfus in this new theme of science and technology, it is important to note the way in which his mind is working and the underlying pattern of his association of ideas.[138] The starting point for the new thought is the advance in understanding from what has hitherto (*jusqu'ici*) been assumed to be true, and the shift to negation of that set of truisms (*c'est faux*) begins with "However" (*cependant*), the announcement of the new epistemological position. This is a variation on what happened when he was talking about photography and the introduction into the discussion of a counterintuitive idea, that the machinery follows both the natural or normative fashion of focusing

138 Whereas the recommended technique of "fantasy analysis" in psychohistory ignores all but the substantive and metaphorical terms in a discourse, especially rubbing out negative and subjunctive or conditional markers, so as to bring to the surface the unconscious dreamlike imagery of repressed thought, in my midrashic readings, I focus on the syntactic markers of process, transformation, and refocalization.

on distant objects and an artificial fashion. What was once thought to be true about the oxidizing of starches proves to be false, but the new understanding comes because the doubts once under the surface of conscious thought have now broken through into moral consciousness.

What was once certain (*on savait bien*) was not all that secure, although it was assumed to be so because the doubts, though present, were hardly there (*on ne se doutait guère*). It was clear that people got fat, but one didn't know how to make them thin again because scientists misunderstood the process by which ingested starches are transformed into bodily fat. The facts don't change; what we believe does. Our assumptions therefore need to be always challenged and questioned so that we learn to see and understand in better ways, so that we come to see the truth and not a fashionable representation of a doubtful truism. Or we need to learn to step out of the obscurity of the old-fashioned *camera oscura*, the dark chamber of ignorance or superstition, into the *camera lucida* Tarde spoke about at the start of this chapter. This is what enlightenment is: not the brilliant and fixed image of truth dominating by a dogmatic assertion of its power but the constant challenging and questioning of assumptions, as Job was forced to do to rid himself of the persecution of his friends, with the ideals of the enlightenment, like Torah and Talmud, as a way of thinking and arguing towards the dynamic and always emerging and developing truth rather than the faithful reception passively of an imposed statement of an iconic truism.

Returning to the "However" where we stopped in our reading of Dreyfus's little double essay on photographic equipment and the mechanism of fat production in the body, what is important to see are these abstracted markers in his text:

> However, it has been recognized . . . because we believed in . . . while all experiments in the laboratory demonstrated the non-existence of these facts. Through multiple experiments, an authoritative chemist arrived at the explanation—quite likely (*assez vraisemblable*). . . .

For Dreyfus, this is the ideal of science: an experimental method that disproves false assumptions and by many experiments (i.e., experiences of testing) builds up a new theory that stands as likely until it too is proven false and another takes its place, and so on *ad infinitum*.[139]

Then a double conclusion. The first is the logical outcome of the preceding essay, and the second is the personal memory evoked by the discussion—one of those very rare moments when Dreyfus permits himself to write about his own childhood and education.

> As all that makes me recall the wishful words formulated by Cahours, my deeply missed teacher at the Polytechnic, in his last books, where he exhorted chemists of [*sic*] to busy themselves with the search for a more perfect knowledge of the blood in order to deduce all its physiological properties.

Perhaps the defective phrase marked *sic* by the modern editors should have had "chemists of the future." What Cahours had taught young Dreyfus in the Polytech was more than a body of knowledge about chemistry, it was a scientific method: from close observation and experimentation through thoughtful extrapolation of general theories to useful application of the knowledge retrieved from nature to human uses. As in art, so in science, the best practice, the beauty of the method, lies somewhere other than in a passive observation and recording of impressions. Beauty is created when it follows an active observation into and a rational transformation of the facts into the next stage of truth. Art and science are not opposites, as science and religion are not; all are variations on the same theme, using different approaches and according to the temperament, talents, and properties of each individual in the time and place of his or her existence.[140]

Can we be absolutely sure this is what Alfred Dreyfus meant here? No, not absolutely, but we can be tentatively comfortable with these speculations when we find them confirmed, refined, and challenged in

---

139 Claude Bernard (1813-1878) and his *Introduction to the Study of Experimental Medicine* (1865) will be discussed further in the next volume in this series.

140 Interestingly, it is Taine who comes close to saying the same sort of thing about what he calls "the ascendancy of involuntary impressions" in art: "Study the sketches, designs, diaries, and correspondence of the old masters, and you will again everywhere find the same inward process. We may adorn it with beautiful names; we may call it genius or inspiration, which is right and proper; but if you wish to define it precisely you must always verify therein the vivid spontaneous sensation which groups together the train of accessory ideas, master, fashion, metamorphose and employ them in order to become manifest" (*The Philosophy of Art*, 80).

subsequent entries in his *cahiers*. For example, immediately following this run of three essays on truth, beauty, and perception and their epistemological, moral, and practical implications, we find two short aphoristic remarks. The first appears in *cahier* 2, folio 37, and the second on the verso of that page.[141]

> Happy those who carry within themselves an ideal of Beauty, and who obey their [sic] ideal of art or the ideal of science.

Aside from the awkward grammatical formulation of this statement,[142] as noted by the modern editor, the import is a clear extension of what has just been said about the way Dreyfus sees all knowledge systems ideally operating towards the same goal of a dynamic truth through different means of approach, not least the broad categories of art and science. Next comes a quotation from Pascal that Dreyfus comments on darkly:

> *De Pascal: "L'âme humaine a des profondeurs insondables." Il eût mieux fait dire que le cœur humain avait des profondeurs de cruauté incommensurables.*

> By Pascal: "The human soul has its unfathomable depths." It would be better to say that the human heart has depths of incomparable cruelty.

Out of the depths of his despair, from amidst the horrible nightmare of his torments in prison, the prisoner reverses the seventeenth-century Christian thinker's aphorism. This is what science cannot understand and what art cannot reproduce in beautiful imagery—the unspeakable evil of the injustices imposed on an innocent Jew. But this way of thinking leads to madness.

In a brief critique of Victor Hugo's *Angelo, Tyran de Padoue*,[143] Dreyfus concludes that this historical play, like others in the Romantic school, makes a flash but then is forgotten, not because it lacks energy

141 *Cahiers*, 75.

142 *"Heureux ceux qui portent en eux un idéal de Beauté, et qui leurs obéissent, idéal de l'art ou idéal de a* [sic] *science."*

143 *Cahier* 2, Folio 38, *Cahiers*, 76.

or style—it has both in abundance—but because everything has been written simply for artificial effect; the whole drama of life has become a fantasy.

This essay is followed by what seems to be a totally unrelated discussion on alcoholism,[144] yet as has happened before, such a scientific essay offers interesting insights into the character and personality of Dreyfus. First, there is a short description of an experiment undertaken over a period of six months in the tiny hut in which the prisoner is kept. He was trying to find an efficient means of producing commercial alcohol and methylated spirits: the attempt was unsuccessful. The discussion then veers in a slightly different direction: he asks himself why the measures of electrical current are named after famous men so that if one wished to write out one's experiments there would be a cacophony: Ohm, Ampère, Latinus Clark . . . Thinking about scientific laws, he is also amused by the words used to designate the facts: this is whimsy, and for too long Dreyfus has been dismissed as a humourless and dour automaton. It is one thing to comment on the artificiality of early nineteenth-century drama and poetry, another to write about alcohol and electricity—but there is a connection in the witty mind of the writer.

After an aborted discourse on Shakespeare's *Othello*, wherein Dreyfus goes no further than writing the title of the essay and then crossing it out, he creates a line drawing of an empty stomach followed by a sketch of the same organ after a hefty meal. This leads into an essay on digestion.[145] From a description of how food is absorbed into the body, he moves to the state of surgery on the stomach, remarking that medical science has not proceeded very far in this regard, lamenting this neglect. Is there a hint here about the poor hygiene and paucity of good food on Devil's Island and Dreyfus's own troubles with indigestion and tropical disease? That would be reason enough to turn away from the Moor of Venice.

A brief notice on Madame de Staël,[146] one of many essays on persons and events connected to the last part of the *ancien régime* and the coming of the French Revolution and its immediate aftermath; this critique admires her because she participated in the progress and the perfect-

144 *Cahier* 2, Folio 39, *Cahiers,* 76–77.
145 *Cahier* 2, Folio 40, *Cahiers,* 77.
146 *Cahier* 2, Folio 43, *Cahiers,* 77.

ability of humanity, clearly something Dreyfus wishes he could enjoy. Then he cites two dozen verses from Hugo's *Odes et Ballades*,[147] beginning "*Que la soirée est fraîche et douce*." (How fresh and sweet the evening is), a sentimental and nostalgic idyll, again perhaps attractive to Dreyfus by its dreamy invitation from the poet to the reader to join him in wandering through the evening landscape together.

From this reverie, Dreyfus glides into another essay on Jules Michelet, this time recounting the historian's biography, emphasizing how his life seemed to be marred by political events, when he was chased out of the Collège de France for refusing to take an oath of loyalty after the *coup d'état*, and thus going into exile, and in that exile—which Dreyfus must have looked on longingly as full of promise and renewal—developing his poetic soul. From this period of his life emerge Michelet's most lyrical, meditative books, such *La Montaigne*, *Le Mer*, *L'Oiseau*, *L'Amour*, and *La Peuple*, impressionistic meditations on nature and society in various forms. It is through these kinds of books, says Dreyfus, that we come to appreciate the beauty of the specifically historical studies Michelet is most famous for; a soul that teaches itself to vibrate in harmony with the environment is preparing itself to understand the moral life of mankind. And, as though comforting himself in his own despondent state, Dreyfus concludes by saying that out of a life defeated and wounded by adversity, "he returned to humanity with a stronger hope, a larger degree of pathos" (*il revient ainsi à l'humanité avec un espoir plus fort, une pitié plus large*).

This leads directly into one of Dreyfus's most important statements about the contemporary spirit:

> Taine, Renan, Darwin, here are the three great minds which have most influenced modern ideas, more or less, following they have been more or less understood. Darwin above all has often been poorly understood.[148]

These are the modern thinkers Dreyfus most admires, to which list he gradually adds a few more, some artists or literary people, but most of them scientists, philosophers, and historians. They are great but they

147 *Cahier* 2, Folio 44, *Cahiers*, 78.
148 *Cahier* 2, Folio 44, Verso, *Cahiers*, 78.

are misunderstood and often neglected, at least in their own lifetimes.

In the second rank behind these three, Dreyfus places John Stuart Mills and the two Spencers in England, Haeckel and Schopenhauer in Germany, and finally Nietzsche (he does not mention where he comes from: born in Germany and living in Switzerland). These all represent a trend in nineteenth-century thought towards hard-headed social, moral, and scientific theory. These foreigners raise the question about where French writers belong. They mostly are specialists who do not venture out of their fields and hardly ever generalize their findings into universal theory. All except Claude Bernard, whose introduction to the scientific method stands out as one of the great books of the century because it sets forth clearly and beautifully a theory of experimental science.[149] Yet, if France is not in the first rank of science and philosophy, it is certainly to be admired for its historians, who have enriched the literature of the age.

Out of this statement comes his next critical piece, on a poem by Sully Prud'homme, "Justice."[150] In this poem, Prud'homme searches for justice until he finds it in the human conscience, an idea Dreyfus approves of, although he might have better expressed it, from what we have seen in earlier essays and their affiliation with rabbinic thought, by indicating that the human soul finds its beauty and strength in justice, that is, in the law. But the poem itself, for all its admirable thoughts, is

---

149 Claude Bernard, "Introduction à l'étude de la medicine expérimentale" (1865), *Oeuvre*, Paris: J. B. Baillière et Fils, 1883. After distinguishing the scientific method from that of the metaphysician, whose scholasticism stands a block to discovering through experimentation the laws of nature, Bernard speaks of "*L'expérimentateur qui se trouve en face des phénomènes naturels ressemble à un spectateur qui observe des scènes muettes. Il est en quelque sorte le juge d'instruction de la nature; seulement, au lieu d'être aux prises avec des hommes qui cherchent à le tromper par des aveux mensongers ou par de faux témoignages, il a affaire a des phénomènes naturels qui sont pour lui des personnages dont il connaît ni le langage ni les mœurs, qui vivent au milieu de circonstances qui lui sont inconnues, et dont il veut cependant savoir les intentions*" (The experimenter finds himself face to face with natural phenomena and so resembles a spectator who observes the examination of men who seek to fool him by false vows, lies or perjury, and he thus deals with natural phenomena that are for him like persons of whom he knows neither the language nor the manners, who live in the circumstances unknown to him, and whom he wishes nevertheless to know the intentions). In other words, a true scientist is both like an investigating magistrate trying to evaluate the testimony of hostile witnesses and an anthropologist who does field studies of persons who speak, think, and feel differently from his own norms. What Dreyfus does is, as we shall see partly in the next chapter but more so in subsequent books of our own, to transfer that scientific method, with due adjustments, to the field of historiography and recreating, inadvertently, a midrashic approach to philosophy, aesthetics, and morals.

150 *Cahier* 2, Folio 45, *Cahiers,* 78.

poorly written, too intricate and scanty: "If the thought is beautiful, the form is weak" (*Si la pensée est belle, la forme est faible*), and for Dreyfus not only must form and content match but beauty needs to be strong—unlike his own mind and body, which he fears will succumb to the torments of his horrible exile. Of Justice like this René Cassin has written, in the very words Dreyfus would have agreed with:

> Centuries have passed. Judaism has, throughout unparalleled trials, preserved its passion for justice and its desire to contribute to the defense of the rights of men of all races and origins, along the lines of the very principle with which it was entrusted two thousand years ago. The Ten Commandments, the first code of the essential duties of man, have suffered many an outrage in history and continue to suffer. Their moral authority remains intact.[151]

Dreyfus's second essay on photography discusses the techniques for enlargement of prints, "*Amplification des épreuves photographiques*."[152] Like the earlier essay, the discussion has both a technical dimension on how to make enlargements and a theoretical component on why such manipulation of artificial images is necessary. A mechanical reproduction of an object out in the world does not adjust itself as the human eye and brain would adjust it in order to give a sense of perspective and depth. What is implied here, but not said explicitly, is that the human mind is creative in its apprehension of natural facts, whereas a camera only records instantaneous perceptions, impressions fixed on glass or chemical film. Photography moves from science to art when it provides the means for correcting the faults of innocent reproduction and from fact to beauty when it gives meaning to the image produced.

Does this have anything to do with the next item in *cahier* 2, a citation of lines from Torquato Tasso in Italian, "*Sprezzata ancella a chi fo piu conserva/Di questa chioma?*" (What good is it to conserve, vile slave, my long hair?) Perhaps a whim or caprice, but also, if we examine the

---

151 "From the Ten Commandments to the Rights of Man, "Shlomo Shoham, *Of Law and Man: Essays in Honor of Haim H. Cohen* (New York: Sabra Books, 1971), 25; cited by José Faur, *The Horizontal Society*, Section 2, 11.

152 *Cahier* 2, Folio 46, *Cahiers*, 78–79.

last lines of this poem, a way for Dreyfus to find a strong expression for his deepest desires to live the heroic life of a soldier, even under the adverse conditions he now has to contend with and despite his tendency to weakness and despair:

> *Della battalglia, entro la turbe ostile*
> *Animo ho bene, ho ben vigior che baste*
> *A conduirti i cavalli, a portar l'aste.*
>
> I will follow you into the fire of battle, in the strongest mêlée of the enemy. I lack neither courage nor force to conduct your horses to carry these lances.

Courage, bravery, and determination: how Dreyfus wishes he could show them in battle! Does he realize the joke here, that the words he inscribes are spoken by a slave, a horse?

Whether he does or not, the next essay[153] seems to be a kind of prose poem of his own, one of several he composes in the course of the *cahiers*. It is followed by a few other brief aphoristic and lyrical comments, the kind of mini-collection he will eventually call the mediations or random thoughts of the Solitary Man, the name he gives to himself or to the literary *persona* created in the workbooks. Although I will analyze these creative efforts more fully in my future work, it is important here, where we are trying to correct false impressions about Dreyfus's character and personality, to spend a few moments on some of these short compositions.

> *Lorsqu'un nuage noir menace la terre et cache sous son voile de sombres brouillards les sommets à la cime ambitieuse, il arrive souvent qu'une douce brise, s'échappant de la terre obscurcie* [four words illegible] *les vapeurs ténébreuses, et prévient, en les divisant, leur chute imminente.*
>
> When a black cloud threatens the earth and hides under its veil the sombre mists the summits of the ambitious peak, it often happens that a soft breeze, escaping from

153 *Cahier* 2, Folio 47, *Cahiers,* 79.

> the darkened earth, [illegible words] the shadowy vapors,
> and prevents, by dividing them, their imminent fall.

This might come from any number of Romantic poets of the early nineteenth century or even some eighteenth-century landscape poems that only partly allegorize their depictions of natural phenomena. This is a rare moment of reverie for Dreyfus, one of his wished-for escapes from the seemingly endless nightmare of his life.

Then comes another composition somewhat more allegorical and tendentious, and written with a nice touch of assonance and syntactic harmony:

> *L'office du Temps est de mètre fin aux haines de détruire les erreurs. La gloire du Temps est de démasquer la fausseté, d'amener la vérité à la lumière, d'imprimer le sceau des siècles sur les choses, de frapper l'injuste obscurcie [?] jusqu'à ce qu'il revienne au droit [six words crossed out].*
>
> The duty of Time is to put an end to hatred, to destroy errors. The glory of Time is to unmask Falsity, to lead truth to the light, to imprint the seal of the centuries on things, to beat down obscure injustice until it returns to the law.

Turlais as editor puts a question mark in square brackets after the phrase *injustice obscurcie* as though that were an unexpected or incomprehensible idea, when, alas, it is the very heart of the matter. Justice has been hidden under a cloud of ignorance and bigotry; it is the enigma of why against all common sense and decency, Dreyfus was convicted of a crime he could not possibly have committed; why the officers of the army and the politicians in the government should have leapt to such illogical conclusions and pursued their quest for punishment to such cruel extremes; why it is taking so very long for Lucie and Alfred's brother Mathieu to bring about a revision of his court-martial; and why heaven and earth do not howl in protest and the voice of God does not break into the world to correct this horrible, unendurable error. In fact, with a minor few editorial changes to orthography and inserted glosses, the prayer to Time could read:

> It is the lawful duty of Time, as *Zman*, an ancient name for God, as the Lord of History and Eternity (*Adon ha kol*), to bring an end to all these hatreds against an innocent man, to destroy the false judgments of the court based on judicial errors. The glory, which is both the honor *(kavod)* and beauty (*hadar)* of the Divine Name, is to unmask the treachery and duplicity of the machinations against a loyal Frenchman, to bring the Truth into the Light, to correct the errors of the world, *tikkun ha'olam,* and to imprint the Seal of the Ages, another liturgical formulaic name for the Divine, on all things, that is, to sanctify this world and signal the beginning of messianic days, to beat down the most black and hateful Injustice that is hidden under the face of military honor and duty to the Republic, so as to hasten the return of rule by law, the dominance and pervasiveness of the Law, the Torah of Israel.

Or as is read out during the regular (nonholiday) evening services of Sabbath:

> We therefore hope in thee, O Lord our God, that we may speedily behold the glory of thy might, when thou wilt remove the abominations from the earth, and the idols will be utterly cut off, when the world will be perfected under the kingdom of the Almighty, and all the children of the flesh will call upon thy name, when thou wilt turn unto thyself all the wicked of the earth.

It would seem difficult to believe any Jew who had grown up with the least attention to the most common prayers of his religion could not have such words, phrases, and concepts resonating in his mind, particularly in times of distress and pain.

Then the third composition in this series, what Dreyfus entitles "*Distique funèbre*," a funeral distich, although it runs more than two lines:

> *La Beauté, la Vérité, la Grâce dans toute la simplicité*

gisent, réduites en cendres.
La mort est son nid, en un cœur loyal repose dans l'éternité.
Vérité et Beauté sont ensevelies.
Qu'à cette urne se rendent les vrais et les beaux et qu'ils soupirent une prière.

Beauty, Truth, Grace in all their simplicity lie here reduced to ashes.
Death is its nest, and a loyal heart reposes in eternity.
Truth and Beauty are wrapped in a shroud.
May this urn transform them into the true and the beautiful and they breathe a prayer.

In what seems a classical graveyard poem, engraved on a tombstone, the poet laments the passing of three key ideals in his philosophy, seeing in their deaths a further stage in their perfection as divine thoughts.

After this melancholy lyrical excursion, Dreyfus returns to a discussion of historiography,[154] at first contrasting two schools of thought: the first, known as the descriptive school, compiles facts without comment and allows the student to draw his own conclusions; the second, the philosophical school, although Dreyfus thinks that name is foolish since there is neither philosophy nor science in it, has the goal of describing the soul of past ages, somehow, by intuition and poetic sensitivity. Unfortunately, Dreyfus does not elaborate on this method here, although he does, of course, elsewhere in the *cahiers*; instead, he slides into "an appreciation" on the old poem *La Pucelle* ("The Virgin") by Chapelain. This contemporary verse on the enthusiastic surge of Mariology and the renewed nationalist interest in Joan of Arc in the second half of the nineteenth century, seen, on the one hand, in the commercialisation of shrines like that of Lourdes and Fatima and, on the other, in a popularization of her figure in monarchist and other pseudomystical politics, as a rather bizarre conclusion to its satire.

La cabale en dit force bien.
Depuis vingt ans, on parle d'elle;

---

154 *Cahier* 2, Folio 48, *Cahiers,* 79–80.

> *Dans six mois, on n'en dira rien.*
>
> The cabal spoke of it with strength, for twenty years one spoke of her, and in six months she will be heard of no more.

The word *cabal* used here to refer to the Catholic mystical movements, say, of the Boulangists and especially of the Jesuits, was also the term of abuse for the Jewish "syndic" or conspiracy. It is difficult to know what Dreyfus means by citing these lines, other than expressing a curiosity of contemporary popular politics, without being conscious of any application to his own condition through anti-Semitic smears—although, as we have noted before, the censors reading his letters and notebooks, not being able to understand the special terms of his love and intellectualism, dismissed his scribbles and his doodles as "*cabalistiques*."

In another short essay on Shakespeare's *Timon of Athens*,[155] after some discussion of the use of Plutarch as a source, Dreyfus shows special interest in the figure of a man subject to bad luck, mistreated by his friends, and susceptible to a cynical view of the world as a consequence, a powerful variation on the Job of the Hebrew Bible. He also understands that the ancients paired Timon with the Cynic philosopher Diogenes as men who tried to put into practice their moral principles, Dreyfus finding in this Greek notion of matching ideas a striking imagery to exemplify the ideas both naive and beautiful. When he considers the way in which Shakespeare depicts Timon as a man thrown into misanthropy by the change in his fortunes, Dreyfus objects, this negative view of the world not being consonant with his own ideals, despite his own tendency to fall into the same despair:

> *La vie n'est ni aix bons, ni aux méchants; les premiers ne reçoivent pas la recompense de leur virtu, les seconds, le châtiment de leurs crimes. La vie est aux indifférents, Cette morale n'est pas gaie.*
>
> Life is neither to the good, nor to the wicked; the first

155 *Cahier* 2, Folio 12, *Cahiers,* 80. Note that this and the preceding composition on *La Pucelle* are on a sheet that seems to have been torn from the bound volume of the *cahier* and numbered Folio 12.

> do not receive recompense for their virtues, the second, punishment for their crimes. Life is to the indifferent. This moral is not gay.

The two troubling words here may or may not be used ironically and the extent of their allusiveness cannot be fully determined, and yet the understanding of the Shakespearian play and Dreyfus's philosophy hinge on them. Those who are *indifférents* may be objective and disinterested, and this would make them scientifically inclined, a necessary and virtuous character in the dispensation of justice in courts of law as well as in laboratories conducting experiments; but they may also be insensible, numbed to the pains and humiliations of others, and consequently cruel in their strict lack of human empathy, making them dangerous persons to deal with. As for *gaie*, this may signal a whimsical understated response to Shakespeare's *Timon* by merely saying that his way of looking at the world is not a pretty or pleasant one, or the word may allude to Nietszche's essay on *The Gay Science*, where the German *fröhliche* plays on the *gai saber* or *gaia sciensa* of Provençal poetry, where it refers to the delightful and pleasurable arts of love. Nietzsche writes with a mòrdant wit, mocking the developments of science and philosophy in his own times, and yet suggesting a way of creatively moving towards a more consolatory and comforting view of the world.

Epilogue

En Europe, les Juifs ont suivi une école de dix-huit siècles, chose que ne peut prétendre aucun autre peuple, et cela de telle sorte que ce n'est pas tant la communauté mais surtout les individus qui ont profité des expériences de cette effroyable période d'épreuves. En conséquence, les ressources spirituelles et intellectuelles des Juifs d'aujourd'hui sont extraordinaires; dans la détresse, ils sont, entre tous les habitants de l'Europe, les derniers à recourir à la bouteille ou au suicide pour échapper a un désarroi profond ce qui est si tentant pur quelqu'un de mois doué. Tout Juif trouve dans l'histoire de ses pères er de ses ancêtres une mine d'exemples du sang-froid et de la ténacité les plus inébranlables au milieu de situations terribles, des ruses les plus subtiles pour tromper le malheur et le hasard en en tirant profit; leur courage sous le couvert d'une soumission pitoyable, leur héroïsme dans le spernare se sperni *(« mépriser d'être méprise ») surpassant les vertus de tous les saints.*

— Friedrich Nietzsche[1]

In Europe, the Jews have followed a single school of thought for eighteen centuries, something which no other people can claim to have done, and have carried this out in such a way that it was not so much the community but individuals who have profited from the experiences of this frightful period of testing. Consequently, the spiritual and intellectual resources of the Jews of today are extraordinary; in their distress, they are, out of all the inhabitants of Europe, the last to escape from

1 Friedrich Nietzsche, *Aurore*, cited in Stephane Zagdanski, "Ânerie d'Arendt: Post-Scriptum a *De l'anti semitisme*" (Paris, 2005-2006) online at http://parolesdesjours.free.fr/arendt.pdf (seen 25 July 2011). *De l'antisemitisme* was published by Julliard, 1995 and again in a new enlarged edition by Climats Flammarion, in 2006. Nietzsche's *Morgenröte – Gedanken über die moralischen Vorurteile*, first appeared in 1881 and is now available in French as *Aurore. Réflexions sur les préjugés moraux*, trans. Giorgio Colli and Mazzino Montinari (Paris: Gallimard, 1989) and in English as *Dawn: Thoughts on the Presumptions of Morality*, trans. Brittain Smith (Stanford, CA: Stanford University Press, 2011).

> profound disorientations through recourse to the bottle or to suicide, which have been such temptations to anyone less endowed. Every Jew find in the history of his fathers and ancestors a mine of examples of self-control and of the most unshakable tenacity, of the most subtle tricks to enable them to triumph over unhappiness and adversity and to profit from it; their courage under the cover of a pitiful submission, their heroism in the *spernare se sperni* ("to scorn being scorned") surpasses the virtue of all the saints.[2]

At this point, where Nietzsche in 1881 seems to pre-empt my descriptions of Dreyfus under duress, in love, and asserting his intellectual prowess, my preliminary excursion into showing how a careful reading of Dreyfus's letters, journals and workbooks allows for a fairly radical re-assessment of his personality and achievements, indeed, his potentiality as a major thinker, must come to an end. The metaphor of the phantasmagoria, which is the one Dreyfus himself used—and which is found repeatedly in the writings of his favourite authors—becomes not only increasingly more apt as we study his style, conceptual framework and psychological profile, but transforms itself into the contours of a midrash. The midrash we are talking about, however, goes beyond the specificities of rabbinical enhancement of sacred texts to include a series of strategies, conscious and unconscious, developed by Jews in Europe under the pressures of persecution and assimilation, to protect and develop their Jewish values, modes of perception, continuities of memory, and creative engagements with the world. These midrashings of experience reveal the most interesting and unexpected features of Dreyfus's character and intellectual activities.

The next volumes in this series will not only continue the close-readings of the *cahiers* begun in this opening book, providing them with an enhanced set of intellectual, psychological and religious contexts, but will probe more deeply into the special, creative relationship between Alfred and his wife Lucie. Though each book can be taken as a separate study, they also each overlap with one another, and deepen the understandings reached in previous exercises.

2 My translation.

Bibliography

Albaret, Céleste, *Monsieur Proust*, as told to Georges Belmont, trans. Barbara Bran. New York: New York Review Books, 2001 (1976) with introduction by André Aciman (1976); originally Paris: Robert Laffont, 1973, 2001.

Albertini, Jean. "Jean-Richard Bloch, de l'Affaire à *La nuit kurde*" in LeRoy, ed. *Les écrivains et l'affaire Dreyfus*, pp. 245–253.

Allen, Jennifer. "Ancient and Modern: The Evolution of Theory and Its Impact on Contemporary Thought." In *Frieze: Contemporary Art and Culture*, No. 125 (September 2009), p. 21.

Améry, Jean. *At the Mind's Limits: Contemplations by a Survivor on Auschwitz and Its Realities*, trans. Sidney Rosenfeld and Stella P. Rosenfeld. Bloomington, IN: Indiana University Press, 1980 (1966).

Améry, Jean. *Intellectuelle à Auschwitz,* trans. Enrico Carri. Torino: Bollati Boringhieri, 1987. Original German title: *Jenseits von Schuld und Sühne—Bewältigungsversuche eines Überwaltigten* (Stuttgart: Ernst Klett, 1977 [Szezesny Verlag, 1966]).

André, Sylvie. "'Et c'est ainsi que Yahve est grand': Chroniques de ma rencontre avec le Midrash" (Coloque d'Étel) *Champ du Midrash* online at http://.lechampdumidrash.net/articles.php?lng=fr&pg=62&prt=2 (seen 08/01/2011).

Anonymous (L. W.) "Anti-Semitism," *Encylopaedia Britannica* (1911) Classic Encyclopaedia. Online at http://www.1911encyclopedia.org/Anti-Semitism (last seen 25/12/2010).

Anonymous. "Dreyfus réhabilité: Chronologie." Online at http://assemblee-nationale.fr.

Anonymous. "Cabinet Accepts Judge Mahon's Resignation: Court Action following Erebus Disaster Inquiry" (May 1981). Online at http://www.nzhistory.net.nz/nmedia/photo/ongoing-debate-about-erebus-disaster (seen 21/10/2010).

Anonymous. "Catalogue de la bibliothèque de feu M. Pierre Dauzwe [pseud]." *Open Library beta,* online at http://openlibrary.org/b/OL6471380M/Catalogue-de-la-bibliotheque-de-feu-M.-Pierre-Sauze-pseud (seen 8/05/2009).

Anonymous. "'J'accuse . . .!' Emile Zola, L'Aurore and the Dreyfus Affair." Online at http://Oxygenee.com (2005).

Anonymous. "Mysterious Rays." Online at http://www.aip.org/history/electron/jjrays (seen 27/01/2011).

Anonymous. "Reproductions de manuscripts." In *Un choix de reproductions de manuscripts à la libraire L'Oiseau-Lire,* online at http://www.loiseaulire.com/Litterature/Manuscrits (seen 8/05/2009).

Anonymous. "Van Gogh as a Letter-Writer." Online at mhtml:file//F:/Van Gogh as a letter-writers—Vincent van Gogh Letters (seen 07/04/2010).

Anonymous. *The History of the Discovery of Cinematography—An Illustrated Chronological History*. Online at http://www.precinemahistory.net/index (seen 1/7/2010).

Anonymous. *World Conquest through World Government: Protocols of the Learned Elders of Zion*, trans. Victor E. Marsden. London: Britons Publishing Company, 1963 (1920).

Anonymous. "Jewish Attitudes to Art." *Jewish Virtual Library: Art*. Online at http://www.jewishvirtuallibrary.org/jsource/judaica.ejud_2002_2002_0_01373 (seen 07/12/2010).

Anonymous. *Anti-Semitism,* ed. Israel Pocket Library, entries chosen from *Encyclopedia Judaica*. Jerusalem: Keter, 1974.

Aron, Raymond. *L'Opium des intellectuals*, intro. Nicolas Baverez. Paris: Hachette Littératures, 2002 (1955).

Artson, Bradley Shavit. "Parashat Va'Yetze—9 Kislev 5766—Lulei: What Keeps Us Going." *American Jewish University*, online at http://judaism.ajula.edu/Content/ContentUnit.asp?CID=902&u=5164&t=0 (seen 28/07/2008).

Assouline, Pierre. *Discovering Impressionism: The Life of Paul Durand-Ruel*, trans. Willard Wood and Anthony Roberts. New York: Magawan Publishing, 2004. Original: Paris: Plon, 2000.

Aubaret, Jean-François. "La question du dessein (1)." *Mag Arts* (April 2003), online at http://webcndp.cndp.fr/magarts/dessin1/lettres.htm (seen 13/01/2007).

Badinter, Robert. *Libres et égaux . . . L'émancipation des Juifs 1789–1791*. Paris: Fayard, 1989.

Bakhos, Carol, ed. *Current Trends in the Studies of Midrash*. Leiden: Brill, 2006.

Bakhos, Carol. "Method(ological) Matters in the Study of Midrash." In Bakhos, *Current Trends in the Study of Midrash* pp. 161–188.

Balluci, Dagoberto Husayn. "Eduard Drumont e la 'France juive.'" *GattoNero* (Libri 2009), online at mhtml:file://:F:\Popolodellarete_it-VediMessaggioSingolo-Perreifllere-Articolidi or http://www/italiasociale.org/ (seen 07/04/2010).

Baltz, Matthew. "The Dreyfus Affair: Its Causes and Its Implications" (25 January 1995). Online at http://www/harwich.edu/dept/history/HHJ/drey (seen 19/05/2009).

Barnes, Rachel, ed. *Cézanne by Cézanne*. Artists by Themselves. Sydney: Angus & Robertson, 1992 (1990).

Baron, Philippe. "L'affaire Dreyfus des *Elie Greuze* de Gabriel Trarieux." In LeRoy, ed. *Les écrivains et l'affaire Dreyfus*, pp. 255–264.

Barraud, Cécile, ed. "Une revue d'élite (*la Revue Blanche*)." *Equinoxes* 9 (2007).

Barrès, Maurice. *Les Déracinés*. Preface par François Broche. Paris: Bartillat, 2010.

Barry, Maurice and Lo Duca, eds., *Méliès, Georges (1861–1938): Créateur du sectacle cinématographique*. Paris: Prisma, 1944.

Beaufort, Raphael Ledos de. *Franz Liszt: The Story of his Life*. Boston: Oliver Ditson & Co., 1887.

Bell, Julien. *Mirror of the World: A New History of Art*. London: Thames & Hudson, 2007.

Belpomme, Judith. "Benda, Julien." *SIHAD: Société internationale d'Histoire de l'Affaire Dreyfus*, online at http://pockcity.ifrance.com/benda (seen 01/09/2009).

Benda, Julien. *Belphégor: essai sur l'esthétique de la présente Société française*, 2eme ed. Paris: Emile-Paul Frères, 1924.

Benda, Julien. *Dialogues à Byzance*, 2eme ed. Paris: Editions de la Revue Blanche, 1900.

Benamozegh, Elijah, *Israel and Humanity*, trans. Maxwell Luria, Preface by Moshe Idel. Mahwah, NY: Paulist Press, 1995; originally *Israël et humanité* (Paris: Association Menorah, 1914). Berkovitz, Jay R. *Rites and Passages: The Beginnings of Modern Jewish Culture in France, 1650–1860*. Philadelphia, PA: University of Pennsylvania Press, 2004.

Bermant, Cahim. *What's the Joke? A Study of Jewish Humour through the Ages*. London: Weienfeld and Nicolson, 1986.

Bernard, Claude. *Introduction à l'étude de la medicine expérimentale* (1865). In *Oeuvre* Paris: J. B. Baillière et Fils, 1881.

Bick, Ezra. "Shiur#08 Egypt." *Understanding Midrash*, Yeshivat Har Etzion, Israel Koschitsky Beit Midrash (VBM). Online at http://vbm-torah.org/archive/midrash/08egypt.rtf (last seen 28/01/2011).

Birnbaum, Pierre. *Le moment antisémite: Un tour de la France en 1898*. Paris: Fayard, 1998.

Birnbaum, Pierre. "Les Juifs d'Etat souls la Troisième République; de l'assimilation sociale aux employés de prestige et d'autoritée." *Romanticisme* 21:72 (1991), pp. 87–95.

Blanche, Jacques-Emile. *Mes Modèles: souvenirs littéraires—Barrès, Hardy, Proust, James, Gide, Moore*. Paris: Stock, 1984 (1928).

Bloch-Dano, Evelyne. *Madame Proust*. Paris: Editions Grasset et Fasquelle, 2004.

Bloom, Harold. "What is Genius," excerpted from, *Genius: A Mosaic of One Hundred Exemplary Creative Minds*. Online at NotAlone, http://www.youarenotalone.com/article/3946 (seen 08/10/2009).

Blum, Anotinette. "L'Ascendant intellectuel et moral de Lucien Herr sur les Dreyfusards" in LeRoy, ed. *Les écrivains et l'affaire Dreyfus*, pp. 159–166.

Bohlman, Philip V. "The Jewish Shechinah, or the feminine sacred in the musics of the Jewish Mediterranean" (9 November 1998). Online at http://research.umbc.edu/eol/MA/index/number3/bohlman_0-3 (seen 25/09/2003).

Bontempelli, Sergio. *Dal razzismo dei colti al razzismo popolare: il "caso Drumont."* Tesi di dottoratio, Universita degli Studi del Salento, Dipartimento de Filsofia e Scienza Sociali. Anno academico 2006–2007.

Borrel, Anne and Senderens, Alain and Naudin, Jean-Bernard. *Dining with Proust*, trans. Wendy Akkatson, Simon Knight, Suer Rose, Isabel Varea and Ros Schwartz.

Bourg, Julian. "Reflections on a Jewish Mirror," review of Jonathan Judaken, *Jean-Paul Sartre and the Jewish Question: Anti-Semitism and the Politics of the French Intellectual* in *H-Ideas* (November 2010). Online at https://www.h-net.org/reviews/showrev.php?id=31252 (seen 23/11/2010).

Bourgeois, André. "Paul Bourget, 1852–1935: 'Littérature engagée.'" *Navigation*, online at http://andrebourgeois.fr@paul_bourget (seen 24/12/2010).

Bourget, Paul. *Crime d'Amour*. no trans. New York: Ace Books, 1953.

Bourget, Paul. *Essais de psychologie contemporaine*, 10ème ed. Paris; Alphonse Lemerre, nd.

Bourrelier, Paul-Henri. "Saint-Cère, l'Affaire Labaudy et Le Cri de Paris," *Blog Revue blanche de Paul-Henri Bourrelier* (15 September 2009). Online at http://revueblanche.over. blog.com (seen 25/11/2010).

Bowen, Elizabeth. "Bergotte." In Quennell, *Marcel Proust, 1871–1922: A Centennial Volume*, pp. 59–75.

Boyarin, Daniel. "De/Re/constructing Midrash: in Bakhos, *Current Trends in the Study of Midrash* pp. 299–322.

Bredin, Jean-Denis. "Préface" to Dreyfus, *Carnets*.

Bredin, Jean-Denis. *The Affair: The Case of Alfred Dreyfus*, trans. Jeffrey Mehlman. New York: George Braziller, 1986; orig. French, Julliard 1983.

Bregman, Marc. "Isaak Heinemann's Classic Study of Aggadah and Midrash" Department of Religious Studies, University of North Carolina (updated 19 March 2008). Online at http://www.uncg.edu/ rel/ contacts/faculty/Heinemann (seen 27/01/2010).

Bregman, Marc. "Aqedah: Midrash as Visualization." *Journal of Textual Reasoning* 2:1 (2001). Online at http://www.bu.edu/mzank/ Textual_Reasoning/tr-archive/tr10/aar2001/Bregman (seen 27/11/2001).

Bressolette, Agnes. "Quand tout s'écroule, la parole peut-elle de survivre?" *Pour librement associer psychoanalyse et grand public*. Online at http://squiggle.be/index2.php?option=com_content&task=view&id=320&pop=1&page... (seen 9 June 2009).

Brichetto, Joanna L. *The Wandering Image: Converting the Wandering Jew*. MA thesis in religion. Nashville, TN: Vanderbilt University, 2006.

Brownson, Ronald, ed. *Claude Monet, Painter of Light*. Auckland: Auckland City Art Gallery, NZI Cup Ltd, 1985.

Bruckner, D. J. R. "Theater Review: Dancing at the Precipice of the End of the World" (26 October 1999). *New York Times* (12 October 2009). Online at http://www.nytimes.com/1999/10/12/12/theater/theater-review-dancing-at-the-precipicep (seen 27 November 2009).

Brun, Bernard. "Marcel Proust et la religion." *Item: Institut des textes & manuscripts modernes*. (19 October 2006). Online at http://www.

item.ens/fr/index.php?id=13957 (seen 16/06/2010).

Brun, Bernard. "A la recherche du Contre Sainte-Beuve." *Item: Institut des textes & manuscripts modernes* (20 March 2007). Online at http://www.item.ens/fr/index.php?id=76070 (seen 16/06/2010).

Buber, Martin. *The Writings of Martin Buber*, selected, edited and introduced buy Will Herberg. New York: Signet/New World Publishing, 1974 (1956).

Burkhardt, Jacob. *The Civilization of the Renaissance in Italy*, 2 vols., trans. S. G. C. Middlemoore. Introduction by Benjamin Nelson and Charles Trinkaus. New York: Harper & Bros/Harper Torchbook, 1958 (1929).

Burns, Michael. *Dreyfus: A Family Affair, 1789–1945*. New York: HarperCollins, 1991.

Cachin, Françoise, *Gauguin: The Quest for Paradise*, trans. I. Mark Paris. London: Thames & London, 1992; orig. Paris: Gallimard, 1989.

Cadot, Michel. "Tschekhov et l'Affaire." In LeRoy, ed. *Les écrivains et l'affaire Dreyfus*, pp. 85–92.

Cahm, Eric. *L'Affaire Dreyfus: histoire, politique et société*. Paris: Livre de Poche, 1994.

Camus, Albert. "Preface," pp. ix-xxxi. Roger Martin du Gard, *Oeuvres completes*, tome I. Paris: Bibliothèque de la Pleiade, 1964.

Carr, Nicholas. *The Shallows: What the Internet is Doing to our Brains*. New York and London: W. W. Norton & Co., 2010.

Cassou, Jean. *La mémoire courte*. Paris: Mille et une nuits/Librairie Arthème Fayard, 2001.

Chabris, Christopher and Daniel Simons. *The Invisible Gorilla and Other Ways Our Intuitions Deceive Us*. New York: Crown, 2010.

Chapman, Guy. *The Dreyfus Trials*. St Albans: Paladin, 1974; orig. B. T. Batsford, 1972.

Charle, Christophe. "La lutte de classes en littérature: *L'Etape* de Paul Bourget et *Vérité* d'Emile Zola." In LeRoy, ed. *Les écrivains et l'affaire Dreyfus*, pp. 225–233.

Chaumont, Jean-Philippe and Jean-Claude Kuperminc, eds. *Zadoc Kahn: un grand rabin entre culture juive, affaire Dreyfus et laïcité*. Paris-Tel-Aviv: Editions de l'éclat, 2007.

Chinaglio, Ruggero. Review of Nadine Shenkar, *L'arte ebraica e la cabala* (Rome: Spirale, 2000). CHIWEB: il sito dell'inedito, online at http://

www.chiweb.net/shenkar (seen 14/06/2004).

Church, Dan M. "Four Faces of a Chambermaid: Mirbeau's Novel and Its Stage and Screen Adaptations" (2003). Online at https://my.vanderbilt.edu/dan_church(seen 18 May 2009).

Claveau, Clive. Bertram Gordon, Talbot Imlau, Norman Ingram, Wendy Perry and David L. Schalk, revs. William D. Irvine, *Between Justice and Politics: The Ligue des droits de l'homme, 1898–1945* (Stanford University Press, 2007). H-Diplo Roundatable Reviews, 7:11 (2007), online at http://www.h-net.org/~diplo/roundables (seen 5 October 2007).

Clegg, Elizabeth. "'Austrian Art' on the Move: The Cultural Politics of International Exhibition 1900–1918." In Natter and Gerunenberg, *Gustav Klimt*, pp. 53–100.

Clemenceau, Georges. *Au pied du Sinaï*. Paris: Georges Crai et Cie, nd.

Clemenceau, Georges. *Contre la justice: l'Affaire Dreyfus*, ed. Michel Drouin, Préface by Jean-Denis Bredin. Montréal: Mémoire du Livre, 2007.

Cogeral, Guy, Sylvie Pafry, Stéfane Guégan and Christine Dixon. *Masterpieces from Paris: Van Gogh, Gauguin, Cézanne and Beyond. Post Impressionism from the Musée d'Orsay.* Canberra, ACT: The National Gallery of Australia, 2009.

Cohen, Jack J. "Exile and Redemption in Modern Jewish Theology." In Levine, Etan, ed. *Dispora: Exile and the Contemporary Jewish Condition*, pp. 91–102.

Col, Norbert. *Burke et la France*. Thèse de doctorat. Université de Paris-IV Sorbonne, Centre de recherches sur la civilisation de l'Europe moderne. 1990–1991.

Colomina, Beatriz. "Sex, Lies and Decoration: Adolf Loos and Gustav Klimt." In Natter and Grunenberg, *Gustav Klimt*, pp. 43–51.

Conner, Tom. "André Gide and his Times: French Intellectuals and the Challenge of Communism." Online at http://e-gide.blogspot.com/p/ressources-en-ligne.html (last seen 09/02/2011).

Conner, Tom. "The Dreyfus Affair and the Emergence of the French Public Intellectual." Online at http://www.unomaha.edu/esc/2006Proceedings/ConmerDreyfus.

Conway, Daniel W. "'Seeing' is Believing: Narrative Visualization in Kierkegaard's Fear and Trembling," *Journal of Textual Reasoning* 2:1 (2003). Online at http://etext.lib.virginia.edu/journals/tr/volume2/number1/conway.html.

Costa-Meyers, Esther da. "Gesamtskunstwerk, or the Politics of Wholeness." In Natter and Gerunenberg, *Gustav Klimt*, pp. 25–31.

Couvrette, Shelly. "Paul Gauguin: *Manao Tupapao* (She Things of the Spirit or The Spirit Watches Over Her)." Online essay at http://www.cat-sidh.net/Writing/Gauguin (seen 12/01/2011).

Crease, Robert P. "The Book of Nature" *PhysicsWeb* (December 2006). Online at http://www.stonybrook.edu/philosophy/faculty/rcrease (seen 08/01/2007).

Cunningham, Antonia. *Essential Impressionists*. Bath, UK: Parragon, 2003.

Cutshall, J. A. "'Celui qui dreyfuse': Alfred Jarry and the Dreyfus Case," *Misia Sert: Symposium* 43 (1989), pp. 20–37. Online at *Questia*, http://www.questia.com/reader/action/readchecked?docld=76963171 (Seen 5/05/2009).

Cutting, James E. "Representing Motion in a Static Image: Constraints and Parallels in Art, Science, and Popular Culture," *Perception* 31 (2002), pp. 1165–1193.

d'Aymery, Gilles. "Julien Benda: The Future of Imagination and Thought," *Swans* (31 March 2003). Online at http://www.swans.com/library/art9/ga153 (seen 20/03/2010).

Damon, Dan. "Chasms of Perdition: How Fernc Liszt tried to Tame the Divine Essence of the Romani Soul," *Central Europe Review* 3:13 (2 April 2001). Online at http://www/ce-review.org/01/13/damon13 (seen 14/11/2010).

Dardorn, Roger. "Une affaire de mystique," In LeRoy, ed. *Les écrivains et l'affaire Dreyfus*, pp. 9–16.

Daspre, André. "L'héroisation du Capitaine Dreyfus" in LeRoy, ed. *Les écrivains et l'affaire Dreyfus*, pp. 217–224.

Daudet, Léon. *L'Entre-Deux-Guerres: Souvenirs des milieux littéraires, politiques, artistiques et médicaux de 1880 à 1905*. Troisième série. PaRIS: Noluvelle Librairie Nationale, 1915.

Davenport-Hines, Richard. *Proust at the Majestic: The Last Days of the Author Whose Book Changed Paris*. New York: Bloomsbury, 2006.

Davidson, Israel. *Parody in Jewish Literature*. New York: Columbia University Press, 1907; repr. New York: AMS Press, 1966.

De Maîstre, Xavier. *Oeuvres Completes*. Paris: Garnier Frères, 1862.

Delandes, Jacques. *La boulevarde du cinema à l'époque den Georges Méliès*. Paris: Editions du Cerf, 1963.

Delhorbe, Cecile. *L' Affaire Dreyfus et les écrivains français*. Neuchchatel et Paris: Editions Victor Attinger, 1932.

Delhorbe, Cécile. *L'Affaire Dreyfus et les écrivains françaises*. Paris et Neufchatel: Victor Attinger, 1932.

Demaison, Gerard. "Secret: The Military History of the Dreyfus Case" (revised 30 December 2003), a review of Jean Doise, *Un secret bien gardé: Histoire militaire de l'Affair Dreyfus* (Paris: Editions du Seuil, 1994). *France at War: The Dreyfus Case and the French* 75, online at http://mailtomikei01@execpc.com (seen 22/02/2010).

Deneen, Patrick J. "Patriotic Vision: At Home in a World Made Strange," *The Intercollegiate Review* (Spring 2002), pp. 33–40.

DesGroseillers, René. "Les écoles françaises" (32002). *La psychanalyse française*, online at http://www.bibliotheques-psy.com/spip.php?article98 (last seen 06/01/2011).

Deutscher, Isaac. *The Non-Jewish Jew and Other Essays*, ed. Tamara Deutscher. London: Oxford University Press, 1968.

Diamond, James Arthur. *Maimonides and the Hermeneutics of Concealment: Deciphering Scripture and Midrash in* The Guide of the Perplexed. Albany: State University of New York Press, 2002.

Dimnet, Ernest. *Paul Bourget*. London: Constable & Company Ltd., 1913.

Dreyfus, Alfred et Lucie. *"Ecris-moi souvent, écris-moi longuement . . . ," Correspondance de l'Ile du Diable (1894–1899),* ed. Vincent Duclert, Avant-propos Michelle Perrot. Paris: Mille et Une Nuits, 2005.

Dreyfus, Alfred. *Carnets (1899–1907): Après le process de Rennes*, édition critique de Philippe Oriol. Paris: Calmann-Lévy, 1998.

Dreyfus, Alfred. *Cinq années de ma vie*. Préface de Pierre Vidal-Naquet, Postface de Jean-Louis Levy. Paris: La Découverte, 1994 (1982).

Dreyfus, Alfred. *Souvenirs et correspondance,* publiés par son fils [Pierre Dreyfus], Paris: Editions Bernard Grasset, 1936.

Dreyfus, Alfred. *Souvenirs et correspondance, publiés par son fils,* Pierre Dreyfus. Paris: Bernard Grasset, 1936.

Dreyfus, Mathieu. *L'Affaire: Telle que je l'ai vécue*. Avant-propos by Jacques Millerand. Paris: Bernard Grasset, 1978.

Drumont, Edouard. *La France juive*, 2 vols. 43rd ed. Paris: Marpon et Flammarion, 1886; repr. by http://UUURGH.net (2008).

Duchatelet, Bernard. "L'echo de l'affaire Dreyfus sans l'oeuvre Romanesque de Romain Rolland" in LeRoy, ed. *Les écrivains et l'affaire Dreyfus*, pp. 287–294.

Duclert, Vincent. *L'affaire Dreyfus,* nouvelle édition. Paris: La Découverte, 2006 (1994).

Dunlop, I. H. E. "Proust and Painting" in Quennell, *Marcel Proust, 1871–1922: A Centennial Volume*, pp. 105–125.

Dunyach, Jean-François, "Histoire et décadence en France à la fin du XIXe siècle. Hippolyte Taine et *Les origines de la France contemporaine*" *Mil neuf cent*, No 14, 1996. *Progrès et decadence*, pp. 115–137.

Elior, Rachel. "From the Covenant of the Rainbow to the Covenant at Sinai, from the Pilgrimage to the Temple to the Vision of the Chariot, from the Blessing of the First Fruits to the Priestly Blessing, and from the *Tiqqun Leil Shavu'ot* to the Revelation of the *Shekhinah*," trans. from Hebrew by Joel Linsider unpublished typescript, thanks to Maru Bing of Hamilton, New Zealand.

Epstein, I., trans. *The Babylonian Talmud, Seder Mo'ed,* Vol. IV. London: Soncino Press, 1938.

Evans, Henry Ridgley. "Introduction: The Mysteries of Modern Magic." In Albert A., compiler and ed., *Magic: Stage Illusions and Scientific Diversions, including Trick Photography*. pp. 1–26.

Evans, Mike, gen. ed. *Art: The Defining Moment in Art. Over a Century of the Artists, Exhibitions, People. Artworks and Events that Rocked the World.* London: Cassell Illustrated/Octopus, 2008.

Ey, Henri. "Le déchifrement de l'inconscient"(1965). *Les Cahiers Henri Ey* No. 2 (2000), pp. 7–23.

Faur, José. "The Targum and Halkha," *The Jewish Quarterly Review* 66 (1976), pp. 19–26.

Faur, José. "God as Writer: Omnipresence and the Art of Dissimulation," *Religion and Intellectual Life* 6 (1989), pp. 31–43.

Faur, José. "Jewish and Western Historiographies: A Post-Modern Interpretation," *Modern Judaism* 12 (1992), pp. 23–37.

Faur, José. "Of Cultural Intimidation and Other Miscellanea: Bar-Sheshakh vs. Raba," *Review of Rabbinic Judaism* 5 (2002), pp. 34–51.

Faur, José. "Rhetoric and Hermeneutics: Vico and Rabbinic Tradition" *Pensar para el nuevo siglo: Giambattista Vico y la cultura europea,* III

(La Citta del Sole, 2001), pp. 917–938. Online at http://betyof.org and http://www.josefaurstudies.org/index.shtml (last seen 26/01/2011).

Faur, José. *Golden Doves with Silver Dots: Semiotics and Textuality in Rabbinic Tradition*. Bloomington, IN: Indiana University Press, 1986.

Faur, José. *The Horizontal Society: Understanding the Covenant and Alphabetic Judaism*, 2 vols. Boston, MA: Academic Studies Press, 2008.

Fauvre, Yves-Alain. "Suarès et son combat dans l'affaire." In LeRoy, ed. *Les écrivains et l'affaire Dreyfus*, pp. 207–215.

Feinstein, Stephen C. "Toward a Post-Holocaust Theology in Art: The Search for the Absent and Present God" (extract). Online at http://fermi.phys/ualberta.ca/ãmk/galles/feinstein (seen 13/12/2010).

Finkielkraut, Alain. "Preface" to Wisse, *If I Am Not For Myself*, p. xi.

Finkielkraut, Alain. *Le Juif imaginaire*. Paris: Editions du Seuil, 1980.

Finkielkraut, Alain. *Le mécontemporain: Péguy, lecteur du monde moderne*. Paris: Gallimard, 1991.

Fischer, Mark. "Real Abstractions: The Application of Theory to the Modern World." In *Frieze: Contemporary Art and Culture*, No. 125 (September 2009), p. 18.

Fonrobert, Charlotte Elisheva. "The Handmaid, the Trickster and the Birth of the Messiah: A Critical Appraisal of the Feminist Valorization of Midrash Aggada." In Bakhos, *Current Trends in the Study of Midrash*, pp. 245–276.

Forth, Christopher E. Review of Ivan Strenski, *Durkheim and the Jews of France* (University of Chicago Press, 1997). *H-Antisemitism* (December 1998), at http://www.h-net.org/reviews/showrev.php?id=2581 (last seen 26 January 2011).

Foxman, Abraham H. "Foreward" to Kotek, *Cartoons and Extremism*, p. xi.

Fraade, Steven D. "Rewritten Bible and Rabbinic Midrash as Commentary." In Bakhos, *Current Trends in the Study of Midrash*, pp. 59–78.

Fraisse, Simone. "L'Antidreyfusisme de gauche entre 1906 et 1910." In LeRoy, ed. *Les écrivains et l'affaire Dreyfus*, pp. 113–121.

France, Anatole. *Crainquebille, Putois, Riquet and Other Profitable Tales*, trans. Winifred Stevens. London: The Bodeley Head, 1925 (1916).

France, Anatole. *Monsieur Bergeret in Paris*, trans. B. Drillien. London: The Bodley Head, 1925 (1921).

France, Anatole. *On Life and Letters*, first series, trans. A. W. Evans. London: The Bodley head, 1924 (1910).

France, Anatole. *On Life and Letters*, second series, trans. A. W. Evans. London: the Bodley Head, 1923 (1914).

France, Anatole. *On Life and Letters*, third and fourth series, trans. Bernard Miall. London: The Bodley head, 1925 (1924).

France, Anatole. *Penguin Island*, trans. A. W. Evans. The Thinker's Library, No. 21. London: Watts & Co., 1931.

France, Anatole. *The Amethyst Ring*, trans. B. Drillien. Minerva Edition. London: The Library Press, 1899.

France, Anatole. *The Elm Tree on the Mall: A Chronicle of our own Times*, trans. M. P. Willcocks. London: The Bodley Head, 1923 (1910).

Franck, Adolph. *The Kabbalah, or The Religious Philosophy of the Hebrews*, rev. and enlarged translation by I. Sossnitz. New York: The Kabbalah Publishing Co., 1926 (orig. in French, 1843, 2nd ed. 1889).

Fry, Roger. *Vision and Design*. Harmondsworth: Penguin Books, 1937 (1920).

Fustel de Coulanges, Numa Denis. *The Ancient City: A Study on Ancient Religion, Laws, and Institutions of Greece and Rome,* no trans. Garden City, NY: Doubleday Anchor Books, 1956 (1864).

Galerner, David. "Mrs. Havermeyer's Legacy: Degas in New York," *City Journal* (Autumn 1995). Online at http://www.city-journal.org/printable.php?id=329 (seen 24/11/2009).

Gauguin, Paul and Charles Morice. *Noa Noa*. (journals from 192) original edition 1901. First translation into English 1919. Now available on Project Guttenberg.

Gauguin, Paul. *The Intimate Journals,* trans. Ruth Pielkovo, ed., Kaori O'Connor. London, Boston, Sydney and Henley: KPI, 1985 (1923).

Gauthier, Robert, ed. *"Dreyfusards!" Souvenirs de Mathieu Dreyfus et autres inédits*. Paris: Collections Archives, 1955.

Gauthier, Robert, ed. *"Dreyfusards!" Souvenirs de Mathieu Dreyfus et autres inédits*. Paris: Collections Archives, 1955.

Gerbod, François. "La reconstruction de l'Affaire dans *Notre Jeunnesse* de Charles Péguy." In LeRoy, ed. *Les écrivains et l'affaire Dreyfus*, pp. 265–273.

Gevritz, Stanley. "Of Patriarchs and Puns: Joseph at the Fountain, Jacob at the Ford" *Hebrew Union College Annual* 46 (1975), pp. 33–54.

Gide, André. *L'Immoraliste*. Paris: Livre de Poche, 1963; original Paris: Mercure de France, 1902.

Gide, André. *If It Die . . .*, trans. Dorothy Bussy. London: Secker & Warburg, 1951. Originally *Si le grain meurt*, 1920; trans. based on 2nd ed of 1924.

Gilbert, Sir Martin. Interview with Ruth Bell in *The Jerusalem Post* (20 February 2007). Online at file:E:\Antisemtism_files\a_002 (seen 08/03/2007).

Goldberg, Jonah. *Liberal Fascism: The Secret History of the American Left from Mussolini to the Politics of Meaning*. New York: Doubleday, 2007.

Goldin, Judah, ed. *The Jewish Expression*. New York: Bantam Books, 1970.

Goldmann, Nahum. Le Paradox juif: conversations en français avec Léon Abramowicz. Paris: Stock, 1976. Internet: AAARGH, 2006.

Gollancz, Victor. *The Case of Adolf Eichmann*. London: Victor Gollancz, 1961.

Golomb, Jacob, ed. *Nietzsche and Jewish Culture*. London and New York: Routledge, 1997.

Gombrich, Wernest H. "Idea in the Theory of Art: Philosophy or Rhetoric?" *The Gombrich Archive*, online at http://www,gombrich.co.uk/showdoc.php?id=24 (seen 07/02/2007).

Goode, Erica. "Stress from Attacks Will Chase Some into the Depths of Their Minds, and Stay" *The New York Times* (18 September 2001). Online at http://www.nytimes.com/2001/09/18/national/18PSYC.hmtl?pagewanted=print (seen 18/09/2001).

Gopnik, Adam. "Trial of the Century: Revisiting the Dreyfus Affair," *New Yorker* (28 September 2009). Online at http://www.newyorker.com/.../2009/09/28/090928crbo_books_gopnik (seen 10 October 2009).

Grimbert, Philippe. *Un Secret*. Paris; Grasset et Fasquette, 2004.

Grunenberg, Christoph. "Luxury and Degradation: Staging Klimt." In Natter and Gerunenberg, *Gustav Klimt*, pp. 33–50.

Gruzinska, Aleksandra. "(Anti-)Semitism 1890s/1990s: Octave Mirbeau and Em. Ciorban," originally in *Rocky Mountain Review* (1997). Online at http://rmmla.wsu.edu/ereview/old/55.1/ articles/gruzinska (seen 24/07/2010).

Guegan, Luc. "La colonne du mystère: Tentative d'épuisement midrashique d'une fresque du Quattrocento" *Le Champ du Midrash* online at http://www.lechampdumidrash.net/articles.php?lng=fr&pg=73 (seen 25/08/2008).

Guetta, Alessandro. "Classical Scholarship and Kabbalistic Pietas in the *Shileta ha-Gibborin* by Avraham Portaleone," Lecture held at the Conference Jewish and the classical tradition in the Renaissance, the Warburg Institute, London 6–7 March 1997, online at http://www,chez.com/jec2/archportaleo (seen 07/11/2005).

Halasz, Nicholas. *Captain Dreyfus: The Story of a Mass Hysteria*. New York: Simon & Schuster, 1955.

Halévy, Daniel. *My Friend Degas*, ed. and trans. Mina Curtiss. Springfield, CT: Wesleyan University Press, 1964. Orig. Paris: La Palatine, 1960.

Halévy, Daniel. *Péguy et les Cahiers de la Quinzaine*. Paris: Bernard Grasset, 1941.

Halévy, Ludovic. *Parisian Points of View,* trans. Edith V. B. Matthews, Introduction by Branden Matthews. London and New York: Harper & Brothers, 1894. Project Gutenberg.

Halévy, Ludovic. *The Abbé Constantin*, Vol. I. no. trans. Project Gutenberg.

Hallstrom, Per. "Presentation Speech, The Nobel Prize in Literature 1927, Henri Bergson." *Nobel Lectures, Literature 1901–1967*, ed., Horst Frenz (Amsterdam: Elsevier, 1969). Online http://www.nobel.se/literatuire/laureates/1927/press (seen 02/08/2004).

Hammond, Paul. *Marvellous Méliès*. London: Gordon Fraser, 1974.

Ha-Nagid, Samuel. "Introduction to the Talmud," Appendix I in Aryeh Carmell, *Aiding Talmud Study*, 5th examined and rev. ed. Jerusalem and New York: Feldheim, 1986.

Hansel, Joëlle. "Défense et illustration de la cabale: Le philosophie et le cabaliste de Moïse Luzzatto," Pardes 12 (1990). Online at http://ghansel.free/dr/luzzato (seen 14/08/2003).

Harrison, Donald H. "Locks and Bagels: No People have been more caught up in the romances and tragedies of the Panama Canal than the Jews," *San Diego Press-Heritage* (12 March 1999). Online at mhtml:file://F:\Jewsinvolvedinthepanamacanal,panama... (seen 18/12/2009).

Hasan-Roken, Galit. "Rabbi Meir, the Illuminated and the Illuminating: Interpreting Experience." In Bakhos, *Current Trends in the Study of Midrash*, pp. 227–244.

Hassine, Juliette. *Esoterisme et écriture dans l'oeuvre de Proust*. Paris: Libraiie Minard, 1990.

Hassine, Juliette. *Marranisme et hébraisme dans l'oeuvre de Proust*. Fleury-sur-Orne: Librairie Minard, 1994.

Haus, Jeffrey. "Culture, Conversion, and the Portrayal; of Jews in Nineteenth-Century France," review of Julie Kalman *Rethinking Antisemitism in Nineteenth-Century France* in *H-Judaic* (November 2010). Online at https://www.h-net.org/reviews/showrev.php?id=29871 (seen 23/11/2010).

Hayoun, Maurice-Ruben. *La liturgie juive*. Paris: Presses Universitaire de France, 1994.

Hayoun, Maurice-Ruben. *Le Judaisme moderne*. Paris: Presses Universitaires de France, 1989.

Heider, Jörg. "Sight Reading: Do Philosophers Understand Contemporary Art?" in *Frieze: Contemporary Art and Culture*, No. 125 (September 2009), pp. 95–99.

Henry, Anne. "Le kaleidoscope" *Cahiers Marcel Proust: Etudes proustienne* III (1979), pp. 27–66.

Herbert, Wray Congdon. "The Uneasy Meeting of Clio and Freud," *The Chronicle of Higher Education* (21 October 1981), pp. 21–22.

Hernando, Alberto. "Peter Quignard: The Outline of Origin and Silence," *Artists\Permalink* (23 January 2005). Online at http://00e00.blogs.com/english/2005/01/alberto_hernand (seen 13/09/2006).

Hirsch, David. *Anti-Zionism and Antisemitism: Cosmopolitan Reflections*. Working Paper No. 1, series ed. Charles Small. New Haven, CT: The Yale Initiative for the Interdisciplinary Study of Antisemitism, nd.

Hitz, Hans-Rudolf. *Les inscriptions de Gozel. Essai de déchiffrement de l'écriture*. I. Tablettes de terre cuite. Ettingen, Switzerland: Editions de l'auteur, 1997. II. Grands galets (pierres), post-à-masques en argile et os, 1998.

Hoffman, Eva. *After Such Knowledge: Memory, History and the Legacy of the Holocaust*. New York: Public Affairs, 2004.

Hoffman, Robert L. *More than a Trial: The Struggle over Captain Dreyfus*. New York: The Free Press and London: Collier Macmillan, 1980.

Homes, A. M. "Seeing the Unimaginable Freezes the Imagination," *The New York Times* (24 September 2001). Online at http:/www.com/2001/09/24/books/24HOME.hmtl?pagewanted=print (seen 24/09/2001).

Hong, Teng-Yueh. "Le dreyfusisme proustien. (Marcel Proust's 'La Revue blanche' and the Dreyfus Affair in France," *Fu Jen Studies:*

literature and linguistics (January 2004). Online at http://www.thefreelibrary.com/Fu+Jen+Studies%3a+literature+%26... (seen 22/01/2008).

Hopkins, Albert A., compiler and ed. *Magic: Stage Illusions and Scientific Diversions, Including Trick Photography.* New York: Benjamin Blom, 1897; repr. 1967.

Hororé, Jean-Paul. "Autour d'Intellectuel." In LeRoy, ed. *Les écrivains et l'affaire Dreyfus*, pp. 149–157.

House, John and Virginia Spate, commentators. *Claude Monet: painter of Light*. Auckland, NZ: Auckland City Art Gallery, 1985.

House, John. "Monet and the Genesis of his Series." In Brownson, *Claude Monet, Painter of Light*, pp. 9–26.

Huneker, James. *Chopin: The Man and His Music* (1900). Project Guttenberg, 2010. Also reproduced by Dover Publications, 1966.

Huneker, James. *Promenades of an Impressionist*. New York: Charles Scribner Sons, 1910. Available on Project Guttenberg.

Hyden-David, Kathleen. "Histoire d'une recontre entre Art et Littérature," *Les amis du livre contemporaine*. Online at http://www.les-amis-du-livre-contemporain.fr/histoire (seen 8/05/2009).

Ilouz, Charles and Laurent Vidal. "Interview with Carlo Ginzburg, 'L'historien et l'avocat du diable'" *Fenêtre* no. 53–54 (2003–2004). Online at http://fr.wikipedia.org/wiki/Carlo Ginzburg (seen 19/09/2008).

Jamet, Claude. "Le Dreyfusisme *Radical* d'Alain." In LeRoy, ed. *Les écrivains et l'affaire Dreyfus*, pp. 177–184.

Jaurès, Jean. *Rallumer tous les soleils*. Textes choisies et présentés par Jean-Pierre Roux. Paris: Omnibus, 2006.

Josephe, Flavius. *Contre Apion,* trad. Leon Blum, ed., Theodore Reinach. Paris: Belles Lettres, 2003 (1930).

Josipovici, Gabriel. "How to See a Blind Man" (A review of Steven F. Kruger, *The Spectral Jew: Conversions and Embodiment in Medieval Europe*) in TLS No. 5421 (23 February 2007), p. 8.

Julliard, Jacques. "Clemenceau, journaliste de l'Affaire." In LeRoy, ed. *Les écrivains et l'affaire Dreyfus*, pp. 167–176.

Kafka, Franz. *The Trial,* trans. Willa and Edwin Muir, Epilogue by Max Brod. London: Secker and Warburg, 1950. Orig. *Der Prozes* Berlin:

Verlag Die Schmiede, 1925.

Kalisch, Isidor, trans. *Sepher Yezirah: A Book of Creation* or *The Jewish Metaphysics of Remote Antiquity*. New York: L. H. Frank & Co., 1877.

Kalmin, Richard. "The Use of Midrash for Social Harmony." In Bakhos, *Current Trends in the Study of Midrash*, pp. 133–160.

Kellman, Steven G. "Reading Kafka's Love Letters as a Key to His Mind." Review of Reiner Stach, Kafja: The Decisive Years, trans. Shelley Frisch. In *Forward* (30 December 2005). Online at http://www.highbeam.com/doc/1P1-118146012 (seen 22/02/2008).

Kelvin, [no other name given]. "Jews of Belle Epoque Paris" *Epicentre* (15 July 2005). Online at http://everything2.com/index.pl?node_id=1736672 (read 11 May 2009).

Keren, Zvi. "Zvi Keren: His Contribution to Israel's Music Scene: An Interview in Honor of his 85th Birthday," ed. Alona Keren-Sagee online at http://www.biu.ac.il/hu/mu/min-ad02/alona (seen 07/05/2009).

Kirby, Michael. "The Dreyfus Case a Century on—Ten Lessons for Ireland and Australia," *Human Rights Lecture 29 June 2006* Law Society of Ireland.

Kleebatt, Norman L., ed. and intro. *The Dreyfus Affair: Art, Truth and Justice*. Berkeley, CA: University of California Press for the Jewish Museum of New York, 1987.

Knobel, Marc. "L'affaire Dreyfus, une affaire toujours actuelle pour l'extrême droite?" *Histoire* (11/05/06). Online at www.comlive.net/L-affaire-dreyfus-une-affaire-toujours (seen 17/02/2010).

Kobrin, Nancy Hartevelt. *The Banality of Suicide Terrorism: The Naked Truth about the Psychology of Islamic Suicide Bombing*. Washington, DC: Potomac Books, 2010.

Kofman, Sarah. *Le mépris des Juifs: Nietzsche, les Juifs, l'antisémitisme*. Paris: Galilée, 1994.

Kolakowski, Leszek. *Bergson*. Oxford and New York: Oxford University Press, 1985.

Kolb, Philip. "The Making of a Novel." In Quennell, *Marcel Proust, 1871–1922: A Centennial Volume*, pp. 25–37.

Kotek, Joël. *Cartoons and Extremism: Israel and the Jews in Arab and Western Media*, trans. Alisa Jaffa. Edgeware, Middlesex: Vallentine Mitchell, 2009 (orig. 1008).

Koviel, Michael. *The Art of World Religions: Judaism*. Poole, Dorset: Blandford Press, 1979.

Kraus, Karl. *In These Great Times*, ed. Harry Zohn, trans. Joseph Fabry, Max Knight, Karl F. Ross and Harry Zohn. Chicago, IL: University of Chicago Press, 1990; Montreal, Que: Engendra Press, 1976.

Kuperminc, Jean-Claude and Jean-Philippe Chaumont, coordinated by Ariel Danan, Danielle Delmaire and Monique Lévy. *Zadoc Kahn: Un grand rabbin entre culture juive, affaire Dreyfus et laïcité*. Paris: Editions de l'Eclat, 2007.

Kurella, Hans. *Cesare Lombroso: A Modern Man of Science*, trans. M. Eden Paul. New York: Rebman Company, 1911.

Kurzman, Charles and Lynn Owens. "The Sociology of Intellectuals" *Annual Review of Sociology* 26 (2002), pp. 63–90.

La Puma, Léonardo. "L'affaire Dreyfus dans la presse salentile (Italie méridionale, région des Popuilles)" in LeRoy, ed. *Les écrivains et l'affaire Dreyfus*, pp. 47–55.

Laborde, Albert. *Trente-nuit années près de Zola: Vie d'Alexandrine Zola*. Paris: Les Editions Français Réunis, 1963.

Ladurie, Emmanuel Le Roy. "Zola et les intellectuals dans la tourmente," *Le Figaro Litteraire—Dossier* (08/01/1998). Online at http://www.asmp.fr/Academie des Sciences morales et politiques (last seen 30 January 2011).

Lanzoni, Remi Fournier. *French Cinema: From its Beginning to the Present*. New York: The Continuum International Publishing Group, 2002.

Lassaigne, Jacques. *Impressionism,* trans. Paul Eve. London: Heron Books,1969 (orig. Lausanne: Rencontre, 1966).

Lazare, Bernard. *L'Antisémitisme: son histoire et ses courses*. Paris: Léon Chailley, 1894.

Lazare, Bernard. *L'Oppression des Juifs dans l'Europe orientale: les Juifs en Roumanie*. Paris: *Cahiers de la Quinzaine*: huitième cahier de la troisième serie, 1902. Online reprint ed. Razvan Paraianu (created January 2001, last revised 2 June 2001 (seen 29 June 2009).

Lazare, Bernard. *Le Nationalisme juif*. Publications du "Kadimah" No. 1. Paris: Stock & Flammarion, 1898.

Le Carré, John. "El teatro del terror," *El Pais*, edition impresa (18 October 2001). Online at http://www.elpais/es/articulo.html?d_date_2001

1018&xref=20011018elpepiopi_6&type=Tesa (seen 20/10/2001).

LeBon, Gustave. *The Crowd: A Study of the Popular Mind*, no trans. 19th ed. London: Ernest Benn, 1947 (trans. 1896).

Lehman, Andrew. "Origins of Autism: What Causes the Condition to Wax and Wane." Online at http://originsofautism.com (seen 12/09/2003).

Leiberman, Shimon. "Kabbala #16 Beauty as Mercy." *Aish.com*, online at http://www/aish.com/SSI/articleToPrint.asp?PageURL=/spiritualuty/kabbala101/Kabb... (seen 24/08/2005).

Lenne, Gérard. *Le cinema fantastique et ses mythologies*. M Paris: Editions du Cerf, 1970.

Lennhoff, Eugene. *The Last Five Hours of Austria*. London: Rich & Cowan, 1938.

Leppert, Richard. "Introduction" to Theodor W. Adorno. *Essays on Music* (University of California Press, 2004). Online at http://www.ucpress.eduy/pages/9275/9275. intro (seen 29/07/2004).

LeRoy, Gervaise, ed. *Les écrivains et l'affaire Dreyfus*. Actes du Colloque organise par le Centre Charles Péguy et l'Université d'Orléans (29–31 Octobre 1981). Paris: Presses Universitaire de France, 1983.

Levi, Anthony. "Peguy, Charles. French, 1873–1914," *Encyclopedia of the Essay*. Online at http://www.custom-essay.net (seen 8/05/2009).

Levi, Anthony. "*Revue des Deux Mondes*, French Journal, 1829–," *Encyclopedia of the Essay*. Online at http://www.custom-essay.net/essay-encyclopedia/Revue-des-Deux-Mondes-Essay (seen on 02 3.08/2010).

Levi, Iakov. "Hatred for Women and Islamic Terror," *Psychohistory* (February 2002). Online at http://www.geocities.com/psychohistory2001/hatredforwomen (seen 27/07/2004).

Levi, Iakov. "Talking Socrates and Jesus," An abstract of discussions on *Sumviva* in July 2000. Online at http://www.geocities.com/psychohistory2001/talkingsociatres (seen 27/07/2004).

Levick, Adam. *Anti-Semitic Cartoons on Progressive Blogs*. Jerusalem Center for Public Affairs. No. 101, 1 September 2010/3 Elul 5770. Online at http://www.cpa.org/JCPA/Templates/ShowPAGE.ASP?drt=3&dbid=1&lngid=1&tmid=111&fid=624&pid=4636&ttl=Aniti-SemiticCartoonsonProgressiveBlogs (seen 25/06/2010).

Levinas, Emmanuel. *Difficile liberté: essai sur le judaïsme*. Paris: Albin Michel, 1976 (1963).

Levinas, Emmanuel. *Ethique et infini: dialogues avec Philippe Nemo*. Paris: Fayard, 1982.

Levinson, Joshua. "Literary Approaches to Midrash." In Bakhos, *Current Trends in the Study of Midrash*, pp. 189–226.

Likin, Max. "Rights of Man, Reasons of State: Emile Zola and Theodor Herzl in Historical Perspective." Online essay at http://www.csub.edu/~mbaker2/HerzlZola.pdf (last seen 26 January 2011).

Lindemann, Albert S. *The Jew Accused: Three Anti-Semitic Affairs (Dreyfus, Beilis, Frank) 1894–1915*. Cambridge, New York, Port Chester, Melbourne, Sydney: Cambridge University Press, 1991.

Liris, Robert. "La Tour foudroyée: image factuelle ou l'Object d'Histoire." *Mentalities/Mentalités* 25:1–2 (2011).

Liris, Robert. *L'Ordinaire de Vichy 1940–1942*. Self-published. Bellerive/Allier: nd. [2010]).

Liszt, Franz. *Friedrich. Chopin*. 4th ed. Leipzig: Breitkopf et Haertel, 1890.

Liszt, Franz. *Life of Chopin*, 2nd ed. trans. John Broadhouse. London: William Reeves, nd.

Lorenzen, Julie, rev. "Growing Up with the Impressionists: the Diary of Julie Manet." Online at http://www.julielorenzen.net/impressionists (seen 10/08/2009).

Löwy, Michael. "Bernard Lazare, Marches et ruptures d'un anarchiste et deux textes issus de *Fumier de Job*," *Incroyables anarchistes* (02/092009). Online at http://sha.federation-anarchiste.org/article16 (seen 26/05/2009).

Magnou, Jacqueline. "L'affaire Dreyfus à travers la presse viennoise: *Die Neue Freie Presse* et *Das Deutsche Volksblatt*—une analyse idéologique." In LeRoy, ed. *Les écrivains et l'affaire Dreyfus*, pp. 75–84.

Maimonides, Moses (Rambam). *The Guide for the Perplexed*. Trans from Arabic, M. Friedlander, 2nd ed., rev. New York: Dover Publications, 1956 (1881).

Mandel, Paul. "The Origins of Midrash in the Second Temple Period." In Bakhos, *Current Trends in the Study of Midrash*, pp. 9–34.

Marcangeli, Alaine. "First Meeting of the Nabis (1888)." In Mike, gen. ed. *Art: The Defining Moment in Art*, p. 28.

Marchiori, Giuseppi. *Gauguin: The Life and Work of the Artist illustrated with 80 Colour Plates*, trans. Caroline Beamish. London: Thames &

Hudson, 1968; orig. Firenze: Sades Edition, 1967.
Martin du Gard, Roger. *Jean Barois*, ed. André Daspre. Paris: Gallimard, 2003; orig. 1921.
Martin, T. Carlaw, "Liszt as Littérateur." In Beaufort, *Franz Liszt*, pp. 207–227.
Masson, Raphaël and Véronique Mattusci, *Rodin*, trans. Deke Disinberre. Paris: Flammarion, 2004.
Maurois, André. *Call No Man Happy*, trans. Denver and Jane Lindley. London: Jonathan Cape, 1943.
Maurois, André. *Pages choisies* avec une notice biographique, de notices littéraires et des notes explicatives par Arsène Chassang et Charles Senningham. Paris: Hachette, 1956.
Maurois, André. *Proust: Portrait of a Genius*, trans. Gerard Hopkins. New York: Harper & Brothers, 1950.
Maurois, André. *The World of Marcel Proust*, trans. Maura Budberg. London: Angus and Robertson, 1974 (orig. Paris: Librairie Hachette, 1960).
Maurras, Charles. "Trois idées politiques: Chateaubriand, Michelet, Sainte-Beuve" (1912). *Action Française*, online at http://www.actionfrancaise.net/projet-tresor-maurras_trois... (seen 06/01/2011).
McCorristine, Shane. "'Dreaming While Awake': The Evolution of the Concept of Hallucination in the Nineteenth Century." University College Dublin. Unpublished essay in typescript.
Méliès, Georges. *"Mes Mémoires" in Barry and Duca, Méliès, Georges (1861–1938): Créateur du spectacle cinématographique.* pp. 161–199.
Mendelsohn, S. Felix, compiler and reteller. *The Jew Laughs: Humorous Stories and Anecdotes.* Chicago, IL: L. M. Stein, 1935.
Mergui, Maurice. "Bonnes nouvelles des parents (extraits d'ouvrages)." *Champ du midrash*, online at http://www.lechampdumidrash.net/mobile/articles.php?lng=fr&pg=90&prt=2 (last seen 27/01/2011).
Mergui, Maurice. "De l'impossibilité de traduire les Epîtres." *Champ du midrash*, online at http://www.lechampdumidrash.net/mobile/articles.php?lng=fr&pg=342. (last seen 27/01/2011).
Mergui, Maurice. "Dictionanaire midrashique du Corpus paulinien." *Le Champ du Midrash*, online at http://www.lechampdumidrash.net/articles.php?lng=fr&pg=234 (seen 25/08/2008).
Mergui, Maurice. "Genèse de la Passion," Premier Colloque d'Etudes

Midrashiques (CHEM 2005), 20–21 August 2005. *Le Champs du Middrash*, online at http://www.lechampdumidrash.net/mobile/articles.php?lng=fr&pg=71 (last seen 27/01/2011).

Mergui, Maurice. "L'atelier du midrash pourt en finir avec les chutes de cheval." *Le Champ du Midrash*, online at http://www.lechampdumidrash.net/articles.php?lng=fr&pg=227 (seen 25/08/2008).

Mergui, Maurice. "Midrash et peinture: Analyse d'une chute de cheval." *Le Champ du Midrash*, online at http:///www.lechampdumidrash.net/articles.php?lng=fr&pg=222 (seen 24/08/2008).

Mergui.Maurice. "Apologie de Paul." *Le Champ du midrash*, online at http://www.lechampdumidrash. net/mobile/articles.php?lng=fr&pg=90&prt=322 (last seen 27/01/2011).

Milikowsky, Chaim. "Reflections on the Practice of Textual Criticism in the Study of Midrash Aggada: The Legitimacy, the Indispensability and the Feasibility of Recovering and Presenting the (Most) Original Text." In Bakhos, *Current Trends in the Study of Midrash*, pp. 79–110.

Miller, Milton L. *Nostalgia: A Psychoanalytic Study of Marcel Proust*. Boston, MA: Houghton Mifflin, 1956.

Mirbeau, Octave. *Combats esthétique,* tome I, 1877–1892, tome 2, 1893–1914. Edition établi, présentée et annotée par Pierre Michel et Jean-François Nivet. Paris: Séguier, 1993.

Mirbeau, Octave. *Romans Autobiographiques.* Preface by R. and R. Wald Lasowski. Paris: Mercure de France, 1991 (1891).

Mix, Elizabeth. Review of Willa Z. Silverman, *The New Bibliopolis: French Book Collectors and the Culture of Print, 1880–1914* (University of Toronto Press, 2008) in *Nineteenth-Century Art Worldwide*. Online at http://www.19thc-artworldwide.org/spring_09/reviews/mix/s (seen 8/05/2009).

Montaigne, Michel. *The Complete Works of Montaigne: Essays, Travel Journal, Letters,* trans. and intro. Donald M. Frame. Stanford, CA: Stanford University Press, 1948.

Montesquiou, Robert de. *L'Art de paraître,* intro. Philippe Thiébaut. Paris: Editions de la Réunion des Musées Nationaux, 1999.

More, Jr., John T. "The Dreyfus and Zola Trials: *The Atlantic* 81:487 (May 1898), pp. 589–602.

Mornard, Henry. *La Révision du procès de Rennes, 15 juin 1906–12 juin 1906 [mémoire]* Paris: Ligue Française pour la Défense des Droits de l'Homme et du Citoyen, 1907.

Morse, Jr., John T. "The Dreyfus and Zola Trials," *The Atlantic Monthly* (May 1898). *Atlantic Unbound* (May 2004), online at www.theatlantic.com/past/docs/issues/1898may/morsen (seen 20/03/2010).

Mucchielli, Alex. *Les Mentalités*. Que sais-je? Collection. Paris: Presses Universitaires de France, 1985.

Murphy, Jonathan Paul. "Proust's Art: Painting, Sculpture and Writing." *In A la recherche du temps perdu*. Oxford, Berlin and Bern: Peter Lang, 2001.

Myers, D. G. "Jean Améry: A Biographical Introduction," originally published in *Holocaust Literature: An Encyclopedia of Writers and Their Work*, ed. S. Lilian Kremer (New York: Routledge, 2000). Online at mhtml:file:F:\Amery, a biographical introduction (seen 1/12/2009).

Nathan, Rabbi. *The Fathers according to Rabbi Nathan (Abot de-Rabbi Natan)*, trans. Judah Goldin. New Haven, CT and London: Yale University Press, 1983 (1955).

Natter, Tobias G. "Gustav Klimt: No More than a Goldsmith: The Cross-pollination of Painting, Architecture and the Applied Arts in Vienna around 1900," trans. Fiona Elliott in Natter and Gerunenberg, *Gustav Klimt*, pp. 13–23.

Natter, Tobias G. and Christoph Grunenberg, eds. *Gustav Klimt: Painting, Design and Modern Life* (London: Tate Liverpool, 2008).

Neusner, Jacob. "Beyond Myth, after Apocalypse: The Mishnaic Conception of History." *Response: A Contemporary Jewish Review* 46 (1984), pp. 17–35.

Neusner, Jacob. *Form-Analysis and Exegesis: A Fresh Approach to the Interpretation of Mishnah*. Minneapolis, MN: The University of Minnesota Press, 1980.

Nguyen, Victor. "Charles Maurras (1808–1952) et l'affaire: Une crise de l'identité française." In LeRoy, ed. *Les écrivains et l'affaire Dreyfus*, pp. 137–146.

Nochlin, Linda. *The Politics of Vision: Essays on Nineteenth-Century Art and Society*. New York: Harper & Row, 1989.

Nourisson, B. *L'Affair Dreyfus: Criminelle machination politique, religieuse, sociale et administrative*. Lausanne: Imprimérie Fritz Ruedi, 1909.

Noy, David. "Joseph bar Mathias's Vision of the Temple." Online at http:inside.bard.edu/religion/facultyproj/temple/temple_hist/josbarma (seen 27/08/2006).

Ouaknin, Marc-Alain. *Concerto pour quatre consonnes sans voyelles: au-delà du principe d'identité.* Paris: Balland, 1997.

Ouaknin, Marc-Alain. *Le livre brûlé: Philosophie du Talmud.* Paris: Lieu Commun. 1993 (1986).

Ouaknin, Marc-Alain. *Lire aux éclats: Elogue de la caresse.* Préface de Léon Chestov. Paris: Quai Voltaire, 1992 (first edition Paris: Lieu Commun, 1989).

Ouaknin, Marc-Alain. *Ouvertures hassidiques.* Paris: Jacques Grancher, 1990.

Ozanne, Marc-Angélique and Frédérique de Jode, *Theo: The Other Van Gogh*, trans. Alexandra Bonfaite-Warren. New York: Magowan Pubolishing, 2004.

Pacheco, José Emilio. "El Affaire Dreyfus y el laberinto de conspiración" *Letras Libres* (March 1999). Online at http://www.letraslibres.com/pdf.php?id=5573 (seen 26/05/2009).

Painter, George D. *Marcel Proust: A Biography*, 2 vols. Harmondsworth: Penguin, 1983 (1959 and 1965).

Painter, Gorge D. *Proust: The Later Years.* Boston and Toronto: Atlantic-Little, Brownin Association with the Atlantic Monthly Press, 1965.

Paléologue, Maurice. *An Intimate Journal of the Dreyfus Case*, trans. Eric Moebacher. New York: Criterion Books, 1957.

Paraf, Pierre. "Preface" de Laborde, *Trente-nuit années près de Zola,* pp. 7–13.

Parkes, James. *An Enemy of the People: Antisemitism.* Harmondsworth: Penguin Books, 1945.

Péguy, Charles. *Notre jeunesse, précède par De la raison.* Paris: Gallimard, 1993.

Péguy, Marcel. *La destin de Charles Péguy.* Paris: Librairie Académique, 1941.

Pellico, Silvio. *My Ten Years' Imprisonment*, trans. Thomas Roscoe. London: Cassell & Co., 1886.

Perrot, Michele. "Preface" to Arthur Mitzman, *Michelet ou la subversion du passé. Quatre leçons au Collège de France (1998).* Paris: Boutique de l'Histoire, 1999. Online at http://ch.revues.org/index205. (last seen 06/01/2011).

Philologus. "Horror is as Horror Speaks" *Forward* (14 September 2001).

Online at http://www.forward.com/issues/2001/01.09.14/arts6/philologus (seen 15/09/2001).

Piperno, Alessandro. *Proust antijuif*, trans. Fanchita Gonzalez Battle. Paris: Liana Levi, 2007 (orig. Italian 2000).

Pissarro, Camille. *Letters to his Son Lucien*, ed. John Rewland, with Lucien Pissarro, trans. Lionel Abel. Santa Barbara, CA and Salt Lake City, UT: Peregrine Smith, 1981 (Pantheon Books, 1944).

Porgès, Jules. Miscellaneous documents online at mhtml:file://F:\JulesPorges (seen 07/04/2010).

Powell, Anthony. "Proust as a Soldier" in Quennell, *Marcel Proust, 1871–1922: A Centennial Volume*, pp. 149–164.

Prontera, Angelo. "'La Civiltà Cattolica' et l'affaire Dreyfus." In LeRoy, ed. *Les écrivains et l'affaire Dreyfus*, pp. 57–64.

Proust, Marcel. *A la recherche du temps perdu*, vol. 1. *Du côté de chez Swann*. Paris: Editions Gallimard/Collection Folio, 1954.

Proust, Marcel. *Carnets*. Editions établis et présentée par Florence Calle et Antoine Compagnon. Paris: Gallimard/NRF, 2002.

Proust, Marcel. *Correspondence*, ed. Jérôme Picot. Paris: Flammarion, 2007.

Proust, Marcel. *In Search of Lost Time*, 6 vols., trans and intro. Ian Patterson. London: Penguin Classics, 2003 (2002).

Proust, Marcel. *Remembrance of Things Past*, 5 vols., trans. C. K. Scott Moncrieff. New York: Random House, 1927.

Proust, Marcel. *Remembrance of Things Past*, vol. 5, *The Past Remembered*, trans. Frederick A. Blossom. New York: Random House, 1959; 1st ed., 1932.

Quennell, Peter, ed. *Marcel Proust, 1871–1922: A Centennial Volume*. New York: Simon and Schuster, 1971.

Quennell, Peter. "Introduction to Quennell," *Marcel Proust, 1871–1922: A Centennial Volume*, pp. 10–24.

Rabi, Wladimir. "Ecrivains juifs face à l'affaire Dreyfus: Etude des comportements." In LeRoy, ed. *Les écrivains et l'affaire Dreyfus*, 17–25.

Rabinowitz, Sima. *From the Depths of my Heart: The Letters of Alfred and Lucie Dreyfus*. Playscript supplied by the author (2009).

Rachum, Stephanie. "Camille Pissarro's Jewish Identity." *Assaph* 5 (2001), online at http://arts.tau.ac.il/.../journals/arthistory/

Assaph5/01rachum. (last seen 30 January 2011).

Regan, Marci. *Paul Durand-Ruel and the Market for Early Modernism*. MA thesis (May 2004), Louisiana State University.

Reinach, Joseph. *Histoire de l'Affaire Dreyfus*, 2 vols. Preface by Pierre Vidal-Naquet, Introduction by Hervé Duchêne. Paris: Robert Laffont, 2006.

Reinach, Joseph. *Récits et portraits*. Paris: Librairie Fëlix Alcan, 1915.

Reinach, Joseph. *Voyage en Orient*., 2 vols. Paris: Charpentier, 1879. Reproduced by Eilbron Classics (USA).

Renan, Ernest. *Souvenirs d'enfance et de jeunesse*, Introduction by Henriette Psichiari, notes Laudice Rétat. Paris: Garnier-Flammarion, 1973.

Renan, Ernest. *The Life of Jesus* (1861), Introduction by John Haynes Homes (New York: Modern Library, 1927) available through Project Gutenberg at http://www.guttenberg.net (22 August 2005).

Renan, Ernest. *Recollections and Letters* of Ernest Renan, trans. Isabel F. Hapgood. New York: Cassell, 1892 (orig. 1889)

Rénouvin, Bertrand. "Maurras, le fondateur" *Mil neuf cent* 11:1 (1993), pp. 77–81. Online at Persee http://www.persee.fr (seen 25 June 2009).

Resture, Resture. "Tahiti: About Paul Gauguin." Online at http://www.janesresture.com (seen 29/06/2009).

Révah, Louis-Albert. *Julien Benda: Un misanthrope juif dans la France de Maurras*. Paris: Plon, 1991.

Rilke, Rainer Maria. *Lettres sur Cézanne*, trans. Philippe Jaccottet. Paris: Editions du Seuil, 1991. Originally *Briefe über Cézanne*, 1952, 1983.

Rivas, Marta. *Un mito proustiana*. Santiago de Chile: Prensas de la Editorial Universitaria, 1968.

Robert, Marte. *From Oedipus to Moses: Freud's Jewish Identity*, trans Ralph Mannheim. Garden City, NY: Anchor Press/Doubleday, 1976 (orig. 1974).

Roche, Anne. "Homme sur un rocher escarpé au milieu de la mer dans le style de Böcklin." In LeRoy, ed. *Les écrivains et l'affaire Dreyfus*, pp. 275–285.

Rodrigue, Aron, "Rearticulations of French Jewish Identities after the Dreyfus Affair," *Jewish Social Studies* No. 2 (1996). Online at http://www.questia.com/PM.qst?a=o&se=gglsc&d=96507314 (last seen 26 January 2011).

Rogers, B. G. "Proust and the Nineteenth Century." In Quennell, *Marcel Proust, 1871–1922: A Centennial Volume*, pp. 129–145.

Rolland, Romain. *Jean-Christophe*, 3 vols in 1, trans. Gilbert Cannan. New York: The Modern Library, 1938; orig. 1910.

Ronnen, Meir. "The Wandering Jew," A review of Jonathan Wilson, *Marc Chagal* (Random House, 2007). H-Judaic online at http://jpost.com/servlet/satellite?cid= 1185379009750&pagename=Jpost%2FJPArticle%2FShowFull (26 July 2006).

Roskill, Mark, ed. *The Letters of Vincent Van Gogh*. London: Flamingo/Fontana/Collins, 1963; orig. 1927–1929.

Rossi, Paolo Aldo. "I Tarrocchi e lúso magico dell'ímmaginazione. *Ut pictura poësis*: il 'Gioco'dei Tarrocchi fra Érmetismo'e 'Teatro della Memoria.'" *Airesis: Il Giardino dei Magi*, online at http://www.airesis.net/IlGiardinoDeiMagi/Giardino/rossitarocchi (seen 01/06/2006).

Roth, Cecil, ed. *Jewish Art: An Illustrated History*. New York, Toronto, London: McGraw-Hill, 1961.

Roth, Samuel. *Now and Forever: A Conversation with Mr Israel Zangwill on the Jew and the Future*. New York: Robert M. McBride & Co., 1925.

Rous, Anya. "The Rising Celebrity of the Artist and the Dreyfus Affair." *Bome*, online at http://www.ecfs.org/bome/cities/paris/hband/Rous/dreyfus2 (seen 05/04/2009).

Rukschcio, Burkhardt and Roland Schachel. *La Vie et l'œuvre de Adolf Loos*, trans. Marianne Braursch. Brussels: Pierre Mardaga, 1982.

Sabiani, Julie. "Féminisme et dreyfusisme." In LeRoy, ed. *Les écrivains et l'affaire Dreyfus*, pp. 199–206.

Safran, Yehuda. "Adolf Loos: The Archimedean Point." In *The Architecture of Adolf Loos: An Arts Council Exhibition.*

Sainte-Beauve, C. A. *Causeries du Lundi*, 3 vols, trans. E. J. Trenchmann. London: George Routledge & Sons and New York: D. P. Dutton & Co., nd.

Sainte-Beuve, "Notice sur Xavier de Maîstre." In De Maîstre, *Oeuvres Completes*, v-xxxvii.

Scharf, Aaron. *Art and Photography*. Harmondworth: Penguin, 1974 (1968).

Scherman, Maurice. "Introduction" to LeRoy, ed. *Les écrivains et l'affaire Dreyfus*, pp. 5–6.

Sepinwall, Alyssa Goldstein. Review of Ilana Y. Zinguer and Sam W.

Bloom, eds., *L'antisémitisme éclairé: inclusion et exclusion depuis l'Epoque des Lumières jusqu'à l'affaire Dreyfus/Inclusion and Exclusion: Perspectives on Jews from the Enlightenment to the Dreyfus Affair*, Leiden and Boston: Brill, 2003. *H-France Review* 4: 80 (August 2004). Online at http://www.h-france.net/reviews/alphatitle (seen 12/05/2009).

Shalom Aleichem. *The Best of Shalom Aleichem*, eds. Irving Howe and Ruth R. Wisse. New York: Washington Square Press, 1982 (New York: New Republic Books, 1979).

Shamah, Moshe. "Understanding Midrash: Parashat Beshalah." *Judaic Seminar*, online at http://www.judaicseminar.org/general/midrash (seen 1/12/2001).

Shank, J. B. Review of Jonathan Israel, *Radical Enlightenment: Philosophy and the Making of Modernity, 1650–1750* (Oxford and New York: Oxford University press, 2001). *H-France Book Reviews*, online at http://www3.uakron.edu/hfrance/reviews/shank (seen 09/08/2002).

Shasha, David. "Dangerous Mystic Motifs in Judaism" SHU (7 July 2010). Online at http://www.huffingtonpost.com/david-shasha/understanding-midrash_b_535249 (seen 10/12/2010).

Shasha, David. "Understanding Midrash," *Huffington Post* (13 April 2010). Online at http://www.huffingtonpost.com/david-shasha/understanding-midrash_b_535249 (seen 10/12/2010).

Shattuck, Roger. "The Work and Its Author," Chapter 1 of Shattuck, *Marcel Proust* (New York: Viking Press, 1974). Online at http://www.studiocleo.com/librarie/proust/crittext (seen 16/03/2010).

Shattuck, Roger. *The Banquet Years. The Arts in France, 1885–1918: Alfred Jarry, Henri Rousseau. Erik Satie, Guillaim Apollinaire*. London: Faber & Faber, 1958 (1955).

Shenkar, Nadine. "The Pomegranate Carpets and the Kabbalah." *Danon Gallery*, online at http:www/danongallery.com/melograni/pomegranates3.asp (last seen 07/02/2011).

Shivanandan, Mary. "Emile Zola: Improbable Defender of Life," *Life and Learning XVII*: The Proceedings of the Seventeenth University for Life Conference (2007). Online at http://www.uffl.org/ vol17/SHIVANANDAN07 (seen 22/02/2010).

Shmidman, Joshua. "Jewish Beauty and the Beauty of Jewishness," *Jewish Action*. Online at http:www. ou.org/publications/ja/5758/

spring98/beauty (seen 05/01/2011). Nordau, Max. "Speech of Max Nordau at the First Zionist Congress, Basle, 29 August 1897." MidEastWeb (2003), online at http://www.mideastweb.org (last seen 06/01/2011).

Sichéry, Sherban. "Israel's Way." In Quennell, *Marcel Proust, 1871–1922: A Centennial Volume*, pp. 79–102.

Signer, Michael A. "How the Bible has been Interpreted in Jewish Tradition," *New Interpreter's Bible* (Nashville, TN: Abingdon, 1994) vol. I, pp. 65–82. Online at http://personal.centernary.edu/~sbrayfor/signer (seen 09/08/2008).

Signer, Michael. "Rashi's Reading of the Akedah." *Journal of Textual Reasoning* 2:1 (2001), online at http:etext.virginia.edu/journals/tr/volume2/signer (seen 16/07/2004).

Silver, Kenneth E. and Romy Golan, eds., with contributions by Arthur A. Cohen, Billy Kliver and Julie Martin. *The Circle of Montparnasse: Jewish Artists in Paris, 1905–1945*. The Jewish Museum, New York. New York: Universe Book, 1985.

Simms, Norman. "Belly Laughs: A Look at the Wit and Wisdom of Jonah," *Mentalities/Mentalités* 8:2 (1993), pp. 13–21.

Simms, Norman. "Parables: Gospel Speech or Rabbinic Joke?" In Samuel Rodin, ed., *Encounters with Judaism: Jewish Studies in a Non-Jewish World* (Hamilton: Waikato University and Colcom Press, 1991), pp. 108–127.

Simms, Norman. "Anti-Semitism: A Psychopathological Disease," Chapter Two in *Judaism and Genocide: Psychological Under-currents of* History—Volume IV, eds., Jerry S. Piven, Chris Boyd and Henry W. Lawton. Writers Club Press, 2002.

Simms, Norman. "Art, Criticism and Psychiatry," review of *Les Cahiers Henri Ey.* Numéro Spécial 12–13. "Psychiatrie et arts plastiques: la psychiatrie devant le surréalisme" in *Mentalities/Mentalités* 19:2 (2005), pp. 81–83.

Simms, Norman. "Jewish Symbolism and Art." *Journal of Literature & Aesthetics* 7:2 (1999), pp. 7–13.

Simms, Norman. "The Little Old Jew at the Bridge, or The Dependence of God on Jewish Jokes and the Place of *Witzenschaft* in Modern Jewish Fiction." *Journal of Literature & Aesthetics* 8:2 (July-December 2000), pp. 37–49.

Simms, Norman. *The Humming Tree: History of Mentalities.* Chicago:

University of Illinois Press, 1992.

Simons, Daniel and Christopher Chabris. *The Invisible Gorilla and Other Ways Our Intuitions Deceive Us*. New York: Crown Publishing Group/ Random House, 1998.

Singer, Peter. *Pushing Time Away: My Grandfather and the Tragedy of Jewish Vienna*. Sydney, NSW: Fourth Estate/HarperCollins, 2003.

Smith, Paul. *Impressionism: Beneath the Surface*. New York: Harry N. Abrames, 1995.

Smolik, Noemi. "Out of the Picture." In *Frieze: Contemporary Art and Culture*, No. 125 (September 2009), pp. 27–28.

Sonino, Michael, ed. *The Batkin Collection of Israeli Art*, curated by Susan Tamarkin Goodman. New York: NY: The Jewish Museum under the auspices of the Jewish Theological Seminary, 1985.

Sonino, Michael, ed. *The Furman Collection of Jewish Ceremonial Art*, exhibited 2 July-6 October 1985. Curated by Susan L. Braunstein. Under the auspices of the Theological Seminary of America. New York: The Jewish Museum, 1985.

Sonino, Michael, ed. *The Schulman Collection of 20th Century American Art*, curated by Susan Tamarkin Goodman. New York: NY: The Jewish Museum under the auspices of the Jewish Theological Seminary, 1985.

Sorel, Georges. *La Révolution dreyfusienne* (Paris: Librairie Marcel Rivière/Bibliothèque du Mouvement socialiste, 1909). Online at mhtml:file//E:\Sorel-Dreyfus_rtf.mht.

Squires, Michele B., ed. and trans. *Marcel Schwob Digital Collection*. Salt Lake City, UT: Brigham Young University, April 2008.

Steevens, G. W. *The Tragedy of Dreyfus*. New York and London: Harper & Brothers, 1899.

Stern, Fritz, ed. *The Varieties of History: From Voltaire to the Present*. 11th printing. Cleveland and New York: Meridian Books/The World Publishing Company, 1964 (1956).

Sternhell, Zeev. "Le nationalisme organique de Maurice Barrès." In LeRoy, ed. *Les écrivains et l'affaire Dreyfus*, pp. 123–135.

Stone, Irving, ed. and Preface, with Jean Stone, *Dear Theo: The Autobiography of Vincent Van Gogh*. New York: New American Library/Signet Book, 1969 (1939).

Strauss, Leo. *Philosophy and Law: Contributions to the Understanding of Maimonides and His Predecessors*, trans. and ed., Eve Adler. Albany:

State University of New York Press, 1995.

Sue, Eugène. *The Wandering Jew: A Tale of the Jesuits*, no trans. London: John Hamilton, 1934.

Suffel, Jacques. "Anatole France et l'affaire Dreyfus." In LeRoy, ed. *Les écrivains et l'affaire Dreyfus*, pp. 235–242.

Sutherland, Christine. *Enchantress: Marthe Bibesco and Her World*. New York: Farrar, Straus & Giraux, 1996.

Sweeney, Marvin A. "Genesis and Modern Holocaust Midrash," Review of Deborah Lee Prescott, *Imagery from Genesis in Holocaust Memoirs: A Critical Study* (Jefferson McFarland & Co., 2010). *H-Net Review*, online at http://h-review@h-net.msu.edu (19 October 2010).

Tabory, Yosef. "History of Prayer" (Spring 2000). Online at http://yucs.org/~jyuter/notes/historyofprayer (last seen 7 February 2011).

Taine, Hippolyte Adolphe. "Introduction to the History of English Literature (1863)." In *Prefaces and Prologues to Famous Books*. New York: P. F. Collier & Son Corporation, 62nd printing 1969 (1938, 1910) (Little, Brown and Co., 1909).

Taine, Hippolyte. *De l'intelligence,* tome second. VIeme ed. Paris: Librairie Hachette, nd. Lexington, KY: Bibliolife Reproduction, 2010.

Taine, Hippolyte. *The Philosophy of Art,* 2nd ed., trans. John Durand. New York: Holt & Williams, 1878.

Taplin, Oliver. "Comedy and the Tragic." In Silk, *Tragedy and Tragic*, pp. 188–202.

Tarde, Gabriel. *L'opinion et la foule.* Introduction par Dominque Renie. Paris: PUF/Recherches Politiques, 1989 (1901).

Tarde, Gabriel. *Les lois de l'imitation: étude sociologique*. Paris: Elibron Classiques, 2005; org. Paris: Félix Alcan, 1890.

Taubes, Isabelle. "De la pensée juive à la psychologie: entrevue de Marc-Alain Ouaknin." *Psychologies* 39 (avril-août 1991), pp. 50-52.

Templ. Stephan and Tina Walzer. *Unser Wien*. Berlin: Aufbau-Verlaf, 2001.

Thomas, Marcel. "Le cas Valéry" LeRoy, ed. *Les écrivains et l'affaire Dreyfus*, pp. 103-112.

Thorne, Sam. "Back and Forward: The Changing Role of Cultural Theory and Its Enduring Importance for Contemporary Art." In *Frieze: Contemporary Art and Culture*, No. 125 (September 2009), p. 13.

Trigano, Shmuel. *L'Ebranlement d'Israël: Philosophie de l'histoire juive.*

Paris: Editions du Seuil, 2002.
Trigano, Shmuel. *Le monothéisme est un humanisme*. Paris: Editions Odile Jacob, 2000.
Trigano, Shmuel. *Le temps de l'exil*. Paris: Manuels Payot, 2001.
Trochimczyk, Maja. "Mazur (Mazurka)." Online at http://www2/fiu.edu/~kneskij/ mazurka (seen 14/11/2010).

Ulmer, Rivka B. Review of Marc Lee Raphael, ed. *Agendas for the Study of Midrash in the Twenty-First Century* (Williamsburg, VA: College of William and Mary, 199). *H-Judaic, H-Net Reviews in the Humanities and Social Sciences* (May 1999), online at http://www.h-net.org/reviews/showrev.php?id=3110 (last seen 09/02/2011).
Urmeneta, Vincente Huici. "Tiempo, espacio y memoria: actualidad de Maurice Halbwachs," paper delivered at the *IV Euskal Soziologia Kongresua—IV Ciongreso Vasco de Socilogia*, Bilbao, 1998, pp. 4380441. Online at http://www.uned.es/ca-bergara/ppropias/vhuici/Temmh (seen 29/07/2004).

Viard, Jacques. "Bernard Lazare et Péguy, ou 'Le sang des prophètes." In LeRoy, ed. *Les écrivains et l'affaire Dreyfus*, pp. 35-43.
Vidal-Naquet, Pierre. *Les Assasins de la mémoire: Un Eichmann de papier et autres essais sur la révisionnisme*. Paris: La Découverte, 1987 (1981).
Vidal-Naquet, Pierre. *Les Juifs, la mémoire et le présente*. Paris: La Découverte, 1981 and 1991.
Villemar, H. *Dreyfus intime*. Paris: P-V. Stock, 1898.
Villemar, H. *Essai sur le colonel G. Piquart*. Paris: Eilbron Classics, 2007; orig. Paris: P-V. Stock, 1988.
Visotzky, Burton L. "Midrash, Christian Exegesis, and Hellenistic Hermeneutics." In Bakhos, *Current Trends in the Study of Midrash*, pp. 111-132.
Vizetelly, Ernest Alfred. *With Zola in England: A Story of Exile*. London: Chatto & Windus, 1899.
Vovelle, Michelle, ed. *Iconographie et histoire des mentalités*. Centre méridional d'histoire sociale des mentalités et des cultures. Université de Provence, Aix-en-Provence. Paris: Edition du Centre de la Recherche scientifique, 1979.

Wagner, Dov. "Sept. 11 and the Jewish Approach to Tragedy"(2002). Chabad-Lubavitch Media Center, online at http://www.kabbalaonline.org/KabbalaWorld\11.09/2002 (seen 12/09/2002).

Walther, Ingo F. and Rainer Metsger, *Vincent van Gogh: The Complete Paintings*, 2 vols in 1, trans. Michael Hulse. Köln, London etc.: Taschen Books, 1990.

Weibel, Peter and Friedrich Stadler, eds. *Vetribung der Vernunft/The Cultural Exodus from Austria*. Vienna: Löcker Verlag, 2993.

Weil, Julien. *Zadoc Kahn (1859–1905)*. Paris: Félix Alcan, 1912.

West, Rebecca. *1900*. New York: Crescent Books/Random House, 1996, 1982.

Weynants, Thomas. *Early Visual Media Archaeology*. Online at http://users.telenet.be/thomasweynants/phantasmaorie-opaque-hauch (seen 20/03/2010).

Wieseltier, Leon. *Kaddish*. New York: Alfred A. Knopf, 1998..

Wilson, Nelly. "Bernard Lazare et le Syndicat." In LeRoy, ed. *Les écrivains et l'affaire Dreyfus*, pp. 27-33.

Winock, Michel. "Les intellectuels dans le siècle." *Vingtième Siècle: Revue d'histoire*, no. 2 (April 1984), pp. 3-14.

Wise, Pyra. "Les lettres de Marcel Proust dans le Fonds Henry Bordeaux à Chambéry: retour sur une amitié et présentation de trios lettres dont deux inédites." *ITEM: Institute des textes & manuscripts modernes* (13 March 2007). Online at http://www.item.ens.fr/index.php?id=76014.

Yadin, Azzan. "Resistance to Midrash? Midrash and Halakhah." In *Halakhic Midrashim: Bakhos, Current Trends in the Study of Midrash*, pp. 35-78.

Yehoshua, Mathias. "Paul Bourget, écrivain engagé," *Vingtième Siècle, Revue d'histoire* No. 45 (Jan-Mars, 1995), pp. 14-29.

Yerushalmi, Yosef Hayim. *Zakhor: Jewish History and Jewish Memory*. Seattle: University of Washington Press, 1982.

Zola, Emile, Ernest Bersot, Salomon Reinach, *Notre Ecole Normale*, ed. Harve Duchene. Paris: Les Belles Lettres, 1994.

Zola, Emile. *L'Affaire Dreyfus: La vérité en marche*, ed. Colette Becker. Montréal: Garnier-Flammarion, 1969.

Zola, Emile. *Les Trois Villes: Lourdes* (1894), *Rome* (1896) *Paris* (1898). All available in Project Gutenberg. *The Three Cities*, trans. Ernest A. Vizetelly, 1894, 1896, and 1898.

Zweig, Stefan. *Balzac*, 2nd ed., trans. William and Dorothy Rose. London: Cassell & Co., 1948 (1947).
Zweig, Stefan. *The World of Yesterday*. Hallam Edition. London: Cassell, 1953 (orig. 1943).

Index

Printed by Libri Plureos GmbH in Hamburg,
Germany

9 781936 235391